# THE GIANT BO

# WORLD FAMOUS
# MURDERS

# THE GIANT BOOK OF
# WORLD FAMOUS MURDERS

Colin Wilson with
Damon and Rowan Wilson

‖ •PARRAGON• ‖

This edition published and distributed by Parragon

This edition first published by Magpie Books Ltd in 1994,
a division of Robinson Publishing

Magpie Books Ltd
7 Kensington Church Court
London W8 4SP

Individual books © Robinson Publishing 1992,
Collection © Robinson Publishing 1993
Illustration © Hulton Deutsch

A copy of the British Library Cataloguing in Publication
Data is available from the British Library.

Printed and bound by Firmin-Didot (France),
Group Herissey. No d'impression : 27505.

# Contents

# GASLIGHT MURDERS

# chapter one

# THE AGE OF GASLIGHT

"*The Age of Gaslight*" – *the words evoke nostalgic images of Victorian music halls and Dickensian hotelries peopled by characters like Sam Weller and the Artful Dodger. In fact, coal gas had been invented at the end of the previous century. It is a fascinating story, and worth telling before we embark on our venture into Victorian murder.*

*When Sir Archibald Cochrane became Earl of Dundonald in 1778, he had no money to go with the title – it had been dissipated by spendthrift ancestors. But at least he had a coal mine near his property at Culross Abbey, not far from Edinburgh. He began making tar for coating ships' bottoms, cooking coal in huge kilns. Unfortunately, the Admiralty decided to start protecting their ships with copper bottoms, and the Earl went bankrupt and died penniless. But while he was still experimenting with the tar-making process, he one day allowed a kiln to overheat. It exploded, and he noticed that the resulting gas burned brightly. If he had grasped the significance of what was happening, he might have ended a rich man instead of dying in a Paris slum. Unfortunately, the Earl lacked imagination.*

*But at least he passed on his interesting observation to a Scottish engineer called James Watt, who had invented a new and improved type of steam engine. Watt in turn mentioned it to his young assistant William Murdock, who sold steam engines in Cornwall. Murdock tried the simple experiment of heating coal in an iron container, and lighting the gas which came out of a pipe leading from the container. Watt liked the idea so much that two years later, in 1801, he installed the first two gas burners in his factory in Soho. The resulting smell became known as "the Soho stink".*

# FIFTY POUNDS
## *REWARD.*

## Horrid Murder!!

### WHEREAS,

The Dwelling House of Mr. TIMOTHY MARR, 29, Ratcliff Highway, Man's Mercer, was entered this morning between the hours of Twelve and Two o'Clock, by some persons unknown, when the said Mr. MARR, Mrs. CELIA MARR, his wife, TIMOTHY their INFANT CHILD in the cradle, and JAMES BIGGS, a servant lad, were all of them most inhumanly and barbarously Murdered!!

A Ship Carpenter's Pean Maul, broken at the point, and a Brickbyer's long Iron Ripping Chisel about Twenty Inches in length, have been found upon the Premises, with the former of which it is supposed the Murder was committed. Any person having lost such articles, or any Dealer in Old Iron, who has lately Sold or missed such, are earnestly requested to give immediate Information.

The Churchwardens, Overseers, and Trustees, of the Parish of St. George Middlesex, do hereby offer a Reward of FIFTY POUNDS, for the Discovery and Apprehension of the Person or Persons who committed such Murder, to be paid on Conviction.

*By Order of the Churchwardens, Overseers, and Trustees,*

## JOHN CLEMENT,

Ratcliff-highway,
SUNDAY, 8th, DECEMBER, 1811.

VESTRY CLERK.

SKIRVEN, Printer, Ratcliff Highway, London.

*So the Age of Gaslight began long before Queen Victoria came to the throne in 1837. By 1805, many Manchester cotton mills were lit by gaslight. And by 1820, most major British towns were illuminated by its yellow, flickering flames, (Gas mantles were not invented until the beginning of the twentieth century, so gaslight looked rather like an outsize candle flame.)*

*At least gaslight made the street safer at night; throughout most of the eighteenth century, late travellers were likely to be attacked by footpads. The most shocking crimes of the early nineteenth century were committed behind closed doors, or in remote areas of the countryside where there was no gas.*

# The Ratcliffe Highway Murders

In 1811, there was a case that made a sensation through the length and breadth of the country, and caused householders everywhere to bolt and bar their shutters. It took place in a house in the Ratcliffe Highway, in the East End of London. On the night of Saturday, 7 December 1811, someone broke into the house of a hosier named Timothy Marr, and murdered Marr, his wife, their baby and an apprentice boy of thirteen. A servant girl who had been sent out to buy oysters discovered the bodies. The incredible violence of the murders shocked everyone; the family had been slaughtered with blows of a mallet that had shattered their skulls, then their throats had been cut. The killer was obviously a homicidal maniac, but the motive had probably been robbery – which had been interrupted by the girl's return. In an upstairs room, a constable of the river police found the murder weapon – a "maul", a kind of iron mallet with a point on one end of the head; they were used by ships' carpenters. The head had the initials "I.P." punched into it. Two sets of footprints were found leading away from the house.

Twelve days later, there was a second mass murder at a public house called the King's Arms, in Gravel Lane, close to the Ratcliffe Highway. The pub was run by a Mr Williamson and his wife, with help from their fourteen-year-old granddaughter, Kitty Stilwell, and a servant, Bridget Harrington. There was

VIEW OF THE BODY OF JOHN WILLIAMS
*the supposed Murderer of the families of Marr and Williamson, and self-destroyer approachin' the hole dug to receive it, in the Cross Road, at Cannon Street Turnpike.*

also a lodger, twenty-six-year-old John Turner. After the bar had closed at 11 p.m., Williamson served a drink to an old friend, the parish constable, and told him that a man in a brown jacket had been listening at the door, and that if the constable saw him, he should arrest him.

A quarter of an hour later, the lodger had gone to his bed in the attic when he heard the front door slam very hard, then Bridget Harrington's voice shouting "We are all murdered." There were blows and more cries. Turner crept downstairs – naked – and peered into the living room. He saw a man bending over a body and rifling the pockets. Turner went back upstairs, made a rope out of sheets tied together, and lowered himself out of the window. As he landed with a crash on the pavement – the "rope" was too short – he shouted breathlessly "Murder, murder!" A crowd quickly formed, and the parish constable prised open the metal flap that led into the cellar. At the bottom of some steps lay the body of the landlord, his head beaten in by a crowbar that lay beside him. His throat had been cut and his right leg fractured. In the room above lay the bodies

In 1815 Eliza Fenning was 21 years old and had been 'in service' since she was 14.

Three weeks after she became cook to the family of Robert Turner of Chancery Lane, London, the mistress of the house threatened to dismiss her because she had been seen going into the bedroom of the menservants in a scanty state of attire. The girl apologized abjectly.

Four weeks later, she offered to make dumplings for the family. This was unusual - the dough was usually bought ready made from the baker; but Mrs. Turner agreed. The dumplings struck them as grey and heavy, but they ate some of them. Soon afterwards, Mrs. Turner, her husband and her father-in-law were all violently sick, and they had to call in a doctor. The next morning the father-in-law went to the kitchen and found the pan in which the dumplings had been cooked. There was a white powder in the bottom, which the family doctor declared to be arsenic.

A packet of arsenic had disappeared from a drawer not long before. The question was: how had it got into the dumplings? Eliza tried to put the blame on the other servants, and her defence pointed out that she had been violently sick, too, after eating from the dumplings. The jury decided that this was probably an attempt to make herself look innocent, and she was sentenced to death. Despite much public sympathy for her, and an appeal for clemency, she was finally hanged, still protesting her innocence.

It has been pointed out that the evidence against her was purely circumstantial, and that the doctor, for example, offered no details of the tests he had conducted to prove that the white powder was arsenic. But a reading of the trial report, contained in The Newgate Calendar, suggests that the jury was probably right to find her guilty of poisoning, if not of attempted murder. From her evidence, Mrs. Turner sounds a highly unpleasant bully; Eliza probably intended to make them all severely ill, by way of getting her own back.

of Mrs Williamson and Bridget Harrington. Both their skulls had been shattered, and both had had their throats cut to the bone. The murderer had escaped through a rear window.

Dozens of sailors and men in brown jackets were arrested on suspicion, among them a young sailor named John Williams, who lodged at the Pear Tree public house in nearby Wapping. He was a rather good-looking, slightly effeminate youth with a manner that sometimes caused him to be mistaken for a "gentleman". There was no evidence against him. But when handbills with pictures of the maul were circulated, John Williams's landlord, a Mr Vermilloe (who happened to be in Newgate prison for debt) said that he recognized it as belonging to a Swedish sailor named John Peterson. Peterson was now at sea, so had a watertight alibi, but had left his chest of tools behind, in the care of Vermilloe.

John Williams was now suspect number one. He had been seen walking towards the King's Arms on the evening of the murders, and had returned to his lodgings in the early hours of the morning with blood on his shirt – he claimed this was the result of a brawl. The stockings and shoes he had worn had been carefully washed, but bloodstains were still visible on the stockings. Williams's room mates said he had no money on the night of the murders, but had a great deal on the following day.

Williams cheated the executioner by hanging himself in prison on 28 December 1811. An inquest declared that he was the sole murderer of the Marrs and the Williamsons – a verdict that may be questioned in view of the two pairs of footprints that were found leaving the Marrs' house. He was given a suicide's burial at a cross roads in East London, with a stake through his heart – the old superstition being that suicides could become vampires.

The details of the Ratcliffe Highway murders are rather less interesting than the effect they produced on the public. It was the first time in English history – probably in European history – that a crime had created widespread panic. Why? Because it was generally accepted that they were committed by one man. In fact, it is rather more probable that they were committed by two, or even by a gang – one witness who lived near the Marrs said he heard several men running away. If that had been believed, there would almost certainly have been no panic –

gangs of thieves were still a familiar hazard in 1811. It was this notion of a lone monster, a man who stalked the streets on his own, lusting for blood, that terrified everybody. Jack the Ripper turned this nightmare into reality seventy-seven years later. But in 1811, the "alienated" criminal had still not made his appearance.

# Thurtell and Hunt

Three more cases would produce this same widespread, feverish public interest during the next two decades. The first was the murder of a sportsman and gambler named William Weare by two more members of the sporting fraternity, John Thurtell and Joseph Hunt. Thurtell, a man of strong character and imposing physical presence, was familiar on the race courses and at barefist boxing matches. Weare had won from him a considerable sum of money at billiards, and Thurtell was convinced he had cheated. So Weare was invited for the weekend to a cottage belonging to a man called William Probert, near Elstree. The four set out from London in two horse-drawn gigs – two-wheeled carriages – and as they arrived, Thurtell shot Weare in the face; the bullet bounced off his cheekbone and Weare begged for his life. Thurtell threw him down, cut his throat with a penknife, then jammed the pistol against his head so hard that it went into the brain, filling the barrel with blood and tissue. The body was then dumped in a pond, and the three men went into the cottage and had supper with Probert's wife and sister-in-law. The next morning, Thurtell and Hunt went to look for the pistol and penknife, without success; but as they left, two labourers found the weapons on top of a hedge. They reported the find to the Bow Street Runners, who soon discovered Weare's body in another pond, into which it had been moved. Probert quickly turned king's evidence, and so escaped. Thurtell was hanged, while Hunt was transported for life.

This commonplace murder aroused such widespread interest

that it was quickly turned into a play that was performed before
crowded houses. A popular ballad of the time – which was sold
at the execution – had the well-known stanza:

> They cut his throat from ear to ear
> His head they battered in.
> His name was Mr William Weare
> He lived in Lyons Inn.

But why *did* it arouse such horrified fascination? It may have
been partly because Thurtell was such a well-known character
in the sporting world. But it was more probably the violence of
the murder – the cut throat, the pistol filled with brains. Again,
the crime touched a sense of nightmare: the ruthless criminal
who ignores the laws of God and man. Yet the sensation it
caused is also evidence that society was changing fast. In
Defoe's time, the murder of Weare would have been merely
one more case to add to the *Newgate Calendar*. But things were
different in 1823. In his *History of Crime in England* (1873), Luke
Owen Pike says:

> "England in the beginning of the year 1820, when
> George III died, was already the wealthiest and, in
> many respects, the most civilized country in Europe
> . . . Stage coaches now traversed all the main roads,
> which were at length beginning to deserve compari-
> son with the great engineering works given to us
> by the Romans . . . Canals intersected the country
> . . . All these changes were, in the main, opposed
> to crime."

In fact, crime was rising steadily – Major Arthur Griffiths
estimates in *Mysteries of Police and Crime* that there was a
ratio of one criminal to every 822 members of the population
in 1828. But most of these crimes were the result of misery
and poverty, of half-starved factory workers and out-of-work
farm labourers. What shocked people about the crimes of John
Williams and John Thurtell was that they were not the outcome
of desperation. They were deliberately committed for personal
gain, for self-satisfaction; in other words, they were acts of

ego-assertion, like the crimes of Caligula or Gilles de Rais.
The age of individual conscience, inaugurated by Bunyan and Wesley, was changing into the age of individual crime.

This was, in fact, something of an illusion. Williams – and possibly a companion – had merely committed murder in the course of robbery: a hundred similar cases could be cited from the previous century. Thurtell's murder was a commonplace gangland execution; Weare was a scoundrel, and all four of them were gamblers and crooks. But the public *wanted* to believe that these were monsters; it stimulated some nerve of morbidity, in an age that was becoming increasingly prosperous and increasingly mechanized.

# Murder in the Red Barn

This also explains the excitement generated by the "Red Barn murder" of 1827. William Corder, a farmer's son who became a schoolmaster, allowed himself to be bullied into marrying Maria Marten, a mole-catcher's daughter who was known in Polstead, Suffolk, as the local tart. She had lost her virginity to one gentleman ("an unfortunate slip" says the *Newgate Calendar*) and then bore a bastard child to another. She also became pregnant to William's brother Thomas, but the child died soon after birth. After Thomas abandoned her, Maria had an affair with a "gentleman" named Peter Matthews, who thereafter paid her an allowance of £20 a year.

William seems to have been an oversensitive mother's boy who was harshly treated by his father and made to work on the farm for a minimal wage. His response was to become something of a petty crook – on one occasion he borrowed money from a neighbour "for his father" and spent it; on another, he secretly sold some of his father's pigs. He was sent away to London in disgrace, but returned to the farm when his brother Thomas was accidentally drowned trying to cross a frozen pond. He soon became Maria's lover, and they spent their evenings making love in the Red Barn on the farm.

**12**  Maria's quarterly £5 note disappeared mysteriously, probably into Corder's pocket, indicating that he cont` ued to look for the easy way out of his problems. Maria beca: .e pregnant again in 1827, and gave birth to a boy; but the chid was sickly, and soon died. Maria's father evidently felt that it was time she became an honest woman, and pressed Corder so hard that he agreed to be married. At which point, he seems to have experienced regrets, and looked, as usual, for the easy way out. He told Maria that they must be married in secret, and persuaded her to meet him in the Red Barn, dressed in a suit of his own clothes. On 18 May Maria kept her appointment in the Red Barn, and was never seen again. Corder returned home and told Maria's family that he had placed her in lodgings in Ipswich for the time being. He told other stories to other enquirers. Then, tired of the gossip, Corder slipped away to London, where he advertised for a wife in a newspaper. The result was a meeting with a young woman called Mary Moore, whom he married. She had enough money to set up a girls' school in Ealing; Corder bought himself some spectacles and became headmaster.

Meanwhile, in Polstead, Maria's mother had been having lurid dreams in which she saw Corder shoot Maria in the Red Barn and bury her there. Her husband recalled that Corder had been seen with a pick and shovel on the day his daughter disappeared, and went and dug at a spot where the earth had been disturbed; he soon unearthed his daughter's body in a sack.

Corder was arrested and hanged – it was an open-and-shut case. His defence – that Maria had committed suicide during a quarrel – deceived no one. Before being hanged, in August 1828, he confessed to murdering Maria Marten.

A book and a play about the murder became instantly popular, and remained so into the twentieth century. Why? Men who killed their pregnant mistresses or wives were by no means uncommon. What thrilled the British public was the piquant mixture of sex and wickedness – the combination that still sells many Sunday newspapers. The *New Newgate Calendar* adopts an almost breathless tone: "The murder for which this most diabolical criminal merited and justly underwent condign punishment, rivalled in cold-blooded atrocity that of the unfortunate Mr Weare, and was as foul and dark a crime

William Corder, his victim Maria Marten and Maria's baby.

## MARIA MARTEN or "THE MURDER IN THE RED BARN"

REVEALED BY A MOTHER'S DREAM

as ever stained the annals of public justice." Then it goes on to describe what a beautiful and "superior" young lady Maria was. In short, it has little or no relation to the actuality – a sluttish countrygirl of loose morals and a weak young man of criminal tendencies. But it was the story everybody wanted to believe, just as they wanted to believe that the "unfortunate Mr Weare" was a respectable businessman who had been lured to his death by two monsters.

> **A popular rhyme at the time of the Burke and Hare murders went:**
>
> **"Burke's the murderer, Hare's the thief And Knox the boy who buys the beef."**

# Burke and Hare

But at least cases like this made the British public aware of the need for a real national police force, instead of local parish constables. And the trial that, more than any other, brought this home to even the most anti-authoritarian liberals was that of the Edinburgh body-snatchers, Burke and Hare. These two Irish labourers met in 1826, and moved into a "beggars' hotel" in Tanner's Close, Edinburgh, together with their common-law wives. Somehow, Hare succeeded in taking over the house when its owner died. And when a tenant called Old Donald died owing his rent, Hare decided to recover the money by selling his corpse to the medical school. The dissection of bodies was forbidden by law; so when someone offered the medical schools a corpse – usually stolen from a newly-dug grave – no one asked any questions. Dr Knox, of 10 Surgeon's Square, paid Hare £7.10s for the corpse, which was more than twice what Old Donald owed. It struck Burke and Hare that this was an easy way of making a living – if only they could come by enough corpses. But graveyards were usually guarded to prevent the theft of bodies. The solution seemed to be to "make" corpses. So when a tenant called Joe the Mumper fell ill, Burke and Hare hastened his end by pressing a pillow over his face. The £10 they received for his body convinced them that they had stumbled upon a more profitable occupation than labouring.

In February 1828, a female vagrant named Abigail Simpson was lured to the house and made drunk. On this first occasion, Burke and Hare lost their nerve, and she was still alive the next morning. But they got her drunk again, and Hare suffocated her, while Burke held her legs. Again, the corpse was sold for

> The early "bobbies" wore top hats lined with steel – not to protect their heads in case of attack, but so that they could stand on them if looking over a wall or through a window above head level.

£10. And over the next eight months, they despatched eleven more victims by the same method. Some of the victims were never identified – like an Irish beggar woman and her dumb grandson; Burke strangled her and broke the boy's back over his knee. Dr Knox probably became suspicious when he was offered the body of an attractive little prostitute named Mary Paterson and one of his students recognized her as someone he had patronized. His suspicions must have become a certainty when Burke and Hare sold him the body of a well-known idiot called Daft Jamie, but he preferred to keep quiet.

The downfall of Burke and Hare came through carelessness; they left the corpse of a widow named Docherty in the house while they went out, and two of their lodgers located it. On their way to the police, they were met by Burke's common-law wife, who saw from their faces that something was wrong and fell on her knees to beg them to keep quiet. The tenants allowed themselves to be persuaded over several glasses of whisky in a pub, but finally went to the police anyway. A search of the house in Tanner's Close revealed blood-stained clothing. Hare quickly turned king's evidence and was not tried. Burke was sentenced to death, and hanged in January 1829. Hare left Edinburgh, and died, an old blind beggar, in London.

This was by far the most gruesome case in British criminal history; yet it was perhaps a little too horrifying for the British public, which preferred tales in which beautiful girls were seduced. So the case of Burke and Hare never achieved the same widespread popularity as the Red Barn murder, or the case of Ellie Hanley, the "Colleen Bawn" ("white girl"), a pretty Irish girl who had been married and then murdered by a young rake in 1819. But it undoubtedly helped to reconcile the British public to the first appearance of the British bobby (so called after the founder of the force, Sir Robert Peel) in September 1829. The new police were told to be firm but conciliatory, respectful, quiet and determined, and to maintain a perfectly even temper. They followed these instructions to the letter,

William Burke.

William Hare.

with the result that the public gradually lost its distrust of its new guardians.

# Police Murders

But it took some time. During these early years, the major problem for the British bobby was simply that he wore uniform and looked "official". This tended to arouse automatic resentment in the slums of England's major cities. In June 1830, Police Constable Grantham saw two drunken Irishmen quarrelling over a woman in Somers Town, north London, and when he tried to separate them was knocked to the ground and kicked in the face with heavy boots. He died soon afterwards, the first British policeman to die in the execution of his duty; the murderers walked away and were never caught. Six weeks later, a policeman named John Long became convinced that three suspicious-looking characters in London's Gray's Inn Road were contemplating burglary, and accosted them. Two of them grabbed him by the arms and one stabbed him in the chest. There was a hue and cry, and another policeman who came on the scene caught a man who was running away. He proved to be a baker called John Smith, who had a wife and six children, and he protested that he had heard a cry of "Stop thief" and joined in the chase. His story was disbelieved and he was hanged a few days later. Under the circumstances, it seems likely he was innocent, and that the early police felt it was better to hang an innocent man than no one at all.

In 1833, the murder of another policeman revealed that the English attitude towards authority remained ambivalent. A mildly revolutionary group called the National Political Union called a meeting in Coldbath Fields, which was promptly banned by the police commissioner. The ban was ignored, and a crowd gathered around a speaker on a soap box. Eight hundred policemen and troops looked on suspiciously. A police spy slipped away from the crowd to report that sedition was being preached, and the man in charge of the police ordered his men to advance slowly, their truncheons at the ready. The crowd booed and pelted them with stones; the police got angry and began hitting out wildly, knocking down women and children as well as men. A man drew a knife as a policeman tried to capture an anarchist banner, and stabbed him in the chest. Police Constable Robert Culley staggered a few yards and fell dead.

A coroner's jury, considering the death, was obviously unsympathetic to the police, feeling they had no right to interfere with freedom of speech. When the coroner was told the jurors were unable to agree on a verdict, he replied that they would have to stay there without food and drink until they *did* agree. Whereupon the jury – which consisted of respectable

Burke and Hare at their trade.

tradesmen – produced a verdict of justifiable homicide against the unknown person who had stabbed Constable Culley. The spectators cheered, and the jury found themselves treated as heroes. The short-term result was to increase the hostility between police and public; but the long term-result was to allow Englishmen to stand on a soap box and say whatever they liked.

# Crime in France: the Great Vidocq

In France, the whole situation would have been regarded as preposterous. They had had their official police force since the time of Louis XIV and the policeman took it for granted that he represented the king's authority and could say and do as he liked. One result of this attitude, of course, was the French Revolution. But the infamous Chambre Ardente affair, with its revelation of mass poisoning and child-sacrifice was evidence that the French needed a police force rather more urgently than the English. (This was, of course, before the introduction of gin caused the English crime wave.) The French chief of police was also the censor of the press, and could arrest newspaper publishers and anyone who printed a "libellous book". (Prohibited books were actually tried, condemned, and sent to the Bastille in a sack with a label – specifying the offence – tied to it.)

The French concentrated on the spy system to keep crime in check – a vast network of informers. M. de Sartines, the police minister under Louis XV, once had a bet with a friend that it would be impossible to slip into Paris without knowledge of the police. The friend – a judge – left Lyons secretly a month later, and found himself a room in a remote part of the city; within hours, he had received a letter by special messenger, inviting him to dinner with M. de Sartines. On another occasion, de Sartines was asked by the Vienna police to search for an Austrian robber in Paris; he was able to reply that the robber was still in Vienna, and give his exact address – at which the Vienna police found him.

The French underworld was also more organized than the

British could ever hope to be. When Louis XVI married Marie Antoinette in 1770, a gang stretched cords across the street under cover of darkness, and crowds attending the celebrations stumbled over them in large numbers. Two thousand five hundred people were trampled to death in the confusion, and the pickpockets moved around rifling the corpses. But the next day, de Sartines's men swooped on known criminals and made hundreds of arrests. They did it so swiftly that they recovered enormous quantities of stolen goods – watches, rings, bracelets, purses, jewellery – one robber had two thousand francs tied up in his handkerchief. It was an inauspicious beginning for a marriage that ended on the guillotine.

After the Revolution of 1789, the police force was disbanded – only to be formed again by Robespierre, who wanted to know what his enemies were doing. Napoleon appointed the sinister Joseph Fouché his police minister, and Fouché's spy network became even more efficient than that of de Sartines.

Under Fouché, the chief of police in Paris was a certain M. Henry. One day in 1809, he received a visit from a powerfully-built young man called Eugène-François Vidocq, who offered information about certain criminals in exchange for immunity. Vidocq was totally frank with Henry; his life had been adventurous, and a hot temper and a love of pretty women had brought him more than his share of trouble with the law. He had been a smuggler, and had escaped from prison, and even from the galleys. Now he wanted a quiet life. Henry could see Vidocq felt trapped; but he wanted him to feel still more trapped, until he would do anything that was asked of him. So M. Henry declined his offer and allowed him to go.

What Vidocq had not told Henry was that he was now involved with a gang of coiners. They denounced him to the police, who called when Vidocq was in bed; he was arrested, nearly naked, on the roof. When M. Henry saw the prisoner, he felt pleased with himself; now Vidocq was well and truly trapped. Henry was now able to state his own terms. And they were that Vidocq should become a police spy and betray his associates. It was hard, but Vidocq had no alternative than to accept. He was taken to the prison of La Force, with the task of spying on his fellow prisoners. It was dangerous work, but freedom depended on doing it well. He did so well, reporting undetected crimes to M. Henry, and the whereabouts of stolen goods, that M. Henry decided to give him his freedom – as a police spy. Vidocq was loaded with chains for transfer to another prison; on the way he was allowed to escape. It made him the hero of the criminal underworld of Paris. His first task was to track down a forger named Watrin, who had escaped and totally disappeared. Cautious enquiries revealed that Watrin had left some possessions in a certain room. Vidocq waited for him to reappear, captured him after a desperate struggle, and dragged him off to M. Henry. There was a large reward. Soon after, Watrin was guillotined. So was another forger named Bouhin – the man who had denounced Vidocq to the police two years earlier. He had been arrested on Vidocq's information.

During the next few years, Vidocq showed himself to be the most determined, efficient and enterprising police agent in Paris. His success aroused intense jealousy in the Police Prefecture, and his colleagues often denounced him as a man who was really in league with the criminals. M. Henry knew better; he knew Vidocq was too attached to his new-found security. He also knew that the rivalry between his men was the greatest threat to the efficiency of the Paris police. Every area in the city had its local station, and there was little co-operation between them. So when Vidocq suggested forming a small force of men who could move freely anywhere in the city, Henry immediately seized upon the idea. Vidocq was allowed four helpers, all chosen by himself – naturally, he chose criminals. There was fierce opposition from all the local police departments, who objected to strangers on their "patches", but Henry refused to be moved. Vidocq's little band was called the Security – Sûreté – and it became the foundation of the French national police force of today.

In 1833, Vidocq was forced to retire, because a new chief of police objected to a Sûreté made up entirely of criminals and ex-criminals. He immediately became a private detective – the first in the world – and wrote his *Memoirs*. He became a close friend of writers, including Balzac, who modelled his character Vautrin on Vidocq.

For the modern reader, the most astonishing thing about Vidocq's *Memoirs* is that the crimes were so singularly un-vicious. This is not to say that criminals were not perfectly capable of murder; only that there was a complete absence of the kind of anti-social resentment that distinguishes so many modern criminals. Burglary or robbery with violence was simply a profession, usually embraced by people who drank too much and liked to keep more than one mistress. Many robbers swore to "get" Vidocq when they came out; no one actually tried it, for their resentment evaporated quickly. During his early days as an informer, Vidocq met two hardened criminals he had known in jail, spent twenty-four hours drinking with them, and agreed to take part in a robbery which would include cutting the throats of two old men. He managed to get a note to M. Henry, and the police were waiting for them as they climbed over a garden wall. Someone fired; Vidocq dropped to the ground, pretending to be hit. And one of his fellow burglars had to be restrained from flinging himself in sorrow on Vidocq's "body". Vidocq often took the trouble to get to know men he had been instrumental in sending to the guillotine or life-imprisonment, performing small services – like taking messages to families – and formed genuinely warm and close relationships with them. He even instituted a custom of standing in the prison yard to watch the men being chained together before they were led off to the galleys. On the first occasion, they raged at him like wild beasts and dared him to come among them. Vidocq did precisely that – while prisoners looking out of barred windows urged the convicts to kill him. Yet no one touched him; they respected his bravery. Vidocq accepted various small commissions – final messages to wives and sweethearts – and parted from the convicts on the friendliest of terms. The socialists were obviously not entirely mistaken to argue that crime was largely a question of social conditions. The criminal with a "grudge against society" had not yet made his appearance.

# Lacenaire

On 16 December 1834, a neighbour of the Widow Chardon, who lived at 271 rue St Martin, noticed a red stain that had seeped under the door, and when his knocks brought no reply, he went to summon the police. They discovered the corpse of a man lying in a pool of blood, his head split open by a hatchet, which lay next to the body. In the next room they found the body of an old woman, covered with stab wounds. She was the mother of the murdered man, who was a homosexual begging letter writer, nicknamed "Auntie". "It was on abject creatures known to share his tastes," says the disapproving Canler, "that suspicion first fell. Several of these filthy fellows were arrested and then released for want of proof." And, for the time being, the police investigation met an impasse.

Two weeks later, on New Year's Eve, Chief Inspector Canler was summoned to investigate an attempted murder. A young bank messenger named Genevey had been asked to call at 66 rue Montorgueil to collect money from a gentleman named Mahossier. On the fourth floor, the clerk found a room with "Mahossier" chalked on the door and knocked. As he entered the room, the door was closed behind him, and some sharp instrument was driven into his back. At the same time, a man tried to grasp him by the throat; he was clumsy, and his hand went into the clerk's mouth. Genevey was a robust young man; he struggled violently and shouted. His assailants became alarmed and ran away. Genevey staggered into the arms of neighbours who came to investigate.

At this time, the Sûreté – Paris's equivalent of Scotland Yard – was a modest organization, with a mere twenty-seven men: it had been founded a few decades earlier by a crook-turned-thief-catcher named Vidocq. Now its chief was a man named Pierre Allard, and he lost no time in appointing Canler to investigate both cases. He began by getting a good description of one of the assailants: a well-dressed man with a high forehead and a silky moustache; his manner, apparently, was polished and courteous. Significantly, he had been carrying a copy of Rousseau's *Social Contract*, the book that had virtually caused the French Revolution. The landlord at rue Montorgueil had not noticed the other man.

Now Canler proceeded to apply the needle-in-the-haystack method. It involved, quite simply, paying a visit to every cheap hotel and doss house in the Paris area, and asking to see the register that they were obliged to keep. Of course, it was obvious that "Mahossier" was not the man's real name, but Canler's knowledge of the criminal classes told him that they often used the same alias many times. And eventually, after trying every lodging-house in Montmartre, Île de la Cité, and the Temple area, he found what he wanted in rue du Faubourg du Temple: the name "Mahossier" in the hotel register. The proprietor shook his head; he had no memory of Mahossier. "How about this name underneath – Fizellier?" The proprietor, a man named Pageot, called his wife, and she was able to tell Canler that Fizellier was a big, red-haired man. Canler could sense that Pageot was not pleased by his wife's helpfulness; he didn't believe in helping the police more than necessary. So Canler thanked them and took his leave.

The description of Fizellier had rung a bell. A big, red-haired man had recently been arrested on a fraud charge, and he was at present in the central police station. Canler's expression was guileless as he entered his cell, notebook in hand, and pretended to search for a name:

"François, you tell me you're innocent of this fraud?"

"That's so."

"All right, then why did you call yourself Fizellier when you stayed at Mother Pageot's?"

"Because there was a warrant out for me, and I'd have been stupid to use my real name."

With quiet satisfaction, Canler went back to his office and made out a report stating that François was one of the two men in the bank messenger case. Then he returned to Mother Pageot's. This time he found her alone, and willing to tell what she knew. Mahossier, it seemed, had a high forehead and silky moustache, and he had stayed there before under the name of Bâton.

There *was* a crook called Bâton, a homosexual thief. "Fizellier" and "Mahossier" had shared a bed, so this might be the man. Canler ordered his arrest. But as soon as he saw him, he knew this was not Mahossier; Bâton was anything but distinguished or courteous. But again, Canler used his knowledge of criminal psychology. If Mahossier had borrowed Bâton's name, then he probably knew him. So, leaving Bâton in custody, Canler made a round of his haunts, and questioned his friends about a distinguished man with a silky moustache. A number of them agreed that this sounded like a person named Gaillard, with whom Bâton had been in prison. Back went Canler to Bâton, told him he was free to go, then asked him in a casual, friendly way about his friend Gaillard. Bâton's description left no doubt that Gaillard and Mahossier were the same person. But where was Gaillard? As soon as Canler began his enquiries, he encountered a difficulty; there were several suspicious characters called Gaillard, and it might be any of them. So, with infinite patience, Canler went back to searching the registers of doss houses. It took him two days to find the signature he wanted, in a hotel in the rue Marivaux-des-Lombards. The proprietress remembered M. Gaillard, a tall man with a high forehead. He had been visited occasionally by a lady. And he had left behind a bundle of Republican songs in his room. She still had them. And they made Canler aware of an interesting aspect of his suspect's character – he was a poet, and not entirely without talent. A letter in the form of a satirical poem made some libellous aspersions about the previous prefect of police. And the handwriting was unmistakably that of Mahossier.

Canler was now told that a prisoner named Avril wanted to talk to him. Avril had heard on the grapevine that Canler wanted to interview Gaillard. He offered to do a deal. If Canler would like to release him, then have him discreetly followed, he would wander around Gaillard's old resorts and see if he could locate him. Canler agreed, and for the next week, Avril was shadowed as he wandered from bar to bar. But when, at the end of that time, there was still no sign of Gaillard, Canler decided he was wasting police expenses, and had Avril put back in jail.

Meanwhile, red-headed François had been convicted, and was doing time in the Sainte-Pélagie prison. Canler decided it was time to renew the pressure. But as he sat beside the prisoner in the cabriolet taking them back to Canler's office, François decided to speak of his own accord. He told Canler that he could give him information about the murder of the Chardons. He had spent an evening drinking with a man who told him that he had murdered the Chardons, while one of his acquaintances kept watch. The man's name? Gaillard . . .

And now, for the first time, Canler realized that his two cases were connected. Mahossier had murdered the Chardons, and attempted to murder and rob the bank messenger. In each crime he had had a different accomplice. In the bank messenger case it had been red-headed François. And in the murder case, Canler had a hunch that the accomplice had been Avril. Now he questioned Avril further, and obtained a new piece of information. "Gaillard" had an aunt, old and quite rich, who lived in the rue Bar-du-Bec; he was even able to tell Canler the number. Canler's chief, Allard, was now so interested in the case that he went with him to visit the old lady. When they rang the bell of her apartment, a panel slid open, and a woman asked them what they wanted. "To speak to Madame Gaillard about her nephew. We are police officers."

In her apartment, Mme Gaillard explained apologetically that she did not trust her nephew, which was why she had had the grill put in the door – he was perfectly capable of murdering her. What, asked Allard, was her nephew's real name? "Pierre-François Lacenaire." It was the first time that Canler had heard the name of the criminal he was hunting for the past three weeks.

A general alert went out. There was no sign of Lacenaire in Paris. But a few days later, on 2 February 1835, the District Attorney in Beaune wrote a letter announcing the arrest of Lacenaire on a charge of passing a forged bill of exchange. He was brought back to Paris in chains. The man Canler and Allard confronted in his cell did not look like a master criminal – more like a gentleman down on his luck. When accused of the attempted robbery of the bank messenger, he admitted it without emotion; like many villains, he felt that it was simply a "job" that had turned out badly, like any unfortunate business venture. Asked the name of his accomplice, he replied: "Gentleman we villains have our code. We do not denounce our accomplices." Canler replied that his accomplices were not bound by a similar code; François had already betrayed him. Lacenaire merely smiled politely; he knew the police were capable of bluffing. All he would say was: "I shall make enquiries." He looked slightly more disturbed when Canler told him that Avril had done his best to betray him, but made the same response. Lacenaire was then transferred to La Force prison.

There his "enquiries" led to his being savagely beaten up by friends of François, so that he had to spend some weeks in the prison hospital. When he next saw Canler, he was ready to obtain his revenge. He made a full confession of both crimes, implicating Avril in the murder of the Chardons, and François in the attack on the bank messenger.

In prison, Lacenaire became a celebrity. The idea of a poetic murderer appealed to the Parisian public; he received many visitors, and discoursed to them on the injustice of the social system – to which he attributed his choice of a life of crime. In the period of the unpopular July Monarchy, with its repressive laws, this kind of thing appealed to Republican intellectuals. Lacenaire revelled in the limelight – it was what he had always craved. The poet Théophile Gautier called him "the Manfred of the gutter" (referring to Byron's noble rebel) and the nickname seemed appropriate. (Pictures of Lacenaire make him look rather like Poe.) In November 1835, Lacenaire, François, and Avril went on trial; Lacenaire and Avril were sentenced to death, François to life imprisonment. Lacenaire admitted frankly that his motive in giving evidence against his accomplices was revenge; he evidently took pleasure in making them aware that if they had observed the code of honour among thieves, none of them would have been in this predicament.

In prison, Lacenaire wrote his *Memoirs*, which were intended to be his justification. He is intent on proving that he is less a criminal than an "Outsider". "A victim of injustice since infancy . . . I had created a view of life very different from other men's. I know only one virtue, which is worth all the rest: it is Sensibility." In fact, the book is full of the emotional, upside-down logic of the typical criminal, a logic based upon self-pity. He loathed his father, and was upset because his parents preferred his elder brother; convinced at the age of sixteen that he would die on the guillotine (to which he liked to refer as his "mistress") he decided to "have the blood of society". But it soon becomes clear that his real trouble was not his philosophy of revolt, but his weakness; when things went well, he was a law-abiding citizen; as soon as they went wrong, he was thrown into a passion of indignation against fate, and tried to take the easy way out by looking around for something to steal. He lacked the ability to face adversity. It is worth commenting on this aspect of Lacenaire's psychology, for we shall encounter it many times in the course of this book.

The execution was carried out, unannounced, on a cold and foggy January morning. Lacenaire watched Avril's head fall into the basket without flinching; but when he himself knelt under the blade, there was an accident that would have broken another man's nerve; as the blade fell, it stuck half-way, and had to be hauled up again; Lacenaire was looking up at it as it dropped and severed his head.

# chapter two

# CRIMINAL TRIALS

*T*he *"Age of Gaslight"* sounds almost modern – after all, it is the age before the coming of electricity. But you only have to read any account of trials in the early nineteenth century to realize that life was closer to the Middle Ages than to the twentieth century.

The Bavarian judge Anselm Ritter von Feuerbach, who was active during the first three decades of the nineteenth century, also wrote a vast work consisting of the trials in which he had been concerned. A small part of it was translated into English in 1846 under the title Narratives of Remarkable Criminal Trials, and it conveys more clearly than any work of history what it was like to live in Bavaria around the turn of the nineteenth century.

The first case in this chapter is so typical that it is worth describing at length, even though the crime itself is brutal and horrific. Let Feuerbach himself set the scene, in order to give some idea of the flavour of his style.

## The Case of John Paul Forster

"Christopher Bäumler, a worthy citizen of Nürnberg, lived in the Königsstrasse, a wide and much-frequented street, where he carried on the trade of a corn-chandler, which there includes the right of selling brandy. He had lately lost his wife, and lived quite alone with only one maid-servant, Anna Catherina Schütz. He had the reputation of being rich.

Bäumler was in the habit of opening his shop at five o'clock in the morning at latest. But on the 21st of September, 1820, to the surprise of his neighbours it remained closed till past six. Curiosity and alarm drew together a number of people before the house. They rang repeatedly, but no one came to the door. At last some neighbours, with the sanction of the police, entered the first-floor windows by a ladder. Here they found drawers, chests, and closets burst open, and presenting every appearance of a robbery having been committed. They hastened down stairs into the shop, where they discovered in a corner close to the street-door the bloody corpse of the maid; and in the parlour they found Bäumler lying dead beside the stove.

As soon as the police were informed of the murder, a commission was appointed to visit Bäumler's house. Immediately on entering the shop, to the right of the door in the corner, between two bins of meal and salt, the maid-servant Schütz lay on her back, with her head shattered, and her feet, from which both her shoes had fallen, turned towards the door. Her face and clothes, and the floor, were covered with blood; and the two bins, between which her head lay, as well as the wall, were sprinkled with it. As no other part of the shop showed any marks of blood, it was evident that she had been murdered in this corner. Not far from the body they picked up a small comb, and at a little distance from that a larger one, with several fragments of a second small one. In the very farthest corner of the parlour, between the stove and a small table, upon which stood a jug, they found the body of Bäumler stretched on his back, with his head, which was resting on a small over-turned stool, covered with wounds and blood. A pipe and several small coins lay under the body, where they had probably fallen when the murderer ransacked the pocket, which was turned inside out and stained with blood, for money or for keys. The floor, the stove, and the wall were covered with blood, the stool was saturated, and even the vaulted ceiling, which was nine or ten feet high, was sprinkled with it. These circumstances, especially the stool on which Bäumler's head still rested, and the pipe which lay under his body, showed that the murderer must have suddenly attacked him unawares and felled him to the earth, as he sat drinking his beer and smoking his pipe on that very spot.

On the table, in the parlour, stood a wine-glass with some red brandy at the bottom, and a closed clasp-knife stained with blood on the back and sides. Two newly-baked rolls were found near the entrance-door.

The baker Stierhof stated that Bäumler's maid had fetched these rolls from his shop the evening before, at about a quarter to ten. His wife, who was examined the next day on this point, recognised the rolls as those bought by the unfortunate maid-servant on the evening of the 20th of September.

On examining the body of the maid-servant, a handsome well-shaped girl of twenty-three, the head was found completely shattered; there were also several wounds upon the neck, breast, and hands, and the breast-bone and three of the ribs were fractured. Bäumler's skull was broken into eleven pieces; and although there were no external injuries upon the chest, the sternum and ribs were fractured, as in the maid-servant. There could not be the slightest doubt that the wounds were mortal. The surgeons gave it as their opinion that the wounds on the heads of both victims had been inflicted with a heavy instrument having a flat surface with sharp edges, probably the back of a hatchet. The ribs did not appear to have been broken with the hatchet, but rather by stamping on the bodies.

The evidence of the baker's wife had led to the conclusion that some man who had stayed until late in the evening at Bäumler's house must have been the murderer. Accordingly, all those who had been at Bäumler's house on that evening were examined, and concurred in saying that a stranger had entered the shop very early, had sat at the farther end of the table, alternately smoking and drinking red brandy out of a wine-glass; and that he had remained there alone at nine o'clock, when the others went away. All agreed in their description of his person; that he was about thirty, of dark complexion, and black hair and beard; that he wore a dark-coloured coat (most of the witnesses said a blue one, which afterwards proved to be a mistake), and that he had on a high beaver hat. With the exception of one witness who had conversed with the stranger about the hop trade and other like matters, and had found him a well-informed, agreeable man, they all stated that he had kept his hat pressed over his face, and his eyes constantly fixed on the ground, and that he had said little or nothing. He stated himself to be a hop-merchant, and said that he was waiting at Bäumler's for his companion, another hop-merchant, who had gone to the play. The witnesses recognised the glass produced in court, as exactly similar to that out of which the stranger had been drinking red clove-brandy."

The first thing that strikes the modern reader about all this is that Bäumler opened his shop at 5 a.m., and that the neighbours wondered what was the matter when he still wasn't open by 6. Elsewhere in the narrative, Feuerbach mentions that the brandy shop stayed open until 11 at night. An eighteen hour day. And it was obviously taken for granted by the rest of the people of Nuremberg, who probably worked roughly the same hours . . .

Feuerbach goes on to say:

"Meanwhile suspicion had fallen upon a certain Paul Forster, who had lately been discharged from the bridewell at Schwabach, and who had been observed for several days before the murder walking about in a suspicious manner before Bäumler's house. His father, a miserably poor day-labourer, lived with two daughters of infamous characters in a cottage belonging to a gardener named Thaler, in the suburb of St John. Forster did not live with his father; but on the morning after the murder he had left the suburb of St John quite early, and had gone to Diesbeck, where he lived with a woman called Margaret Preiss, who had been his mistress for many years. At her house he was arrested by the police on the 23rd of September, the third day after the murder. In her room were found, among other things, two bags of money, the one containing 209 florins 21 kreuzers, the other 152 florins 17 kreuzers. Besides these Preiss's illegitimate daughter, a girl of about fourteen, gave up a small purse containing some medals and a ducat which Forster had given to her when he returned to Diesbeck.

On the following day, when the gens d'armes were escorting Forster and his mistress through Fürth, the waiter of the inn recognised the prisoner as the man who had come to the inn at about eight or nine in the morning of the 21st of September, dressed in a dark grey cloth greatcoat, went away again in about an hour, and then returned dressed in a dark blue coat, and gave him a brown one which he carried under his arm to take care of, requesting him to keep it safe, and to be sure not to show it to any one; adding that in a week he would return and claim it. The waiter now informed the magistrate at Fürth of this circumstance, and produced the greatcoat, which was much stained and in some places soaked with blood.

The description given of the suspicious-looking stranger, who had sat out all the others on the evening of the 20th of September, exactly resembled Forster."

So the murderer was caught easily enough; it could hardly have been easier if he had given himself up.

Now comes one of the oddest parts of the case:

"As soon as the prisoners reached Nürnberg, at about

4 p.m. of the 24th, they were conducted, according to legal practice, to view the bodies lying in Bäumler's house. The corpses were laid in their coffins, with the faces exposed and the bodies covered with their own bloody garments; Bäumler on the right, and the maid-servant on the left hand, thus leaving a passage open between the coffins.

Paul Forster was brought in first: he stepped into the room, and between the two corpses, without the slightest change of countenance. When desired to look at them, he gazed steadfastly and coldly upon them, and replied to the question whether he knew the body on the right, 'No, I know it not; it is quite disfigured: I know it not.' And to the second question, 'Do you know this one to the left?' he answered in the same manner, 'No, she has lain in the grave; I know her not.' When asked how he knew that the body had lain in the grave, he replied, pointing to the face, 'Because she is so disfigured; the face is quite decayed here!' On being desired by the judge to point out the exact spot which he thought so decayed, with a constrained air, but with the coarsest indifference, he grasped the head of the murdered woman, pressed the brow, the broken nose, and the cheeks with his fingers, and said quite coolly, 'Here: you may see it clearly!' He attempted to evade every question addressed to him by the judge, by affecting that the idea of murder was so utterly foreign to him, that in all innocence and simplicity he mistook the deadly wounds for the result of decay.

All the endeavours of the judge to wring some sign of embarrassment or feeling from this man, as he stood between his two victims, were vain: his iron soul was unmoved. Only once, when asked, 'Where, then, is the corn-chandler to whom the house belongs?' he appeared staggered, but only for a moment. The judge went so far in his zeal, as to desire him to hold the hands of both corpses, and then to say what he felt. Without a moment's hesitation, Forster grasped the cold hand of Bäumler in his right, and that of Schütz in his left hand;

and answered, 'He feels cold – ah, she is cold too;' an answer which clearly contained a sort of contemptuous sneer at the judge's question. During the whole scene, the tone of his voice was as soft and sanctimonious, and his manner as calm, as his feelings were cold and unmoved.

His mistress's behaviour was very different: she was much shaken on entering the room. When desired to look at the dead bodies, she did so, but instantly turned away shuddering, and asked for water. She declared that she knew nothing of these persons, or of the manner of their death. She said that she had learned that she was supposed to be implicated in the horrible deed from the populace, who crowded in thousands round the carriage which brought them from Fürth to Nürnberg, calling her a murderess, striking her with their fists and sticks, and ill-using her in every way. But that God would manifest her innocence, and that she could bring witnesses to prove that she had not left her home at Diesbeck for some weeks. Her evident compassion for the victims, and horror of the crime, spoke more in favour of her innocence than her tears and protestations. An alibi was subsequently most clearly proved."

This method of getting the suspected murderer to view – and even touch – the corpse was common all over Europe at this period. Feuerbach comments that in cases of infanticide, this has never been known to fail. But this murderer was a hardened criminal, and was unaffected.

It was, of course, an open-and-shut case. The police were able to prove that Forster's sister had given him the axe with which he killed Bäumler and the maidservant. Forster continued to deny knowing anything about the murders until he saw that all these denials would only make things worse. So at this stage he changed his story, and explained that the murders had actually been committed by two men called Schlemmer, who had offered to take him with them to Bohemia, where their rich relations would give him a job. He had met them later in the day, and they had offered to look after his axe while he took a letter to the post. They then vanished with his axe. He met them later at the brandy shop, after all the other guests had gone, and they sent him to go and look out for their cart, which was due to arrive about ten. While he was still waiting for the cart, the Schlemmer's joined him, carrying a trunk and a white parcel. The cart now arrived, and they drove off to the city gate, where the Schlemmer's told him they would not take him to Bohemia after all, but would give him a present . . . This was the white parcel, and when Forster got it home, he found that it contained some bloodstained clothes, and the bags of money that were found in his mistress's house.

It was an absurd story, but the judges had to check it out. They suspected, in any case, that Forster had had accomplices, because Bäumler was reputed to be a very rich man, and should have had far more than the 350 or so florins found in Forster's possession. They checked – with German thoroughness – but finally concluded that the Schlemmer's were a figment of Forster's imagination.

Still Forster fought every inch of the way. He had good reason: a man could not be executed unless he confessed. And by 1820, torture had been abolished in Bavaria. (Feuerbach had been responsible for that, in 1806.) Eventually, he was found guilty, and sentenced to life imprisonment in chains, with hard labour. His sister was sentenced to a year in prison as an accomplice.

And that seems to be the end of the case. But in fact, the most interesting part is still to come. Feuerbach goes on to quote at length from an autobiography written by Forster when he was in jail for burglary two years earlier. And this makes it clear that Forster was far from being a brutal and basically stupid killer. He calls it *The Romance of My Life and Loves*, and even Feuerbach is compelled to admit that parts are very well written indeed.

John Paul Forster explains that as a child, he was quiet and thoughtful. A baron came to live in a house in which Forster's father was the gardener, and Forster got to know the baron's two children, and greatly enjoyed acting as a kind of servant to them. The baron liked this so much that he used to invite Forster over every day. His schoolfriends and even his brother began to call him a snob, and refused to play with him. But John Paul had glimpsed a way of life that filled him with longing. And when he left school, the baron offered him a job as a servant. He dressed in grey livery, and accompanied his master and mistress

to "balls and assemblies". He was in the seventh heaven, says
Feuerbach.

Then came the blow that would eventually turn Forster into a criminal. His father, who was religious, decided that John Paul ought to become a shoemaker. John Paul flatly refused; but he finally agreed to learn the trade of gardening, because that gave him an opportunity of "coming into contact with gentlefolks". And he was apparently an excellent gardener – until he was conscripted into the army (This was about 1805, when all Europe was in arms against Napoleon.)

From then on, things went from bad to worse. He hated army life, with its beatings and semi-starvation. (Again, we have to remember that soldiers were beaten as a matter of course.) He was always in trouble with the NCOs, always being flogged or thrown into jail. One day he stole away to spend the night with a cook named Babetta, with whom he was in love; he returned the next day, but his absence had been noted, and he received twenty lashes.

In 1810 he fell in love again, this time with Margaretha Preiss. He badly wanted to leave the army, but was not allowed to. He began trying to get himself thrown out of the army by thieving. He also deserted several times, and was sentenced each time to "run the gauntlet" (which was as painful as being flogged) and sentenced to serve another six years in the army. Finally, his crimes caused so much trouble that he was drummed out in disgrace.

That, of course, was what he wanted; but ten years of cheating, lying and deserting had undermined his character, and made him bitter. He was soon in jail for three and a half years for burglary. There he wrote the autobiography, intended as a legacy for his beloved Margaretha. Feuerbach sneers that it illustrates how important he thought he was, and quotes with contempt passages about the "soft murmuring of the evening breezes and the melting harmony of the senses." In fact, they reveal that Forster was genuinely a tragic "outsider" figure, a man who had had a glimpse of freedom and then had it snatched from him. The amount of poetry that he quotes reveals that he was highly literate.

The murder, admittedly, was utterly stupid, the act of a man who wanted to get rich quick and marry his Margaretha. Like Raskolnikov in Dostoevsky's *Crime and Punishment*, he was hoping that one single crime would bring him thousands of florins, enough to give him a start in life. Instead, he was to spend the rest of his life in chains. But even the account of his years in jail make us aware that he was no common criminal. Feuerbach says: "For years Forster had borne in dogged silence the hardships of imprisonment, the misery of civil death, the burden of his chains, and the still heavier burden of a troubled conscience." All attempts to make him confess were a failure. His life was totally ruined, yet he told his fellow prisoners: "Steadfastness of purpose is the chief ornament of a man. He should not easily give up life; however wretched, life is a noble thing. Believe me, comrades, whenever I look upon my ball and chain, I feel proud to think that even on my death bed my last breath shall be drawn with courage." He even polished his chains until they "shone like silver". At first he used to enthrall his fellow prisoners – who all regarded him with the deepest respect – with amazing stories "of enchanted princes and princesses"; then he suddenly decided to speak only in monosyllables, and kept up this resolution "out of pride" for the rest of his life (or what we know of the rest of it.)

His stubbornness was unbending. When given work he considered too hard for him he refused to do it. He was lashed, "receiving the severest blows without moving a muscle or uttering a sound, and returned to his cell just as if nothing had happened." He was beaten again and again, each time he refused to do the work; at last the authorities were forced to give way, and allow him to do the work he preferred.

Feuerbach ends his account by telling us that Forster's face is "vulgar and heavy", the lower part so long that it gives him the look of an animal. Although a humanitarian, he obviously regards John Paul Forster as a contemptible ruffian. For the modern reader, Forster's story is one of tragically wasted powers. He had "ideas above his station", and he had the kind of courage and determination that might have brought him fame and success. Instead, he spent the rest of his life – he was still alive when Feuerbach described the case – mouldering in Lichtenau jail. Life in the year 1820 could be devastatingly cruel.

# Anna Zwanziger

The same point is made by Feuerbach's most remarkable story:
his account of the mass poisoner Anna Zwanziger. Again, I
quote his account of her crimes:

"In the year 1807 a widow, nearly fifty years of age,
calling herself Nanette Schönleben, lived at Pegnitz
in the territory of Baireuth, supporting herself by
knitting. Her conduct gained her a reputation which
induced Justice Wolfgang Glaser, who was then
living at Rosendorf separated from his wife, to
take her as his housekeeper, on the 5th March,
1808. On the 22nd of the following July Glaser was
reconciled to his wife, who had been living with
her relations at Grieshaber near Augsburg. Soon
after her return to her husband's house, though
a strong healthy woman, she was suddenly seized
with violent vomiting, diarrhœa, &c., and on the 26th
August, a month after the reconciliation, she died.
Anna Schönleben now left Glaser's service, and
on the 25th September she went to live as housekeeper with Justice Grohmann at Sanspareil. Her
new master, who was unmarried, was thirty-eight
years of age, and though a large and powerful man,
had suffered from gout for several years, and was
often confined to his bed. On these occasions Anna
Schönleben always nursed him with the utmost care.
In the spring of 1809 he was seized with an illness
more violent than any he had had before, and
accompanied by entirely new symptoms, – violent
vomiting, pains in the stomach, diarrhœa, heat and
dryness of the skin, inflammation of the mouth and
throat, insatiable thirst, and excessive weakness and
pains in the limbs. He died on the 8th May, after an
illness of eleven days, and his housekeeper appeared
inconsolable for his loss. Every one, the medical men
included, took it for granted that Grohmann, who
had long been ailing, had died a natural death.

Anna Schönleben was once more out of place, but her reputation for kindness, activity, attention and skill as a sick-nurse soon procured her a new home. At the time of Grohmann's death the wife of the magistrate Gebhard was just expecting to be brought to bed, and asked Anna Schönleben to attend her as nurse and housekeeper during her lying-in. Anna Schönleben, always willing to oblige, readily agreed, and from the day of the confinement she resided in Gebhard's house, dividing her time between the care of the household and of the child. Madame Gebhard was confined on the 13th May, 1809, and both the mother and the child were doing very well until the third day, which the mother fell ill. Her illness became more alarming every day; she was seized with violent vomiting, nervous agitation, distressing heat in the intestines, inflammation in the throat, &c.; and on the 20th May, seven days after her confinement, she died, exclaiming in her agony, 'Merciful Heaven! you have given me poison!' As Madame Gebhard had always been sickly, and moreover had died in childbirth, her death excited no suspicion, and, like Madame Glaser and Grohmann, she was buried without more ado. The widower, embarrassed by his household and the infant which was left upon his hands, thought that he could do nothing better than to keep Anna Schönleben as his housekeeper. Several persons endeavoured to change his resolution. They said that this woman carried death with her wherever she went; that three young persons whom she had served, had died one after the other within a very short time. No one made the smallest accusation against her; their warnings arose from a mere superstitions dread of an unfortunate sympathetic influence exercised by her upon those with whom she lived: her obliging deportment, her piety, and her air of honesty, humility and kindness, protected her from every breath of suspicion. Thus she remained for several months in Gebhard's service unsuspected and unaccused.

During her residence in Gebhard's house various

suspicious events occurred, without, however, exciting attention. On the 25th August, 1809, a certain Beck, and the widow Alberti, dined with Gebhard. Soon after dinner they were both seized with violent vomiting, colic, spasms, &c., which lasted until late at night. About the same time she gave the messenger Rosenhauer a glass of white wine, and not long after he had swallowed it he was attacked in precisely the same manner, and was so ill as to be forced to go to bed. On the very same day she took Rosenhauer's porter, a lad of nineteen named Johann Kraus, into the cellar and gave him a glass of brandy. After drinking a small quantity he perceived a sort of white sediment in it, and therefore left the rest, but in a short time he felt very sick. During the last week of August, one of Gebhard's maid-servants, Barbara Waldmann, with whom Anna Schönleben had had several trifling disputes, was taken ill after drinking a cup of coffee, and vomited every half-hour during the whole day. The most remarkable occurrence, however, took place on the 1st September. Gebhard, while playing at skittles with a party of his friends, sent for a few pitchers of beer from his own cellar. He and five other persons drank some of the beer, and were seized soon after with sickness and internal pains; some of the party, among whom was Gebhard, were so ill as to require medical aid.

This first inspired distrust and dislike of Anna Schönleben. On the following day, chiefly at the instigation of one of his fellow-sufferers at the skittle-ground, Gebhard dismissed her from his service, but gave her a written character for honesty and fidelity.

She was to leave Sanspareil for Baireuth on the next day – 3rd September. She expressed her surprise at so sudden a dismissal, but was civil and obliging as usual, and busied herself during the whole evening in various domestic arrangements. Among other things she took the salt-box out of the kitchen (which was no part of her usual duty), and filled it from a barrel of salt which stood in Gebhard's bedroom. When the maid-servant Waldmann commented upon this, Anna Schönleben said, in a jesting manner, that she must do so, for that if those who were going away filled the salt-box, the other servants would keep their places the longer. On the morning of her departure she affected the greatest friendship for the two maid-servants, Hazin and Waldmann, and gave each of them a cup of coffee sweetened with sugar which she took out of a piece of paper. While the carriage was waiting for her at the door she took Gebhard's child, an infant five months old, in her arms, gave it a biscuit soaked in milk to eat, then let it drink the milk, and finally parted from it with the most tender caresses, and got into the carriage which was to convey her to Baireuth, and which Gebhard paid for, besides giving her a crown dollar and some chocolate.

She had been gone scarce half an hour when the child became alarmingly ill and vomited terribly, and in a few hours more the two maid-servants were attacked in the same manner; and now, for the first time, suspicion was excited. On hearing from his servants how Anna Schönleben had busied herself, Gebhard had the contents of the kitchen salt-box analyzed by a chemist, and a large quantity of arsenic was found among it. The salt-barrel was likewise found at the trial to contain thirty grains of arsenic to every three pounds of salt."

Anna Zwanziger was caught fairly easily. After wandering around for a few months, hoping that Judge Gebhard would send for her – she was obviously slightly insane – she made the mistake of returning to Nuremberg, where she was arrested. Two packets of arsenic were found in her possession. The science of toxicology – detecting poisons – had recently made enormous strides, and when Frau Glaser's body was exhumed, large quantities of arsenic were found. Faced with this evidence, she finally confessed, and was executed by sword in 1811.

Once again, Feuerbach's account of her life throws an entirely new light on the case, and even if we end by feeling no sympathy for the mass murderess, we at least begin to understand why she did it. Born in Nuremberg in August, 1760, the daughter of an innkeeper, Anna was orphaned by the time she was five. After living for five years with various relatives, she was taken at the age of ten into the house of her guardian, a wealthy merchant, and there received a good education. She was more fortunate than John Paul Forster, for she actually lived the kind of life Forster only dreamed about. But when she was fifteen, her guardian decided to marry her to a drunken lawyer named Zwanziger, who was more than twice her age. She objected, but finally had to give way.

Spending most of her days alone, while her husband was out drinking with cronies, she became an avid reader of novels and plays. She was so moved by Goethe's *Sorrows of Young Werther* – which had caused an epidemic of suicide ten years earlier – that she was also tempted to kill herself. She also read Richardson's novel *Pamela*, about a servant girl whose master tries hard to seduce her, but is finally so overcome by her virtue and goodness that he marries her. This also exercised a powerful influence on her. And she was deeply moved by Lessing's tragedy *Emilia Galeotti*, about a girl who is pursued by a wicked prince (who has murdered her fiancée) and ends by persuading her father to kill her to prevent rape.

Her husband soon spent her inheritance – he was capable of drinking ten bottles of wine a day, and was soon a hopeless alcoholic. Anna was now forced to become a high class prostitute to support her husband and two children – although she claimed she only slept with gentlemen. This, at least, was better than starving; she learned to use her physical charms to persuade men to support her. She even thought up a brilliant scheme involving a lottery of watches (we would call it a raffle), which

James Marsh, the British chemist who invented an incredibly sensitive test for arsenic – so sensitive that it could detect a thousandth of a milligram of arsenic – was a scientific prodigy who was never appreciated. He worked all his life for thirty shillings a week at the Royal Military Academy. For his great discovery he was given the gold medal of the Society of Arts – but would have undoubtedly preferred cash. Frustration turned him into an alcoholic and when he died at 52, he left his wife and children destitute.

once again made them prosperous; but her husband again spent the money. One lover, a lieutenant, persuaded her to leave her husband, but her husband then persuaded her to return. When she divorced him, he persuaded her to remarry him the next day. Clearly, Anna was not the ruthless bitch Feuerbach represents her as. She admits that she ended by feeling very fond of him.

Finally, Zwanziger died, and after eighteen years, Anna was left on her own. There was no national assistance or social security in Bavaria in 1796. she had to find a way to support herself and her children. She tried to set up a sweetshop in Vienna, but it failed. She became a housekeeper, but had to leave when she had an illegitimate child by a clerk – she put it into a foundling's home, where it died.

Anna was now thirty-eight, still attractive to men. She found a "protector" who installed her in lodgings, and tried to supplement her income with doll making. Tired of being a kept woman, she accepted an excellent job as a housekeeper in the home of a minister, but left after a few months – Feuerbach says because of her dirty habits, but more probably because she gave herself "airs and graces". For, as Feuerbach remarks perceptively, "the insupportable thought of having fallen from her station as mistress of a house and family to the condition of a servant, worked so strongly on her feelings as to cause her to behave like a madwoman." In short, the ups and downs of her life caused her to suffer a mental breakdown. "She laughed, wept and prayed by turns. She received her mistress's orders with a laugh, and went obediently away, but never executed them."

Anna was now definitely insane, and in her misery, she retained one basic obsession: to have a man to look after her and protect her. But her physical charms were fast disappearing. Her old "protector" took her back for a while and got her pregnant again, then left her to chase an actress. She had a miscarriage. After that she attempted suicide by drowning, but was rescued by two fishermen. She was ill with fever for several weeks.

At the age of forty-four, no longer attractive, Anna was forced to take an ill-paid job as a housemaid; now she was at a kind of rock bottom. She stole a diamond ring and absconded. Her master reacted by placing a notice in the newspapers naming her as a thief, which destroyed any remnants of reputation she still possessed. Her son-in-law, with whom she was staying, threw her out.

In the following year, it looked as if fate had finally smiled on her. Working as a needlework teacher, she attracted an old general and became his mistress. Again she dreamed of security and being in charge of her own household. But he walked out on her, and ignored her letters.

And so, in 1807, after more miserable wandering from place to place, she found herself in Pegnitz, near Baireuth, where she was offered a job by Judge Glaser. (To explain her preference for judges, we have to remember that her first husband was a lawyer.) At fifty, the craving for security had given her the cunning of a madwoman. She poisoned the wife of Judge Glaser, hoping he would marry her – an insane hope, since she was now skinny, sallow and ugly. She moved on to the home of Judge Grohmann, who was unmarried and twelve years her junior. Now, surely, she had found the man who was destined to bring security to her old age . . .? Grohmann suffered from gout, and she enjoyed nursing him. She enjoyed nursing him so much that she began slipping small quantities of arsenic and antimony into his food. Eventually, she overdid it – this seems clear, since she can have had no reason to kill her meal ticket – and he died. Feuerbach says she appeared inconsolable, and this is almost certainly because she was.

And so it continued – the tragedy of a madwoman who remembered that she had once been a mistress with servants, an attractive women whom men had once desired, and who was now incapable of facing reality. In our own society, she would have been confined in an asylum after her trial, and so found some kind of security in her final years. As it was, she knelt down at the block, and her head fell into the headsman's basket. Perhaps the woman who had identified with Emilia Galeotti and Pamela felt that it was more appropriate than dying in a workhouse.

# Andrew Bichel

Feuerbach records another case of a multiple killer that has the odd distinction of being possibly the first recorded instance of what we would now call the sex murder. This statement must immediately be qualified by saying that there have always been sex crimes, particularly during wars, and that the sixteen century Nuremberg executioner Hans Schmidt records a number of cases in which robbers have also raped their female victims. But the sex crimes of the past were usually committed by drunks, or (as in the case of Schmidt's robbers) with rape as the secondary aim. Bichel's crimes seem to have been motivated by some odd sexual perversion which was certainly not understood at the time.

The case was discussed by Major Arthur Griffiths, one of the best of the late nineteenth century historians of crime, whose *Mysteries of Police and Crime*, published in 1898, is still highly readable. Here is his description of the Bichel case.

> "One of the earliest cases recorded is that of Andrew Bichel, who lived at Regendorf, in Bavaria. His character was strangely contradictory. Until his terrible misdeeds were finally brought home to him, he did not enjoy a bad reputation. He was not a drunkard, nor a gambler, nor quarrelsome; he was married to a wife with whom he lived on good terms, had children, and was esteemed for his piety. But below the surface he was a pilferer and petty thief; suspected of robbing his neighbours' gardens, he was caught by the master he served, an inn-keeper of Regendorf, stealing hay from his loft. His nature really was abjectly and inordinately covetous; he was a coward who persisted in his crimes because he seemed to have secured perfect immunity from detection. They were committed on the defenceless; his victims were helpless, credulous women, who trusted him and made no attempt to defend themselves. Cunning in him was allied to great cruelty, and both were backed by such extraordinary greed that he thought

the pettiest plunder worth the greatest crime. 'A man thus constituted will commit no crimes requiring energy or courage,' writes the judge who tried him. 'He will never venture to rob on the highway, or break into a house; but he would commit arson, administer poison, murder a man in his sleep, or, like Bichel, cunningly induce young girls to go to him, and then murder them in cold blood for the sake of their clothes or a few pence.'

No suspicion was roused against Bichel for years. Girls went to Regendorf, and were never heard of again. One, Barbara Reisinger, disappeared in 1807, and another, Catherine Seidel, the year after. In both cases no report was made to the police until a long time had elapsed, and a first clue to the disappearance of the last-named was obtained by a sister, who found a tailor making up a waistcoat from a piece of dimity which she recognised as having formed part of a petticoat worn by Catherine when she was last seen. The waistcoat was for a certain Andrew Bichel, who lived in the town, and who now followed the curious profession of fortune-teller.

Catherine Seidel had been attracted by his promises to show her fortune in a glass. She was to come to him in her best clothes, the best she had, and with three changes, for this was part of the performance. She went as directed, and was never heard of again. Bichel, when asked, declared she had eloped with a man she met at his house.

Now that suspicion was aroused against Bichel, his house in Regendorf was searched, and a chest full of women's clothes was found in his room. Among them were many garments identified as belonging to the missing Catherine Seidel. One of her handkerchiefs, moreover, was taken out of his pocket when he was apprehended.

Still there was no direct proof of murder. The disappearance of Seidel was undoubted, Reisinger's also, and the presumption of foul play was strong. Some crime had been committed, but whether abduction, manslaughter, or murder was still a hidden mystery.

Repeated searchings of Bichel's house were fruitless; no dead bodies were found, no stains of blood, no traces of violence.

The dog of a police sergeant first ran the crime to ground. He pointed so constantly to a wood-shed in the yard, and when called off so persistently returned to the same spot, that the officer determined to explore the shed thoroughly. In one corner lay a great heap of straw and litter, and on digging deep below this they turned up a quantity of human bones. They went a foot deeper, and found more remains. Near at hand, underneath a pile of logs by a chalk pit, a human head was found. Not far off was a second body, which, like the first, had been cut in half. One was believed to be the corpse of Barbara Reisinger, the other was actually identified, through a pair of pinchbeck earrings, as that of Catherine Seidel.

Bichel stood defiant before the searching questions of the judge; he lied continually, and was proved to have lied. Still he would make no avowal. Even when confronted with the corpses of his alleged victims, as was then the custom in Bavaria, he would not yield. Although so greatly agitated that he all but fainted on the spot, he had yet the strength of will to master his emotions, and when again asked if he recognised his handiwork, he protested that he had never seen the corpses before. 'I only trembled,' he protested, when taxed with the weakness, 'I only trembled at the sight. Who would not tremble on such an occasion?' But he could not stand; he sank into a chair. All his muscles quivered; his face was horribly contorted.

Yet a deep impression had been left on his mind, and when relegated to prison 'his imagination,' as Feuerbach says, 'overcame his obstinacy.' He made full confession of these two particular crimes. Reisinger he had killed when she came seeking a situation as maid-servant. He was tempted by her clothes. To murder he had recourse to his trade of fortune-telling, saying he would show her in a magic mirror her future fate, and producing a

board and a small magnifying glass, placed them
on a table in front of her. She must not touch
these sacred objects; her eyes must be bandaged,
her hands tied behind her back. No sooner had she
consented than he stabbed her in the neck, and it
was all over with her.

This success emboldened him to repeat the operation. He sought to entrap other girls, choosing always
the best dressed, and putting forward the bait of the
magic mirror. But he failed with three, and then
caught Catherine Seidel in the toils. The process was
exactly the same as with Barbara Reisinger, but this
victim was not killed so easily. The after part was
the same.

Bichel now resolved to adopt murder as a trade,
and looked about him for fresh victims. But although
the motive was strong and his cunning great, he does
not seem to have enticed many more within reach of
his knife. The police heard of several cases in which
he had used the same lure of the magic glass upon
girls who promised to go to him dressed in their best,
but who, fortunately for themselves, thought better
of it. They escaped, some by want of faith in the
mirror, others by a secret aversion to Bichel, a few
by mere accident.

Bichel, was found guilty and condemned to be
broken on the wheel, but the sentence was commuted
to beheading."

Why did Bichel murder girls? Feuerbach seems to accept
Bichel's own explanation. "My only reason for murdering
Reisinger and Seidel was desire for their clothes." But the
next sentence contradicts this. "I must confess I did not want
them; but it was exactly as if someone stood at my elbow and
whispered: "Do this and buy corn." Which makes it sound as
if Bichel's extreme poverty drove him to crime. But if that *was*
his motive, then why did he keep the clothes?

A modern psychiatrist would have interviewed Bichel until
he understood his motives. Was he, perhaps, fascinated by his
sister's clothes as a child, and enjoyed dressing up in them?
Did he have some deep resentment of well-dressed women that

**50**  aroused a kind of sadistic desire to kill? Or is it possible that the motive was simply rape? At this distance in time, we shall never know. And unfortunately, Feuerbach himself has failed to provide us with the biographical clues that he unearthed in the case of Forster and Anna Zwanziger . . .

# chapter three

# NOTORIOUS AMERICAN CASES

*C*riminally speaking, America in the early nineteenth century is relatively uninteresting. There were plenty of violent deaths, of course, but they were mostly the work of bandits and common criminals. Soon after World War II, a New York publisher issued a series of volumes on murders in major cities – New York murders, Chicago murders, Denver murders, and so on.
But few of them contain any cases before 1850.

The same applies to the best compilation of American crime in the nineteenth century, Thomas S. Duke's Celebrated Criminal Cases of America, published in San Francisco in 1910. The book is full of marvellous accounts of riots and robberies and Indian massacres, of political assassins and murderous thugs. But there are few cases that rate as criminological classics, on the level of Burke and Hare or Lacenaire or Anna Zwanziger.

One of the rare exceptions is the amazing story of the murder in the Harvard Medical School. Thomas Duke was an ex-policeman, and his down-to-earth, factual way of telling the story adds to its impact.

In North Carolina, Lavinia Fisher has become a legend, like Calamity Jane or Bonnie Parker. Lavinia and her husband John Fisher were members of a gang of highwaymen who, in 1818, operated from Six Mile House, north of Charleston, and robbed passing travellers. Cavalry surrounded the house and ordered the gang to leave. They did so quietly, and the cavalry left behind a young man called David Ross to guard the house. The next day the gang came back and threw him out; the beautiful Lavinia attacked him and pushed his head through a pane of glass. The enraged lawmen returned and forced the gang to surrender. Most of them were sentenced to death for highway robbery. But Lavinia persuaded the susceptible prison governor to allow them to occupy a more comfortable – and less secure – part of the jail. In September 1818, they knocked a hole in the wall, and John Fisher and some others escaped down a rope made of sheets. But the rope broke before Lavinia could follow, and John refused to escape without her. Although they received one reprieve, both met the hangman in February 1819, Lavinia fighting and screaming to the last. She seems to have been a bad tempered termagant – but to the people of Charleston she is still the beautiful highwaywoman who went to her death without flinching.

# Professor Webster

"On Friday, November 23, 1849, one of the most prominent physicians in Boston, Dr George Parkman, mysteriously disappeared. Being very methodical in his habits, his family immediately suspected foul play.

He was the owner of many tenement houses and was rather exacting in his attitude toward his tenants, many of whom were of the rougher class. As he collected the rents himself, the authorities proceeded on the theory that he had antagonized some of these tenants to such an extent that they murdered him for the double purpose of revenge and robbery, and then concealed his body.

The river was dredged and the doctor's tenements and the buildings adjacent thereto were thoroughly searched, but no trace was found of the missing man, although large rewards were offered.

When the doctor left home, about noon on November 23, he stated that he had an appointment with a person at 2:30 p.m., but did not divulge the name of the person.

About 1:30 p.m. he entered the grocery store conducted by Paul Holland, at Vine and Blossom streets, and after leaving an order, he asked permission to leave a paper bag containing a head of lettuce at the store for a few moments, but he never returned for it. This grocery store was but a short distance from one of the leading medical colleges in Boston, the college being located on Grove street. Elias Fuller, who conducted an iron foundry adjacent to the medical college, and his brother, Albert, saw Dr Parkman in front of the college about 2 p.m. on the date of his disappearance.

Dr John Webster was the professor of chemistry at this college and also at Harvard College. His standing in the social and professional world was equal to that of Dr Parkman, and their families were on terms of considerable intimacy.

Notwithstanding the fact that Dr Parkman called on Dr Webster at the college at 2 p.m. on Friday, the 23rd instant, and his subsequent disappearance was the principal topic of conversation in Boston the next day and for some time afterward, Dr Webster did not inform the almost distracted members of the Parkman family of this visit until the Sunday evening following, although it was proven that he saw an account of the doctor's disappearance in the Boston Transcript on Saturday afternoon.

Dr Webster then stated that Dr Parkman called on him for the purpose of collecting $450 which Webster had previously borrowed, giving as security a mortgage on a piece of real estate.

He claimed that he paid Dr Parkman the full amount due, from the proceeds of the sale of tickets to his course of lectures in the college.

Dr Parkman held a note for this amount, which he

had in his possession when he called on Dr Webster
and which the latter subsequently produced to prove
that he had paid the money. He added that Dr
Parkman stated that he would proceed forthwith to
Cambridge and cancel the mortgage.

Dr Webster also claimed that he saw Dr Parkman
go down stairs and leave the college after this
transaction.

Webster made many conflicting statements as to
the denomination of the money paid and as to the
circumstances under which it was paid, but his
standing in the community was such that it was
difficult to believe him guilty of any wrong-doing
and it would have been considered preposterous at
that time to even suspect him of being implicated in
the murder of his friend and benefactor.

Merely as a matter of form, the authorities decided
to search the medical college, but before proceeding
with the formal search an apology was made to Dr
Webster for the intrusion.

When Ephraim Littlefield, the janitor of the building, observed the farcical search, he looked on with
disapproving eyes, and intimated that a more thorough search would result in sensational discoveries.

The authorities then questioned Littlefield closely,
and he made the following statement:

"I have known Dr Parkman for many years. On
Monday evening, November 19, 1849, I was assisting
Dr Webster when Dr Parkman entered the room. He
appeared to be angry at Dr Webster and without any
preliminary conversation, abruptly said: 'Dr Webster,
are you ready for me tonight?'

"Webster replied, 'No, I am not, doctor.'

"I then moved away, but I heard Dr Parkman
reprimand him for selling mortgaged property, and
in a final burst of anger said: 'Something must be
done to-morrow,' and he then left.

"On the morning of Friday, November 23, I saw
a sledge hammer which belonged in the laboratory,
behind Dr Webster's door. I had never seen it there
before and have been unable to find it since.

"At 2:15 p.m. I was at the front door and saw Dr Parkman approaching the college, but I went inside and did not see him enter the building. About one hour afterward I went to Dr Webster's laboratory to clean up, but found the door bolted from the inside.

"I knocked loudly but received no response, although I heard someone walking inside who, I supposed, was Dr Webster. I then tried all the different doors leading to his laboratory, but they were all locked from the inside – a most unusual occurrence.

"At 4 o'clock I tried the doors again, with the same result. At 5 p.m. I saw Dr Webster leave the building from the back exit.

"I went to a party that night, and at 11 p.m. returned to the college, where my wife and I are domiciled. I again tried Dr Webster's door and again found it locked.

"On the next day, Saturday, Dr Webster was in his laboratory all day, but I did not go near him. That evening I met him on the street, and we discussed the article in the evening paper about the disappearance of Dr Parkman.

"Formerly he would look me in the face when talking, but on this occasion he hung his head and was pale and agitated. On Sunday and Monday the doors to the laboratory were still locked. On Tuesday I found the doctor's room open and mentioned the fact to my wife.

"On this day he was exceptionally friendly toward me and gave me an order for a Thanksgiving turkey. This was remarkable, as I had known him for eight years, and it was the first time I ever knew of him giving anything away.

"On Wednesday, Dr Webster came to the college early and again locked the door.

"The flue from his furnace is between the walls near the stairs leading to the demonstrator's room, and when I passed up the stairs the wall was extremely hot."

The janitor's statement in regard to the door to the

laboratory being constantly locked for several days subsequent to the disappearance of Dr Parkman was corroborated by several persons who had called during that period.

· These disclosures were made on Thursday, November 29, and the officers proceeded at once to Dr Webster's laboratory, and after vigorous knocking, the door was unbolted from the inside and the officers were admitted by Dr Webster, but nothing was said regarding the janitor's statement.

At this time a bright fire was burning in the furnace. Nothing was found on this date, and the search was resumed on Friday in the absence of Dr Webster.

In the meantime the furnace had become cool enough to permit of an examination, which resulted in the finding of a fractured skull containing a full set of mineral teeth.

By means of a trap door, the officers descended to the cellar, where they found a right leg.

In a tea chest they found the upper part of a man's body and the left leg. The shape of the body corresponded with that of Dr Parkman.

Dr Winslow Lewis and two other reputable surgeons stated that the manner in which the body was separated indicated that it was done by someone having knowledge of anatomy.

The fact that these remains were found concealed in the chemical laboratory where no such subjects were required, made it apparent that they were the remains of some victim of foul play, and Dr Ainsworth, the demonstrator of anatomy at the college, stated that they were not parts of any subject used in the college for dissection.

Dr N. C. Keep, who had made a full set of false teeth for Dr Parkman, inspected the plate and teeth and identified them as work he had done for Dr Parkman, because of a peculiarity of the lower jaw, which caused him much trouble. But to be positive, he produced the model, which fitted the plates exactly.

The result of the police investigations were not

made public until it was proven beyond all doubt that the remains of Dr Parkman had been found. Police Officer Clapp was then sent to Dr Webster's home at Cambridge to arrest him for murder.

When the public learned of the arrest of the eminent professor, it was at once concluded that a grave mistake had been made and that too much credence had been given to the statement of the janitor, who possibly was attempting to shield himself.

At the trial it was proven that notwithstanding his outward show of prosperity, Dr Webster was financially embarrassed. It was proven that he had committed a felony by selling the property upon which Dr Parkman held a mortgage for $450 and that the latter threatened to prosecute him for this offense if he did not immediately pay the principal and interest, amounting to $483.60.

It was proven that it was utterly impossible for Dr Webster, who saw the state prison and ruin staring him in the face, to raise this small amount of money.

It was proven that he lied when he stated that he paid this amount from the proceeds of the sale of tickets to his course of lectures at the college, as he had received no such amount, and a large portion of what he *did* receive was paid to others.

It was proven that Dr Webster called at Dr Parkman's house and requested the latter to call at the college at 2:30 p.m. on November 23 for the purpose of making a final settlement.

Dr Webster could give no reason for keeping a roaring fire in the furnace for several days after Dr Parkman's disappearance, and during the Thanksgiving holidays, when all of the other professors were enjoying a week of recreation.

While it was the duty of the janitor to build the fires, the latter was barred from Dr Webster's apartments, who personally attended to the building and feeding of the fire.

It was proven that the upper part of the body and left leg found in the tea chest were tied together by a peculiar kind of twine and that Dr Webster had, on November 27, purchased similar twine and several fish hooks which were found in his apartments.

It was proven that when the officers approached the room in which the tea chest containing a greater part of the body was found, Dr Webster endeavored to discourage them from searching that room by stating that highly explosive chemicals were stored there.

A pair of trousers belonging to Dr Webster was found in a closet and subjected to a microscopical examination with the result that human blood was found.

While the search was being made for Dr Parkman, the City Marshal of Boston received three anonymous letters.

One, supposed to have been written by an illiterate person, suggested that a search be made on "brooklynt heights," another stated that Dr Parkman had gone to sea on the ship "Herculian," and a third, signed "Civis," stated positively that the missing doctor had been seen at Cambridge.

Handwriting experts swore positively that all three letters were written by Dr Webster.

The defense produced witnesses to prove the previous good character of Dr Webster and also introduced testimony to the effect that Dr Parkman had been seen after the defendant claimed he left the college. After producing medical experts to contradict the medical testimony introduced by the prosecution, the case was submitted.

Chief Justice Shaw then delivered his charge to the jury, and his instructions regarding circumstantial evidence were so able, comprehensive, and discriminating that they have since been regarded as a model by many of the leading jurists of America. When the cause was finally submitted to the jurors, they almost immediately agreed that the defendant was guilty. As Justice Shaw was also officially connected with Harvard College and had been friendly with Dr Webster for years, he almost collapsed while pronouncing the death penalty on his erstwhile friend.

The date of execution was set for August 30, 1850. Notwithstanding efforts made to obtain executive clemency, Dr Webster went to the gallows on that day, publicly protesting his innocence, although it was claimed that he confessed his guilt to a clergyman."

# The Bender Family

London's legendary Sweeney Todd, the Demon Barber of Fleet Street, who precipitated customers into the basement from a swivelling barber's chair, then cut their throats, never existed except in the imagination of his creator, the playwright George Dibdin Pitt. But thirty years after the first production of that famous play in 1842, a real American family, the Benders, achieved a gruesome notoriety that rivals that of the Demon Barber.

On 9 March, 1873, Dr William York left his brother's house in Fort Scott, Kansas to return home on horseback. Fort Scott

The most famous murder in American history took place literally by gaslight. As Abraham Lincoln sat in Ford's Theater in Washington on the night of 14 April, 1865, a 26-year-old actor named John Wilkes Booth walked into Lincoln's box and shot him behind the left ear with a one-shot Derringer pistol. Then, shouting "*Sic semper tyrannis*" ("Ever thus to tyrants") he leapt on to the stage. Unfortunately, his spur caught in the curtain and he fell, fracturing his left shinbone. The injury slowed his escape back to the south, and twelve days later, he and fellow-conspirator David Herold were surrounded by Union soldiers in a barn in Virginia. When Booth refused to surrender, the barn was set on fire. Then a shot rang out, and Booth fell dead – whether he shot himself, or was killed by one of the soldiers, was never discovered with certainty.

marked the border of the Indian territories, but Dr York's journey was through safe, settled prairie and ought to have been uneventful. However Dr York did not arrive back in Independence, his home town. Weeks passed and nothing was heard from him. Something was evidently wrong. Colonel York, the doctor's brother, organized groups to search the area between Independence and Fort Scott. It was Colonel York himself who stopped at the Wayside Inn near Cherryvale to ask after his brother.

The inn was actually a tiny log cabin, roughly sixteen by twenty feet, surrounded by some farmland and an orchard. It was owned by European immigrants, the Bender family. The local people did not know exactly where they came from, only noticing that they spoke in thick guttural accents. The household consisted of Ma and Pa Bender, fifty and sixty respectively, and two grown-up children, both born in America. Kate Bender, the daughter, was a spiritualist and gave lectures on the subject as Professor Miss Kate Bender. She also advertised in the local paper as a faith healer who could not only cure disease, but also blindness and deafness. Their son was less gifted, only helping his father around the farm and inn. The whole family was heavily built and florid.

Colonel York knew that his brother had planned to stay at the Wayside Inn and thus made it one of the first places at which he enquired. Old Man Bender denied any knowledge of Dr York, pointing out that the Indians where still a real danger and that there were bandits everywhere. He and his son offered to help dredge the nearby river for Dr York's body. The Colonel was convinced and left to search elsewhere.

Soon another of the organized search parties called at the Benders' inn and asked after Dr York. Again they denied all, but after the party had left, they packed possessions into their covered wagon and fled.

No-one noticed they had gone for some while; guests were infrequent. Then on 9 May yet another search party noticed that the Wayside Inn seemed deserted, and that the cattle were making distressed noises. On entering, they found that the house stank of decomposition. At the back the cattle and sheep had been left penned for some time, and many were dead of thirst or hunger. Then someone noticed that the dry half-acre of orchard to the right of the house looked strange. The topsoil had been ploughed between the trees, and due to heavy rain some of the ploughed ground seemed to have subsided. The subsidence was in the shape of a grave.

Digging soon revealed the body of Dr York. His skull was crushed and his throat had been cut. Before nightfall seven other bodies had been recovered from the orchard's soil. All had been killed in the same way, except one small child who had been asphyxiated. From her position it seemed clear that she had been thrown into the grave alive, her murdered father thrown in on top of her, and both then covered over.

The next day another body of a child was unearthed. This one was so badly decomposed that only its sex and approximate age could be ascertained. It was an eight-year-old girl. Unlike the other adult victims this girl seemed to have been deliberately mutilated, her right knee disconnected and her breastbone driven in.

Upon searching the inn, officers discovered that the smell was not only coming from the neglected animals. A trapdoor in the floor led down to a cellar – in fact a roughly-dug pit – coated in rancid blood.

The story behind the bodies soon emerged through deduction. The Bender family murdered guests who looked like they had some money. They would do this in an ingenious way. The dining area of the tiny cabin was divided from the sleeping area by a thick curtain suspended from the ceiling. The dining table was positioned within the small space in such a way as to make the diner sit with his back directly against the curtain. If the guest seemed worth the risk, either Old Man Bender or his son would wait in the sleeping area for a clear outline of the victim's head against the curtain and then smash the skull with a heavy stone-breaker's hammer. After searching the corpse for money, they would cut its throat in order to be certain that no life remained and then throw them down through the trapdoor in to the cellar to await nightfall and burial. The orchard turf was kept constantly ploughed in order to hide any signs of grave-digging.

Naturally the community of Cherryvale and its surroundings was horrified. Local farmers were quick to form a vigilante group and scour the area for signs of the Bender's flight. Four groups set out north, south, east and west to find their tracks. Another group "arrested" a Mr Brockman, an acquaintance of the Benders and an accomplice in the eyes of the local townsfolk because he had once been Bender's business partner. The vigilantes hanged him from a tree until he was almost dead in an attempt to force information from him.

Other local people began remembering strange events that at the time were ignored. A Mr Wetzell remembered answering Kate Bender's advert in the newspaper. He suffered from acute facial neuralgia, and decided to try Kate's mystic powers as a cure. He and a friend visited the inn, where Kate greeted them in a friendly and charming manner, telling him that she could easily cure his neuralgia, but would he not prefer some dinner first? The two guests sat down, whereupon Old Man Bender and his son, who had been watching them closely, disappeared behind the curtain. For a reason neither of them could adequately explain, the two guests decided to stand up and eat their dinner at the bar. At this Kate became angry and abusive, and the rest of the family looked on threateningly. Sensing that something strange was going on the two men quickly left.

Apart from this first-hand account of the Bender's methods, another piece of evidence was unearthed by officers. Some time before the discovery of the Bender's secret the body of a man had been found deliberately concealed under the ice of a frozen creek. The skull had been smashed and the throat so severely cut that the head was almost detached. A hole had been cut in the ice and the body pushed through it. Tracks in the snow of the river bank showed that the murderer's cart had a severely skewed wheel; one of the ruts had a decidedly zig-zag appearance. When tested the Bender's farm cart left the same tracks. It would seem that during the winter the ground in the Bender's orchard was too frozen to dig.

Officially the Bender's were never found. The search continued sporadically for the next fifty years, with many pairs of unhappy travelling ladies identified as Ma and Kate Bender.

However it seems possible that the Benders did meet justice. In his book *Celebrated Criminal Cases of America* (1910), Thomas Duke prints two letters from local police chiefs in response to his question: what happened to the Benders? One reports, "There was a vigilance committee organized to locate the Benders, and shortly afterwards Old Man Bender's wagon was found by the roadside riddled with bullets. You will have to guess the rest."

of them are still here, but they will not talk except to say that it
would be useless to look for them, and they smile at reports of
some of the family having been recently located."

It is possible that the vigilantes killed the Benders and kept
it a secret. However it is also possible that living so close to the
scene of such gruesome and heartless murder, the locals had to
create a happy ending.


# The Kidnapping of Charley Ross

The word kidnap, meaning to "nap" (or nab) a child, came into
use in the late seventeenth century, when homeless children
were nabbed and sold to the plantations in North America.
But the first case of kidnapping, in our modern sense of the
word (to seize someone for ransom) occurred in Philadelphia
in 1874.

Charley and Walter Ross, four and six years old respectively,
disappeared from their suburban Philadelphia home on 1 July,
1874. Walter was soon home again, recovered by a Mr Henry
Peacock who had found him crying loudly in front of a
downtown sweet shop. Walter's story was, for the period,
a strange one. For the past four days two men had been
driving past the front lawn of the Ross's stone mansion and
offering the children sweets. On the fourth day Walter had
suggested that they go into Philadelphia to buy some fireworks
for the approaching Independence Day celebrations. The two
men readily agreed, and took the children to "Aunt Susie's",
a sweet shop on the corner of Palmer and Richmond street.
Walter was given twenty-five cents to spend and gleefully ran
into the shop. When he came out the carriage had gone.

The idea that Charley had been kidnapped did not at the time
seem plausible. In fact the crime was not really established as
existing; Pennsylvania had no specific law against it. The other
reason why extortion seemed unlikely was that despite owning
a large stone house, Christian Ross, the boy's father was only
moderately wealthy. He had made his money in selling groceries

but had recently gone bankrupt. At the time of the abduction he was only just beginning to break even again.

Then, on 3 July, a note from the kidnappers arrived. It was hand-written and only semi-literate. Despite the uneducated appearance of the spelling and grammar, the style was florid: ". . . if any aproch is made to his hidin place that is the signil for his instant anihilation. if you regard his lif puts no one to search for him yu money can fetch him out alive an no other existin powers . . ." The note demanded money without stating an amount, or specifying a method of payment. It was obvious that the kidnappers wished to bargain.

Ross gave the letter to the police and they made the contents public. The community was outraged in a way that perhaps is no longer imaginable. When the police decided to closely search the whole local area, the inhabitants voluntarily allowed officers to search their homes, something that the police would have had legal difficulty in compelling them to do. Anyone who refused the police entry was looked upon with suspicion. Although the child was not found, a great deal of stolen property was, and prosecutions followed.

Three days after the last another note arrived, demanding $20,000 and threatening to kill the child if any detectives were set on their trail. Ross was directed to enter a personal ad in *The Philadelphia Ledger* when he was ready to negotiate. It was decided that the longer an exchange of notes could be maintained the better the chance of forcing the kidnappers into a blunder. Therefore the ad read: "Ross will come to terms to the best of his ability."

A reply soon arrived, saying that the abductors were getting very impatient, and that the reason for the evasive reply was obvious to them. Despite this Ross continued to publish ambiguous answers. In fact, he had made up his mind not to compound a felony by paying the criminals, and went as far as to announce the fact publicly. This in effect severed the link of communication with the kidnappers and put Charley Ross' life in a great deal of danger.

Seeing that the worry of this situation was driving his wife into an early grave, Ross relented. Through the small ads he signalled his willingness to hand over the money. Shortly another note arrived, remonstrating with Ross for behaving so recklessly and postponing any deal. The reason given was that the phase of the moon was not propitious for business transactions.

On 30 July the instructions arrived at last. Ross was to put the money in a white painted suitcase and board the night train to New York with it. For the entire journey he was to stand on the rear platform of the last carriage, looking back down the track. He was to throw the suitcase off the train at the signal of a torch. It was clear that the kidnappers had been waiting for a moonless night, in order to avoid being followed.

Ross complied, and waited for the whole journey without receiving a signal. On his return a note awaited him, chiding him for failing to keep the deal. It seemed that the kidnappers had read a newpaper report "revealing" that Ross intended to go with the police to follow up a clue somewhere entirely different. Consequently they themselves had not taken the trouble to turn up. Even if the kidnappers had got hold of the case, they would have found that it contained only a letter demanding a simultaneous exchange of money for child. Ross now communicated this demand to the kidnappers. They replied that simultaneous transfer was impossible, and again threatened to kill the child.

Meanwhile the New York police had found an informer capable of identifying the handwriting of the ransom notes. According to this man the writing belonged to a William Mosher. The informant said that a few years previously Mosher and a man named Joseph Douglas had approached him to be an accomplice in abduction of a millionaire's child. The information seemed promising, and the police traced Mosher to 235 Monroe Street, Philadelphia where he lived with his family. Douglas lived in the same house. Unfortunately, by the time police searched the building the Moshers and Douglas had moved to New York.

At about the same time a final communication reached Ross. It instructed him to place an ad in *The New York Herald* reading "Saul of Tarsus: Fifth Avenue Hotel" followed by the date that he would be there with the money. Ross did as he was told, sat in the hotel all of 15 November, but there was no visitation. The kidnappers remained silent.

On 14 December the summer home of a Mr Van Brunt situated on the Upper East Side of New York was burgled. Mr Van Brunt was in residence, and heard the intruders climbing down into his cellar over the sounds of a storm. By the time that the burglars re-emerged from the cellar, there were five armed men waiting for them. Mr Van Brunt shouted "Halt!" The burglars fired two shots, both of which missed, and tried to escape out of the window. Van Brunt shot the nearest man with his shotgun, nearly blowing him in half, while his son jumped on the other burglar and accidentally shot him through the chest with a handgun. It was clear that both men were dying. Although in terrible pain, the burglar with the chest wound refused to be moved, and asked for an umbrella to keep himself dry during his last moments. In between fits of pain the man spoke: "Men, I won't lie to you. My name is Joseph Douglas and the man over there is William Mosher. He lives in New York, and I have no home. I am a single man and have no relatives except for a brother and a sister whom I have not seen for twenty years. Mosher is married and has four children" (here pain for a moment overcame his speech) "I have forty dollars in my pocket that I made honestly. Bury me with that." After another fit he continued: "Men, I am dying now and it's no use lying. Mosher and I stole Charley Ross." Van Brunt asked him why they had done it. "To make money." was the simple reply. When asked where the boy was Douglas told them to ask Mosher. He was told that Mosher was already dead, and his blasted body was dragged over in order to prove it. Douglas said that they had known that the police had them cornered. All he would say about Charley was that: "the child will be returned home safe and sound in a few days." Douglas survived over an hour of agony in the rain. Eventually he lapsed into unconsciousness and died.

The bodies were taken to the morgue, where a terrified Walter Ross identified them as the men who had taken Charley. Despite Douglas' dying assurances, and a reward of $5,000 and no questions asked for anyone who returned the child, Charley was never seen again.

Mr Ross carried on searching for his child, heartened by a statement made by William Westervelt, Mosher's brother-in-law and the man with whom Mosher and Douglas had lived in New York. He had told Ross that the day before he died, Mosher had said that he would arrange a simultaneous transfer if that was the only way to get the money. This pre-supposes that the boy was still alive.

Westervelt was tried as an accomplice in New York, and despite a lack of any firm evidence he was sentenced to seven years in solitary confinement.

It has to be assumed, despite Westervelt's statement, that Charley Ross was dead long before Mosher and Douglas were shot. Perhaps he was killed when Christian Ross announced publicly that he had no intention of aiding a felon. An unconfirmed story reports that Charley Ross was delivered into Westervelt's hands almost immediately after his kidnap, Mosher and Douglas remaining in Philadelphia to arrange ransom notes and payment. Westervelt, according to the story, became nervous and drowned the child in the East River. This was impossible to confirm however, as Westervelt disappeared after serving his sentence.

Christian Ross spent the rest of his life and his money checking up reports of Charley, travelling as far afield as Europe.

On 25 February, 1875 Pennsylvania Legislature officially recognized kidnapping as a crime.

# chapter four

# POISONINGS AND RAILWAY MURDERS

*O*n 25 July, 1814, a strange contraption with iron wheels groaned and hissed into life, and dragged eight wagonloads of coal along parallel iron tracks. That first railway engine, christened "Blücher" and affectionately known as Puffing Billy, also dragged its inventor into the limelight of world history.

George Stephenson, the self-educated son of a Northumbrian miner, was not only an inventive genius; he also proved himself an inspired prophet when he told the British House of Commons: "People will live to see the time when railroads will become the great highways for the King and all his subjects . . ." What he did not foresee was that his great invention was inaugurating a new and fascinating chapter in the history of murder.

Oddly enough, the classic cases of "murder on the railway" – Müller, Dickman, the Merstham tunnel mystery, the Rock Island express murder – now have a nostalgic fascination for students of crime. We can anticipate the day when railway stations will disappear and give way to airports – as they have already disappeared in many parts of America – and the thought of a steam engine chugging between green fields has all the charm of a pleasant daydream.

# The First Railway Murder

England's first train murderer was a twenty-five-year-old German tailor named Franz Muller; indeed, he may be the world's first train murderer, for his crime was committed in 1864, and it was almost another ten years before Jesse James committed the world's first train robbery and brought a new kind of risk into the lives of railway passengers.

On the night of 9 July, 1864, at Hackney railway station, two men entered a first class compartment of a train that had come from Fenchurch Street, and noticed a bloodstained black beaver hat lying on the seat; under the seat they found a heavy walking stick with bloodstains on it. Obviously, some crime had taken place.

Soon after this, the engineer of another train noticed a bundle lying beside the line. It proved to be an old gentleman with a fractured skull. He died twenty-four hours later. Letters in his pocket identified him as Thomas Briggs, the seventy-year-old chief clerk of Robart's Bank, in the City.

The only clue was the hat made of beaver fur, which was too old and worn to belong to Mr Briggs. It seemed that the murderer had snatched up Mr Briggs's hat by accident, and left his own behind. Mr Briggs's colleagues at the bank were able to tell the police that he wore gold-rimmed glasses and carried a gold watch and chain. These were missing. His hat, apparently, was also quite distinctive, having been specially made for him; its lining was unique and easily recognizable. A few days later, a Cheapside jeweller named John Death told the police about a young foreigner who had come into his shop, and exchanged a gold watch chain for a less expensive one and a cheap ring. The watch chain was identified as belonging to the dead man.

But who was the young foreigner? Newspaper publicity about the bloodstained hat solved this problem too; a cabman named Matthews identified the beaver hat as belonging to a German called Franz Muller, who had courted his daughter for a time. Matthews had, in fact, bought the beaver hat for Muller.

# UNDER THE PATRONAGE
## Of the NOBILITY.

### INSTANTANEOUS COMMUNICATION,

Between PADDINGTON and SLOUGH, a distance of nearly Twenty Miles, by means of The

# ELECTRIC
# *TELEGRAPH*

Which may be seen in operation Daily, from Nine in the Morning till Eight in the Evening, at The

## GREAT WESTERN RAILWAY,
### Paddington Station—and The
## TELEGRAPH COTTAGE,
### Close to the Slough Station.

---

### Admission. — ONE SHILLING,
### Children and Schools Half-Price.

---

Since this very interesting Exhibition has been opened to the Public, it has been honoured by the visits of His Royal Highness Prince Albert, the Emperor of Russia, the King, and Prince William of Prussia, the Duke of Montpensier, His Royal Highness the Duke of Cambridge, the Duke of Wellington, Sir Robert Peel, the Foreign Ambassadors, and most of the Nobility, &c.

In no way has the Science of Electricity been made so subservient to the uses of man, as in its application to the purposes of Telegraphic Communication, which is now brought to the height of perfection. The working of this beautiful Apparatus is not in the least degree affected by the weather, intelligence can be sent by night equally well as by day; distance is no object; by its extraordinary agency communications can be transmitted, to a distance of a Thousand Miles, in the same space of time, and with the same ease and unerring certainty, as a signal can be sent from London to Slough. According to the best authorities, the Electric Fluid travels at the rate of

## 280,000 Miles in a Second.

The Electric Telegraph has been adopted by Her Majesty's Government, and the Patentees have just completed a line of communication between London and Portsmouth, agreeably to directions received a short time ago, from

### The Right Hon. the Lords of the Admiralty.

In the late trial of John Tawell, at Aylesbury, for the Murder at Salt Hill, near Slough, the Electric Telegraph is frequently mentioned in the evidence, and referred to by Mr. Baron Parke in his summing up. The Times Newspaper very justly observes, "That had it not been for the efficient aid of the Electric Telegraph, both at the Paddington and Slough Stations, the greatest difficulty, as well as delay, would have been occasioned in the apprehension of the prisoner." Although the train in which Tawell came to town was within a very short distance of the Paddington Station, before any intelligence was given at the Slough Telegraph Office, nevertheless before the train had actually arrived, not only had a full description of his person and dress been received, but the particular carriage and compartment in which he rode were accurately described, and an officer was in readiness to watch his movements. His subsequent apprehension is so well known, that any further reference to the subject is unnecessary.

---

The Telegraph Office, at Paddington Station, is at the End of the Up-Train Platform, where a variety of interesting apparatus may be seen in constant operation.

T. HOME, Licensee.

S. G. Fairbrother, Printer, 31, Bow Street, Covent Garden.

The police rushed to Muller's lodgings, only to find that he **71** had already left. His landlady said he had sailed for Canada, and was now on his way to New York. Fortunately, the *Victoria* was a fairly slow boat; two detectives pursued him on the much faster *City of Manchester*, together with the jeweller and the cabman. So as Muller disembarked from the *Victoria*, he was identified by Mr Death, and the detectives arrested him.

At his trial – paid for by the German Legal Protection Society – the prosecution pointed out that Mr Briggs's watch had been found sewn in a piece of canvas in Muller's trunk. This fact made a not-guilty defense virtually impossible, and the jury lost no time in bringing in a guilty verdict. Muller protested his innocence until he stood on the gallows; then, a moment before the trap dropped, he said in German: "I have done it." As the body swung on the end of the rope, the clergyman who had administered the last rites shouted: "Confessed! Confessed!"

Muller must have been one of the most incompetent murderers of all time. The crime was committed for money, yet he only took thirty shillings and the gold watch; he left four guineas and a valuable snuffbox in his victim's pocket. By exchanging the watch chain and taking the wrong hat, he ensured his own conviction. Yet his ultimate piece of stupidity was to keep Briggs's hat, with its distinctive lining – he was actually wearing it when he was arrested.

# John Tawell – Murder by a Quaker

The message that alerted train drivers to look out for Mr Briggs's body was sent by telegraph. Nineteen years earlier, one of the

The most sensational of all train murderers was the Hungarian train wrecker Sylvestre Matushka, who blew up trains because it caused him erotic excitement. Jailed for life in 1932 for causing two train wrecks in which twenty-two people were killed and over one hundred injured, he was released during World War II. He went on to work for the Americans as an explosives expert during the Korean war.

first telegraphs led to the arrest of a particularly ruthless killer. He became known as "Quaker Tawell."

John Tawell, who began life as a druggist, was transported to Australia for forgery in 1814, but by the time he returned to England, had amassed a fortune of £30,000. His wife fell ill and died, and during her illness, Tawell began a liaison with the attractive girl who nursed her, Sarah Hadler. She later bore him two children, and Tawell moved her to a cottage at Salthill, near Slough. Meanwhile, he married a second time, a Miss Catforth, from whom he took care to conceal the liaison. He paid Sarah Hadler (now known as Hart) £1 a week. After Tawell paid Sarah a visit in September 1844, she fell ill and vomited, but recovered from the attack.

On New Year's Day, 1845, Tawell went down to Salthill from his home in Berkhamsted; a neighbour saw him arrive, and a little later, met Sarah on her way to buy stout, and remarked how happy she looked. Soon after dusk, the neighbour heard Sarah scream, and went to her door with a lighted candle; she met Tawell, hurrying away, and found Sarah writhing on the floor in agony. Before the arrival of the doctor, she was dead.

A telegraph line – one of the first – had recently been constructed from Slough to Paddington, and a message was sent, asking the police to look out for a man in Quaker dress. When Tawell arrived at Paddington, he was followed to the lodging he had taken for the night, and arrested the next morning. He immediately made his first mistake by denying that he had left London the previous day.

Meanwhile, Sarah Hadler's body had been opened, and the bitter smell of prussic acid had been noted. The analyst, Mr Cooper, mixed the stomach contents with potassium ferrosulphate, and obtained the deep Prussian blue colour of potassium ferrocyanide. His conclusion was that Sarah Hadler had been poisoned by prussic acid, probably administered in stout. When it was proved that Tawell had bought the acid at a chemist shop in Bishopsgate, the case against him looked black.

The defending, counsel, Fitzroy Kelly, advanced an ingenious defence, saying that apple pips contain prussic acid, and that there had been a barrel of apples in the room in which Sarah Hadler had died. At this, both sets of medical experts proceeded to distil apple pips to see how much cyanide they could obtain.

The prosecution said that the amount distilled from 15 apples
was not even dangerous; the defence replied that they had
succeeded in distilling two-thirds of a grain of pure hydrocyanic
acid from 15 apples, and that such a dose could be toxic.

The jury took the view that all this was irrelevant, and
sentenced Tawell to death. Shortly before his execution, he
confessed to the murder, and to an attempt to poison Sarah
Hadler with morphine the previous September. His motive
had been financial – his Australian investments had dropped
in value, and he wanted to save the £1 a week he paid
his mistress. Tawell was hanged in April 1845, and is now
remembered mainly as the first murderer to be trapped by the
electric telegraph. The defence lawyer became known forever
afterwards as "Apple Pip Kelly".

# Dr Palmer of Rugeley

If Muller and Tawell were both incompetents, Dr William Palmer
– who became infamous as "Palmer the Poisoner" – was, on the
contrary, one of the most successful criminals of the century of
gaslight. During his nine-year career of crime, Palmer committed
at least a dozen murders, and would probably have committed
a dozen more if he had not been arrested. This came about in
1855, when he was accused of poisoning a friend named Cook
with strychnine.

On 13 November 1855, Palmer and John Parsons Cook
attended the races at Shrewsbury, and Cook's mare, Polestar,
won. Back in a hotel in Rugeley, where they were celebrating,
Cook took a swallow of his brandy and jumped to his feet
crying: "Good God, there's something in that that burns my
throat." Palmer retorted "Nonsense", and drained the rest of
the brandy. But Cook became increasingly ill. And after taking
some pills offered to him by Palmer, his body convulsed so
violently that his head touched his heels, and he died a few
minutes later. Palmer was not slow to claim that the dead man
had negotiated £4,000 for his benefit, and produced a document
to prove it.

ILLUSTRATED AND UNABRIDGED EDITION

OF

# The ⚜ Times

## REPORT

OF THE

# TRIAL OF WILLIAM PALMER,

FOR POISONING JOHN PARSONS COOK,

AT RUGELEY.

THE TALBOT ARMS, RUGELEY, THE SCENE OF COOK'S DEATH.

FROM THE SHORT-HAND NOTES TAKEN IN THE CENTRAL CRIMINAL COURT
FROM DAY TO DAY.

LONDON: WARD AND LOCK, 158, FLEET STREET.
1856.

It was some days before Cook's stepfather became suspicious and demanded an autopsy. Palmer was arrested on a money-lender's writ. Yet, incredibly, he was not only permitted to be present at the autopsy, but to sneak out of the room with the jar containing Cook's stomach – he was caught only just in time.

Now it was recalled that Palmer had been associated with a long series of sudden deaths, and with many dubious financial transactions. As a trainee doctor he had fathered no fewer than fourteen illegitimate children, and one of these had died unexpectedly after a visit to Palmer. An acquaintance named Abbey had died in the Staffordshire Infirmary after drinking a glass of brandy with Palmer.

Back in Rugeley with his medical diploma, Palmer had married an heiress, the illegitimate daughter of an Indian army officer; but apparently she was not as rich as he had hoped. Three years later, he invited his mother-in-law to stay with them, and she died suddenly during the visit. Her money passed to her daughter – and in turn to Palmer. In the following year, a bookmaker named Bladon died with equal suddenness when staying with Palmer. A large sum of money disappeared, and so did Bladon's betting book, in which Palmer figured as a heavy loser. His wife was heard to enquire wearily: "Where will it end?" – her own sudden death would occur three years later. But in the meantime, sudden deaths continued to occur with suspicious frequency – a creditor named Bly, an uncle named "Beau" Bentley, and four of Palmer's children, who died in convulsions. Then, in 1853, Palmer insured his wife for £13,000, and she died soon afterwards. The ease with which he had acquired this money – and staved off bankruptcy – evidently decided Palmer to insure the life of his brother Walter for £82,000. But when Walter died suddenly, after a drinking bout, the company was suspicious, and refused to pay. Palmer succeeded in insuring a friend called George Bates for £25,000, who also died unexpectedly; but when a detective employed by the company learned from a boot boy that he had seen Palmer pouring something into Bates's drink, they once again refused to pay. Palmer then had a drinking session with the boot boy, who was severely ill after it.

It was after these setbacks that Palmer attended the Shrewsbury races with Cook, who died in agony a week later.

The bodies of Palmer's wife and brother were now exhumed;

and a considerable quantity of antimony was found in Anne Palmer. There was no poison in Walter Palmer, but Taylor pointed out that prussic acid would escape from the body after death in the form of gases.

Cook's stomach had been sent to the well-known Professor of Medical Jurisprudence, John Swain Taylor, at Guy's Hospital. It had been turned inside out before it had been thrown in the jar, and Palmer had then succeeded in taking the jar out of the room before anyone noticed; when it was returned, there were two slits in its parchment cap. Taylor was able to find a small quantity of antimony in the stomach – not enough to kill a man – but no strychnine. Palmer was still at large when Taylor's letter, containing his results, arrived in Rugeley, and he succeeded in intercepting the letter, and sending the coroner a present of game, pointing out that no strychnine had been found.

If the case had depended solely on Taylor's evidence, there can be no doubt that Palmer would have been acquitted. But the circumstantial evidence was overwhelming. It was proved that he had forged Cook's signature on a cheque for £350 while his friend lay ill, and also forged the document showing that Cook owed him £4,000. So although Taylor's evidence came in for some derision, there was never any doubt about the verdict, and Palmer's guilt. He was hanged at Stafford on 14 June 1856.

# Dr Pritchard

Palmer is a strange phenomenon because, although born into a wealthy middle class family, he seems to have been a born crook. The same is true of that other famous Victorian poisoner, Dr Edward William Pritchard – although in his case, dishonesty seems to have been compounded with mental instability.

Pritchard was born in 1825, son of a captain in the Royal Navy. When he was twenty-one he was commissioned as an assistant surgeon in the Royal Navy, and served until he was twenty-six. At Portsmouth he met a pretty Scottish girl, whom he married. She was Mary Jane Taylor, and the husband and wife moved

to Hunmanby, near Filey in Yorkshire. They had five children.
Pritchard soon became known as a habitual liar and boaster
in Hunmanby, and his frequent amours did much to ruin his
reputation as a responsible medical man. He was a freemason,
and used his membership of that body for self-advertisement.
In 1858 Hunmanby became too hot to hold him and he sold his
practice. For a year he travelled abroad as a medical attendant
to a gentleman, and then started to practise in Glasgow.
Here he soon made himself as unpopular as he had been in
Yorkshire. His vanity seems to have been overwhelming, like
his mendacity. He would lecture on his travels, and distribute
photographs of himself to anyone who showed any tendency to
admiration. He even gave one to a stranger he encountered on
a train. He claimed to be a friend of Garibaldi (who had never
heard of him), and when he applied for the Andersonian chair
of Surgery, he submitted as testimonials the names of many
eminent English doctors, who had certainly never heard of him.
(He did not get the appointment.) He manufactured evidence
for his friendship with Garibaldi by presenting himself with a
walking-stick engraved, "from his friend General Garibaldi".

On 5 May 1863 his failing professional reputation was further
damaged when a servant girl mysteriously died in a fire at his
home at II Berkely Terrace, Glasgow. A verdict of death by
misadventure was returned; but the girl had made no attempt
to leave her bed, so it seems probable that she was unconscious
when the fire started; moreover, Mrs Pritchard was absent from
home that night.

Pritchard pressed a claim against a suspicious insurance
company and won it.

In 1864 Pritchard moved to Sauchiehall Street, where he
bought a house with money supplied by his wife's mother,
Mrs Taylor. There, in the same year, his wife caught him
kissing a fifteen-year-old servant-girl, Mary M'Cleod, whom
he had seduced. (She became pregnant, but allowed Pritchard
to perform an abortion.)

In November 1864 Mrs Pritchard fell ill, and went to stay
with her family in Edinburgh, where she got better. On
returning to Glasgow, she became ill again and took to her
bed, where she stayed until her death in March 1865. On 8
December Pritchard bought an ounce of Fleming's Tincture of
Aconite, and made three similar purchases during the next three

months. A Dr Gairdner was summoned, and was so suspicious of her symptoms that he suggested to Mrs Taylor's son (also a doctor) that Mrs Pritchard should be removed from the house. Pritchard claimed that she was too ill to move, so Mrs Taylor, who was a healthy and powerful woman, although seventy years old, moved in to nurse her daughter. On the day of her arrival, she ate some tapioca (which was later found to contain antimony) and promptly fell ill. She finally died during the night of 24 February. A Dr Patterson who called suspected that she was under the influence of some powerful narcotic, and refused to give a death certificate, which Pritchard finally supplied himself, stating cause of death as apoplexy. On the week of 13 March Pritchard decided to finish poisoning his wife, which he did to such good effect that she finally died on the night of 17 March. But a cook and housemaid who had tasted some of the food eaten by Mrs Pritchard became ill, and there was considerable suspicion of the doctor. He certified the cause of death as gastric fever, and took the body to Edinburgh to be buried. On his return he was arrested on suspicion of murder. Someone had written an anonymous letter to the police (probably Dr Patterson, although he denied it). The bodies of Mrs Taylor and Mrs Pritchard were examined and both found to contain antimony and aconite. (Pritchard had declared that Mrs Taylor's death may have been caused by an overdose of a medicine containing opium.)

The trial opened at the High Court of Justiciary, Edinburgh, in July 1865, before the Lord Justice Clerk (Right Honourable John Inglis). Prosecuting were Lord Ardmillan and Lord Jerviswoode, the Solicitor-General Mr Gifford, and Mr Crichton. Defending were Mr Rutherford Clerk, Mr Watson, and Mr Brand. It was noted that the organs of both victims were impregnated with antimony, although there was no trace of it in the stomachs, pointing to poisoning over a period. During the trial, Dr Patterson showed himself extremely hostile to the prisoner. The defence tried to blame Mary M'Cleod for the poisoning, a suggestion which the judge dismissed in his summing-up. The jury found Pritchard guilty after an hour's deliberation. In prison he applied himself to his devotions, and confessed to the murders, attempting, in one confession, to implicate Mary M'Cleod, although he later admitted that he alone was responsible for the murders.

The motive of the murders is obscure, although Pritchard must surely have been a man who felt the ground slipping away from underneath him as his lies and attempts to gain admirers brought only dislike and pity, and might have decided that he needed to make a completely fresh start. He was certainly slightly insane, and his hypocrisy sometimes savours of total self-delusion; for example, when his wife's death was announced, he cried: "Come back, my dear Mary Jane. Don't leave your dear Edward." When the coffin was about to be taken to the station, Pritchard kissed his wife's lips repeatedly, muttering words of love.

His execution in Jail Square, near Hutcheson Bridge, was attended by a record crowd of 100,000.

# chapter five

# INFAMOUS AUSTRALIAN CASES

*A*ustralia's early record of crime, like that of America, consists *mainly of acts of highway robbery and burglary. A list of the 165 criminals executed in the Melbourne jail between 1842 (the year it was opened) and 1900 includes many cases labelled "robbery with violence", "robbery with wounding", "shooting with intent to kill", "attemped murder", and in one case, "ambush of the McIvor gold escort". (The year 1880 naturally includes the execution of legendary outlaw Ned Kelly.) Rape was then a capital offense, and there are half a dozen cases of rape and carnal knowledge, including rape of a girl of ten, of a girl under six, and one entry that states simply: "Carnally knowing daughter." The severity of sentences for wounding and attempted murder is an indication that, even in 1850, this was a "frontier society" in which crime was treated with the utmost severity.*

## The Man They Couldn't Hang

Many of the early settlers were convicts who had been "transported" to the Botany Bay penal colony. A widely publicized case of 1803 involved a Jewish Cockney convict named Joseph Samuels, who had been transported for seven years for housebreaking in 1801, at the age of nineteen.

One night in August 1803, a local prostitute named Mary Breeze returned from a hard evening's work to find that her cottage had been ransacked; among other items missing was a portable desk with twenty-four guineas hidden in it. Mary Breeze alerted the local constable, Joseph Luker, who set off in search of the robbers. It seems that he did not get far. The next morning, his body was found on the trail near Mary Breeze's cottage. He had been killed by sixteen savage blows to the head with a cutlass.

The newspaper accounts merely state that "various clues" led the police to the cottage of a member of the "convict constabularly" – presumably an ex-convict who had now become a policeman – named Isaac Simmonds. They found Simmonds with Joseph Samuels, and two other men named William Bladders and Richard Jackson. All four were charged on "suspicion of robbery and murder". The following day in court, Samuels admitted burgling Mary Breeze's cottage, but denied the murder of Constable Luker.

Bloodstains on their clothes led to Simmonds and Bladders being charged with murder. But at their trial, they "explained away" the stains (probably alleging that they were animal blood), and were found not guilty. Twenty-one-year-old Samuels was the only one to be found guilty – of housebreaking. And since most crimes in 1803 were capital, he was sentenced to death.

At 9 a.m. on 26 September, 1803, Samuels was led out to be hanged. Simmonds was in the crowd. And when the chaplain asked him to confess his crimes before his execution, Samuels pointed at Simmonds and shouted that *he* had committed the murder, and that he and Simmonds (a fellow Jew) had taken a Hebrew oath of secrecy on the night of their arrest. (They had been kept in a cell together.)

It was too late to charge Simmonds, so the preparations for the execution went ahead. The horse pulling the cart on which Samuels was standing was urged forward. For a moment, Samuels dangled in the air. Then the rope snapped and he fell to the ground. The hangman was summoned again; he placed a second noose around Samuel's neck, and again the horse walked forward. This time, the rope somehow unravelled, and Samuels again landed on the ground. At the third attempt, Samuels was held by two men as the cart moved away, then dropped. The rope snapped again.

The Provost Marshall stopped the proceedings, and reported the strange events to the governor, who ordered a reprieve. Samuels went back to the penal settlement to a lengthened term of imprisonment. A few years later, he drowned near the Newcastle penal settlement when he and a number of other convicts stole a boat which sank in a storm.

# The Kinder Case

The classic Australian murder of the age of gaslight is a typical eternal triangle – although in this case, it might be better compared to a square. It has another remarkable feature – the murderer, Louis Bertrand, was cast in the mould of the true Victorian villain – in a work of fiction he would be regarded as quite unbelievable.

Henry Kinder was a bank clerk who also happened to be an alcoholic. He and his attractive wife Ellen had moved from New Zealand to Sydney at about the same time that a dental assistant named Henri Louis Bertrand had arrived from

England's case of "the man they couldn't hang" occurred in 1885. John Lee of Babbacombe, Devon, had been sentenced to hang for the murder of his employer, Miss Emma Keyse, who had been found dead on 15 November 1884 with her throat cut. Lee was sentenced on circumstantial evidence. On 22 February, 1885, Lee was taken to the scaffold, and the hangman pulled the lever. The trapdoor – which had been repeatedly tested – refused to open. Lee was removed and the trapdoor tested; it worked perfectly. Berry the hangman tried again; again the trap jammed. There were more successful tests, then Berry tried again. When the trap refused to open a third time, Lee was taken back to his cell. His sentence was commuted to twenty-two years, and he was released on 17 December 1907. He always insisted that he had dreamed that the trap would not work the night before it happened. There was one major difference between this and the Samuels case: Lee was almost certainly guilty.

England. Bertrand even looked like a stage villain – he had dark
wavy hair, parted down the middle, and a little moustache; if
his pictures are to be believed, he also had dark smouldering
eyes. In Sydney, the Frenchman married a girl named Jane
Palmer. Apparently he treated her badly, and sometimes beat
her. Nevertheless, his dental business prospered, and the two
of them lived in fashionable Wynyard Square.

Unlike the gentle Jane Bertrand, Ellen Kinder required more
than one man. In New Zealand she had had a lover named
Frank Jackson. And when, in January 1865, she met the good
looking Frenchman, she lost no time in allowing him to join her
in bed. Bertrand does not seem to have concealed the affair from
his wife – in fact, he even forced her to get into bed with himself
and his mistress. It was later suggested that he possessed some
hypnotic power over her. What is certain is that he dominated
her completely.

Six months after the two became lovers, Ellen Kinder's
previous lover, Frank Jackson, arrived in Sydney and went
to stay with the Kinders. When Henry was at the bank, Jackson
and Ellen Kinder retired to her bed.

When Bertrand found out that his mistress was being doubly
unfaithful, he was indignant. There was a showdown, which
ended with Bertrand demanding that she choose between them.
With downcast eyes, Ellen admitted that she preferred the
dentist. Jackson accepted this philosophically, and moved out.

The cunning Bertrand now saw that Frank Jackson might be
of use to him. If Jackson would seduce Jane Bertrand, he would
have an excuse for casting her off. Accordingly, he invited Frank
Jackson to move in with them. But apparently the seduction
failed to occur – either because Jackson was not attracted to Jane,
or because Jane was shy and unsuited to infidelity. Bertrand
shook his head. "It's a pity my wife is virtuous. It makes it so
hard to get rid of her."

In fact, the devious Frenchman's plans were even more
sinister. He had found a bundle of love letters from Ellen in
Jackson's belongings, and was tormented with jealousy. Now
he decided to kill Ellen's husband, and to implicate Jackson.
After all, if Kinder was murdered, and the letters were found
by the police, Jackson would be the obvious suspect . . .

Incredibly, the villainous dentist took his young assistant,
Alfred Burne, into his confidence. One evening, Alfred rowed

him across the harbour, and Bertrand vanished in the direction of the Kinder's cottage in St Leonards, clutching a tomahawk. He returned looking disgruntled. The intended victim had been drunk – probably in bed – and Bertrand's nerve had failed him. A week later Alfred rowed him to the north shore again; for some obscure reason, the dentist had blacked his face and donned a red shirt. He asked Alfred to come along and help him with the murder. His assistant declined, and Bertrand cursed and ordered him to row back.

Now Bertrand bought a brace of pistols, and began practising by firing at a sheep's head. He also warned Frank Jackson that he intended to kill Henry Kinder, and gave him the money to go to Melbourne. His intention was to make it look as if Jackson had fled. In fact, Jackson only went as far as Maitland, a hundred miles away.

Now, at last, Bertrand was ready. On Monday 2 October – the Australian spring – Jane Bertrand spent the day at the Kinder's cottage – Henry was home suffering from a hangover. Louis Bertrand came over later. He and Henry went to a hotel for a drink, and later the two couples sat in the parlour, Kinder and Bertrand playing cards while the women arranged flowers. There was a sudden loud report. The women looked round in time to see Henry Kinder slump on to the carpet. Bertrand bent down and replaced Kinder's pipe in his mouth. A smoking pistol lay on the carpet. Ellen Kinder fled from the room, while Jane knelt down and tended Henry Kinder, who was still alive.

A doctor who was called a few hours later was told that Kinder had shot himself. (Bertrand apparently hoped he would have bled to death by then, but Henry remained stubbornly alive.) The dentist told the doctor that the Kinders had been quarrelling about a man just before it happened – he was obviously still determined to implicate Jackson. The doctor accepted his story – after all, it was supported by both wives. He did not notice that Kinder's wound was at an angle – behind the ear – that made it highly unlikely that he had fired the pistol.

Henry Kinder was still able to speak, and told the police that he had *not* shot himself; they decided that he was delirious and ignored him. But, to Bertrand's chagrin, Kinder now began to recover. Jane Bertrand was nursing him faithfully. So Bertrand ordered her to put poison in Kinder's milk. Whether she did or not was never established; at all events, the following day,

Kinder was dead. It was assumed, naturally, that he had finally
died from his wound.

So it seemed that the scheming dentist had committed the
perfect crime. Now all he had to do was to get rid of his wife,
and he could marry his mistress. But a new complication arose.
Frank Jackson heard of Kinder's death, and wrote to Bertrand
threatening to denounce him unless Bertrand paid him £20 to
leave the country. But Bertrand felt secure in the suicide verdict.
He handed the letter over to the police, who charged Jackson
with blackmail; he was sentenced to twelve months.

The dentist's sister Harriet Kerr now came to stay with him.
She adored her brother, and it was natural that he should tell
her of his love affair with Ellen. But when she saw the way he
treated his wife, she was disgusted – and even more so when
Jane removed her dress and showed her whiplash marks on
her back. Unaware that he was losing her admiration, Bertrand
even admitted that he had killed Henry Kinder. His sister burst
into tears.

One morning soon after this, Harriet returned from a walk
to hear her brother shouting at his wife. He was brandishing
a heavy stick, and she was whimpering: "Don't kill me – you
promised you wouldn't." Harriet burst in, and was ordered out.
She went as far as the landing, and heard her brother order Jane
to write a note saying that she had poisoned herself. His next
move, clearly, was to force poison down her throat. But Jane
refused. Moments later, Bertrand stormed out of the room.

Three weeks after her husband's death, Ellen Kinder and her
two children left Sydney for Bathurst, where her parents lived.
She and her lover exchanged passionate letters. She was sensible
enough to burn his; he kept hers, and they were later produced
at his trial.

And now, in the best tradition of Victorian melodrama, the
villain began to go to pieces. He declared he was being haunted
by the ghost of Henry Kinder, and he once pushed aside a glass
of wine, saying that it reminded him of blood. He also forgot
himself so far as to attack a woman named Mary Robertson –
who made some slighting remarks about Ellen Kinder – with a
knife. For this he received a sentence of fourteen days in jail.

Also in prison, Frank Jackson was telling the police about
the murder plot. But before their investigation had progressed
beyond a few enquiries, Bertrand's sister Harriet went to the

police and reported his confession. Her brother was still in jail, so there was no need to arrest him. But Ellen Kinder was arrested in Bathurst, and Jane Bertrand was also taken into custody. Both women were later discharged for lack of evidence against them.

Bertrand's trial, with its scandalous evidence about adultery – even of forcing his wife to join him in bed with Ellen Kinder – was Australia's trial of the century. Bertrand deliberately behaved in a deranged manner, striding up and down the dock. And in spite of the damning evidence of his sister, Frank Jackson and Alfred Burne, the jury was unable to agree on a verdict.

At the second trial, the evidence from the first was read aloud. This time, the jury took two hours to reach a verdict of guilty. But the attempt to save time by reading the evidence aloud was to backfire. After Bertrand had been sentenced to death, the local Jewish community, led by Bertrand's wealthy uncle, briefed a barrister to try to overturn the death sentence. The main objection was that the jury should have heard the evidence from witnesses, not at second hand from transcripts of the first trial. Bertrand's sentence was commuted to life imprisonment. At which point, he brought the melodrama to a fitting conclusion by admitting his guilt.

Twenty-eight years later, he was released from prison, and immediately boarded a steamer for England. What became of him after that is unknown.

The cause of all the trouble, Ellen Kinder, returned to New Zealand, and is said to have supported herself as a barmaid.

# Frederick Bailey Deeming

If the murder of Henry Kinder was Australia's crime of the century, Frederick Bailey Deeming, hanged in Melbourne jail on 23 May, 1892, was certainly its criminal of the century. He shared with Palmer the Poisoner a delight in devious criminal schemes that is reminiscent of Conan Doyle's Professor Moriarty.

Little is known of Deeming's early life. He himself claimed that both his mother and father had been in mental homes, and

that as a child his own abnormality earned him the nickname,
"Mad Fred".

His career of crime seems to have started relatively late. In
1883 he was about thirty years of age, and had left his recently
married wife in Birkenhead while he went to Australia to seek
his fortune. In Sydney he worked as a gasfitter, and very
quickly spent some time in jail for stealing fittings. This is
the only crime that can be said to be unworthy of Deeming's
flamboyant personality; for, like Dr Pritchard, he was a braggart
and inventor of tall tales worthy of Munchausen. After a brief
term in jail, he made an attempt to earn an honest living,
having now been joined by his wife. This failed, owing to
his total unreliability, which sent his trade to his more staid
rivals. He filed a petition for bankruptcy, and was arrested for
fraud. Released on bail, he fled with his wife and children to
Port Adelaide. There, under the name of Ward, he stayed in
January 1888. It seems that he decided quite definitely on a
criminal career at this time. He left there for St Helena, and on
the voyage defrauded two brothers named Howe of £60. From
St Helena the family moved to Cape Town, where he obtained
work from a firm of engineers. He soon tired of this, and
moved around to Port Elizabeth, Kimberley, Johannesburg, and
Durban, always "talking big" and managing to support himself
with various minor frauds. His chief prey were jewellers, and he
was soon wanted for frauds amounting to £1,000 by jewellers in
Cape Town, Durban, and Johannesburg. His usual method was
to pose as the manager of a diamond mine.

In Johannesburg he offered lavish hospitality to big business
men and gained a large sum through a swindle worked on the
National Bank.

Next he obtained a post as manager of a gold-mining company
at Klerksdorp. Here he devised a new swindle; he offered to sell
certain gold mines to a rich financier. When the financier set
off for Cape Town to investigate Deeming's claims, his agent,
a man named Grice, received a telegram instructing him to pay
Deeming "not more than £2,200". Grice actually paid up £2,800
for some deeds of property. Soon, Grice received a telegram
from Deeming saying he intended to meet a Mr Leevy in Cape
Town; soon after that, "Leevy" himself telegraphed to say that
Deeming had died after a brief illness.

Deeming now sent his wife and children (there were now

four) to England, and went to Aden on a coal vessel, then to Southampton. Detectives were on his trail, and he went from Hull to Birkenhead, then to Camberwell, Stockton-on-Tees, sailed for Australia, doubled back at Port Said and returned to England.

At Hull and Beverley in Yorkshire, he was a millionaire and a relative of Sir Wilfred Lawson. He proposed marriage to the landlady of his hotel, who had the sense to refuse him; another woman, a Miss Matheson, accepted him and he married her bigamously. A few months later he deserted her. Shortly before the marriage he was in Antwerp posing as Lord Dunn. After the marriage he and his "wife" stayed at Gosport at the Star Hotel under the name of Lawson; he paid the hotel bill with a bogus cheque and returned to Hull.

In Hull, he swindled a jeweller out of £285 worth of jewellery (paid for with a bouncing cheque) and hastily embarked for South America. On this trip he became well known to the passengers as a hospitable and wealthy man, manager of a diamond mine in South Africa; he arranged a concert in aid of the Seamen's Orphanage and headed the subscription list with a generous donation. His fellow passengers were startled when he was arrested at Montevideo. He wrote indignantly to his counsel that the prison fare was doing "considerable hingery" to his health. (Deeming seems to have been almost illiterate.) On the way back to England he tried all kinds of ruses for escaping; he even told the sceptical detective hair-raising adventure stories in which he had killed men.

At Hull Assizes, on 16 October 1890, he was sentenced to nine months in jail. On 16 July 1891 he was released. He now went to the Commercial Hotel, Liverpool, where he posed as O. A. Williams, who was an inspector of regiments in South Africa (or India – his story varied), who had come to England to take a house for a Colonel Brooks who would be shortly retiring. Deeming was certainly now planning to murder his wife and family, for he found a cottage, Dinham Villa, at Rainhill, and specified that he was to concrete the kitchen floor since the colonel hated uneven floors. His wife came to visit him at Rainhill and had meals with him in the hotel, where she was introduced as his sister. (Deeming was already courting a Miss Mather, daughter of a widow who kept a newsagent's, shop.) Towards the end of July 1891, Mrs Deeming and the children

moved into Dinham Villa, and were murdered and buried under
the kitchen floor. Deeming then cemented the floor himself,
getting workmen to help with the finishing touches. Before
leaving the hotel, where he had made many friends, he gave
a dinner party that was reported in the local papers. This was
a month after the murders. He spent two weeks in London,
where he wrote to his murdered wife's father, saying that he
intended to visit him soon with his wife, and then returned to
Rainhill, where he married Miss Mather. He took her to see
Dinham Villa, and danced a little jig on the kitchen floor.

They decided to sail for Australia. Before leaving England,
Deeming tried one more fraud; he sent a picture by rail, and
then tried claiming that it was damaged, and demanded £50
compensation. The railway company called his bluff, and he
left England without the money.

Miss Mather appears to have been extremely happy with her
lively husband; but by the time they reached Australia – ten
days before Christmas, 1891 – she must have had her doubts. A
neighbour who saw her described her as a silent woman whose
eyes seemed red from weeping. She must have suspected her
husband's true character from the fact that he now insisted on
an alias of Droven or Drewen. They took a house in Andrew
Street, Windsor, Melbourne. In a very short time indeed, Miss
Mather found her way under the bedroom floor, where she was
cemented in.

On 5 January, Deeming moved out. He applied to a matri-
monial agency for a wife, but then left Melbourne suddenly
and sailed for Sydney. On the boat he met his next prospective
victim, a Miss Katie Rounsfell, who quickly agreed to marry him.
She knew him as Baron Swanston. He travelled to Sydney with
her, then left her and obtained a job with Fraser's gold mine,
Southern Cross. She was actually on her way to join him
when chance – in the form of the discovery of Miss Mather
– saved her.

Eight weeks after Deeming had moved out of Andrew Street,
the agent, a man named Connor, went to look over the place,
having heard of an offensive odour in the bedroom. The newly
cemented fireplace was crumbling – the heat of an Australian
summer had dried it too quickly. Connor kicked away a few
lumps of soft concrete and found himself looking at the face of
a dead girl.

"Drewen" had left many clues behind him, including a card labelled O. A. Williams, with the Rainhill address on it. This soon led to the discovery of the bodies in Dinham Villa. Detective-Sergeant Considine, of the CID in Melbourne (who was in charge of the case) has declared that three houses in which Deeming had lived in Johannesburg also revealed bodies of women under the hearths. If so, it is not known who these women were. At the time Deeming lived in Johannesburg, his wife was with him.

Considine soon discovered that "Drewen" was a confidence swindler who had defrauded a Melbourne firm of valuable jewellery, and had tried to swindle another firm of £2,000. He had also tried to blackmail the shipowners whose boat had brought him to Melbourne, declaring that his wife had lost a £1,000 necklace on the trip. (No doubt this accounted for Emily Mather's disillusion, for she must have been called upon to substantiate Deeming's story.)

Deeming was traced to Southern Cross and arrested there. He was taken to Melbourne – great crowds gathering to watch his arrival – and tried there. He suffered from fits (as he had on the voyage back from Montevideo), but detectives suspected these were faked. At one point he narrowly escaped lynching. He wrote to Miss Rounsfell, declaring his innocence and asking her to believe in him; he also asked for money. (Miss Rounsfell was an heiress.)

His defence tried an insanity plea, and Deeming declared that the apparition of his dead mother frequently appeared to him, and had once urged him to kill all his woman friends. He also made a speech declaring that Emily Mather was still alive and that the people in court were the ugliest he had ever seen in his life. He was sentenced to death. In jail he confessed to being Jack the Ripper – an impossibility since he was in jail at the time of the murders.

# chapter six

# THE SCIENCE OF DETECTION

*T*he most remarkable achievement of the Age of Gaslight was undoubtedly its development of the science of detection. Scientific crime detection had been taking slow, hesitant steps since the last quarter of the eighteenth century, when a number of brilliant chemists – Scheele, Hahnemann, Metzger, Rose – learned how to detect arsenic, even after it had been absorbed by the human body – it was this new knowledge that convicted Anna Zwanziger. By 1820, the great Mathieu Orfila had created the science of toxicology, which meant that poison was no longer the murderer's most reliable weapon.

The art of photography also came to play an important part in crime detection. By the 1870s, most police forces in Europe added a photograph of a criminal to his file. Their main problem was the popularity of beards – a photograph of one bearded, scowling face looked very much like another. Moreover, an archive of a hundred thousand photographs is useless unless they are classified in a way that enables the police to decide where to start looking.

Alphonse Bertillon.

When parts of a woman's body – including her head – were found in the river Seine in 1887, photographs of the head were sold at newsagents in an attempt to identify her. Hundreds were bought. This led to her identification as the wife of an old soldier called Billoir. His defense was that he had kicked her in the course of a drunken quarrel and that she had collapsed and died. But medical examination showed that her heart had still been beating when she was dismembered. Billoir was sentenced to death, remarking gloomily: "The doctors have done for me."

# Alphonse Bertillon

When the twenty-five-year-old Alphonse Bertillon became a clerk at the Sûreté in 1879, most of the old identification procedures were practically useless. Bertillon was a dreary, pedantic young man whom most people found rather repellent; but he came from a cultured and scientific family, and the chaos irritated him. He was certain there *ought* to be some simple way of arranging the hundred thousand photographs and descriptions.

Bertillon's story would be ideal for Hollywood. He compared photographs of criminals to see if there was some way of classifying noses and faces. Then he thought it might be a good idea to take measurements of criminals when they were arrested – height, reach, circumference of head, height sitting down, length of left hand, left foot, left leg – Bertillon chose the left-hand side because it was unlikely to be affected by work. He was subject to constipation, stomach upsets, headaches and nosebleeds; but he had a certain stubbornness that made him ignore the knowing smiles of colleagues. A doctor named Adolphe Quetelet had asserted that the chances of two people being exactly the same height are four to one. If that was so, and the same thing applied to the other statistics, then you needed only two or three measurements of each criminal to raise the odds to a hundred to one. When the prefect of police ignored Bertillon's letter about this method, Bertillon bought himself a set of filing cards, and started to work on his own, staying in the office until late at night. His boss Gustave Macé revealed a lack of insight when he read Bertillon's report, and said it was too theoretical. The prefect, Andrieux, told Bertillon to stop making a nuisance of himself. And three years went by before Bertillon could persuade a new prefect, Jean Camecasse, to give him an interview. Camecasse was as sceptical as his predecessor, but he was impressed by the clerk's persistence. He told Bertillon that they would introduce his method experimentally for three months. This was obviously absurd; it would take more than three months to build up a file, and a method like Bertillon's depended on accumulation. But with Macé himself opposed to the whole idea, he knew his only chance lay in working on and praying for luck. His card index swelled at the rate of a few hundred a month. But with more than twenty thousand criminals in Paris alone, the chances of identifying one of them was low. Towards the end of the third month, Bertillon had towards two thousand cards. Theoretically, his chance of identification was one in ten – fairly high. But it must be remembered that a large number of his criminals were sent to jail, often for years, so most of his file was lying fallow, so to speak.

On 20 February 1883, luck was with him. His system led him to identify a petty criminal who had been measured three months earlier. It was a very small triumph, but it was enough to make Camecasse decide to allow the experiment to continue. This was not far-sightedness. The post of prefect was a political appointment; Camecasse was hoping for fame. Unfortunately, a new prefect had been appointed by the time Bertillon became a celebrity; but history allows Camecasse the credit. As the file swelled, identification became more frequent. Before long, it averaged one a day. But what Bertillon needed was a really sensational case.

He had to wait until 1892 for it, but when it came, it spread his name all over the world. And the reason for the notoriety of the case was more or less accidental.

Since the early 1880s, a terrifying group of people known as the Anarchists became steadily more well known. People were not all that interested in their idealistic doctrine of the inherent goodness of human nature – which means that man does not need Authority to keep him virtuous. In 1881, Russian anarchists – they called themselves Narodniki – blew up Tsar Alexander II with a bomb; in Chicago, in May 1884, someone hurled a home-made bomb into a crowd of policemen who were about to break up a meeting of strikers, killing seven of them. Eight anarchists were condemned to death; one of them blew himself up with a bomb, and wrote in his own blood: "Long live Anarchy!" Four of the anarchists were eventually hanged. In France, anarchists like Malatesta, Grave and Reclus spoke darkly of the "propaganda of the deed", and the bourgeoisie shuddered. On May Day 1891, three anarchists were arrested for taking part in demonstrations at Clichy, and badly beaten-up by the police. At their trial, the prosecuting attorney Bulot demanded the death penalty for all three – although no one had been killed in the riots. The judge, Benoist, acquitted one of them and gave the other two prison sentences of three and five years. In March the following year – 1892 – a tremendous explosion shook the house in which Judge Benoist lived, destroying the stairway. Two weeks later, another explosion blew up Bulot's house in the Rue de Clichy. Luckily, no one was killed in either explosion. But the panic was tremendous. Large quantities of dynamite had been stolen from quarries at Soiry, and the Parisians wondered where the next explosion would occur. A Left-Wing professor was arrested for the first explosion, and he agreed that he had planned it; however, a man named Ravachol had carried it out. Ravachol was known to the police – not as an anarchist, but as a burglar who was suspected of murder; he had killed an old miser and his housekeeper, two women who kept a hardware store, and an old miser who lived in a forest hut. He was also believed to have robbed the tomb of a countess to steal her jewellery. The alias of this forty-year-old criminal seemed to be Konigstein.

On the day of the Rue de Clichy dynamiting, Ravachol dined in the Restaurant Véry in the Boulevard Magenta, and tried to convert a waiter named Lhérot to anarchism. Two days later, he returned, and Lhérot noticed a scar on his thumb, which had been mentioned in descriptions of Ravachol. He notified the police, and the man was arrested.

Here was Bertillon's chance to prove his system to the world. Luckily, "Konigstein" had been briefly under arrest at St Etienne as a suspect in the murder of the old man, and the police there had taken his measurements before he managed to escape. Bertillon himself measured Ravachol, and the measurements corresponded exactly. The idealistic anarchist

Ravachol was the murderous criminal Konigstein, and for the time being, at least, the anarchist movement was discredited. On the evening before Ravachol's trial, the Restaurant Véry was blown up by a bomb, which killed the proprietor and a customer – it was obviously retaliation for the arrest of Ravachol, and an attempt to intimidate the judges. It succeeded; Ravachol was only condemned to prison. But the judges of St Etienne were less scared of anarchist bombs; with Bertillon's proof in their hands, they were able to bring home the five murders to Ravachol, and he was executed on 10 July 1892. For the next few years Paris rocked with bombs – there was even one in the Chamber of Deputies – and President Carnot himself was assassinated. Bertillon luckily escaped the wrath of the anarchists.

# The method of Fingerprinting

But, absurdly enough the method known as "Bertillonage", which had revolutionized almost every police force in the world, was already out of date by this time. In India in the 1860s, a civil servant named William Herschel had observed that no two fingerprints are ever alike. He put it to use in his job of paying off pensioned Indian soldiers. These men could seldom write, and they all looked alike to English eyes. And when they realized this, the pensioners began collecting their pensions twice, or returned and collected other people's pensions. When Herschel noticed that fingerprints were always different, he made them sign for their pensions by placing the index finger on an inked pad, and pressing it gently at the side of his name on the list. The swindling ceased. Some years later, a Scot named Henry Faulds made the same discovery, and wrote a letter to *Nature*, declaring that this might be a means of identifying criminals. The year was 1880, two years before Bertillon was allowed to start making his experiments in measurement. Faulds and Herschel were later to be involved in bitter disputes about priority, but these do not concern us here.

A disciple of Darwin, Sir Francis Galton, became interested in Bertillonage because he thought it would help in the study of problems of heredity. He became friendly with Bertillon, and this interest in police work led him to write to Herschel about his methods of fingerprinting; he had read the exchange of letters between Herschel and Faulds in *Nature*. Galton settled down to the study of fingerprints, and soon decided that there were only four basic classifications; the core of his method was the triangle, or "delta", in the centre of a fingerprint. In 1892, Galton's book *Fingerprints* came out. So in the year of his greatest triumph, Bertillon had become redundant. He refused to acknowledge it – for years he fought grimly for his system, betraying an unfortunate lack of the truly scientific spirit. But fingerprinting was bound to prevail in the end; it was so much simpler than Bertillonage.

The first murder ever to be solved by a fingerprint took place in Necochea, Argentina. A twenty-six-year-old woman named Francesca Rojas ran into the hut of a neighbour saying that her children had been murdered. The two children, aged four and six, lay dead in bed, their heads beaten in. She accused a man named Velasquez, who was in love with her. She wanted to marry another man, and she claimed that Velasquez had threatened to kill "what she loved most". She had returned from work to find the children dead . . .

Velasquez was arrested and badly beaten, but he denied the murders, while agreeing to the threat. The police methods in Necochea were primitive; they tortured Velasquez for a week, without result; then the police chief tried making moaning noises outside the woman's hut, hoping to frighten her into confession by pretending to be a ghost.

A police inspector named Alvarez went out to investigate from La Plata. And he knew something about the work of a Dalmatian named Juan Vucetich, head of the Statistical Bureau of Police in Buenos Aires, who had developed his own fingerprint system after reading an article by Galton. Alvarez went into the woman's hut and searched for clues. All he could find was a bloody thumb-print on a door. Alvarez sawed off the portion of the door and took it back to headquarters. Then he sent for Francesca Rojas, and made her give her thumb-print. Alvarez knew very little about classification, but it was quite obvious that the two prints were identical. When he showed

Alfred Stratton.

Albert Stratton.

the woman the two prints through a magnifying glass, she broke down and confessed – she had murdered her own two children because she wanted to marry a young lover who objected to them. This Argentine Lady Macbeth, who tried to rid herself of illegitimate children and an unwanted lover with one blow, obviously deserves to stand very high on a list of the world's worst women.

# The Stratton Brothers

The first English murder case involving fingerprints took place in Deptford in 1905. At 7.15 a.m., on 27 March of that year, a passing milkman saw two men emerge from a shop at 34 High Street, Deptford, and slam the door behind them. It was a paint shop, and the manager, an elderly man called Farrow, ran the shop with his wife.

At half past eight, the shop boy arrived and found the place closed up; he went to fetch the shop's owner, and they forced a kitchen window. Farrow was found dead on the ground floor, his head battered in; his wife was found dead in bed. What had happened was clear enough. The two men had broken into the shop, and Mr Farrow had heard the noise and hurried downstairs – where he was beaten over the head with jemmies and left for dead. The men went upstairs, and killed his wife in the same way. They found the cash box under her husband's pillow and emptied it. Farrow was not dead; after the men left the shop he staggered to the door and looked outside, where he was seen by a little girl who thought nothing of a bloodstained man; then he locked the shop door, and died.

The police were on the scene by 9.30, and soon found a thumb-print inside the cash box. It was photographed and enlarged. The police now checked on local criminals, and discovered that two brothers named Stratton were missing from their usual haunts. They were known as a violent and brutal pair, who had been in the hands of the police several times. They were picked up later in the week and fingerprinted. The thumb-print in the cash box was identical with that of the elder brother, Alfred. The police had no other evidence against them, since the milkman had been unable to identify them. Sergeant Collins, the fingerprint expert, would be the most important prosecution witness.

It was obviously an important case, and the future of fingerprinting might stand or fall by it – for a few years at least. Neither the judge – an elderly gentleman named Channell – nor the jury knew anything about fingerprints. The defence decided to take no chances, and called two of their own fingerprint experts. One of these was none other than Henry Faulds, the Scot who had discovered fingerprinting and declared that it should be used for police work. Through an unfortunate accident, he had never received the credit that was his due. When Sir Francis Galton had written to ask *Nature* for the addresses of the two men who had been conducting a correspondence about fingerprinting, the editor accidentally sent him only the address of Herschel. Herschel, like Galton, was a generous and disinterested sort of person, who immediately handed Galton all his results – with the consequence that Galton never had reason to consult Faulds. But Faulds, unfortunately, was an obsessive egoist who wanted credit for his discovery. (It will be remembered that Herschel actually discovered fingerprinting first, but Faulds was the first to publish the discovery.) For years, Faulds fought a violent battle to gain recognition; the British felt this was rather unsporting, and ignored him. So now Faulds decided to make himself felt by opposing the Crown case. The other "expert" was yet another disappointed egoist, Dr Garson, who had first sneered at fingerprinting (he was a champion of Bertillonage), then decided to change horses, and invented his own system. And it was Garson's appetite for recognition that swung the case against the Strattons. Sergeant Collins gave a lecture on fingerprints and drew sketches on a blackboard. Garson and Faulds made no attempt to deny that no two fingerprints are ever alike, but they *did* assert that the print on the cash box was not identical with the print of Alfred Stratton's thumb. To the judge and jury, all fingerprints looked alike, and they were inclined to credit the assertion that the two prints were not really identical. Collins replied that the discrepancies were the kind that are bound to occur when fingerprints are taken, because lines will look thicker or thinner according to the pressure applied and the angle at which the finger is

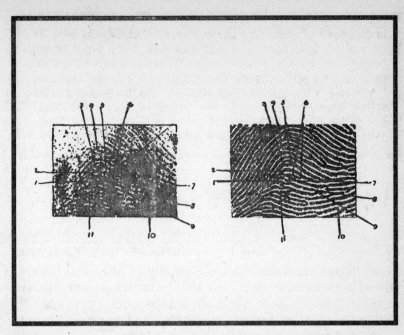

The fingerprint that made legal history. *Left*: the thumb-print left by Thomas Farrow's murderer on the cash box that he robbed. *Right*: the thumb-print of Alfred Stratton. A convincing eleven points of similarity prove beyond any doubt that they were made by the same person.

pressed on to the paper. He demonstrated this convincingly by taking fingerprints of the jury on spot, and showing exactly the same discrepancies. But the seeds of doubt had been sown. The prosecutor now played his trump card. Garson was called back to the stand, and was asked whether it was not true that he had written a letter offering to testify for the prosecution? Yet he was now testifying for the defence. Clearly, this was a man who would change his opinions for the sake of being an important witness in an important trial. The judge remarked that he was obviously untrustworthy. And the last hope of the Stratton brothers vanished. They were found guilty, and both of them proceeded to shout abuse at the court, dissipating the impression of wronged innocence they had been aiming for. The judge sentenced them to death. England's first fingerprint murder had established that a fingerprint alone is enough to hang a man.

In *Mysteries of Police and Crime*, Major Arthur Griffiths tells the story of a robber who was detected by means of a finger he left behind. The thief was climbing over a factory gate with iron spikes on top when a policeman saw him and shouted. The thief ran away; it was only in the next days that his finger was found on one of the spikes. It had stuck into it as he tried to escape, and his own weight had pulled it off. The fingerprint proved to be in Scotland Yard's collection, and the thief was captured and sentenced to jail.

# The Murder of PC Cole

Another new science was aiding the law in its battle against crime; it was called ballistics – the study of guns and bullets. When Louis Bertrand used a one-shot pistol to kill Henry Kinder in 1865, such weapons were already becoming obsolete. By 1840, a young man named Samuel Colt had invented the colt revolver. By 1870, mass produced revolvers were producing a crime epidemic like the poisoning epidemic of the seventeenth century. The revolver seemed a boon for criminals, since every bullet apparently looked alike. Yet even before scientists learned to study the "rifle marks" on bullets under a microscope, the police were learning that a bullet could convict a criminal just as surely as a fingerprint. Major Arthur Griffiths cites the classic case that has become known as "Orrock's chisel."

On 1 December 1882, the cobbled, gaslit streets of east London were wrapped in choking fog as a young constable set out from Dalston police station on a beat that took him down a narrow thoroughfare called Ashwin Street. As he turned the corner, he came to a sudden halt as he saw a man placing a lantern on top of the wall outside the Baptist chapel, and beginning to scramble over. PC Cole took a swift step forward, laid his hand on the man's shoulder, and asked: "What do you think you're doing?" For a moment, the man – who seemed little more than a youth – looked as if he was going to resist; then he changed his mind and agreed to "go quietly". But PC Cole and his captive had only gone as far as the pub on the corner when the man broke loose and ran. Cole ran after him and grabbed him by the left arm; as he did so, the man reached into his pocket, pulled out a revolver, and fired three shots. A woman who was walking towards them screamed and fled; as she ran, she heard another shot. Moments later, she encountered two policeman in Dalston Lane, and led them back to the scene of the shooting. PC Cole was lying on the pavement outside the Baptist chapel, his head in the gutter; a trickle of blood ran from the bullet hole behind his left ear. He died five minutes after being admitted to the local German Hospital.

Inspector Glass, who took charge of the case, ordered a search of the area where the policeman had been found; on the wall of the Baptist chapel, the burglar had left his dark lantern; behind the railings, a chisel, a jemmy, and a wooden wedge had been left on the ground. The only other clue was a black billycock hat, which the burglar had lost in the course of the struggle. The woman who had seen him running away described him as short and slightly built; another witness gave the same description.

There was one man in the Dalston police station who believed he knew the identity of the murderer. Only minutes before Cole had arrested the burglar, Police Sergeant Cobb had been walking along Ashwin Street with another sergeant, Branwell, when they had noticed a man standing under a streetlamp. Cobb recognized him as a young cabinetmaker named Tom Orrock, and when he saw the policeman, he looked furtive and uncomfortable. Orrock had no criminal record, but he kept bad company – thugs and professional criminals – and it seemed a reasonable assumption that he would one day try his hand at crime. As they passed Orrock that night, Cobb had been tempted to arrest him for loitering. But standing under a streetlamp was no crime, and Cobb had decided against it. Now he regretted it, and was inclined to blame himself for the death of PC Cole, who was a young married man with children.

Informed of Sergeant Cobb's suspicions, Inspector Glass was inclined to be dismissive – to begin with, he disliked Cobb, regarding him as too unimaginative and too conscientious. But he ordered Tom Orrock – who was nineteen – to be brought in for an identity parade. When the witnesses who had glimpsed Cole's captive failed to identify him, Orrock was released. Soon after that, he disappeared from his usual haunts.

Months after the murder, the investigation was at a standstill. The clues seemed to lead nowhere. The hat bore no marks of identification, and the chisels and the large wooden wedge might have belonged to anybody. But the bullets looked more promising. All four had been recovered – two from the policeman's skull, one from his truncheon, another from the truncheon case. They were unusual in that they had been fired from a revolver that was little more than a toy – the kind of thing ladies sometimes carried in their handbags. The science of ballistics was unknown in 1882, but the rarity of a gun suggested that it might one day provide a valuable piece of evidence.

When studied through a magnifying glass, one of the chisels also yielded an interesting clue. A series of scratches near the handle looked like an attempt at writing, probably with a sharp nail. And when the chisel was photographed for the case file, the letters could be seen more clearly, and they resolved themselves into a capital R, followed by what looked like an o, a c, and a k. Rock. Could it be short for Orrock? Cobb began calling in every tool shop in the Hackney and Dalston area, asking if they recognized the chisels, but met with no success.

Cobb refused to give up. A year after the murder, he was talking with an acquaintance of the missing cabinetmaker named Henry Mortimer, who occasionally acted as a police informer. And Mortimer's rambling discourse suddenly arrested the sergeant's attention when he mentioned that Tom Orrock had possessed a revolver – a nickel-plated, pin-fire miniature affair. Orrock had seen it advertised in the *Exchange and Mart*, and he and Mortimer had gone to Tottenham to purchase it from the owner for the sum of half a guinea. They had also been accompanied by two men named Miles and Evans, both professional – if unsuccessful – criminals. On the way home, the four men had stopped on Tottenham Marshes and used a tree for target practice. At Cobb's request, Mortimer accompanied him to Tottenham and showed him the tree. The following day, Cobb returned alone, and dug some bullets out of the tree with his penknife. One of them was relatively undamaged, and was obviously of the same calibre as the bullets that had been fired at PC Cole.

Now Cobb was sure he had his man, and that view was confirmed when Mortimer admitted that Orrock had virtually confessed to killing PC Cole. When Mortimer had expressed disbelief, Orrock had replied: "If they can prove it against me, I'm willing to take the consequences." This is precisely what Cobb now set out to do.

The first step was to lay the new evidence before his immediate superior. Inspector Glass was still inclined to be indifferent, but he agreed to ask for help from New Scotland Yard in trying to trace the shop that had sold the chisel. And it was the Scotland Yard team that finally located a woman named Preston, a widow who carried on her husband's tool-sharpening business. She recognized the chisel because she always made a practice of scratching the name of the owner near the handle; she remembered the young man who brought in the chisel for grinding had given the name Orrock, which she had shortened to "Rock".

Now at last, they had the kind of evidence that might impress a jury. All that remained was to locate Tom Orrock. Scotland Yard was asked to circulate his description to every police station in the country. This would normally have brought prompt results, for in those days before the population explosion, most police stations were aware of any strangers who had moved into their district. So when another year failed to bring news of the wanted man, Glass was inclined to assume either that he was dead or that he had gone abroad. Cobb refused to believe it. And one day he had an inspiration. One place where a man could "lie low" with reasonable chance of escaping recognition was prison. Once again, Cobb began painstaking enquiries – enquiries that entitle him to be ranked with Canler and Macé as a distinguished practitioner of the needle-in-the-haystack method. And he soon learned that a man answering Orrock's description had been serving a term for burglary in Coldbath Fields for the past two years. Coldbath Fields, in Farringdon Road, was one of London's newer prisons, and had a reputation for severity. The name under which the prisoner was serving his sentence was not Tom Orrock, and when he was summoned to the governor's office, the man denied that he was called Orrock or had ever been in Dalston. Sergeant Cobb attended an identity parade, and had to admit reluctantly that he was unable to recognize Orrock among the seven uniformed convicts who now faced him. But as the men filed out again, they passed under a light, and Cobb suddenly recognized the profile of the man he had last seen standing under a gaslamp in Dalston more that two years earlier. He stepped forward and laid his hand on the shoulder of Thomas Henry Orrock.

Now it was a question of building up the web of circumstantial evidence. Orrock's sister, Mrs Bere, was questioned, and admitted that on the night of the murder her brother had returned home with a torn trouser leg, and without his hat, claiming that he had been involved in a street brawl. Orrock's two friends Miles and Evans were questioned separately. They admitted that they had spent the day of the murder drinking with Tom Orrock in various pubs, and that soon after 10 o'clock in the evening, the three had been in the Railway Tavern in Ashwin Street when Orrock boasted that he intended to embark on a criminal career by "cracking a crib" – stealing the silver plate of the Baptist church, which he attended regularly, and taking it to his brother-in-law to be melted down. Orrock had then left the pub. Not long after, Miles and Evans heard the sound of revolver shots, but claimed they had taken them for fog signals. All the same, they had left the pub and been among the crowd that gathered around the wounded policeman. Three weeks later, when a reward of £200 had been offered for information leading to the capture of the murderer, Orrock went to Evans and begged him not to inform on him; Evans swore that he would not "ruck" on a comrade even for a thousand pounds.

But all this was merely hearsay evidence. The vital link between Tom Orrock and the murder of PC Cole was the revolver. This had disappeared – one witness said that Orrock admitted throwing it into the River Lea. But the police were able to track down the man who had sold Orrock the revolver – his name was McLellan – and he unhesitatingly identified bullets and cartridge cases as being the calibre of those he had sold to a young man in the last week of November 1882, one week before the murder. McLellan's description of the purchaser fitted Thomas Henry Orrock.

A few decades later, all this corroborative evidence would have been unnecessary. Examination of the bullets under a comparison microscope would have proved that the bullet found in the tree at Tottenham was identical with the bullet that killed PC Cole. But in the year 1884, no one had yet thought of studying the pattern of rifle marks on the side of a bullet; it would be another five years before Professor Alexandre Lacassagne would provide the evidence to convict a murderer by studying bullet grooves under a microscope. Nevertheless, when Tom Orrock came to trial in September 1884, it was the bullet evidence that carried most weight with the jury. The bullet found in the tree at Tottenham was "precisely similar to the one found in the brain of the dead constable", said the prosecution. "If the prisoner purchased the revolver, where was it? A man did not throw away a revolver that cost him 10 shillings without good cause." The jury was convinced. On Saturday 20 September 1884, Thomas Orrock was convicted of the murder of PC Cole and sentenced to be hanged. The jury added a special recommendation to Sergeant Cobb for his persistence in tracking down the killer. But the chronicler relates that, in after years, Inspector Glass liked to claim credit for capturing Orrock, and "has often remarked that the man who in reality put the police in possession of their information to this day is ignorant that he disclosed to them this knowledge" - from which it would appear that Glass continued to resent the success of his subordinate and to deny him any of the credit.

# chapter seven

# THE MYSTERY OF JACK THE RIPPER

*B*y the 1880s, the Age of Gaslight was drawing to a close. In 1881, Edison developed the first electric power plant in the world. In 1890, electric lights were switched on in the Chamber of Horrors at Madame Tussaud's waxworks in London – they had to be shaded in green to produce the same "creepy" effect as the flickering gaslamps.

But the most sensational British crime of the century occurred in the final years of the gaslamp. The nature of the crimes was so horrific that the soubriquet of the unknown murderer was soon famous around the world.

## Jack the Ripper

In view of our complete ignorance of the identity of Jack the Ripper, it is strange that the case has continued to exercise such fascination for over half a century. Many people suppose that the Ripper crimes took place over many years and that his victims ran into dozens; whereas, in actual fact, the murders took place over a few months in 1888 and the victims were certainly not more than seven in number – quite possibly only four. The present writer has read an article in a spiritualist newspaper called *Two Worlds*, in which it is alleged that a medium, Mr Lees, helped to catch the Ripper; the article speaks of the murders as extending over several years and running into hundreds. Similarly, an article in the surrealist magazine of the 1920's, *Minotaur*, by Maurice Heine, speaks casually of "the eleventh victim", and includes a dubious photograph of the "eleventh victim".

The facts, briefly, are these: between 31 August 1888 and 8 November 1888 five murders took place within an area of half a mile in Whitechapel in the East End of London. All the women were mutilated with a knife and on several occasions some of the internal organs were taken away. After 8 November the murders ceased abruptly.

During the early part of 1888 there were two murders of women in Whitechapel that may possibly have been the work of the Ripper. The first was of an unfortunate woman named Emma Elizabeth Smith, aged forty-five, who was returning home in the early hours of the day following Easter Monday (3 April) when she was attacked. Twenty-four hours later she died in hospital of peritonitis, some sharp instrument like a spike having penetrated her abdomen. She claimed she was attacked by four men in Osborn Street at about four in the morning as she was returning home from a public house; they took her money (only a few coppers) and mistreated her. Her account of the four men seems circumstantial enough; she described one of them as being only nineteen.

The murder which is often regarded as the Ripper's first crime took place in Gunthorpe Street (then known as "George Yard") in the early hours of the day following Bank Holiday Monday, 7 August. A prostitute named Martha Turner (or Tabram) was picked up by a soldier on Bank Holiday night and seen in The Angel and Crown drinking with him. Several hours later (at about 5 a.m.) her body was found on the first landing of George Yard Buildings. She had been stabbed thirty-nine times; the murderer had used two weapons, one a bayonet or long-bladed knife, the other some kind of surgical instrument. He was also ambidextrous. The soldier who had been seen with her was traced, but had an alibi; all the soldiers in the Tower were paraded, but no arrest was made. It is impossible to state with any certainty whether this was the Ripper's first crime in Whitechapel, but most writers on the case are inclined to believe that it is the work of the Ripper. The present writer is inclined to doubt it.

At 2.30 a.m. on Friday 31 August, a woman friend saw a prostitute named Mary Anne Nicholls (known as "Polly") at the corner of Osborn Street; she admitted to having had "no luck". Three-quarters of an hour later, her body was found by a carter named Cross in Bucks Row (now called Durward Street), lying in the entrance to the Old Stable Yard at the west end of the street. In the mortuary of the Old Montague Street Workhouse it was discovered that she had been disembowelled. Death was due to severing of the windpipe. She was identified by her husband, a printer's machinist, from whom she had been separated for seven years. She was forty-two years of age, and known as a habitual drunk. When her husband saw her body, he was heard to say, "I forgive you for everything now I see you like this." It was revealed that she had been staying at a dosshouse in Thrawl Street, where a bed could be had for fourpence a night. On the previous evening she had been turned away from the dosshouse because she had no money. She commented, "Don't worry, I'll soon get the money. Look what a fine bonnet I've got."

A bruise on her face indicated that the murderer clamped his hand over her mouth before cutting her throat. A woman sleeping in a bedroom only a few yards from the murder heard no sound.

The next murder took place on 8 September. Annie Chapman, aged forty-seven was turned away from a lodging house in Dorset Street, having no money to pay for a bed. It seems probable that the murderer accosted Chapman outside the yard where the murder took place – at 29 Hanbury Street. She accompanied him down a passageway at the side of the house some time after 5 a.m. The body was found shortly after 6 a.m. The head had been almost severed from the body, and then tied in place with a handkerchief. The body was cut open, as in the case of Mary Nicholls, and the kidney and the ovaries had been removed. Two front teeth were missing (repeating a curious feature of the Nicholls murder) and two brass rings and some coppers were laid at her feet. In another corner of the yard was the torn corner of a bloodstained envelope, containing the crest of the Sussex regiment. Under a tap was a leather apron. It seems possible that these last two items were intended to mislead the police. A soldier had been suspected in the Tabram case, and Whitechapel gossip named a man called "Leather Apron" as the murderer. (He was actually a Polish Jew named Pizer, a shoemaker, who was arrested and then released.) Again the murderer had carried out the crime with extreme coolness and had made no sound. There were sixteen people living at 29 Hanbury Street and a scream would have quickly brought help to the victim.

On 28 September a letter was sent to the Central News Agency signed "Jack the Ripper" and threatening more murders. "I am down on whores and shant quit ripping them till I do get buckled." Whether or not it was by a practical joker, the name caught the public imagination when it first appeared in the newspapers (after 30 September).

The murders caused a universal panic. Meetings were held in the streets, criticizing the police and the Home Secretary. Bloodhounds were suggested, but they promptly lost themselves in Tooting. The newspapers of the time gave extremely full reports of the murders and inquests, and were tireless in offering theories.

A description of the murderer offered by someone who saw Annie Chapman talking to a man outside 29 Hanbury Street included a large moustache and a "foreign appearance".

On the morning of 30 September two murders were committed in Whitechapel. The first was of a Swedish woman called Elizabeth Stride. A hawker named Louis Deimschutz drove his horse and cart into the back yard of the International Workers Educational Club in Berner Street. (A council school now stands on the site.) He saw a woman's body on the ground and rushed into the club to give the alarm. The woman's throat had been cut and she had been killed very recently – so recently that it is possible that "Jack the Ripper" was interrupted and made his escape as Deimschutz entered the club. This was at 1 a.m.

At this time a forty-three-year-old prostitute named Catherine Eddowes was released from Bishopsgate police station, where she had been in charge for drunkenness. She was picked up by the Ripper and taken into a narrow alleyway that extends between Mitre Square and Duke Street, known as Church Passage (now St James Passage). Police Constable Watkins passed through the passage on his beat at one-thirty. A quarter of an hour later he again passed through the square, and found the body of Catherine Eddowes in the corner of the square near Church Passage. Her face had been badly mutilated – perhaps to delay identification – and the body cut open in the usual way; the left kidney and entrails had been removed and taken away. It was some time before she was identified, and in the meantime, one of the newspapers published a report that she was thought to be a certain "Mary Anne Kelly". This is a

remarkable co-incidence, since the name of the final victim was Mary Jeanette Kelly.

A householder who lived in Berner Street (off the Commercial Road and the farthest afield of the Ripper's murders) testified that she saw a young man carrying a shiny black bag away from the scene of the crime. (Men carrying black bags were sometimes attacked in the street in Whitechapel at this time, and the Ripper murders made this type of bag go quite conclusively out of fashion.)

After the murder the Central News Agency received another letter signed "Jack the Ripper", regretting that he had been interrupted with his victims, and had not been able to send the ears to the police. (There had been an attempt to cut off the ear of Catherine Eddowes.) He also mentioned that "number one squealed a bit", which is borne out by a witness in Berner Street who heard the cry. The letter was posted only a few hours after the murders, and was written in red ink.

The murders had caused unprecedented excitement, and bands of vigilantes patrolled the streets of Whitechapel at night. But as weeks passed without further crimes, the panic died down. (One theory suggests that the Ripper was incarcerated in a mental home during these weeks.) On 9 November the last of the murders took place at a house in Millers Court, which ran off Dorset Street (now Duval Street), probably between Dorset Street and Whites Row to the south. Mary Jeanette Kelly was younger than the other victims, but of the same class. She was twenty-four. On the morning of 9 November at 10.45 a.m. a man knocked on the door of Mary Kelly to collect the rent. Getting no reply, he peered in at the broken window. What remained of Mary Kelly lay on the bed. The head had been almost severed from the body; the heart had been placed on the pillow. The entrails had been draped over a picture frame. The murderer had apparently worked by the light of a pile of rags, the ashes of which were burnt in the grate. Neighbours testified to hearing a cry of "Murder" at about 3.30 a.m. The inquest revealed that no parts of the body had been taken away this time.

The panic caused by the murder led to the resignation of Sir Charles Warren, the unpopular Chief of Police.

There were three other crimes that some writers on the case believe may have been committed by the Ripper. In June 1889,

> The final words of Dr Neil Cream – poisoner of four London prostitutes in 1891 – were: "I am Jack the . . ."; then the trap dropped. *Could* Cream have been Jack the Ripper? Apparently not: he was in Joliet Penitentiary, in Chicago, serving a life sentence for poisoning a patient, at the time of the murders.
>
> But a Canadian professor has noted that Joliet was a notoriously corrupt prison, where a rich prisoner could buy his freedom. And in 1897, the year before the Ripper murders, Cream's father died, and left him £5,000 . . .
>
> So it is *just* possible that Cream's last words were true after all.

parts of a female body were found in the Thames. The head was not found, but a scar on the wrists enabled the police to identify the victim as Elizabeth Jackson, a prostitute who lived in a lodging house in Turks Row, Chelsea.

On 17 July the body of Alice McKenzie, known as "Clay Pipe Alice", was found in Castle Alley, Whitechapel; her throat was cut and there were gashes across her abdomen. In his introduction to *The Trial of George Chapman*, H. L. Adam quotes the McKenzie case as one of the Ripper murders.

Finally, on 13 February 1891, the body of Frances Coles, a prostitute of about twenty-five, was found under a railway arch at Swallow Gardens in Whitechapel; her throat had been cut and there were injuries to her abdomen. She was still alive when found, but died soon afterwards.

There have been many theories about the Ripper's identity. One of the earliest was put forward in 1929 in *The Mystery of Jack the Ripper* by Leonard Matters, a Member of Parliament. He claimed that the Ripper was a certain Dr Stanley, who had confessed to the crimes on his deathbed in Buenos Aires. According to Matters, Stanley's son had contracted syphilis from Mary Kelly – the last victim – and Stanley set out to track her down. Whenever he questioned a prostitute about her, he killed her so she could not warn Mary Kelly. And eventually he found Mary, and slaughtered her with vengeful ferocity . . .

Unfortunately, Dr Stanley is not to be found in the Medical Register for 1888, and was almost certainly a figment of Matters' imagination. Moreover, if Mary Kelly had been syphilitic, it would certainly have been recorded in the post mortem report.

What *was* noted in that report is that Mary Kelly was three months pregnant. And this led an artist named William Stewart to the conclusion that Jack the Ripper was a woman – a sadistic midwife, who had gone to Miller's Court to perform an abortion. To demonstrate that a woman would be capable of sadistic violence, he cites the case of Mrs Eleanor Pearcey, who killed the wife and baby of her lover Frank Hogg in October 1890, almost decapitating Phoebe Hogg. A bloodstained axe established her guilt and she was hanged on 23 December, 1890. But Mrs Pearcey's crime was committed out of jealousy. The notion of a female Jack the Ripper, killing out of pure sadism, is psychologically unrealistic.

A writer named William Le Queux had claimed in 1923, in *Things I Know*, that the Ripper was a mad Russian called Alexander Pedachenko, sent to London by the Tsar's secret police to embarrass the British police. He explained that he had unearthed this information in a manuscript on great Russian criminals written in French by the "mad monk" Rasputin, and discovered in the cellar of his house after his assassination in 1917. But Rasputin spoke no French, and his house did not have a cellar – he lived in a flat. In 1959, a journalist named Donald McCormick revived the Pedachenko theory, with "new evidence" from a manuscript called *Chronicles of Crime* by a Dr Thomas Dutton. But although Dutton certainly existed, his manuscript has vanished. And in 1988, the year of the Ripper centenary, McCormick declined to appear on television to defend his theory, which would seem to suggest that he has abandoned it.

One of the most interesting theories was first publicized by the television interviewer Dan Farson in 1959. Farson had tracked down the manuscript notes for *Days of My Years*, the autobiography of Sir Melville Macnaghten, the CID chief who joined Scotland Yard soon after the murders. Macnaghten mentioned that there were three major suspects, against two of whom "the case was weak". The third, who had committed suicide in the Thames soon after the last murder, was almost certainly – according to Macnaghten – Jack the Ripper. Macnaghten did not mention the actual names in his book.

Macnaghtens's original notes contained the three names; the two "weak suspects" were called Ostrog and Kosminksi, while the leading suspect was one "M. J. Druitt", "a doctor who lived with his family, and who drowned himself immediately after the murder of Mary Kelly."

Farson looked into the history of Montague John Druitt, and discovered that he was a barrister who committed suicide late in 1888. His career as a barrister had been a failure; he had taught in a private school in Blackheath, but had been dismissed for unknown reasons just before his suicide.

Both Farson and a journalist named Tom Cullen wrote books naming Druitt as the Ripper. But the objections against this are overwhelming. To begin with, it is obvious that Macnaghten is writing from mere hearsay. Druitt was not a doctor, he did not live with his family (he had rooms in the Temple), he did not commit suicide immediately after the Kelly murder, but a month later. We also know that he committed suicide because his mother had become insane, and he was afraid that the same thing was happening to him.

But perhaps the strongest objection to the Druitt theory is that Druitt was a member of the upper middle class. The study of "serial murder", which has received much attention in recent years, has revealed the interesting fact that all serial killers have been working class, and often suffered traumatic poverty and abuse in childhood. So far, at any rate, there has been no middle or upper class serial killer.

That observation also seems to dispose of an interesting theory held by a doctor named Thomas E.A. Stowell, who contacted the present writer in 1960. For various reasons, Stowell was convinced that Jack the Ripper was Queen Victoria's grandson, the Duke of Clarence, (known as Eddie), who would have become king of England if he had not died in the 'flu epidemic of 1892. Stowell had unearthed information that seemed to indicate that the Queen's physician, Sir William Gull, suspected Eddie of being the Ripper. He told me that Gull's private papers – which he had seen – revealed that Eddie had not died of 'flu, but of softening of the brain due to syphilis.

Stowell swore me to silence – in case it "upset her majesty" – but in 1970, finally published his theory in a magazine called *The Criminologist*. He called his suspect "S", but dropped enough hints to make it clear that he had Eddie in mind. The tremendous public furore that resulted – the story appeared in newspapers all around the world – killed him soon after the article appeared.

Another expert on the Victorian period, Michael Harrison, studied Stowell's article and decided that Stowell had misread Sir William Gull's papers, and that "S" was not the Duke of Clarence. It was probably Gull himself who referred to the suspect as "S"; but why call Clarence "S" when his name was Eddie? Harrison concluded that "S" was, in fact, Eddie's close friend (and tutor) James Kenneth Stephen, who died insane after a blow on the head from the vane of a windmill. Harrison unearthed some fascinating information about Stephen (the cousin of novelist Virginia Woolf, who also had mental problems and committed suicide), including some oddly sadistic poetry about women. But Jim Stephen sounds nothing like the descriptions of the Ripper given by woman who saw him. And if the observation that serial killers tend to be working class is correct, then his upper class origins make him a highly unlikely candidate.

Clarence was involved in a complicated theory put forward by journalist Stephen Knight in *Jack the Ripper: The Final Solution*, in 1976. According to Knight – who based his theory on the statements of a man called Joseph "Hobo" Sickert, son of the painter Walter Sickert – Clarence had secretly married an artist's model named Annie Crook. When the Palace found out, the model was kidnapped and confined in a mental home, and Sir William Gull was entrusted with the task of murdering Mary Kelly and a number of other prostitutes who knew the secret and were trying to blackmail the Palace. He did this in association with a coachman called John Netley, killing the women in the coach, and leaving deliberate clues associated with Freemasonry.

There is, in fact, some evidence that Clarence was the father of an illegitimate child, who in turn became the mother of "Hobo" Sickert. But Sickert himself admitted that the rest of his story – about Jack the Ripper – was a hoax. This should have been clear all along from the fact that Gull suffered a stroke in the year before the murders.

In the year of the Ripper centenary, a television production company, David Wickes Productions, announced that it had gained access to "secret Ripper files" and had established his identity beyond all possible doubt; this would be revealed in a fictional "documentary" in which Michael Caine would play Inspector Abblerline, the officer in charge of the case. The production company was later forced to acknowledge that their claims were "less than truthful", and to make a shamefaced climb-down. When the "documentary" finally appeared, it proved to be a well scripted but almost totally fictional account of the murders, in which Jack the Ripper proved to be Sir William Gull, in association with John Netley. All reference to the Annie Crook theory of "Hobo" Sickert were dropped; Gull's motive was reduced to insanity. As entertainment it was excellent; as a serious study of the murders, it must be dismissed as spurious and exploitatory.

Another Ripper expert, Robin Odell, advanced the theory that the killer was a Jewish slaughterman, a *shochetz*, who used ritualistic slaughter techniques on his victims; he defended this notion in *Jack the Ripper: Summing Up and Verdict*, (1988) co-authored with myself. The problem with Odell's interesting theory is that his evidence is purely circumstantial; all Whitechapel records that might have proved the existence of his hypothetical *shochetz* have been destroyed.

In *The Crimes, Detection and Death of Jack the Ripper*, Martin Fido, has argued that "Kosminski", another of Macnaghten's three suspects, was "Jack the Ripper, on the evidence of remarks made by Sir Robert Anderson, Assistant Commissioner of Police, who is recorded as saying that Jack the Ripper was a Polish Jew. Fido tracked down information about a man named Aaron Kozminski, who was committed to an asylum in 1891, and speculated that he might have been identical with a violent madman named David Cohen and a syphilitic named Nathan Kaminsky. Once again, the problem is simply lack of any concrete evidence to connect the suspects with the murders.

In *The Ripper Legacy*, Martin Howells and Keith Skinner return to Farson's theory that Druitt was Jack the Ripper, and add the speculation that he was murdered by former Cambridge friends to prevent the scandal from becoming known. Their research is excellent, but does not overcome the objections to the Druitt theory stated above.

Equally well researched is Melvin Harris's book *Jack the Ripper: The Bloody Truth*. He takes up a theory first advanced by the "magician" Aleister Crowley, and later elaborated by Richard Whittington Egan, to the effect that the Ripper was a doctor and adventurer named Roslyn D'Onston Stevenson, who committed the murders as part of a ritual to obtain "supreme magical power". Stevenson actually existed, but is on record as believing that the Ripper was a doctor named Morgan Davies. There is no real evidence to identify D'Onston (as he preferred to call himself) as the Ripper, and if the "working class" theory is correct, then it is virtually impossible, since he was from a wealthy middle class background. The same objection applies to a theory put forward by Jean Overton Fuller to the effect that the painter Walter Sickert was himself Jack the Ripper.

Other candidates for "Ripperhood" include John Netley himself (Tim Wright), Mary Kelly's common law husband Joseph Barnett (Bruce Paley) and Oscar Wilde's artist friend Frank Miles (Thomas Toughill). In all three cases, the evidence offered is once again purely circumstantial, without the kind of concrete facts that might support it. In the opinion of the present writer, the likeliest candidate is the father of a seventy-seven year old man who wrote to Dan Farson from Melbourne, Australia, and signed himself G.W.B. The letter reads:

> "When I was a nipper about 1889 I was playing in the streets about 9 p.m. when my mother called, 'Come in Georgie or JTR will get you'. That night a man patted me on the head and said, 'Don't worry Georgie. You would be the last person JTR would touch'." (This man was apparently the writer's own father.) "I could not remember the incident but it was brought to my mind many years later. My father was a terrible drunkard and night after night he would come home and kick my mother and us kids about something cruelly. About the year 1902 I was taught boxing and after feeling proficient to hold my own I threatened my father that if he laid a hand on my mother or brothers I would thrash him. He never did after that, but we lived in the same house and never spoke to each other. Later, I emigrated to Australia. I was booked to depart with three days' notice and my mother asked me to say goodbye to my father. It was then he told me his history and why he did these terrible murders, and advised me to change my name because he would confess before he died. Once settled in Melbourne I assumed another

name. However my father died in 1912 and I was watching the papers carefully expecting a sensational announcement". But this never came; his father died without confessing.

In Melbourne, "Georgie" changed his name, but after the death of his father, changed it back again.

"Now to explain the cause of it all. He was born 1850 and married 1876 and his greatest wish was his first-born to be a girl, which came to pass. She turned out to be an imbecile. This made my father take to drink more heavily, and in the following years all boys arrived. During the confession of those awful murders, he explained he did not know what he was doing but his ambition was to get drunk and an urge to kill every prostitute that accosted him."

Georgie's father seems to have been a collector of horse manure. On one occasion, after killing a woman, he was wearing two pairs of trousers. He removed the bloodstained outer pair and buried them in the manure. Later, when he and his mate stopped at the Elephant and Castle, where they usually ate sausage and mash, his father told his mate he was not hungry, and would bury himself in the manure to keep warm. While he was hidden there he heard a policeman asking questions about Jack the Ripper, and was "scared to death".

This letter certainly sounds authentic, and it is hard to imagine why a seventy-seven-year-old man in Melbourne should take the trouble to write a long anonymous letter if it was not true – it could hardly be a craving for attention. (Presumably, in spite of the anonymity, it should not be too difficult to discover G.W.B's name by studying sailing lists of ships to Melbourne in 1902.) Assuming, then, that "Georgie" believed every word he wrote, is it not conceivable that his father invented the story about being Jack the Ripper simply to get a kind of revenge on his son after years of ignoring one another? This is obviously a possibility. Yet in all other ways, Georgie's father sounds like the kind of suspect who *could* be Jack the Ripper – a highly dominant type, a heavy drinker, a bully where his family was concerned, and capable (as Charlotte MacLeod suggested) of

holding down a job. Many serial killers and sadists have been
heavy drinkers and have committed their acts of violence when
drunk. If Georgie's father was not Jack the Ripper, then it is
at least possible to state that he was the type of person who
easily *could* have been. That is probably as far as we shall ever
be able to go in solving the problem of the identity of the most
notorious killer of all time.

> Perhaps the most sensible comment on the identity of Jack the
> Ripper was made by London policeman Donald Rumbelow, author
> of *The Complete Jack the Ripper*. He remarked that if, on the Day
> of Judgement, the Archangel Gabriel says: "Stand forth, Jack the
> Ripper, and tell us your name", everybody in the audience will
> say: "*Who?*"

# CRIMES OF PASSION

# Introduction

*C*rime *passionel* – the crime of passion. The words conjure up dark-skinned southerners like Rudolph Valentino, and sultry girls with daggers concealed in their stockings. "The passion killer is characterized by emotional immaturity and a simplistic moral outlook", said Dr Magnus Hirschfeld, an expert on sex crime. Perhaps this explains why criminologists have paid so little attention to the *crime passionel*. It seems too simple, too straightforward. A hot-tempered man strangles his flirtatious lover. What is there to exercise the ingenuity of a psychologist?

A great deal more than appears on the surface. It *is* true that southerners are more prone to commit crimes of passion than northerners. We say this is because northerners are more cerebral and calculating, while southerners are more hot-blooded and emotional. But in that case, why is the rate of sex crime higher in northern countries? A man who commits murder for the satisfaction of a momentary physical impulse cannot really be called more cerebral or calculating than a man who plans how to kill his mistress' husband.

No, the real explanation is more complicated and more interesting. To begin with, geography and climate play an important part. In northern countries, with their cold and difficult conditions, men and women have tended to develop as equals. They work hard together; and the women, muffled in their winter clothes, do not draw attention to their physical attractions. Perhaps this explains why the Eskimos, according to early travellers used to offer their wives to the guest. In warmer countries, the difference between male and female is more obvious. The sun-bronzed peasant of Italy or Spain wears his open-necked shirt; the girl wears her brightly-coloured skirt and off-the-shoulder blouse. Sexual maturity comes earlier in the warmer climate. The consequence is that southern men and women see one another as two separate races, almost separate species.

Now when this happens, their view of one another becomes strangely intermingled with illusions and idealizations. Maxim Gorky has caught this with great psychological accuracy in his story *Twenty Six Men and a Girl*. The men are baker's assistants confined all day in a damp cellar and they are all in love with a girl called Tanya who calls there every day. One day, a swaggering soldier tells them that he could seduce Tanya – and he does it. Suddenly the twenty six men hate her; they turn on her and scream insults at her. And Tanya haughtily walks off, never to return. *She* is the realist. The soldier may have treated her like a whore, but he has given her pleasure. These men treat her like an angel, and then abuse her when she fails to live up to it.

Now this tradition – of regarding woman as a romantic goddess – has its roots deep in the southern cultural tradition. The "troubadours" were poets who flourished in southern France and northern Italy as early as the eleventh century, and they invented the tradition of "courtly love". The troubadour's "lady" was his absolute ruler; at a word from her, he would ride off round the world. The stories of King Arthur and his knights of the round table were first written in French, by poets who were inspired by the troubadours and their attitude to women. Scholars believe that the whole tradition of troubadour love originated among the Arabs of north Africa.

There is another – and less pleasant – side to the romantic view of Woman. She is supposed to be quiet, obedient and infinitely yielding. The Italian poet Petrarch told a story that remained popular for centuries. A marquis who distrusts women finally marries a poor peasant girl called Griseldis. Then he proceeds to "test" her to see how obedient she is. First, he takes her children from her as soon as they are born. Then he announces that he intends to divorce in order to marry another woman. Patient Griseldis agrees to everything – even attending his wedding and praising the beauty of the bride-to-be. Finally, overcome by her gentleness and patience, the marquis admits that he has merely been testing her. He takes her back, and "they live happily ever after".

Even if it *is* only a story, it captures the medieval attitude to women in a country like Spain or Italy. To modern ears it sounds sadistic and slightly insane. Surely the marquis could tell that she was a sweet, obedient girl without subjecting her to such humiliations? But that would not have satisfied Petrarch's readers, male or female. For Griseldis was

supposed to be their idea of a perfect woman – beautiful,
obedient, long-suffering, entirely dependent upon Man, her
master.

It is because these deep-rooted attitudes still persist in the
southern temperament that southerners are prone to commit
crimes of passion. The women who swooned over Rudolph
Valentino or John Boles had no idea of what it would really
be like to be married to a Sheik. The rape in the desert might
be exciting, but the rest could be hell – as Marie Laurent
discovered when she married Prince Ali Kamel Bey Fahmy
(*see* page 83). But at least it was Prince Fahmy who ended
up with three bullets in him. In so many parallel cases it is
the woman who dies.

In 1972 Francisco Pineda, a car mechanic of Guadalahara,
Mexico, walked into the bedroom of his employer, Fernando
Ortega, a thirty-two-year-old hunchback. His employer lay
stretched on the floor in his pyjamas, dead. Francisco's pretty
stepdaughter Maria Pineda, lay dead on the bed, her skirt
around her thighs. Police discovered that both had died of
cyanide poisoning: Ortega had forced her to drink cyanide
at knife point, then drank it himself. Ortega was suffering
from tuberculosis; Maria was acting as his nurse, administering
injections. Ortega fell violently in love with her, but she was
not attracted to the hunchback. She may have thought that the
drink he forced on her contained knockout drops, and that his
intention was simply to rape her. In fact, in spite of the position
of her dress, Maria had not been sexually molested. Ortega
could have raped her before he killed himself; but that was
not what he wanted. He loved her, and wanted to join her in
death. The tragedy was stupid, pathetic – and typical of the
southern temperament. And we can clearly see the southern
attitude to women. He adored her, she was his goddess. But
she also had to pay with her life for the sin of disobedience to
the male.

To the northern, pragmatic way of thinking, there is something absurd about "crimes of passion". It always seems to the
northerner that there is a simpler way out. This explains why
the Emmett-Dunne case aroused so little interest in England
in 1954, although the newspaper-buying public had followed
the activities of Heath, Haigh and Christie with rapt attention.
Emmet-Dunne was the army sergeant who killed a fellow
sergeant with a karate chop, then hanged him to make the
death look like suicide: all this in order that he could marry
the dead man's widow. The newspapers headlined the murder

trial but the British public was apathetic – it was as if they felt that a man must be a bit weak in the head to risk his neck by committing a murder merely in order to marry a woman. Significantly, Emmet-Dunne was an Irishman – a Celt; and, racially speaking the Celts are "southerners".

# chapter one

# ELIZABETHAN & 18TH CENTURY CRIMES OF PASSION

*Four centuries ago, it was quite different. The Elizabethans had an enthusiastic – not to say morbid – interest in crimes of passion, and the Elizabethan dramatists made the most of it. From Shakespeare's* Othello *to Webster's* Duchess of Malfi, *you could almost say that the favourite Elizebethan plot was about a husband murdering his wife, or vice versa. But one of the most popular of these bloody tragedies is virtually unknown today, although some scholars believe it was written by Shakespeare; this is the anonymous* Arden of Feversham *(1592), which was based on a true case that was discussed all over England. It is described by the famous Elizabethan chronicler Raphael Holinshed, who provided Shakespeare with so many of his plots.*

## The Murder of Thomas Arden

Thomas Arden was a Kentish gentleman, the Mayor of Faversham, who married Alice North, the sister of the North who translated Plutarch. Arden was more interested in money than sex, and Holinshed suggests that he married Alice for her powerful family connections rather than because he was in love with her. Probably her dowry was generous. And having secured her, he went back to his main business of accumulating money and land – he managed to defraud a man named Greene of some abbey lands by using his influence to get a Chancery grant of them. Alice now met a tailor called Thomas Morsby (or Mosbie, as it is spelt in the play) and became his mistress; Morsby was in the service of her father, Sir Edward North. Arden was perfectly happy about handing over his marital duties to Morsby. He invited Morsby to come and live in his house, and left him there to console Alice when he had to go on business trips. He certainly knew what was going on; there was an occasion when he saw Alice with her arms around Morsby's neck, and heard them referring to him as a cuckold. What pleased him less was the discovery that the couple were thinking of murdering him; however, he didn't take this too seriously, and continued to encourage Morsby to keep up the good work. Presumably this left Morsby too tired to do the murder himself; for he approached Greene – the man who has been defrauded – and Greene, in turn, hired two assassins with the beautiful names of Black Will and Shagbag. These proved to be a pair of incompetents, and Charlie Chaplin could have made a superb comedy out of their attempts to kill Arden. Even Shakespeare – or whoever dramatized the case – has a preposterously funny scene in which the two murderers wait for Arden by a market stall, and the stall-keeper swings his shutter into place and cracks the skull of Black Will.

Morsby tried various sophisticated and over-subtle methods of killing Arden – a poisoned crucifix, poisoned pictures, etc – but finally, they were forced to summon Black Will and Shagbag to the house to kill Arden as he sat at table. Morsby finished him

The murder of Thomas Arden in 1550.

off with a blow on the head from a flat iron, after he had been stabbed and throttled. They then dragged the body to a nearby field. It was snowing, so the footprints were obvious, and one of the accomplices forgot to throw the bloodstained knife and towel into the well. The law took violent retribution. Murder of a husband by his wife was regarded as a form of treason, and the penalty was to be burned alive. The servants who had helped in disposing of the body were also tried. Shagbag, Greene and the painter who had supplied poisons managed to escape; the last lines of the play mention that Shagbag was murdered in Southwark. The law was so anxious to make an example of everyone concerned in the murder that an innocent servant named Bradshaw was tried with the others, and sentenced to death, although the rest of the conspirators all asserted that he was not concerned. "These condemned persons were diversely executed in sundry places," says Holinshed; the servant Michael hung in chains at Faversham; a maid servant who had been an accessory was burnt alive, "crying out on hir mistresse that had brought hir to this ende". Morsby and his sister were hanged at Smithfield in London; Alice Arden was burnt at Canterbury on 14 March, and Black Will was also burnt on a scaffold at "Flishing in Zeland". Greene – the man who had procured the murderers – returned some years later, and was promptly executed and hung in chains. Even a man named Adam Foule, who had merely acted as Alice's messenger to Morsby, was sent to London with his legs tied under the horse's belly and imprisoned in the Marshalsea. Holinshed adds the legend that the imprint of Arden's body could be seen in the grass for many years afterwards; he also notes that Arden had stolen the field in which his corpse was found from a poor widow. The archives of Canterbury contain the entry: "For the charges of brenning Mistress Arden and execution of George Bradshaw [the innocent servant], 43 shillings."

The play itself is remarkably successful as drama; but it can hardly be called a realistic presentation of the case. Arden – who was obviously a vicious miser – is portrayed as a doting husband who loves his wife so much that he closes his eyes to her infidelities. Alice is made to repent fulsomely when she sees her husband's body; in fact, it was Alice who accused the innocent Bradshaw – hardly the act of a repentant woman.

In short, it is necessary to read between the lines to get the facts of the case. Arden married Alice for money, and then deliberately found her a lover. Alice was almost certainly a nymphomaniac. Why did she accuse Bradshaw, whom the others declared to be innocent? Was it because she had made advances to him and had been rejected? Why was Adam Foule imprisoned, although he had been only a messenger? Was it because the judges suspected that any male connected with Alice might have been her lover?

We also learn something of the Elizabethans from the fate of the maid, who had been merely an accessory after the fact. She was burned alive, while Morsby, the instigator, was only hanged. Why such severity over the murder of a highly unpleasant miser? It is surely a reasonable inference that it was the sexual aspect of the case that aroused this universal morbid interest. The Elizabethan public was very like the public of today, except that it was far less sophisticated, since there were no sensational newspapers to spread the details of every divorce case. There is an immense reservoir of sexual frustration under the surface of working class life, and this case offered it an outlet. Alice Arden was one of these upper class women who spend their days in the arms of lovers; probably every woman in the case was somebody or other's mistress . . . They all deserved burning. So when the story was made into a play, Arden had to be whitewashed – otherwise the sexual motive was made less important, and nobody wanted that . . .

# The Mystery of Amy Robsart

Queen Elizabeth I herself may have been party to a murder. Her lover, Sir Robert Dudley, (later the Earl of Leicester), was an extremely handsome but thoroughly spoilt and undisciplined character. When he was only seventeen, he had married Amy Robsart, the daughter of Sir John Robsart, a Norfolk squire – apparently they married for love, and remained in love for some years. But Dudley became involved in the conspiracy to make Lady Jane Grey queen of England. It failed, and Dudley's father, the Earl of Warwick, was executed for his part in it. Dudley was also sentenced to death, and his wife had to visit him in the Tower of London. However, he was pardoned, and redeemed himself by fighting against the French at the Battle of St Quentin (1557). When Elizabeth came to the throne in the following year, Dudley lost no time in hurrying to court, where the twenty-five-year-old queen became violently infatuated with him. Soon he had been appointed Master of the Queen's Horse and made a Knight of the Garter. The Spanish Ambassador wrote to Philip of Spain to tell him that Robert Dudley would probably be king in the near future.

Two years later, in 1560, the Dudleys moved to Cumnor Place, near Abingdon, Oxfordshire. On 4 September of that year, Queen Elizabeth told a foreign envoy that Amy Robsart was dying – an odd statement in view of the fact that she seems to have been in normal health, and apparently on excellent terms with her husband.

---

The great Elizabethan scandal was the murder in the Tower of London of Sir Thomas Overbury – a murder that involved adultery, poison and homosexuality.

King James the First, who succeeded Queen Elizabeth in 1603, was a homosexual. In 1606, while the king was watching a tournament, a page named Robert Carr broke his leg. A tall, good-looking young man, he was soon enjoying the king's favour.

Carr was already involved with another homosexual, Thomas Overbury, eleven years his senior. Overbury now became Carr's secretary, reading the king's mail and secret dispatches.

In 1610, the beautiful fifteen-year-old Frances Howard, daughter of the Earl of Suffolk, came to court. She was already the wife of the teenage Earl of Essex – an arranged marriage which had not yet been consummated. It was Carr who consummated it. When the husband returned from France and took her to the country, she refused to grant him his marital rights. Eventually, the Archbishop of Canterbury was persuaded to grant a divorce.

Overbury became frantic at the thought of Carr marrying Frances Howard; he made so much fuss that the king had him thrown in the Tower.

There Frances arranged to have him poisoned, with the connivance of the Governor of the Tower, Sir Gervase Elwes. On 15 September, 1613, Overbury died after five months of agony.

Eighteen months after Carr married Frances, the chemist's assistant who had administered the final dose of mercuric sublimate made a deathbed confession. Elwes and three accomplices were put on trial and executed in the autumn of 1615. Carr and his wife were tried in the following year and both sentenced to death. Confined in the Tower for six years, they were then allowed to return to their country home. But love had turned to hatred; they never spoke to one another. Frances died of a disease of the womb at the age of thirty-nine; Carr lived on gloomily for many years more; when he went to see the king, James broke down and cried on his shoulder.

Four days later, on 8 September, 1560, Amy is said to have sent all the servants to Abingdon Fair – her husband was at court. When they returned, they found her body at the foot of the stairs with a fractured skull. Apparently she had slipped on the stairs. The coroner's jury found her death to be accidental. And as the relations between Robert Dudley and the Queen became closer, rumours abounded that Dudley had had his wife murdered, with the Queen's connivance. The actual killer was rumoured to be Sir Anthony Forster, Dudley's Comptroller of the Household at Cumnor, in association with his mistress, Mrs Oddingsells.

For whatever reason, the Queen decided not to marry Dudley. He was probably her lover anyway (although historians deny this), and she had no desire to share power with a husband. She even tried to marry Dudley off to Mary Queen of Scots, but he declined. In 1564, Dudley was created Earl of Leicester.

In 1575, Dudley laid on the famous entertainment for the Queen at Kenilworth Castle, an entertainment described at length by Sir Walter Scott in his novel of that name. The eleven-year-old Shakespeare is said to have witnessed it. But Scott goes on to take some major liberties with English history. He makes Dudley marry Amy secretly, and a villain called Varney later arranges her murder by means of a booby trap outside her bedroom door.

Was Amy murdered? The historian Ian Aird argues that her death was an accident, due to the cancer of the breast from which she is known to have been suffering. But the Simancas Archives indicate that there was a plot to poison Amy, and this may be what the Queen had in mind when she said that Amy was dying. On the other hand, she may merely have known about the cancer of the breast.

Dudley's future career was not particularly glorious, but at least he escaped execution – the fate of Elizabeth's other favourite, the Earl of Essex. When the English went to help the Dutch against the Spanish in 1586, Dudley proved arrogant and incompetent as their commander, and returned home in virtual disgrace. But he had one more triumph – he stage-managed the Queen's famous visit to her troops at Tilbury – when the Spanish Armada was on its way – when she made her famous speech describing herself as "a weak and feeble woman", but with "the heart and stomach of a king". A few months later, in August 1588, Dudley was dead, at the age of fifty-five, of a "burning fever".

Whether or not Dudley planned the murder of his wife, there

seems no doubt that he was one of the most unpleasant and **135**
treacherous characters in English history. When Mary Queen of
Scots was in prison in 1587, Dudley tried to persuade the Queen
to have her quietly poisoned. And with the evidence of a poison
plot against Amy in the Simanca Archive, it seems more than
likely that her death was no accident.

# Catherine Hayes

In 1725, another case of husband-murder created the same
kind of nationwide sensation as the Arden of Faversham case.
The sheer gruesomeness of the murder, and the fact that the
murderess had had several lovers, again titillated the morbid
sexuality of the British public, and contributed to making the
loose-living lady an almost legendary villainess.

Catherine Hayes was born Catherine Hall, in Birmingham,
the daughter of poor parents. In 1705, when she was fifteen,
she was noticed by some army officers, who persuaded her
to return to their quarters; there she became their collective
mistress for a while, until they moved on. She then found a job
as a servant with a Warwickshire farmer named Hayes. The son
of the house, a carpenter, fell in love with her; one morning, they
went secretly into Worcester, and were married. John Hayes was
then twenty-one. After six years in the country, his young bride
began to dream of London, and persuaded her husband to move
there. She was so excitable and quarrelsome that her in-laws
raised no objection. In London, John Hayes became a successful
coal merchant, pawnbroker and moneylender. His success in
this latter occupation lends colour to his wife's assertion that
he was unbearably mean. At all events, Hayes was successful
in business, and in a little over ten years, made enough money
to sell his shop in the Tyburn Road and take lodgings nearby.
His relations with his wife had deteriorated badly. This may
have been due to his meanness and her desire for luxury, or
there may have been deeper causes. She later told one of her
accomplices in the murder that Hayes had murdered two of his
children in the country – presumably when they were newborn.
*If* Hayes was pathologically mean, there might just possibly be
some truth in this story.

Early in 1725, a young man named Thomas Billings, a tailor,

came to their house, and Catherine Hayes declared him to be an old friend, or relative. He stayed with them, and when Hayes went to the country on business, Billings took his place in Catherine's bed. The two lovers made the most of their freedom, throwing parties and spending a great deal of the money that Hayes had taken so long to accumulate. When Hayes returned, he was furious, and gave his wife a beating. But for some reason, he did not turn Billings out of the house.

Another friend from Warwickshire now arrived, a Thomas Wood. It was to him that she told the story of her husband killing her two children, and she mentioned that Hayes had also killed a man. Wood also became her lover, and her promise that her husband's estate – some fifteen hundred pounds, a fortune for those days – would be put at his disposal when she became a widow finally made him agree to help her kill her husband.

On 1 March 1725, Wood came back from a visit to the country, and found Billings, Catherine and John Hayes in the midst of a drinking session. Wood, who was young and boastful, declared that he had just drunk a guinea's worth of wine and was still sober, and Billings challenged Hayes to drink the same amount – six bottles. If Hayes could do it without getting drunk, Billings would buy the wine; if not, Hayes should pay for it. Hayes accepted the offer; perhaps the prospect of six bottles of free wine was too much for his miserly soul. Billings, Wood and Catherine Hayes set off for a tavern in New Bond Street, and on the way, she pointed out that this would be a good opportunity to kill her husband.

In the Brawn's Head the three of them drank a pint of "best mountain wine", and asked for six pints to be sent up to their lodgings. Catherine Hayes paid 10s 6d for it – perhaps its quality was only half as good as the stuff Wood claimed he had been drinking.

Hayes downed the six pints of wine without much trouble, while the other three drank beer; his wife quietly sent out for another pint which Hayes, now too fuddled to count the bottles, also drank. He then fell down on the floor, woke up after a few minutes, and staggered off to bed in the next room. The bed was probably the kind that Hogarth portrayed, with its lower end actually on the floor. Hayes fell asleep on his face. Billings came in with a coal hatchet, and hit him on the back of the head with it. The blow fractured his skull, and Hayes began to kick his feet in agony, making such a noise that the woman in the room overhead came down to investigate. By this time, Wood had seized the hatchet and given Hayes two more

Etched by J Chapman.

Catherine Hayes.

blows, which completed the work of killing him. When Mrs Springate complained that the thudding noise had awakened them, Catherine Hayes explained that her husband had some noisy guests, but that they were about to leave. It must have been a tense moment, and both Wood and Billings were badly unnerved.

The next problem was what to do with the body. They had to get it down two flights of stairs to the street. Then suppose they bumped into a member of the watch? As soon as Hayes was recognized, they were done for. But Catherine Hayes refused to be panicked. She pointed out that if they cut off her husband's head, and disposed of that first, the body would not be identifiable, even if they had to flee from the watch and leave it in the street.

The two men were already nauseated. The bed was drenched with blood; blood had even shot up to the ceiling with the hatchet blows. Catherine Hayes suggested that they decapitate her husband with his neck over a bucket to catch the blood. The two men must have been wishing that this business had never started; but there was obviously no way out except to dispose of the body. So they placed the body on the bed so the head hung over. Catherine Hayes held the bucket underneath the neck, Billings twisted his fingers in the blood-soaked hair, and Woods sawed away at the neck with a carving knife – hatchet blows would have brought Mrs Springate down again. When the head was off, they dropped it in the pail, and left the headless body to bleed into it.

Catherine Hayes recognized that there was still danger. If the head was identified, it would be traced back to her. She proposed boiling it in a pot until the flesh came away – a revolting but sensible idea – but the others were too nervous. They became even more nervous when Mrs Springate shouted down irritably to know what was going on. Here Catherine Hayes showed a presence of mind that entitles her to be ranked with Alice Arden and Lady Macbeth; she called back that her husband had been suddenly called away on a journey, and was getting ready to go. Now the two Thomases could hardly wait to get out of the house. They poured the blood from the bucket down the sink, then had to tiptoe up and down the stairs half a dozen times to get water from the well to wash it down. When that was done, the men crept downstairs, one of them holding the bucket under his coat, while Catherine Hayes walked down behind them, talking in her normal voice, saying goodbye to her husband, in case any of the neighbours was listening. According to the sharp-eared Mrs

Springate, she put up an excellent and convincing performance.
Then the two men made off as fast as they could, and Catherine
Hayes hurried upstairs to clean up the blood before it clotted. It
was a long task, because the unpolished floorboards had soaked
up the blood like a sponge; even when she had washed it and
scraped it with a knife, the marks were still visible.

Meanwhile, Billings and Wood hastened towards the river
– a long walk, from the present day Oxford Street down to
Whitehall. It was nearly midnight. People of that time tended
to go to bed early, and the watch were likely to challenge people
who were out after midnight. Billings must have looked as if he
was pregnant, with the pail under his greatcoat. They reached
Whitehall, but the dock gates had already been closed. The tide
was out, and the foreshore of the river was mostly mud; wading
across that would attract attention. They walked on along the
river, past Westminster, to the Horseferry wharf – at the end of
the present Horseferry Road, under Lambeth Bridge. They went
to the end of the dock, and threw the head over. Instead of a
splash, there was a thud as it landed on mud. But they were too
frightened to worry. They threw the bucket after it, and hurried
away. The nightwatchman on the wharf heard the thud, and a
man on board a boat saw them throw the bucket; but it was a
dark night, and no one was very curious. Billings and Wood
hastened back home, now feeling slightly better. They found
Catherine Hayes still scraping at the floorboards, trying not to
make too much noise. The headless body still lay across the
bed. The two men made up a makeshift bed in the other room,
and tried to sleep. Catherine Hayes sat by them, brooding. She
must have been wishing that they had disfigured the face with a
knife to prevent recognition. But with luck, the head was already
on its way out to sea . . . She was still sitting there when the two
men woke up at dawn.

And also at dawn, the nightwatchman, a Mr Robinson, walked
to the edge of the dock to stretch his legs, and saw the bucket and
the head lying in the mud. A small crowd soon gathered, and the
lighterman from the boat mentioned seeing a man throwing the
bucket into the river.

Back in the lodgings, the murderers were discussing what to
do with the body. The first and most obvious thing was to
conceal it in case someone came into the room. Mrs Hayes went
out and got a large box; but it was not big enough. They cut off
the arms, and the legs at the knees; but the body was still too
long. They hacked off the thighs, and finally managed to pack
most of the pieces into the box, leaving some of the smaller items

in an old blanket. That evening, at 9 o'clock, Wood and Billings crept downstairs with the trunk in a blanket. It was early and there were too many people about; but they were not going to risk being stopped by the watch. This time they went north – fortunately there was not far to go before they were in the fields of Marylebone. They tossed the trunk into a pond that Wood had located during the day, then went back and collected the rest of the body. It was Mrs Springate who let them in at midnight; fortunately, she had no reason to be suspicious, even though her husband had found clots of blood in the drain that morning. Blood was common enough.

The next day, Wood made off to the country to soothe his shattered nerves. Billings resumed his place in his mistress's bed.

The parish officers of Westminster had not been idle. They ordered the blood and dirt to be washed from the head and – a macabre touch – the hair to be combed. Then the head was set on a stake at St Margaret's churchyard in Westminster. It drew a fascinated crowd, but no one recognized it. But the next day, a young apprentice named Bennett saw it, and flew to tell Catherine Hayes that he thought it looked like her husband. She told him angrily that he could get himself into serious trouble if he spread such reports – her husband was alive and well. Bennett apologized and promised to say nothing about it. And a Mr Patrick also thought he recognized the head, and went along to a pub called the Dog and Dial in Monmouth Street – at which Hayes and his wife used to drink – to mention his suspicion. Billings happened to be working there at the time, and someone replied that the head couldn't belong to John Hayes, because Billings was his lodger, and he would know if anything had happened to Hayes. Billings immediately confirmed this, saying that he had left Hayes in bed that morning.

Mrs Hayes must have been feeling nervous; but she recognized that flight would be a mistake. When a neighbour asked after her husband, she said he was out taking a walk; the visitor mentioned the head in the churchyard, and Mrs Hayes expressed horror at the wickedness of the age. "Why, they even say they've found bits of a woman's body in a pond at Marylebone," she declared, and the neighbour said she hadn't heard about that.

Wood came back to town on the 5th – two days after he had fled. Catherine Hayes gave him some of her husband's clothes, and five shillings. She told him that the head had been found, but that no one had yet identified it.

The head was beginning to stink; worse still, the features were

The head of John Hayes, murdered by his wife, was mounted on a pole in Westminster for the purpose of identification.

already beginning to turn black. The parish officers had it placed in a large jar full of spirit – perhaps gin – and continued to exhibit it to anyone who was interested. For a short period it looked as if the mystery was solved when a woman said she thought it was her husband; but after a long look at it, she said she couldn't swear to it.

Catherine Hayes remained remarkably cool. Less than a week after the murder, she left her lodgings and moved to another in the neighbourhood, taking Billings, Wood, and Mrs Springate. No doubt she was afraid that the latter might gossip; she even paid a quarter's rent for the lady. She then proceeded to collect as many of her husband's debts as possible, even threatening to sue her husband's brother-in-law for money he owed. She wrote various letters in her husband's name to other debtors.

Inevitably, Hayes' friends began to wonder what had become of him. A man called Ashby called on her to enquire. She then told him, in strict confidence, that her husband had killed a man in a quarrel, and had fled to Portugal. Mr Ashby asked if the head found in the river belonged to the murdered man, but Mrs Hayes said no, they had buried the body entire.

All this was bound to arouse suspicion. Ashby communicated with the neighbour who had already enquired; they talked with another neighbour. And finally, a Justice of the Peace was informed. They hurried to Catherine Hayes' lodgings and knocked on the door. She was in bed with Billings; she dressed and went to the door. Billings was sitting on the edge of the bed without shoes or stockings when the officers came in. When asked if he had been sleeping with her, she said no, he was mending his stockings. The Justice remarked that he must have been doing it in the dark, since there was no candle or fire.

Wood was not present, but they arrested Catherine Hayes, Billings and Mrs Springate, and took them off to different prisons, to prevent them concocting a story. Catherine Hayes continued to assert her innocence, and asked if she might see the head from the churchyard. The Justice agreed, and they took her to the barber-surgeon – a Mr Westbrook – who was keeping the head. Here, Catherine Hayes called upon all her histrionic powers, and shouted: "Oh, it is my dear husband's head!" and proceeded to kiss the jar. Mr Westbrook came in and said he would take the head out of the jar – it was generally believed in those days that murderers would reveal their guilt if forced to touch the corpse. But Catherine Hayes was equal to anything; she seized the head and kissed it, then asked if she could have a lock of its hair. Her performance must have been a little too dramatic; the barber-surgeon replied sardonically that she had already had too much of his blood; at which Catherine Hayes fainted, or pretended to. She had already run through the emotional spectrum; it was the only thing left for her to do.

While all this was taking place, someone saw the blanket floating in the Marylebone pond, and pulled it out. The rest of the body was soon recovered. But Catherine Hayes and Thomas Billings continued to assert their total innocence.

Wood was the weak link in the chain. On the following Sunday, he came back to London from Harrow, and went along to Catherine Hayes' old lodgings. They told him she had moved to a house nearby, and someone offered to show him. His informant took him to the wrong place – to the house of Mr Longmore, one of the neighbours who had caused the arrest. There the terrified Wood was dragged off his horse, and taken to the Justice who had been questioning the others. At first, Wood declared himself innocent; but in Newgate, his nerve broke, and he made a full confession. He explained that Mrs Hayes had told him that her husband was an atheist and freethinker, and that "it would be no more sin to kill him than to kill a dog". When the other two were told of the confession, they decided that there was no further point in keeping silent – especially as it might lead to torture – and also confessed. Mrs Springate was released.

It was after this that Catherine Hayes suddenly realized that the charge against her was not of murder, but petty treason – the killing of her lord and master; and that the penalty for this was to be burned alive. But she still hoped that her crime might be regarded simply as murder, since she had not struck any of the blows that killed her husband. At her trial, with the fear of a painful death hanging over her, she denied that she had any hand in the actual killing of her husband, and said that she had kept silent only because she was afraid that Wood and Billings would kill her too. When it was clear that all three would be sentenced to death, Wood and Billings begged that they might not be hanged in chains, and she again repeated her plea to be hanged rather than burned. But the judge sentenced her to be burned, and she screamed all the way back to Newgate.

She revealed a better side to her nature before her execution; she sent messages to her two ex-lovers, regretting that she had involved them in all this. When she saw Billings in chapel, she sat holding his hand and leaned her head on his shoulder. She was obviously in love with Billings.

A few days before her execution, she somehow managed to

Catherine Hayes burned at the stake for murder.

get a bottle of acid into her cell. Unfortunately, a fellow prisoner
saw it and tasted it. A little spilt on a handkerchief burnt it. So
the prisoner smashed the bottle on the floor.

Wood caught a fever in prison, and died before he could
be executed. He is the only person in the case who seems to
deserve much sympathy. His age is not recorded, but it seems
fairly certain that he was still in his teens. He seems to have
been a good-natured, easy-going young man who was too easily
influenced.

Billings was also young. Osborn records that when he first
came to stay at the Hayes' lodgings, there was a rumour that he
was Catherine Hayes' son by a previous "connection". He was
executed before Catherine Hayes, and when the executioner –
Richard Arnet, Laughing Jack's predecessor – came to fetch her,
she asked him if he had killed her "dear child" yet.

Her last moments give the case a final touch of horror. It was
customary to strangle a woman condemned for petty treason
before burning her. Arnet lit the brushwood around her, then
started to pull the strangling rope from behind; but the fire
reached his hands too quickly, and he had to let go. The
spectators watched her trying to push the burning faggots
away while she screamed. More faggots were thrown on, to
try to put her out of her misery soon, "but", says Wilkinson,
"she survived amidst the flames for a considerable time, and
her body was not perfectly reduced to ashes in less than three
hours".

# chapter two

# THE USE OF POISONS

*The violent method chosen by Catherine Hayes to despatch her husband has few parallels among crimes of passion. Most women who wished to get rid of an unwanted spouse chose poison. Not only was it likely to attract less attention; it had the enormous additional advantage of being practically undetectable. Science had not yet invented a sure method of identifying poisons once they were in the human system. And even before they entered the human system, the usual method of testing them was to try them on a dog or cat, and see if the animal went into convulsions.*

## The Affair of the Poisons

While the English remained rigidly puritanical in the matter of extramarital love affairs, the attitude of the French was altogether more lax. This was never more true than at the court of the Sun King, Louis the Fourteenth, where a wife without a lover was even rarer than a husband without a mistress. In most cases, both spouses accepted the situation with good humoured tolerance. But there were inevitably a few cases where the husband or wife decided that a permanent change of partner would be desirable, and that murder would solve the problem more conveniently than divorce. In 1673, the thirtieth year of Louis's reign, such deaths reached epidemic proportions.

It was in that year that Nicholas de la Reynie, Louis's Chief of Police, was informed by two priests that many penitents were asking absolution for poisoning their spouses. A young lawyer who was having dinner with a fortune-teller known as La Vigoreux, wife of a tailor, was startled to hear another fortune-teller, Marie Bosse, declare: "What a marvellous trade! Duchesses, marquises, princes! Three more poisonings and I'll be able to retire." The lawyer passed on this information to Desgrais, who sent the wife of one of his officers along to ask Marie Bosse's advice about her husband's cruelty. On the second visit, Mme Bosse handed over a phial of a colourless poison, together with precise instructions for using it. And finally, on 4 January 1669, the police descended on Marie Bosse in the early hours of the morning and placed her under arrest. La Reynie was shocked to be told that Marie had been found sharing a huge bed with her two sons and her daughters, for it was believed that magical powers could be passed from one member of a family to another by incest. La Vigoreux was also arrested, and she and Bosse proved more than willing to talk. At first, La Reynie thought he was dealing with a harmless matter of witchcraft – love potions and magic spells – for although belief in magic was still common among the uneducated class, the aristocracy of the Age of Reason was already inclined to dismiss it as pure imagination. But as La Reynie listened to the confessions, he realized with alarm that Marie Bosse had not been exaggerating when she talked about her clients: this affair involved the "highest in the land". Moreover, Bosse and La Vigoreux were associated with an eminent fortune-teller called Catherine Deshayes, known as La Voisin, whose wealthy and aristocratic clients included members of the court. One client, Mme de Poulaillon, was the wife of the Master of Forests and Waterways in Champagne, while another two, Mme Leféron and Mme Dreux, were the wives of Paris magistrates who would probably be called to try these "witches". Finally, with astonishment, La Reynie heard the names of two of the king's mistresses, Louise de la Vallière and Mme de Montespan, and at that point he knew that the king himself must be informed. And when the king heard the details, he decided immediately that this could not be tried in open court; all this talk of poisons and love potions could only bring the monarchy into discredit. La Vigoreux was tortured – she died under torture – and so were Marie Bosse and La Voisin. They told amazing stories of poison and magic spells. The pretty Mme Poulaillon, burdened with an ageing husband and a demanding lover, had been given shirts treated with arsenic, which would cause her husband to scratch himself, and a "healing ointment" that would kill him in ten weeks. But her husband had come to suspect her designs, and had her confined in a convent. And Mme de Montespan, for ten years the king's favourite mistress, had called on the sorceresses whenever the king's affections had seemed to be diminishing, and had been supplied with love potions and aphrodisiacs, including Spanish fly, mashed blister beetles, cocks' combs and cocks' testicles. And there was worse to come. Montespan had raised the question of whether the queen and Louise de la Vallière might be killed by witchcraft. This was beyond the powers of the fortune-tellers; they sent her instead to the "high priest of devil worship", an evil old man called Abbé Guibourg. The essence of the black masses performed by Guibourg was the sacrifice of a newborn baby. Mme de Montespan was made to lie naked on a bed, her feet dangling on the floor, with the sacred chalice on her groin. La Voisin brought in a baby, and Guibourg slit its throat over the chalice, into which he drained its blood, reciting the names of Mme de Montespan and the king. The child's entrails were removed, and its body burned in a furnace; the entrails were used for distilling a magic potion – which included the Host used in the black mass – and this was given to Mme de Montespan to administer to the king.

La Voisin's daughter, who described all this, also told how a lady of the court named Mme des Oeillets had come for a magic potion, accompanied by a man; Guibourg had explained that he would need to mix the sexual discharges of both into the potion. But since Mme des Oeillets was menstruating, he accepted instead some of her menstrual blood, which he mixed with the sperm which the man had produced by masturbating into the chalice.

The king was horrified. If this became known, he would be the laughing stock of Europe. He therefore gave orders that the case should be tried in private. The trial began in April 1679, and dragged on until July 1683; 104 defendants appeared before a selected panel of twelve judges in a chamber of the old Paris Arsenal; since this was lit by candles and torches it became known as the Chambre Ardente (lighted chamber). Many other priests were found to be involved, and the king was shocked to discover the astonishing extent of black magic in France. Thirty-six death sentences were handed out, and four life sentences to the galleys; another thirty-four prisoners were sentenced to banishment or heavy fines. No word of the proceedings leaked outside the walls of the "Poison Chamber", but the long and grim series of executions left the public in

of Mme de Montespan was never mentioned; she had been
replaced by a new favourite, Mme de Maintenon – who had
been her protégé – and retired to a convent. In 1709, the king
ordered that all papers relating to the case should be destroyed;
but by some error, the minute-book of the clerk of the court was
overlooked; it was finally published in the second half of the
nineteenth century, revealing for the first time one of the most
incredible stories of murder and black magic in the recorded
annals of crime.

# Mary Blandy

The first poisoning case in which medical evidence played the
decisive role was the trial, in 1751, of Mary Blandy, charged
with poisoning her father with arsenic. In 1746, at the age
of twenty-six, Mary was still unmarried, although she was an
heiress to a fortune of £10,000; her father, a prosperous lawyer
of Henley-on-Thames, took exception to most of the young men
who showed signs of interest in his plain but good-natured
daughter. But in that year, Mary made the acquaintance of
a Scottish captain, the Honourable William Henry Cranstoun,
who immediately began to pay her attentions. Cranstoun had
many disadvantages; he was small, pock-marked, cross-eyed,
and already married; none of this prevented him from deciding
to win Mary's hand. The first step was to rid himself of his
wife, who was being supported by her relatives in Scotland.
He wrote to her explaining that his chances of advancement in
the army were poor while he was married, and begging her to
write him a letter stating that she had merely been his mistress.
She was finally persuaded to do this, whereupon Cranstoun
circulated copies to his and her relatives, and instituted divorce
proceedings. His wife opposed it and proved that their marriage
was legal. And Mr Blandy, who had been prepared to accept
Cranstoun as a son-in-law – after all, he was the brother of
a Scottish peer – indignantly reproached the ugly little Scot
and indicated that the engagement was at an end. Cranstoun
nevertheless continued to call, and he and Mary continued to
regard themselves as secretly engaged, although she declined
his suggestion that they should run away and marry. Mrs Blandy

became the captain's ardent ally after he had given her £40 to pay a debt she had contracted on a visit to London. Soon after this visit, in September 1749, Mrs Blandy became suddenly ill and died, begging her husband to allow Mary to marry Cranstoun. When Cranstoun wrote to Mary, telling her that he was besieged by the bailiffs, and needed his £40, she borrowed the money and sent it to him.

From this point on, we must accept either the version of those who believe Mary guilty, or those who are convinced she was an innocent dupe. Cranstoun explained to her that he knew a fortune-teller called Mrs Morgan, whose magic potions could be relied upon to make her father change his mind. And on a visit to the Blandy household in 1750, Cranstoun apparently demonstrated the efficacy of a magic powder by slipping some of it into the old gentleman's tea. He had been in the worst of tempers at breakfast, yet overflowing with benevolence at dinner. Mary allowed herself to be persuaded to continue the doses. And in April 1751, Cranstoun sent Mary some "Scotch pebbles" – a fashionable ornament at the time – together with a white powder for cleaning them. Mary began to administer the powder to her father in small doses. And the fact that Francis Blandy began to suffer acute stomach pains must have made her aware that the potion was less harmless than her lover claimed. And when the servant, Susan Gunnel, tasted some of the gruel that Mr Blandy was about to eat, she also became ill. After that, Susan poured out the gruel from the pan and noticed a gritty white powder in the bottom; she took this to a neighbour, who sent it to an apothecary. But since no reliable chemical test was known for arsenic, no immediate analysis was attempted. Nevertheless, Susan went to Mr Blandy and warned him that she thought he was being poisoned by his own daughter. And when Blandy asked Mary if she had put anything into his tea, she became pale, and hurried from the room.

Incredibly, Mr Blandy took no steps to prevent Mary from meddling with his food. And when he was shown a letter Mary had written to Cranstoun, begging him to take care of what he wrote, he only smiled and said: "Poor lovesick girl! What a woman will do for the man she loves." Then he continue to sink. And when Mary, now in a panic, threw some letters and powder into the kitchen fire, the cook rescued the powder as soon as she left the room. Mr Blandy asked to see Mary, who fell on her knees and begged him not to curse her; he told her that he blessed her, and hoped God would forgive her. Two days later, he died.

That same afternoon, Mary begged the footman to accompany her to France, and offered him £500, which he refused. The following morning, she ran out of the house and tried to escape, but was soon surrounded by an angry crowd. Her lover was more successful; when he heard news of her arrest, he fled to France.

When Mary was tried, on 3 March 1752, the main witnesses against her were four doctors. They agreed that the condition of Mr Blandy's inner organs suggested arsenic poisoning, and that the white powder they had analysed was arsenic. But the only test they had been able to apply involved touching a red-hot iron to the powder, and sniffing the vapour, which they declared to be that of arsenic. In later years such evidence would have been unhesitatingly rejected. On the other hand, servants were able to state, in considerable detail, when and how Mary had administered poison to her father – to such an extent that it now seems astonishing that Mr Blandy was not warned in time. Mary made a passionate speech in which she flatly denied administering poison although she admitted that she *had* put a powder into her father's food "which had been given me with another intent". She gave her father the powder, she said, to make him fond of Cranstoun. The prosecution rejected this with contempt, pointing out that she had attempted to destroy the powder as soon as she knew she was suspected. And after thirteen hours, the jury took only five minutes to find Mary guilty.

Six weeks later, her hands bound with black ribbon, she mounted the gallows outside Newgate, insisting to the end that she had no intention of killing her father. Her last words were to ask the hangman not to hang her too high "for the sake of decency". Cranstoun survived her by only six months, dying "in considerable agony" at Furnes, in Flanders, in his fortieth year.

Where Cranstoun was concerned, it was the old gentleman who had the last laugh. While Mary was awaiting her trial she was told that her father's estate amounted to less than £4,000. The fortune of £10,000 – which had attracted Cranstoun – had either never existed, or been long spent. This was almost certainly the reason that Frances Blandy had set his face against so many aspiring suitors – because he was unable to provide the promised dowry. The irony of the situation must have come home to him on his deathbed; he had wronged his daughter by witholding the truth, and now she had poisoned him to obtain a non-existent fortune. This would seem to explain why he asked

Mary Blandy, hanged for murder in 1752.

the weeping girl: "How canst thou think I could curse thee?";
after all, he had only himself to blame.

It was not until the end of the eighteenth century that poison ceased to be the favourite weapon of the domestic murderer. This was because a number of scientists – notably Karl Scheele, Samuel Hahnemann and Johann Metzger – had devised methods of testing for the most popular of all poisons, arsenic. In 1809, a German poisoner named Anna Zwanziger was trapped when one of her victims was exhumed and found to be full of arsenic. Anna had been killing off the wives and fiancées of her male employers in the hope of supplanting them; she was executed by the sword in 1811.

# The Praslin Case

Other scientific developments were also helping to bring killers to justice. In 1847, it was the remarkable new invention called the microscope that provided the solution of the most sensational *crime passionel* of the decade.

Charles-Louis Theobald, the Duc de Choiseul-Praslin, married his wife Fanny – a daughter of one of Napoleon's generals – in 1824, when she was sixteen and he nineteen. She was a woman of fiery temperament, with lesbian inclinations, and by the time she was thirty-four, and had borne nine children, she was corpulent and wrinkled. The duke, an introverted, withdrawn man, found her dominant ways intolerable, and ceased to frequent her bed. Yet there can be no doubt that the duchess continued to love her husband. Matters became increasingly strained when an attractive girl named Henriette Deluzy was engaged as the children's governess, and it soon became clear that the duke was strongly attracted to her. Whether she became his mistress is not known, but it seems certain that the duchess thought the worst. She told her husband to dismiss the girl; he replied that if Henriette left, he would go too. The duchess wrote him a number of pathetic letters, which make it clear that this was not the first time the duke had shown interest in other women, and that in spite of this, she still loved him.

Finally, the duchess got her way; Henriette Deluzy was dismissed – without even a reference. The duke continued to call on her, and the affair became the talk of Paris society.

In June 1847, the duchess announced that she intended to seek a divorce, on the grounds of her husband's adultery with the governess. The duke was mad with fury; he would lose his children and his position at one blow. On the evening of 17 August, he went to see Henriette Deluzy, and returned home in the early hours of the morning. As dawn was breaking, the servants were electrified by a piercing scream. Then the bell connected to the duchess's bedroom began to ring. There was another scream. It looked as if burglars had broken in. The duke's valet and the duchess's maid crept to her door, and heard the crash of something falling over. They knocked and called, but there was no reply. They tried another door, but it had been wedged. A number of servants rushed to the garden, and looked up at the bedroom window; as they did so, the shutter opened, and several of them saw a man they recognized as the duke. It seemed that he had also heard the burglars and had entered his wife's bedroom. The servants rushed back indoors to help him fight the intruders. To their surprise, the bedroom door was now open. The room was in chaos, with overturned furniture, and splashes of blood on the walls. The duchess was sitting on the floor, half-propped against her bed; she was obviously dead. Her throat had been slashed, and her face bruised and battered.

As they were examining her, the duke walked into the room, and gave a scream as he saw his dead wife. "Some monster has murdered my beloved Fanny! Fetch a doctor." He claimed that he had only just been awakened by the noise.

Two passing gendarmes noticed that the front door was open, and came in to investigate. Soon the house in the rue Faubourg-St-Honoré was full of policemen, including M. Allard, Vidocq's successor as head of the Sûreté. It took him very little time to dismiss the theory about burglars – to begin with, the duchess's jewels were untouched. Under the sofa, he found a Corsican pistol, covered with blood.

"Does anyone know whom this belongs to?", asked Allard.

To his surprise, the duke answered: "Yes, to me."

To this Allard asked: "But how did it get here?"

The duke's story was that he had heard cries for help, and rushed into his wife's bedroom, brandishing his pistol. Seeing that she was covered in blood, he had dropped the pistol to raise her up. As a result, he had become covered in blood. Seeing that his wife was dead, he went back to his bedroom to wash off the blood . . .

It was just plausible – except, of course, that he had told the servants that he had only just awakened. Allard went to the duke's bedroom, and pointed out that bloodstains led to his door. The duke replied that he had been dripping with his wife's blood as he had returned. But the state of the duke's bedroom left little doubt of his guilt; there was a bloodstained handkerchief, the bloodstained hilt of a dagger, and a piece of bloodstained cord. And when the severed end of the bell-pull from the duchess's bedroom was found under her husband's shirt, Allard told the duke he was under arrest.

But suppose his story were true? Or suppose, at any rate, that he continued to insist that it was true? Was there any point at which his account could be positively disproved? He could claim that the servants had misunderstood him when they thought he said he had only just been awakened by the noise. He could claim that the shock of discovering his wife's dead body had led him to act in a strange and confused manner, carrying off the bloodstained cord and the bell-pull. A court might disbelieve him, yet still have difficulty proving that he murdered his wife.

---

One night in 1957, a 17-year-old chemist named Humphry Davy was heating a mixture of damp iron filing and nitric acid. Cautiously, he bent forward to sniff the retort. The gas smelt sweetish, and seemed to have no ill-effect - which surprised him, since he had been warned it could kill. He sniffed more deeply, and was suddenly filled with a sensation of lightness. There was a buzzing noise in his ears, and objects in the room seemed to be getting bigger and falling towards him. Oddly enough, he was not alarmed; on the contrary, he felt a tremendous gaiety, and burst out laughing. Then he passed out. When he woke, up, he exclaimed: 'What a wonderful discovery! Laughing gas.

Laughing gas - or 'nitrous air', as its discoverer, Joseph Priestley, had called it - became a craze. The apparatus was cheap, the chemicals easily obtainable. Unfortunately, they were often impure: the nitrous oxide gas became contaminated with the deadly nitrogen peroxide. Many people were, poisoned; some died. And the gas-sniffing craze ended as suddenly as it had begun. Humphry Davy didn't know it, but he had inaugurated the Age of Drugs.

The bloodstained pistol was turned over to the eminent pathologist Ambroise Tardieu, who had written the first treatise on hanging, proved the guilt of Dr de la Pomerais, and discovered "Tardieu spots", the spots of blood that form under the heart of people who have been suffocated. What the police wanted to know was whether the pistol had been dropped in the duchess's blood, or used as a weapon to batter her to death. With characteristic thoroughness, Tardieu studied the pistol, first under a magnifying glass, then a microscope. The first thing he discovered was a chestnut hair close to the butt. Near the trigger guard, he found fragments of skin tissue. Further microscopic examination revealed a bulb, or root, of human hair, and more fragments of flesh. One of the fragments melted when heated, and formed a grease spot on a piece of paper. Moreover, some of the contused wounds on the dead woman's forehead had been made with a blunt instrument like the butt of the pistol. In short, there could be no possible doubt. The microscope revealed that the duchess had been battered to death with the pistol.

Tardieu's medical investigations revealed exactly what had happened that night. The Duc de Praslin had slipped into his wife's bedroom, probably through the bathroom, intending to kill her with one sweep of a sharp knife. But his nerve failed him, or perhaps she woke up as he bent over her. The blade made a deep cut in her throat, but failed to sever the windpipe; she screamed, and began to fight. He stabbed her again and again with a dagger, then began to beat her with the butt of the pistol; as she writhed on the floor, she bit his leg (a medical examination revealed her teeth marks). By this time the whole house was aroused; the servants were knocking on the door. His original plan – of killing her, then opening the front door and making it look like a burglary – had to be abandoned; instead, he decided to leave an open window. But as he threw back the shutters, he saw the servants in the garden. At least this allowed him to escape back to his own bedroom. And now he made yet another mistake. He rushed into his wife's room, pretending that the noise had awakened him, and screamed at the sight of his wife's body. And when the police arrived, and he was forced to change his story, he knew that his last chance of getting away with murder had vanished . . .

Before being taken off to the Luxembourg prison, the duke succeeded in swallowing a dose of arsenic. He died three days later, still refusing to admit to the murder. But Tardieu's microscope had made such a confession superfluous.

# Madeleine Smith

In Glasgow in 1855, an attractive but bored nineteen-year-old girl named Madeleine Smith, daughter of a well-to-do architect, was introduced in the street to Pierre L'Angelier, a young Frenchman from Jersey, who had gone to considerable trouble to engineer the introduction. Soon afterwards, Madeleine received a letter from L'Angelier declaring his love; she replied encouragingly, using the maid as a go-between. The course of true love was far from smooth; when her parents found out, they ordered her never to communicate with him again. But the lovers continued to snatch brief and frustrating meetings, during which they exchanged hasty kisses and caresses. By December she was addressing him as "My own darling husband". But no real intimacy was possible between them until the following summer, when the Smiths went to their country house at Row; here Madeleine had a chance to take unchaperoned country

---

When London typist Elsie Cameron called on her lover Norman Thorne at his chicken farm at Crowborough, Sussex, to announce her pregnancy, she disappeared from sight. Her father telegraphed to ask her whereabouts; Thorne telegraphed back: "Not here . . . can't understand". Questioned by police and press, he insisted that he had not seen her.

When, a month later, a female neighbour reported that she had seen Elsie Cameron walking through the gate of the chicken farm on the day of her disappearance, police began digging. They found her dismembered body in a chicken run – buried in the exact spot at which Thorne had been photographed by a newspaper, feeding the chickens.

Thorne now claimed that he had stormed out of the hut after a quarrel with Elsie, and found her hanging from a beam when he returned.

Police pathologist Sir Bernard Spilsbury pointed out injuries to her face and head indicating heavy blows. Thorne's credibility was further dented by the discovery that there was no rope mark on the beam – on the contrary, the dust on top of the beam was undisturbed. If Thorne had pleaded manslaughter, he would probably have escaped with a prison sentence; as it was, his insistence on the suicide story led inevitably to a guilty verdict. He was hanged in April 1925.

In fact, Elsie had been bluffing; she was not pregnant.

walks. A letter to L'Angelier in June 1856 begins: "If we did wrong last night, it was in the excitement of our love", and went on to note prosaically: "I did not bleed in the least but I had a good deal of pain during the night."

But later that summer, disillusionment – or perhaps merely satiety – began to set in. This may have had something to do with the attentions of a wealthy bachelor named William Minnoch, a close friend of her father's, who eventually proposed. Madeleine accepted. And at this point, L'Angelier played into her hands with a fit of petulance that led him to return one of her letters; she promptly replied that their engagement was at an end. "My love for you has ceased." L'Angelier's response was to threaten to write to her father revealing all. Madeleine hastily agreed to meet him again; again her letters address him as "dearest pet" and "sweet love"; but no longer as "My darling husband". For the truth was that she loathed the ungentlemanly blackmailer with her whole heart. They had two more meetings, each in the basement of Madeleine's house, and on each occasion he drank a cup of cocoa prepared by Madeleine. After the first meeting, L'Angelier was ill; after the second, in March 1857, he returned home in agony, bent over and clutching his stomach; by 11 o'clock the next morning he was dead. His doctor insisted on a post-mortem, and eighty-seven grains of arsenic were found in his stomach – the lethal dose being three grains.

Madeleine's letters were found; she immediately became the chief suspect, and was arrested on 31 March. The notion of a young girl becoming the mistress of a Frenchman horrified Scottish public opinion. Her guilt seemed obvious. Yet although it was proved that she had purchased three lots of arsenic, as rat poison, they had been mixed with soot or indigo. And no signs of soot or indigo were found in the dead man's stomach – but one medical witness commented that the grains of indigo could easily be washed from the arsenic with cold water. Madeleine insisted that her lover was in a habit of taking small quantities of arsenic for health reasons (arsenic is a stimulant and improves the complexion), but the defence offered no proof of this assertion. The jury eventually brought in a verdict of "not proven" – peculiar to Scotland – which implied that they regarded her as guilty, but found the proof insufficient. The crowd in court cheered, evidently feeling that L'Angelier deserved what he got.

Madeleine did not marry William Minnoch. Instead, she went to London, where she married a man named Hora, and became a successful hostess. The artist George du Maurier is said to have attended a Hora soirée and, unaware of the identity of his hostess, remarked "Madeleine Smith's beauty shouldn't have **159** saved her from the scaffold." She later married an artist, George Wardle, who became manager of William Morris's silk weaving firm, and she developed an interest in socialism; Bernard Shaw once ate at her table. She died in America at the age of ninety-two.

> Cesare Borgia was an adept in the use of poisons. Some of them could make the victim die a lingering death, making his hair and teeth fall out; others could kill immediately, with all the symptoms of a stroke or heart attack. It is satisfactory to record that his downfall came through poison. Cesare and his father - the Pope were invited to dine with a cardinal, Adriano de Corneto. They fell violently ill after the banquet. (So did the cardinal - but that was probably political wisdom.) The Pope died. And Cesare, who believed himself invincible and invulnerable, suddenly saw his castle of fantasy collapse.
>
> His troops deserted him. He was made prisoner by a new Pope. He fled to Spain, and was imprisoned for his brother's murder. He escaped and joined a small army belonging to his brother-in-law; in a minor skirmish, he was seriously wounded, stripped and left to die. He was 32 years old, and had been responsible for dozens of murders. His sister Lucrezia married again, became famous for her kindness and piety, and lived happily ever after - or at least for 11 years, until she was 39.
>
> It is ironic that this gentle, affectionate girl should have become known as one of the great poisoners of history, when there is no evidence that she ever harmed anyone except, possibly, herself.

# chapter three

# THE ETERNAL
# TRIANGLE

*M*ost famous crimes of passion involve an "eternal triangle" – husband, wife and lover (or mistress) – and in the majority of these, the murderer and the lover are partners in crime. But there is another type of eternal triangle in which the lover – or mistress – remains innocent, a mere catalyst who happens to inspire the crime. The most celebrated example of the "catalyst" effect occurred in the Crippen case, which we shall examine in the next chapter. But an earlier case, that of Dr Cross, provides an equally interesting example.

## Dr Cross and the Catalyst Effect

A retired army surgeon, sixty-two years of age, Dr Philip Cross lived comfortably with his wife and six children at Shandy Hall, near Dripsey, County Cork. His wife was twenty-two years his junior; they had been married eighteen years, and it had been, on the whole, a satisfactory marriage. In October 1886, Mrs Laura Cross engaged a new governess for the children, a twenty-year-old girl named Effie Skinner. Effie, like Ethel Le Neve, was the catalyst type: not particularly pretty, but with something soft and yielding about her. As soon as he saw her, the military, rather forbidding Dr Cross felt like a hawk eyeing a sparrow. For the first time, he realized that his marriage had been merely satisfactory, never ecstatic. It had never provided him with any real outlet for his male dominance.

One day, as Effie stood talking to him about the children, he bent and kissed her. He was afraid she would tell his wife or leave immediately. But she stayed, and his desire to possess her increased. His wife noticed it, and she took what seemed to her the sensible course: she sacked Effie. The girl was shattered, she went to Dublin, and when Dr Cross visited her there, she finally gave herself to him. Possession did not cool his desire; he wanted to be married to her, living in comfort in Shandy Hall.

Early in May, 1887, Mrs Cross began to suffer attacks of vomiting. Her husband told her she had a weak heart. She died on 1 June, and was buried three days later. Less than two weeks after this, he married Effie Skinner in London. At first, he decided that they had better keep the marriage a secret and live separately, but when he got back to Dripsey, he discovered the news had preceded him.

There seemed no point keeping Effie in London, so he moved her to Shandy Hall. Inevitably, there was gossip, and the police finally decided to act. Laura Cross was exhumed, and the coroner found 3.2 grains of arsenic in her body, as well as strychnine. There was no trace of heart disease.

The police were also able to trace the firm from whom Dr Cross had bought arsenic "for sheep dipping". Tried at the Munster Assizes in Cork, he was found guilty on 18 December, 1887, and hanged in the following January. Effie was so shocked by the realization that she had been the cause of the murder that she refused to see him in the condemned cell, and Cross's hair turned white overnight.

# Adelaide Bartlett

At the time Dr Cross was engaged in seducing Effie Skinner, another celebrated crime of passion was exciting the usual fever of morbid interest among British newspaper readers – in fact, moreso than usual, since the third member of the triangle was a clergyman who showed a regrettable lack of chivalry towards the woman with whom he may or may not have committed adultery.

Theodore Edwin Bartlett was a hard-working and highly ambitious grocer. By the time he was twenty-nine, he and his business partner owned a chain of small shops in south London. This explains why, although he was a good-looking man, fond

The classic murder case on which Theodore Dreiser based his famous novel *An American Tragedy* took place on 11 July, 1906. Chester Gillette, a twenty-two-year-old labourer with aspirations to rise in the world, worked in his uncle's skirt factory in Courtland, New York. There he had an affair with eighteen-year-old secretary Billie Brown and made her pregnant. By this time, Gillette had met an attractive young socialite at a dance and become engaged to her. When Billie threatened to disclose her condition to his uncle, Chester invited her out for a day's boating on Big Moose Lake. Later that day, he was seen walking in the woods, his clothes dripping wet. Checking into another hotel he asked the clerk "Has there been a drowning reported?" The clerk said no.

Billie's body, her face battered, came to the surface the following day, and an inquest found that she had been murdered. Gillette's replies to police questions were evasive. Charged with murder, his defence was that Billie had committed suicide. But he then changed his story and claimed that the boat had capsized accidentally. The tennis racket with which he had beaten her was found buried near the lake, and proved crucial in contributing to the guilty verdict. Gillette was electrocuted in March 1908. Seventeen years later, he was immortalized by Theodore Dreiser, whose *American Tragedy* became a best-seller.

of the open air, he had never married; life was too busy for romance. Then, one day in the early 1870s, he went to call on his brother Charles, who lived in Kingston, and was introduced to a dazzlingly attractive eighteen-year-old girl named Adelaide Blanche de la Tremoile. She had dark curly hair, large appealing eyes, and a sensual mouth. Edwin found her fascinating. But it seems likely that, at this stage, marriage did not enter his head. Adelaide was definitely a "lady", and therefore far above him socially. Then he learned that there was some odd secret in her background. Adelaide's mother had borne her out of wedlock. Her father was a wealthy Englishman who preferred to keep his identity secret – it has been suggested that he was a member of Queen Victoria's entourage when she visited France in 1855, and was therefore probably titled. Now Adelaide lived with a guardian in a house in Richmond – she was staying in the Kingston house as a guest of Charles's sixteen-year-old daughter. So it seemed that, although she was a "lady", her chances of being accepted into English society were minimal. Edwin saw his chance, and pursued it with single-minded vigour. He called on her when she returned to Richmond, and seems to have persuaded her guardian, or her father, that a virtuous and successful grocer would make a desirable husband. To Adelaide he explained solemnly that his intentions were more than pure – there was no element of carnal desire in his feeling for her, and when they were married, their relationship would be wholly platonic. And by way of proving his good faith, Edwin Bartlett packed off his newly-wedded bride to a ladies' finishing school in Stoke Newington. She came to stay with her husband during the school holidays but, according to Adelaide, their relationship was like that of father and daughter. And when she had finished at the Stoke Newington school, Edwin sent her off to a convent in Brussels. She stayed there until 1877, two years after their marriage, when she returned home to a newly furnished flat above Edwin's largest shop in Herne Hill. And for just one month, life was pleasant and peaceful, and Adelaide no doubt enjoyed being a young married woman in charge of her first home. Then Edwin's mother died, and the dutiful son invited his father to come and live with them.

It was a mistake. The old man was a bad-tempered old sponger, and he had never liked Adelaide. He made himself so unpleasant that Adelaide ran away from home – there is evidence that she went to stay in the house in Kingston where Edwin had first met her. And this seems to have led to further trouble. Edwin's younger brother Frederick also lived in the house, and the old man suspected a love affair. One writer on the case states that she became Frederick's mistress, but there is no evidence whatsoever for this assertion. All we know is that the old man accused Adelaide of having an affair with Frederick, and that Edwin was so incensed that he made his father sign an apology, which was drawn up by a solicitor. Then an uneasy peace reigned in the household.

Four years later, in 1881, two things broke the monotony of their lower middle class lives: Edwin had a nervous breakdown (brought on, according to his father, by laying a floor), and Adelaide had a stillborn baby. The latter accident was Edwin's fault; the nurse he engaged to look after his wife had sensed that this might be a difficult birth, and begged Edwin to call in a doctor. But the Victorian Edwin was rather shocked at the idea of another man "interfering with her", and refused. By the time a doctor was finally called in, the baby was dead.

Soon after this, perhaps to distract her, they moved to the village of Merton, near Wimbledon. Edwin's motive may also have been to get rid of his father – he selected a house that had no spare bedroom. So the old man was forced to find a home elsewhere.

There have been spectacular lonely hearts cases - but perhaps the most extraordinary of them involved the death of a mother and daughter, who may both have been mistresses of the killer. The daughter, Maria Domenech, was a pretty 28-year-old social worker from New York; her body, clad only in black panties, was found at the bottom of the cliffs of Moher, on the west coast of Ireland, on May 24, 1967.

It took more than a week for the Irish police to identify her, with the aid of Interpol, and by that time her mother, 51-year- old widow, Mrs. Virginia Domenech, had also vanished from her New York home. The trail led the police to Orly Airport, Paris, where Maria had prepared to fly to Ireland on the afternoon of May 22, in company with a man. Careful detective work revealed that they had arrived in Dublin hours later, hired a car, driven across Ireland, and arrived at the cliffs at five in the morning.

There he had knocked her unconscious, taken a large sum in traveller's checks from her pocketbook, and thrown her to the beach below. He then caught a plane from Shannon back to Paris a few hours later. He thought the alibi was perfect; but when the police established his identity as Patrick D'Arcy, an Irish-American who had been having a tempestuous affair with Maria before she left America - as well as showing marked attention to her mother - he realized the gamble had failed. D'Arcy committed suicide in a motel room in Florida a few weeks after the murders. Virginia Domenech's body has never been found.

Early in 1885 – the Bartletts had now been married ten years – the couple decided to try another place of worship one Sunday morning. They attended the Wesleyan chapel in Merton. The preacher that day was a young man named George Dyson. He had a black moustache, a receding hairline, and was of slight build. Dyson made a pastoral call soon after that. And when he told Edwin Bartlett that he was about to go to Trinity College, Dublin, to take his degree, Bartlett was deeply impressed. He had an almost pathetic admiration for anyone with education – he himself was an avid but disorganized reader. He cross-questioned Dyson about his studies, and pressed the young man to come and visit them again as soon as he returned from Dublin. Slightly overwhelmed – for he was modest and not very clever – Dyson agreed. And a warm, if rather peculiar friendship, began between these three rather lonely people.

Dyson found Edwin Bartlett "exceedingly odd". He seemed to have eccentric ideas on all kinds of subjects. For example, he was a devotee of a work called *Esoteric Anthropology* by Thomas Low Nichols, whose long sub-title declared it to be a "confidential" treatise on the passionate attractions and perversions of the most intimate relations between men and women. It was not, as the judge later assumed, disguised pornography, but an early "women's lib" discourse on the unfairness of using women as sexual objects. It recommended birth control, and suggested that sexual intercourse should only be practised for the purpose of begetting children. Another of Edwin's rather peculiar beliefs was that men should have two wives, one for "use" and one for intellectual companionship. He was also, like many Victorians, interested in hypnotism, and in the doctrines of Anton Mesmer, according to which human beings possess a "vital magnetic fluid" that can be passed from one to another.

Soon, Edwin Bartlett was professing the warmest affection for the Reverend Dyson. In fact, he proposed that Dyson should continue Adelaide's education, teaching her geography, history, Latin and mathematics. Dyson, who was making a mere hundred pounds a year, agreed. He would arrive in the morning while Edwin was out at business, and often stay all day. During most of this time, he was alone with Adelaide. Whether she became his mistress depends on one's final view of her guilt or innocence, but certainly she often sat at his feet, with her head on his knee, and he often kissed her, alone and in her husband's presence. And, oddly enough, Edwin seemed delighted with the whole arrangement. His wife was lonely – she had only one close female friend, a Mrs Alice Matthews – and now he had found her a male friend and teacher who could be trusted implicitly. Edwin had unlimited faith in clergymen. If he found Edwin still in the house when he came in for supper, he warmly pressed him to stay for the evening. When the Bartletts went to Dover for a month, Edwin tried to persuade Dyson to come too, and offered him a first class season ticket so he could rush down every time he was free. Dyson refused, but Edwin still found time to travel to Putney (where Dyson lived) and whisk him off to Dover as an overnight guest. And he asked Dyson to be an executor of his will, in which, naturally, he left everything to Adelaide.

That September, the Bartletts moved into a new lodging – it was to be their last – in Victoria. Edwin told their new landlady, Mrs Doggett, that they would be having a regular visitor, a clergyman, as a dinner guest. And George Dyson continued to call as regularly as ever, travelling from Putney, where he was now in charge of his own church, on a season ticket presented by Edwin Bartlett. They even kept a special jacket and slippers for him to change into. Dyson was finding this close friendship with a young married woman disturbing, and he confessed openly to Edwin that he was growing attracted to Adelaide and that it was upsetting his work; he felt he ought to stop seeing them. Edwin dismissed the idea, assuring Dyson that Adelaide had become a better and nobler woman since she had known him. He seemed to be trying to throw them into one another's arms. And Mrs Doggett noticed one day, after Dyson had left, that the window curtains were not merely drawn, but pinned together. It is hard to imagine why they should do this unless, at the very least, they had been engaging in some heavy petting.

And now, suddenly, Edwin became ill. One day he felt so exhausted at work that he hurried home. The next morning, he and Adelaide and Dyson went to a dog show – dogs were one of Edwin's main interests – but he felt so ill that they had to return home. Adelaide went out to fetch a doctor. She found a young man called Alfred Leach, whom she had never met before, but who immediately accompanied her back home. Edwin was suffering from sickness, diarrhoea and bleeding of the bowels; he had also had toothache. When Dr Leach looked into his mouth, he observed a blue line round the gums, a symptom of mercury poisoning. When he asked Edwin if he had taken mercury, Edwin denied it, but admitted that he had swallowed a pill he had found in a drawer – he had no idea what it was for. Leach arrived at another explanation. Edwin's teeth were in an appalling condition and his breath smelt foul. Apparently the dentist who made his false teeth had failed to draw the stumps; for some reason, he had sawed off the teeth at the gums. When these had rotted, the dentist merely made more false teeth, and the condition of his mouth made it impossible for Edwin to clean his remaining teeth. Leach's theory was that Edwin had, at some time, got a dose of mercury into his system, and that the sulphides produced by his rotting teeth had combined with it to form mercuric sulphide, hence the blue line. A dentist who was called in verified that Edwin was suffering from mercury poisoning, and extracted fifteen roots and stumps.

So throughout December the patient remained in bed. On Christmas Day, 1885, he received an unpleasant shock when he went to the lavatory and passed a round worm. He was naturally something of a hypochondriac, and this gave him "the horrors". He swore that he could feel worms wriggling in his throat, and became deeply depressed.

On the last day of December, and the last day of Edwin's life, he went to the dentist for yet another tooth extraction. Young Dr Leach, who had become a devotee of Adelaide, went with them. On the way, Adelaide remarked that they had just been saying that they sometimes wished they were unmarried, so they could have the pleasure of getting married again. Later, when Edwin got home, his appetite had improved, and he ate a large meal of oysters, jugged hare and cake, with a helping of chutney. He told Mrs Doggett that he would have a haddock for his breakfast, Obviously, he was at last on the road to recovery.

Just before 4 a.m. on New Year's Day, Adelaide knocked on the Doggett's bedroom door. "Go and fetch Dr Leach. I think Mr Bartlett is dead." She explained that she had fallen asleep, holding Edwin's foot, which apparently soothed him, as she sat beside his bed. She had awakened and felt that he was cold. She had tried to revive him with brandy, but without success. Dr Leach observed a glass of brandy on the shelf, with a smell of chloroform.

The moment old Mr Bartlett heard of his son's death, he concluded he had been murdered. He sniffed his son's lips, then turned to Dr Leach and said, "We must have a post mortem".

The post mortem revealed a baffling and astonishing fact: that Edwin Bartlett had died of chloroform poisoning. This was so astonishing because chloroform is an unpleasant-tasting substance that would be almost impossible to swallow; moreover, it causes vomiting. If chloroform was poured down someone's throat when he was unconscious, for example, from the fumes of chloroform, it would get into the lungs. And there was no chloroform in Edwin Bartlett's lungs. Which seemed to point to the completely mystifying conclusion that Edwin Bartlett had drunk the chloroform voluntarily. Yet his cheerfulness before he went to sleep, and the fact that he had even ordered his breakfast, made it unlikely that he intended suicide.

And where had the chloroform come from? This was soon revealed. The Reverend Dyson had bought it, at Adelaide's request. He had even gone to three separate chemists to get a fairly large quantity, claiming that he wanted to use it as cleaning fluid. Adelaide had told him she wanted it to make her husband sleep. And now, when he heard that chloroform had been found in Edwin's stomach, Dyson was panic stricken. He saw it as the end of his career. He rushed along to see Adelaide, and when Mrs Matthews came unexpectedly into the room, she heard Dyston saying: "You did tell me Edwin was going to die soon." And when Adelaide denied it, he bowed his head on the piano and groaned: "Oh, my God!" Later that day, he saw Adelaide alone, and she asked him to say nothing about the chloroform. Dyson refused, and said he was going to make a clean breast of it.

And so he did. And the result was that Adelaide Bartlett found herself on trial for murder. When, in the spring of 1886, it became known that she was to be tried for poisoning her husband, and that the Reverend George Dyson would probably stand in the dock beside her, public excitement was intense. It had all the signs of being a thoroughly scandalous murder case, complete with revelations of secret adultery and a plot by the lovers to kill the husband. And when it was known that the great advocate Edward Clarke would defend Adelaide, people nodded significantly. Clarke was not one of those barristers who depended on verbal fireworks and bullying to win his cases; he was known for a certain quiet sincerity. Yet for all that, he had a formidable reputation. It was obvious that no suburban grocer's wife could afford his services, which could only mean that her mysterious father had intervened.

In the event, Adelaide finally stood alone in the dock; Dyson had managed to clear his own name by shamelessly doing his best to hand her over to the hangman. Edward Clarke had an apparently impossible task: to convince a Victorian jury that this pretty Frenchwoman, quite probably an adulteress, was innocent of her husband's murder. He had only one thing on his side: the total mystery of how even the most cunning murderess could have got the chloroform into Edwin Bartlett's stomach.

Clarke's defence was brilliant. His line of argument was that

Edwin was a highly eccentric man who had almost thrown his wife into the arms of the clergyman, and who had actually told them that he expected them to get married when he was dead. He had insisted that his marriage to Adelaide should be purely platonic, and they had only had sexual intercourse once, as a result of which a baby had been born. But in the last days of his illness, Edwin had suddenly shown a desire for sexual intercourse. Adelaide felt this was wrong, since she now regarded herself as affianced to Dyson. So she asked Dyson to get her chloroform, so she might wave it in his face if he made sexual demands. However, she had been unable to go through with it. She had never been able to keep a secret from Edwin, and on that last evening of his life, had confessed her intention and showed him the bottle of chloroform. Edwin had been rather sulky about it, and had placed the bottle on the mantelpiece. And somehow, while Adelaide dozed by his side, holding his foot to comfort him, some of that chloroform had got into Edwin's stomach. (She admitted she had disposed of the rest by throwing it from the window of a train.) The main point of the defence was that Edwin was eccentric to the point of insanity, and that such an unpredictable man might easily have swallowed chloroform, perhaps simply to upset his wife and gain attention.

Amazingly enough, the jury swallowed this unlikely story of a wife too virtuous even to permit her own husband sexual intercourse, even when it was revealed that Edwin had rubber contraceptives in his pocket and undoubtedly used them in making love to Adelaide. But the central point of the defence, of course, was that baffling mystery of the chloroform: if Adelaide poisoned her husband, how did she get it into his stomach? To that question the prosecution had no answer. After that, there could only be one verdict. "Although we think there is the gravest suspicion attaching to the prisoner, we do not think there is sufficient evidence to show how or by whom the chloroform was administered." So the verdict had to be not guilty. The judge had to reprove the court sternly as it burst into cheers.

The question of Adelaide's guilt or innocence has been argued by criminologists ever since. Some, like Nigel Morland, have no doubt that she was innocent, and that Edwin took the chloroform himself in a spirit of resentment or mischief. The majority are inclined to believe that Adelaide was poisoning Edwin from the beginning with some mercury compound, and only decided on the dangerous expedient of ether when he looked like recovering. And one, Yseult Bridges, believes that

In 1972, Francisco Pineda, a car mechanic of Guadalajar, Mexico, walked into the bedroom of his employer, Fernand Ortega, a 32-year-old hunchback. His employer lay stretched of the floor in his pyjamas, dead. Francisco's pretty step-daughter Maria Pineda, lay dead on the bed, her skirt around her thighs Police discovered that both had died of cyanide pdisoning Ortega had forced her to drink cyanide at knife point, then drank it himself.

Ortega was suffering from tuberculosis; Maria had been acting as his nurse, administering injections. Ortega fell violently in love with her, but she was not attracted to the hunchback. She may have thought that the drink he forced on her containec knockout drops, and that his intention was simply to rape her

In fact, in spite of the position of her dress, Maria had no been sexually molested. Onega *could* have raped her before he killed himself; but that was not what he wanted. He loved her and wanted to join her in death.

Adelaide somehow used hypnosis to induce Edwin to swallow the chloroform. None, as far as I know, have hit upon what seems to be the simplest and most obvious solution.

Let us try to reconstruct a hypothetical scenario. When Edwin Bartlett meets the beautiful Adelaide, he is too shy to hope that she will become his mistress as well as his wife, and so he assures her that their relationship will be a purely platonic one. But after two years of marriage, he is less humble and self-effacing, and insists on his marital rights. As a result, Adelaide becomes pregnant, but due to her husband's peculiar ideas about doctors, she loses the baby.

Edwin's curious attitude, his feeling that a doctor who examined his wife would be "interfering with her", indicates a powerful physical jealousy. It is surely the attitude of a man who has the utmost difficulty in persuading his wife to permit him the use of her body, so the idea of another man examining her intimately arouses intense jealousy. Adelaide, for her part, finds sex with her husband rather unpleasant, perhaps because his rotten teeth cause permanent halitosis, and she does her best to persuade him to abide by their "platonic" contract by petting him, fussing over him, showing him a great deal of affection, in fact, everything but allowing him into her bed. (At the trial, it was emphasized that they seemed to be an extremely happily married couple.) She makes use of the standard excuse, that she is afraid of becoming pregnant again, but Edwin counters that by buying contraceptives.

For Edwin, life becomes a permanent siege on his wife's virtue, with very infrequent successes. In his efforts to soften her, he deliberately introduces the Reverend George Dyson into their household, and encourages a flirtation. In effect, he is asking the clergyman, whom he trusts implicitly, to "warm her up". While she is feeling kindly and grateful to her husband, she can hardly refuse him the occasional embrace.

Edwin falls ill; we do not know whether, as Yseult Bridges believes, she has been administering small doses of lead acetate or some mercuric poison. But it gives her a flash of hope, she sees the end of her martyrdom in sight. Then he begins to recover and to indicate that his sexual appetites are returning to normal. Perhaps she finds the contraceptives in his pocket.

And it is at this point that she asks Dyson to buy the chloroform. Presumably the idea of killing Edwin is at the back of her mind – it is hard to believe that she intends to soak a hankerchief in the drug and try and press it over his nose whenever he becomes amorous. But she also knows Edwin well enough to know that, as a hypochondriacal invalid, he quite enjoys taking "medicines". He is in a state of neurotic depression about his "worms". Dr Leach has given him all kinds of medicines for them, without effect – Edwin is convinced he is still swarming with worms. All Adelaide needs to do is to produce the chloroform, and tell Edwin that Dr Leach has recommended this to get rid of worms. Perhaps only the lightest of hints is needed. Perhaps she offers him a little chloroform mixed with brandy, but he finds it unpleasant. Then, as she sits beside him, holding his foot and breathing deeply, he decides that he will win her approval by taking his medicine, and he cautiously reaches out for the bottle.

Sir James Paget, a well-known doctor, made the famous comment: "Now the case is over, she should tell us in the interests of science how she did it". The answer is surely that she did not do it, Edwin did. Whether it was at Adelaide's suggestion we shall never know.

# Mrs Maybrick

Because she was suspected of adultery, Adelaide Bartlett was fortunate to avoid meeting the hangman. Because she undoubtedly *had* committed adultery, her younger contemporary Florence Maybrick came an uncomfortable shade closer to the gallows. Both women were married to drug-taking hypochondriacs, but Mrs Maybrick's defence failed to convince the judge or jury at her trial for murder.

Florence Chandler, born in Mobile, Alabama in 1862, was a "southern belle" in the tradition of Scarlett O'Hara; her father was a wealthy banker, and her main aim in life was to secure a rich husband. He appeared on the scene when she was eighteen – an overweight, forty-one-year-old English cotton broker named James Maybrick, whom she met on a

---

The great American *cause célèbre* of 1904 was the trial of *Floradora* girl Nan Patterson for the murder of her lover Caesar Young in a hansom cab. The shot that killed gambler Caesar Young was fired at about 8 o'clock on the morning of 4 June, 1904; he was dead by the time he reached hospital. Nan Patterson claimed he committed suicide but the police disbelieved her – to begin with, the revolver was in Young's pocket, and it seemed unlikely he would have placed it there after shooting himself.

Young, who was married, had met Nan Patterson on a train to California two years earlier. It was a passionate affair, but by 1904, Young wanted to terminate it; to that end he booked passage for Europe for himself and his wife on the *Germanic*. He and Nan spent a last evening quarrelling violently. He nevertheless met her for a breakfast of brandy and whiskey, after which they called the hansom, and Young was shot soon after. Under the circumstances, Nan's story that he killed himself because he was upset about leaving her seemed unlikely – the bullet had entered at the wrong angle. At her first trial, a juror became ill, so a mis-trial was declared. Her second trial ended with a hung jury. When the third trial also ended in deadlock, all charges against her were dropped. In retrospect it seems clear that Nan was acquitted, not because she was innocent, but because the men on the jury felt she was too pretty to hang.

Nan cashed in her notoriety by accepting leading roles in various musicals, but proved to lack talent, and soon vanished into obscurity.

ship crossing the Atlantic. When she accepted his proposal,
Florence may have suspected that he was not a virgin, but she
was certainly unaware that he had an American mistress named
Mary Hogwood, by whom he had sired three children.

For a while the newlyweds lived in Norfolk, Virginia, where
Maybrick spent his days at the cotton exchange. A male child
was born there. When they moved back to Liverpool two years
later, another child, this time a girl, arrived. It was soon after
this that Florence learned that her husband had a mistress
named Mary Hogwood, and that Mary had given birth to
two more children since James Maybrick's marriage. She was
upset, but accepted the "double standard" that was current in
the late Victorian age. And for another four years, life continued
uneventfully at Battlecrease House, their home in the Liverpool
suburb of Aigburth.

The Maybricks often gave dinner parties, and it was at one of
these in December 1888 that Florence met a tall, good-looking
man named Alfred Brierley, a thirty-eight-year-old bachelor who
was, like her husband, a successful cotton broker. She saw him
a great many times that winter, and when the spring came,
Brierley accompanied the Maybricks on a tour of the spring
race meetings. Brierley's obvious admiration was welcome; her
husband was frequently bad tempered, and had ceased to treat
her with the courtliness a southern belle expected. Brierley, on
the other hand, behaved like a medieval knight.

So when her husband went to London alone on 12 March,
1889, and Brierley took the opportunity to tell Florence he
loved her, she admitted shyly that she returned the feeling.
Brierley went on to press her to go away with him – but he
was not thinking of an elopement, only of a dirty weekend.
By this time, Florence was as eager to commit adultery as he
was, and agreed.

It happened a week later. Telling her husband that she was
going to stay with an aunt who was about to have an operation,
Florence checked into a small hotel in London. Brierley's took
another suite. That night, Mrs Maybrick spent the night in
Brierley's suite; the following night, he slept in hers. But
although both suites had been reserved for a week, they
checked out after only three days. This may have been because,
having satisfied their curiosity, they were tired of one another,
or possibly because Florence wished to establish an alibi. She
went to stay with her cousin Margaret Baillie.

The day after she returned home, she and her husband
attended the Grand National at Aintree. Brierley was also there,

Mrs James Maybrick.

and he offered to take Florence to take a look at the Prince of
Wales in the grandstand. By this time, Maybrick seems to have
begun to develop belated suspicions; when his wife returned,
he told her angrily that she had been away too long.

That evening, the Maybricks had a noisy quarrel, and he
ordered her to leave the house, sending for a cab. In fact,
the cab was finally dismissed, and Florence spent the night
in a room next to the nursery. The next morning, she had
a black eye. That day, Mrs Maybrick told a female confidant
that she wanted a divorce. The family doctor intervened, and
the Maybricks apparently made up their quarrel – even when
Mrs Maybrick revealed that she was heavily in debt to money
lenders. But harsh words were exchanged again the next day.
After sounds of a noisy altercation, the servants found Florence
in a faint. She spent a week in bed.

On 8 April, Florence went to see Alfred Brierley to display her
black eye; she was evidently hoping that he would propose an
elopement. Instead he looked embarrassed and got rid of her as
soon as possible.

In mid-April, James Maybrick went to London to pay off
another of his wife's creditors. He also took the opportunity
to see a doctor about pains in the head and numbness in the
limbs. The doctor prescribed various medicines for indigestion
and constipation. He does not seem to have been aware that
Maybrick made a habit of dosing himself with arsenic and
strychnine, both of which are stimulants when taken in small
quantities, and which can produce the symptoms Maybrick
complained about. He seems to have been concerend enough
to re-draft his will – although he now left most of his estate to
the children.

Soon after this, Florence bought no less than two dozen fly
papers from the local chemist – the old fashioned type consisting
of a sheet of paper soaked in a solution of arsenic. A servant
noticed that the fly papers were soaking in water in a sink. A
week later, Mrs Maybrick ordered yet another two dozen. Three
days later, on 27 April, 1889, James Maybrick had a severe attack
of vomiting. He attended the Wirral races, but his hand was so
shaky that he spilt his wine when dining with friends.

As the attacks of indigestion continued on into May, the
servants – who were inclined to be hostile to Florence – informed
some of Maybrick's friends that they suspected his wife of poisoning him. Maybrick's brother Michael arrived from London,
and ordered that no one but a nurse was to attend the sick
man. When he caught Florence pouring medicine from one

bottle to another, he shouted at her and took charge of the medicine, refusing to accept her explanation that it had so much sediment that a bigger bottle was more convenient for shaking. Michael took the medicine for analysis, but it proved to contain no poison. Neither did some food that Michael confiscated and took to the same doctor.

Nevertheless, on 11 May, James Maybrick died. A post mortem showed stomach inflammation due to "some irritant substance". On 14 May, Florence was arrested and charged with his murder.

One thing was quite clear: that Maybrick had been for years in the habit of taking various dangerous substances as stimulants, including arsenic and strychnine. In any modern court of law, this would have been sufficient to ensure his wife's acquittal. Moreover, even the Home Office expert, Dr Thomas Stevenson, admitted that arsenic is a cumulative poison that will be stored up in the system; this in itself should have been enough to acquit Florence Maybrick.

Unfortunately, her three nights in London with Alfred Brierley had become known. Three days before her husband's death, she had written him a letter describing her husband as "sick unto death", and telling Brierley that there was "no fear of discovery". A servant intercepted it and handed it to Michael Maybrick. And although the letter contained no evidence that Florence was poisoning her husband it virtually condemned her. Before a hostile jury, and an audience that hissed her, Mrs Maybrick heard Mr Justice Fitzjames Stephen read the sentence of death on Wednesday 7 August, 1889. The date of execution was fixed for 26 August.

The verdict caused nationwide indignation. But in those days there was no court of appeal. Thousands of people signed a petition for mercy. Even Maybrick's ex-mistress, Mary Hogwood, wrote from Virginia to say that he took arsenic all the time, and that she had fully expected him to die of it. Three days before she was due to hang, Florence Maybrick's sentence was commuted to life imprisonment.

She was released in 1904, and returned to America, where she wrote a book called *My Fifteen Lost Years*, and became a popular lecturer, never failing to move her audience with her simple statement: "I swear to you I am innocent." She spent the later years of her life as a recluse, surrounded by cats, dying in 1939. Her son Jim, convinced that she had murdered his father, forbade her to see her daughter Gladys; he carried a photograph of his father with him to the day of his death. Oddly enough, he

also died of poison. Working in a laboratory in British Columbia, **177**
Canada, in 1911, he accidentally picked up a beaker containing
cyanide – instead of water – to wash down a sandwich, and died
soon after.

America differed from England in never having had a "Victorian age". Nineteenth century America was noisy, vulgar and
almost painfully alive. Mrs Fanny Trollope – mother of the
novelist – and Charles Dickens took one look at the United
States, and hurried back to England to write highly critical
travel sketches. But American crudeness was counterbalanced
by sheer inventiveness and an endless capacity for innovation.
This was as apparent in its crimes of passion as in its railroads
and dime stores. In 1895, a Sunday school teacher named
Theodore Durrant lured two virtuous girls – separately – into
the Baptist church on Bartlett Street in San Francisco, where
he killed and raped them. The first, Blanche Lamont, was
placed in the belfry; the second, Minnie Williams, was left
in the library where she had been stabbed to death. Durrant
had been seen with both girls just before they vanished, and
was found guilty and sentenced to death. In the days when sex
crime was virtually unknown, the Durrant case made headlines
all round the world.

In 1897, a Chicago sausage maker named Adolph Luetgart,
who had more than one mistress, decided to dispose of his
wife in such a way that her body would never be found; he
boiled her in one of his sausage vats, turning her into soft
soap with a solution of caustic potash. He overlooked one
small detail: his wife's rings. These were found in the bottom
of the vat, together with a false tooth and a sesamoid bone
from the human foot. Nevertheless, Luetgart's ingenuity was

In France, the most sensational murder trial of 1890 was that of
a pimp named Michel Eyraud and his attractive but unscrupulous
mistress Gabrielle Bompard. She lured a wealthy businessman
named Gouffé to her room, where Eyraud strangled him. The corpse
was then placed in a trunk and dumped in a wood near Lyon. By the
time the trunk was found, the body was so decomposed as to be
unrecognisable. But brilliant forensic work by the great pathologist
Alexandre Lacassagne revealed a legbone malformation that proved
the body to be that of the missing Gouffé. Eyaraud fled to America,
was recognised in Cuba through a newspaper photograph, and was
taken back to Paris to face the guillotine; his mistress received life
imprisonment.

not entirely wasted, because he was convicted on purely medical evidence, he escaped the death penalty and was sentenced to life imprisonment.

# The Guldensuppe Case

It was also in 1897 – on 26 June – that two teenagers who were swimming in the East River near the foot of 11th Street discovered a floating parcel that proved to contain human remains. The headless torso was wrapped in a red and gold oilcloth with a cabbage rose pattern, and the hairy chest had a patch of skin missing, suggesting that a tattoo had been removed; the mutilations seemed to indicate surgical skill. The next day, the lower half of the body, minus the legs, was found in woods near 176th Street – the legs were later found by another two boys swimming off the Brooklyn shore.

The newspaper magnate William Randolph Hearst, virtually the inventor of the "Yellow Press", saw an opportunity to sell more of his newspapers, and assigned a "murder squad" of reporters to the case. One of these, George Arnold, was inspecting the remains (now complete except for the head) in the city morgue when he observed that the hands and the fingers were heavily calloused. Arnold was a devotee of the Turkish baths, and he knew that masseurs develop the same kind of callouses. Since the big man on the slab looked vaguely familiar, he hurried down to his favourite establishment in Murray Hill and asked if any of the masseurs had failed to report for duty. The answer was that a man called Willie Guldensuppe had not been in for two days. And he had a tattoo on his chest. Guldensuppe had lived at a boarding-house at 439 Ninth Avenue, which was run by an unlicensed midwife called Augusta Nack.

Hearst's "murder squad" now set out to trace the distinctive oilcloth in which the remains had been wrapped, and the newspaper, the *Journal*, published appeals for information, and a coloured reproduction of the oilcloth. It was a Hearst reporter who was making a round of dry goods stores on Long Island who found the dealer who had sold the oilcloth; the man's name was Max Riger, and he described the woman who had purchased it as a well-built but not unattractive lady. Since this description fitted

Augusta Nack – who had the dimensions of an opera singer –
Hearst reporters galloped off to the Ninth Street boarding-house,
narrowly forestalling those of a rival newspaper, the *World*, and
persuaded Augusta Nack to accompany them to the police
headquarters. To keep rival reporters away, Hearst rented the
whole boarding-house and placed guards on the door; they even
severed the telephone wires.

The police decided on shock tactics, and took Mrs Nack to view
the remains. Pointing to the legs, the detective asked: "Are those
Willie's?"

Mrs Nack looked at him haughtily. "I would not know, as I
never saw the gentleman naked."

But the *Journal* reporters had heard another story from the
inhabitants of the boarding-house and from neighbours. They
asserted that Mrs Nack and Willie Guldensuppe had been lovers
for years. But they had quarrelled recently, the cause apparently
being a fellow lodger, a young barber named Martin Thorn.

The police managed to forestall the *Journal* reporters at the
barber shop where Thorn worked. There another barber named
John Gotha told them that Thorn had confessed the murder of
Willie Guldensuppe to him. Thorn's story was that Mrs Nack
had seduced him when her regular lover, Guldensuppe, was
away. But when Guldensuppe had found them in bed together,
the brawny masseur had beaten Thorn so badly that the barber
had to go into hospital. And when he reported for work with
two black eyes, he was dismissed. Thorn decided to change
his lodgings. But Mrs Nack had continued to visit him there.
And Thorn had purchased a stiletto and a pistol, determined to
revenge himself . . .

Martin Thorn was arrested, and the *Journal* headline declared:
MURDER MYSTERY SOLVED BY JOURNAL. By now, both the
*Journal* and the police had located the spot where the murder
took place. It was in a pleasantly rural area on Long Island called
Woodside, not far from the store where the oilcloth had been
purchased. A farm stood next to the cottage, and on the day
Willie Guldensuppe's torso had been recovered from the river,
the farmer had been puzzled to see that his ducks had turned
a pink colour. The reason, he soon discovered, was that they
had been bathing in a large pool of pink-coloured water, which
had issued from the bathroom drainage pipe of the cottage next
door. But it was not until the farmer read of the arrest of Martin
Thorn and Augusta Nack that he connected this event with a
couple who had rented the cottage two weeks earlier. They
had called themselves Mr and Mrs Braun, and had paid $15

rent in advance. But they had only visited the cottage on two occasions, the second on the day of the disappearance of Willie Guldensuppe . . . Belatedly, the farmer decided to pass on his suspicions to the police.

A revolver, a carving knife and a saw were found in the cottage; but, advised by their respective lawyers, the two declined to confess. Thorn succeeded in escaping to Canada and was brought back; yet even when shown the "confession" he had allegedly made to John Gotha, he continued to insist on his total innocence.

The difference between the Nack-Thorn trial and that of Eyraud and Bompard is a measure of the difference between Paris and New York in the *fin de siècle* period; the French would have been horrified by the carelessness and levity of the American courtroom. Thorn was represented by a brilliant but not over-scrupulous lawyer named Howe, whose line of defence was simply that the two defendants were unacquainted with one another, and that neither of them knew the victim anyway. What evidence was there, asked Howe, that the assorted arms and legs belonged to Willie Goldensoup? (On other occasions he pronounced it Gludensop, Gildersleeve, Goldylocks and Silverslipper.) They might belong to any corpse. What evidence was there that the victim had ever existed?

This audacious line of defence might well have succeeded – New York jurors liked to be amused, and Howe had talked innumerable clients out of the electric chair – except that Mrs Nack decided to confess. Hearst had sent a Presbyterian minister to see her in prison every day, and one day he had brought his son, a curly-haired child of four, who climbed on to her lap and begged her to clear her conscience; Hearst naturally printed the story a day ahead of his rivals. And on the second day of the trial, Mrs Nack declared that she had seen the light, and gave a gruesomely detailed account of the crime. On the day before the murder, she and Martin Thorn had rented the cottage on Long Island. She then told Willie Guldensuppe that she had decided to run it as a baby farm, and asked him to come and give his opinion. When Willie entered the building, Thorn was waiting behind a door, and shot him in the back of the head. Then they threw him into the empty bathtub and, while he still breathed stertorously, Thorn sawed off his head. While Mrs Nack went out to buy oilcloth, Thorn dismembered the body – he had once been a medical student, which explained the surgical skill noticed by the police surgeon. He left the taps running, under the impression that the water would run down a drain and into the sewers; in fact, there was no drain, and it formed a pool in the farmyard, where the ducks were delighted at the opportunity of a midsummer bathe. Thorn then encased the head in plaster of Paris, and threw it in the river . . .

The narrative so upset one of the jurors that he fainted and had to be carried out of court. This caused a mis-trial, and when the case was resumed, Thorn had changed his story. He now declared that the cottage had been rented only as a love nest, and that on the day of the murder, he had arrived to find Mrs Nack already there. "Willie's upstairs. I've just killed him." Once again, Howe rested his defence upon the assertion that there was no proof that the corpse was that of Willie Guldensuppe, and for a while it looked as if the absence of an American Lacassagne might sway the issue in favour of the accused. But the jury chose to be convinced by the negative evidence of the missing tattoo, and found them both guilty. Martin Thorn went to the electric chair; Mrs Nack was sentenced to twenty years. The *Journal* was jubilant, but the *World* took the view that Thorn was the victim of a scheming woman.

Mrs Nack was apparently an exemplary prisoner, and was paroled after ten years; she returned to her old neighbourhood on Ninth Avenue and opened a delicatessen shop; but for some reason, the neighbours found her cooked meats unattractive, and she retired into obscurity.

---

In 1914, 138 articles and cartoons appeared in the Paris newspaper *Le Figaro* deriding the finance minister Joseph Caillaux. On 13 March, 1914, Mme Henriette Caillaux, his wife, strode into the office of *Le Figaro* and shot dead its leading columnist – and the man largely responsible for the lampoons – Gaston Calmette.

Tried the following July, Mme Caillaux pleaded great provocation, and that the gun had gone off accidentally. She was acquitted.

## • chapter four •

# SEXUAL DEVIANTS

*In 1902, Queen Victoria had been dead for only a year, and Britain was still governed by Victorian morality. This meant inevitably that any crime that involved an element of sex scandal aroused far more excitement than a crime that merely involved violence against the person. Which in turn explains the widespread press coverage given to "the Peasenhall mystery" – although in the age of the serial killer, its details seem commonplace enough.*

## The Peasenhall Mystery

1 June, 1902, was a bright, sunny morning after a night of storm. William Harsent, a carter, walked through the peaceful Suffolk village of Peasenhall, on his way to take clean linen to his daughter Rose. He walked through the wet garden of Providence House, where the girl was in service, and pushed open the back door. What he saw made him drop the linen. Rose Harsent lay, half naked, at the foot of the stairs. Her throat was cut from ear to ear, and deep gashes covered her bare shoulders. She had been wearing a nightdress, but this had been partly torn from her, and partly burnt away. A broken medicine bottle lay on the floor beside the body.

The local policeman arrived, followed by the doctor. The

policeman discovered that the broken medicine bottle had
contained paraffin – which had apparently been used in the
attempt to burn her. The girl's bed had not been slept in, but
there were three letters in the room, one of which made an
appointment to come and see her at midnight.

The signature made it clear that the author was William
Gardiner, a young foreman carpenter who lived nearby; he
had a wife and six children, and was known as a devout
Methodist. Medical examination revealed that Rose Harsent
had been dead at least four hours, and that she had been
pregnant.

No one had any doubt that the father of the unborn child
was William Gardiner, for in the previous year he and Rose had
been the subject of scandal in Peasenhall. Two youths had seen
them walking towards an empty cottage known as the "Doctor's
Chapel", which stood alone in a field. The youths had hidden
behind a hedge until the two had gone inside, then crept closer.
They were unable to see what was happening, but the sounds
made it clear. There was a rustling of clothes, then the girl gasped
"Oh, oh."

The silence that followed seemed to suggest a state of mutual
satisfaction. Gardiner was heard to ask her what she was
thinking. She answered: "What you were reading last Sunday."
He asked her what he had been reading, and she replied: "About
what we are doing now." She then went on to quote the verses
from Genesis, chapter 38, about how Onan "spilled his seed on
the ground".

When the story was repeated in Peasenhall, the villagers, who
knew their Bible, had no doubt that Gardiner and Rose Harsent
had either been engaged in extremely intimate "petting", or that
the youths had overheard an act of *coitus interruptus*. Gardiner
was a Sunday School teacher; Rose Harsent was one of his
choir girls.

The scandal was so great that an enquiry had been conducted
by the Reverend John Grey; Gardiner had denied the story,
saying that he had been in the "chapel" with the girl only to
help her move a stiff door. Gardiner had been told "Let this
be a warning to you for life", and had appeared to be suitably
chastened. Yet although he promised to have nothing further
to do with the girl, it was plain to people who observed them
closely that they were still on intimate terms.

The day after Rose Harsent's body was found, a superintendent of police called on Gardiner, and asked him if the
handwriting on one of the letters was his; Gardiner denied it.

The policeman asked if the envelope in which a certain letter was contained was not identical with those used by Gardiner's building firm; again he denied it. But the next day, he was arrested and charged with Rose's murder.

Certainly, the case against him looked black. His clasp knife was found to be stained with blood, although he claimed he had been cutting up rabbits: in 1902, there was no way of testing whether a bloodstain was from a human being or an animal; Paul Uhlenhuth *had* discovered the basic principle in 1900, but it had never been used outside Germany.

Various witnesses said that they saw a large fire burning at the back of Gardiner's house on the morning after the murder; the prosecution argued that this explained why no bloodstained clothing was found in the house; Gardiner's wife testified that there had been a fire, but that it was only the usual fire they lit on Sundays; but she did not explain why they needed a fire on a hot June morning.

Gardiner's defence was an alibi, supported by his wife; he said he had been at home all evening, and been in bed beside his wife all night. Gardiner was lucky. In those days the jury's verdict in a murder trial had to be unanimous, and one member of the jury stubbornly refused to be convinced of his guilt. The judge had to order a retrial, and once again the jury failed to agree.

Gardiner should have been tried a third time; but the authorities decided he had been through enough, and entered a *nolle prosequi* – which meant no further prosecution would take place. It was equivalent to the Scottish verdict of "not proven". Gardiner and his wife moved to a London suburb, where they opened a shop. Whether they prospered or not has never been recorded.

Was Gardiner guilty? We can never know. Certainly, Gardiner was not the only man who might have made Rose pregnant. Highly indecent verses were found in her room, and proved to have been written by the youth next door, who was in love with her. She was no blushing wallflower, but a forthright country girl who had no objection to keeping obscene verses. She may well have had other lovers beside Gardiner – a solution adopted by Brian Cooper in *Genesis 38* his novel about the murder, which suggests that the dissenting jury man who saved Gardiner's neck at the first trial knew the identity of the real murderer.

Only one thing is clear: Gardiner came close to the gallows, not because the evidence against him was particularly strong, but because the jury found it hard to forget that this Sunday

# The Crippen Case

In the year 1908, a young medical assistant succeeded his superior, Dr Pepper, as pathologist at St Mary's Hospital, London. Bernard Spilsbury was recently married, and had been receiving a salary of only £200 a year. Two years later, Spilsbury achieved sudden fame as a result of the most sensational murder trial of the decade.

Dr Harvey Hawley Crippen was an American whose medical degrees, if they existed, would not have allowed him to practise in England; his diploma came from a college of homoeopathy, still regarded by many members of the medical profession as a crank aberration. He was a thirty-year-old widower when, in 1892, he met a nineteen-year-old Polish girl who had anglicized her name to Cora Turner.

She was the mistress of a stove manufacturer, who had set her up in a flat and was paying for her singing lessons – Cora was convinced she would become a great singer. The notion of being a doctor's wife appealed to her, and she induced Crippen to propose by telling him that her lover wanted her to run away with him. The great depression of 1893 made life difficult; when they were forced to move in with Cora's parents, she told him it was time to forget general practice and become a quack. Crippen remained, basically, a quack and a confidence man for the rest of his life. He worked as a salesman for a patent medicine company, and in 1897, became manager of its London office. His employer called himself Professor Munyon, and his cure for piles, advertised by a picture of himself with an upraised finger, gave rise to many ribald jokes. But Munyon fired Crippen when he found he was the "manager" of a music-hall singer – Cora was now calling herself Belle Elmore and was on the stage – and from then on, Crippen was forced to struggle on as a low-grade quack selling worthless nostrums. He became a consultant to a firm of dubious ear specialists, Drovet's, and a magazine editor who called on Crippen had his ears examined with a filthy speculum which he made no attempt to disinfect. He was also startled by Crippen's flamboyant dress – the loud

The Seddon poisoning case (1912) and the Brides in the Bath case certainly deserve a place in any collection of twentieth-century crime. Seddon was a miser, who killed his lodger - another miser named Eliza Barrow - with arsenic for the sake of some India stock. Seddon's defence argued that be was already well-off and did not need the money, but Seddon's performance in the witness box made it obvious that he was an obsessional miser who would probably have killed for a five pound note. When, after his appeal against the death sentence had been dismissed, he heard the poor price that his property had fetched, he exploded: "Well, that finishes it".

George Joseph Smith was a confidence man who married lonely spinsters, relieved them of their cash, then deserted them. When one lady, Bessie Munday, refused to part with her money, he persuaded her to make a will in his favour, and drowned her in a zinc bath tub in July 1912. In December 1912, his next wife, a nurse named Alice Burnham, was also found drowned in her bath. In December 1914, the third and last victim, Margaret Lofty, was found drowned. And when a relative of Alice Burnham read the report, she went to the police. Inspector Arthur Neil decided to experiment to see how a woman could be drowned in her bath; they found that it was remarkably simple - the killer simply had to grab her knees and raise them. The experiment almost cost the life of a "volunteer" in a bathing suit. But the jury were convinced; in any case, it was impossible to believe that the deaths of three wives in zinc bathtubs could be coincidence, and Smith was hanged, still tearfully protesting his innocence.

shirt and yellow bow tie, the enormous diamond stick-pin. For **187**
a quiet, unassuming little man, Crippen had an odd taste in
clothes. He also had a reputation for meanness – he made a
habit of offering to buy a drink, then discovering he had left
his money at home, and borrowing half a crown. The editor
commented on Crippen's "flabby gills and shifty eyes".

The "ear specialist" Drovet went bankrupt when the firm
was convicted of gross negligence in the death of a locksmith
and other examples of what amounted to medical homicide.
But it was there that Crippen met a seventeen-year-old typist
named Ethel LeNeve (whose real name was Neave). She was a
moaning hypochondriac whose endless complaints of headache
and catarrh had earned her the nickname "Not very well thank
you". She had been a miserable child, painfully conscious of a
deformed foot, and hating her father because he insisted that
it would cure itself if she walked properly. (He proved to be
right.) She was also jealous of her vivacious younger sister. Yet
underneath these unpleasant traits, she had a highly dominant
character, and this is undoubtedly what attracted Crippen to
her. Crippen was something of a masochist in his relations with
women. This is presumably why he did not divorce Cora when
he found she had taken an ex-prize-fighter as a lover, and why
he put up with a series of lodgers who shared his wife's bed.
With bankrupt stock purchased from Drovet's, Crippen set up
his own business, with Ethel as his bookkeeper.

As Belle Elmore, Mrs Crippen became a moderate success in
the London music-halls. The British liked the American act, and
Belle seems to have been the sort of person that everyone liked
anyway – immensely vital, good natured, embarrassingly frank.
She earned the enduring friendship of Marie Lloyd and many
other music-hall artists. But at home, she became inclined to
bouts of screaming temper. And most of her friends detested
her husband, regarding him as a sponger.

Ethel was in love with her employer, and in some ways they
were well suited. Crippen was a crook, although as a result
of weakness rather than moral delinquency, and Ethel was a
pathological liar, whose biographer Tom Cullen writes that she
"lied from sheer perversity – in fact she seemed incapable of
telling the truth". But she was also determined not to yield
her virginity until they were legally married. It was not until
Crippen discovered his wife in bed with the German lodger –
and Ethel, presumably, had reason to feel that his marriage was
at an end – that she consented to become his wife in the physical
sense of the term; the date was 6 December 1906, seven years

after their first meeting. It seems to have happened in a hired hotel room during the day, as did their subsequent intimacies – Crippen continued to return home at night.

Crippen became a dentist, and Ethel his assistant. At one point, Ethel became pregnant; she was determined to have the baby, and for a while it looked as if it might transform their lives, and bring about the inevitable break with Belle. Then she had a miscarriage. And to make things worse, Belle went around telling the Music Hall Ladies' Guild members that no one was sure which of Ethel's many lovers was responsible.

If the Christine Keeler affair was the great British political scandal of the 1960s, the Max Garvie affair was its equivalent among crimes of passion. Garvie, a wealthy farmer, lived with his wife Sheila and their three children at West Cairnbeg in east Scotland. But when Garvie began to develop an interest in nudism – he founded a local club – pornography, homosexuality and abnormal sex, the marriage began to founder. In 1967, Garvie connived at an affair between his thirty-three-year-old wife and a twenty-two-year-old schoolteacher, Brian Tevendale (to whom he was also attracted). Tevendale in turn introduced Garvie to his married sister, Trudy Birse, who became his mistress, her policeman husband apparently accepting the situation. (At a party, Garvie provided him with a girl, "so the foursome turned into a sextet".) On one occasion Garvie and Tevendale tossed up to decide who would make love to Sheila first.

When Sheila Garvie and Brian Tevendale ran away together, Garvie was upset and finally persuaded her to return. He paid to have Tevendale beaten-up twice.

On 14 May, 1968, Garvie disappeared after a Scottish National Party meeting. Eventually, Sheila Garvie admitted to her mother that her husband was dead and, after a struggle with her conscience, Mrs Watson went to the police. Garvie's body was discovered in an underground tunnel at Lauriston Castle. Sheila Garvie, Brian Tevendale and Tevendale's friend Alan Peters were charged with murdering him by striking him with a rifle butt or an iron bar.

Mrs Garvie's defence centred on her husband's sexual perversions, and the newspapers made the most of the affair, with its "sixsome" and wife-swopping. The defence did her no good; a puritanical Scottish jury found Sheila Garvie and Brian Tevendale guilty, and they were sentenced to life imprisonment (in practice, about ten years). Alan Peters was released on a verdict of "not proven". An outraged crowd chased Trudy Birse and her husband down the street, and they had to take refuge in a newspaper office.

This may well have been the last straw. Instead of leaving her, which would have been the obviously sensible course, Crippen decided to murder her. On 17 January 1910, he bought no fewer than seventeen grains of hyoscine, a vegetable poison that he had seen administered to calm the violently insane at London's Royal Bethlehem Hospital. There is a strong probability that Ethel knew that her lover intended to kill his wife – she may even have planned it. On the evening of 31 January 1910, two of Belle's music-hall friends came to dinner at the Crippens' house at 39 Hilldrop Crescent, Camden Town. They said goodbye to Belle at 1.30 the next morning; it was the last time Belle was seen alive. The following day, Crippen pawned Belle's diamond ring and ear-rings, and Ethel slept at Hilldrop Crescent. The following day, letters were received by the Secretary of the Music Hall Guild, signed Belle Elmore and resigning her membership; they explained she was leaving for America to nurse a sick relative. Just before Easter, in the third week of March, Crippen told his friends that Belle was dangerously ill in Los Angeles; soon after, he announced her death.

Belle's friends were suspicious. Someone checked with the shipping lines, and discovered that no one of that name had sailed for America in February. A music-hall performer called Lil Hawthorne paid a visit to New York with her husband John Nash, and they also made enquiries, which achieved no positive result. Back in London, they talked to Crippen, who sobbed convincingly, but told contradictory stories about precisely where Belle had died. The Nashes decided to go to Scotland Yard. There they spoke to Chief Inspector Walter Dew of the CID, who agreed to go and talk to Crippen. And Crippen smoothly admitted that his wife was still alive. She had simply walked out on him and gone to join her former prize-fighter lover in Chicago. Dew was completely taken in. A thorough search of the house convinced him that there were no suspicious circumstances. When Dew left the house, he was more than half convinced that Belle was alive.

Then Crippen made his greatest mistake; he decided to flee. He and Ethel left for Antwerp, and took a ship for Canada. Ethel was dressed as a boy. When Dew returned two days later, and found the house deserted, he called in his team of diggers. Beneath the coal cellar floor, buried in quicklime, he found the remains of Mrs Crippen.

On board the SS *Montrose*, Crippen's secret had already been discovered by Captain Henry Kendal, who quickly realized that "Mr Robinson's" son was a girl in disguise. In a copy of the *Daily*

*Mail* which he had taken on board, the captain found a picture of the wanted "cellar murderer" Crippen. He handed his radio operator a message that began: "Have strong suspicion that Crippen London cellar murderer and accomplice are among saloon passengers." So it came about that Crippen was the first murderer to be caught by means of wireless telegraphy, for which Marconi had received the Nobel prize in the previous year. On the morning of 31 July 1910, as the ship lay off the mouth of the St Lawrence river, Crippen went on deck, and was greeted by Dew, who greeted him with "Good morning, Dr Crippen."

On the morning Cora Crippen's remains were found, Bernard Spilsbury was preparing to leave for a holiday in Minehead with his wife and child. Then he received a summons from his eminent colleagues Drs Pepper, Willcox, and Luff, to go and view the body. Richard Muir, who had prosecuted the Stratton brothers, was in charge of the prosecution. (When Crippen heard this, he remarked dolefully, "I fear the worst.")

Crippen was defended by the brilliant but unscrupulous Arthur Newton, who would later go to prison for forging Crippen's "Confession" and selling it to a newspaper. As a defendant, Crippen was certainly his own worst enemy. His only chance of escaping the rope was to admit everything except intent to kill. But if Crippen pleaded guilty, the whole sordid story about Belle and Ethel would emerge. Crippen chose to protect Ethel and enter a plea of innocence. His defence was that Belle had left him, just as he said, so the body in the cellar must be that of some other woman, buried by some previous tenant, or hidden there during his tenancy. It was obviously an absurd story, and it amounted to suicide. And, of course, it left to the prosecution the fairly light task of proving that the corpse *was* that of Cora Crippen. So the forensic evidence lay at the heart of the case. On one side was the formidable team of Pepper, Willcox, Luff, and Spilsbury, on the other, Drs Turnbull, Wall, and Blyth. Turnbull had been accosted by the defence at a bridge party, and had casually agreed to give his opinion as to whether a piece of skin was from the stomach, and contained an operation scar; he decided it was from a thigh, and that the scar was merely a fold. Since the operation scar was almost enough in itself to identify Mrs Crippen, the defence was delighted. When Arthur Newton broke his promise not to call Turnbull as a witness, the doctor was horrified and tried to change his mind. But unless he was willing to make a public confession of error, it was too late.

The ideal solution to the murderer's problem would be to make the body disappear into thin air; next on the list, to hide it where it could never be found. Putting it in a trunk, where it is sure to be discovered, is no way to conceal a murder. This was the view held by the Chief Constable of Brighton when, on June 17, 1934, he was called to the Brighton left- luggage office to examine the nude torso of a woman that had been found in a plywood trunk. Railway clerks could recall nothing about the man who had deposited the trunk there on Derby Day - June 6th - the busiest day of the year. But there seemed to be an abundance of clues. Sir Bernard Spilsbury examined the remains. They were of a young woman in her early twenties. The head, arms and legs had been removed; but the torso suggested that the girl belonged to the middle or upper classes. She had a good figure, with no slack flesh, and the muscles were well developed, suggesting plenty of exercise. The golden brown of the skin also indicated that she spent much of her time in a warmer climate than England. At the time of death, she had been four months pregnant.

An alert sent out to all other cloak-rooms in England led to the discovery of the legs in a case at King's Cross station in London. Each had been severed at the thigh and the knee, and they confirmed the view that the girl had been athletic and well-proportioned. The conclusion that the trunk had been left by a man was reached by weighing it; only a strong man could have lifted it without help.

There were two important clues. On a sheet of brown paper - in which the body had been wrapped - there as the word 'ford'. It looked as if it was the second half of a place name, like Guilford or Watford. In the trunk, there were two newspapers. The copies of the *Daily Mail* dated May 31st and June 2nd were of an edition that was circulated only within fifty miles of London.~When a porter recalled helping a man to carry the trunk on Derby Day, it began to look as though a solution was near but this mystery has never yet been solved.

Willcox had found hyoscine in the remains, and Crippen was proved to have bought seventeen grains of the drug not long before his wife's disappearance. Spilsbury, an expert on scar tissues, had no doubt whatsoever that the fragment of skin was from a stomach, not a thigh. And when they found part of a rectus muscle of the abdominal wall attached to the skin, the identification was proved beyond doubt. In court, Turnbull identified the skin as coming from the thigh, and the scar as a fold. Spilsbury, with the calm, grave manner that later led juries to think him infallible, pointed out the older man's errors with a pair of forceps, and the harassed Turnbull left the box with an embarrassed flush. He was followed by Dr Wall, who admitted that he had changed his mind about the piece of skin, and that it came from the abdomen. Dr Blyth disputed the presence of hyoscine in the body, but made a poor showing. It was Pepper's team that carried the day, and it was the junior member of that team who made the most powerful impression in court.

Crippen's downfall was not due entirely to this medical team. Part of the body had been wrapped in a piece of pyjamas jacket, and it contained the maker's name. One pair of Crippen's pyjamas had a missing jacket, but Crippen insisted that these had been purchased years before, in 1905 or 1906 – the intervening years would explain why the jacket was now missing. But Muir was able to establish that the pyjamas to which the jacket belonged had been purchased in 1909. Crippen was caught out in a direct lie, and this did as much as anything to convince the jury of his guilt. It took them only 27 minutes to reach their verdict. Crippen was hanged on 23 November 1910. Ethel was tried separately, but acquitted.

Ethel LeNeve emigrated to Canada, but she returned to England in 1916, took a job in a furniture store in Trafalgar Square, and married an accountant there. Her husband is said to have borne a strong resemblance to Crippen. They lived in East Croydon, and in 1954, she revealed her identity to the novelist Ursula Bloom, who had written a novel called *The Girl Who Loved Crippen*. Miss Bloom became a close friend, and it was to her that Ethel LeNeve remarked one day that she had never ceased to love Crippen. She died in 1967, at the age of eighty-four.

Many writers have pointed out that the great mystery remains: why did Crippen kill his wife when he could simply have walked out of her life? In his novel, *Dr Crippen's Diary*, Emlyn Williams settles for the explanation that Crippen gave her hyoscine tablets in mistake for aspirin. Dr Ingleby Oddie, who worked with Muir for the prosecution, had a more plausible theory. It was his belief that Crippen intended to kill his wife with hyoscine, convinced that her death would be ascribed to a heart attack – which is highly likely. What Crippen did not realize is that a large dose of hyoscine does not invariably act as a sedative, but can have the opposite effect. Witnesses claim to have heard screams coming from 39 Hilldrop Crescent on the morning of the murder, and another neighbour heard a loud bang. Crippen possessed a pistol and ammunition. Oddie speculates that the dose of hyoscine, given in a "night cap", caused her to become hysterical and start screaming. If neighbours rushed in, all Crippen's plans would collapse; there would be an inquest, and hyoscine would be discovered. Crippen salvaged what he could of the murder plan, and shot her through the head – the skull was never found. Then he had no alternative but to dismember the body and seek a place to hide it . . .

# Bywaters and Thompson

After the trial of Crippen, the next crime to arouse a comparable sensation was the case of Thompson and Bywaters – in fact, it is arguably the widely publicized *crime passionel* of the period between the two wars.

A little after midnight on 4 October, 1922, a couple were returning to their suburban home in Ilford, Essex, after an evening at the theatre. Suddenly, a man sprang out of the shadows and attacked the husband. The woman was heard to scream: "Oh don't! Oh don't!", but it was too late. Her husband lay on the pavement, and the man ran off into the darkness.

Passers-by helped her and called a doctor; he discovered that the man was already dead. The woman, twenty-eight-year-old Edith Thompson, was escorted home by the police; she was in shock, and told them she had no idea what had happened. Her husband had simply collapsed, she said; she thought he had had one of his heart attacks.

The next morning, the police informed her that her husband, Percy Thompson, had died of number of stab wounds; she still maintained that she had no clear memory of what had happened. But eventually she was able to recall that her husband had been "attacked by a strange man".

By now, the police had heard a name that interested them:

Dr Arnold Axilrod, a Minneapolis dentist, broke one of the major rules of dental surgeons and often administered anaesthetic to female patients without the presence of a nurse. One seventeen-year-old girl complained that she had been given a pill that knocked her out for several hours.

On 23 April, 1955, the body of twenty-one-year-old Mary Moonen was discovered lying by the side of the road. She had been strangled. Medical examination revealed that she had recently had sexual relations, and that she was three months pregnant. Her husband, a soldier, had been in Korea for more than three months. When it was discovered that Mrs Moonen had had an appointment with Axilrod the evening before, he was arrested.

Axilrod admitted that she had been to see him the previous evening, to tell him she was pregnant, then claimed he had "blacked out". When newspapers reported the case, twenty more women came forward to complain that they had been put to sleep by Dr Axilrod for a period of hours. And Mary Moonen's sister, who had recommended Dr Axilrod to Mary, admitted that Axilrod had anaesthetized her for long periods, then talked "suggestively" to her. "I thought he was kidding".

In court, the prosecution accused Axilrod of habitually having sex with female patients under anaesthetic. Axilrod was sentenced to a period of from five to twenty years in prison.

Frederick Bywaters, a young man who had once lodged with the Thompsons, but had left after a quarrel with the husband. Percy Thompson's brother Richard believed that Bywaters – a laundry steward on a P & O liner – was at present at sea. But Superintendent Frederick Wensley, the detective in charge of the case, soon ascertained this was not true. In fact, Bywaters, a young man of twenty, was soon traced to the home of Edith's parents. Brought in for questioning, he seemed arrogant and irritable; in spite of his youth, he was obviously a highly dominant character. But when some spots on the sleeve of his jacket were identified as blood, Wensley informed him that he was going to be detained. He insisted he knew nothing of the death of Percy Thompson.

By this time, the police had obtained a search warrant; and what they found in Edith Thompson's home would eventually condemn her to death: a series of letters written by Edith Thompson to Frederick Bywaters, and signed "Peidi". They made it clear that these two were lovers.

It was Edith who broke first. Crossing the yard at the Ilford police station, she caught a glimpse of Bywaters through the library window. She suddenly cried: "Oh God, what can I do? Why did he do it? I didn't want him to do it. I must tell the truth." And minutes later, in the CID office, she had admitted that the man who stabbed her husband to death was Frederick Bywaters. Soon afterwards, Bywaters also confessed. He admitted waiting for the couple at the end of the road, then grabbing Thompson and asking him to divorce his wife. They grappled, he said, and he pulled out a knife. "He got the worst of it." Mrs Thompson, he insisted, knew nothing about the murder; she had been standing at some distance, "spellbound", at the time . . .

If that had been all, Frederick Bywaters would have hanged alone for the murder of Percy Thompson. But the letters shed an altogether more sinister complexion on the affair. For, if they were to be believed, Edith had been attempting to get rid of her husband by poisoning him with ground glass – a light bulb pounded into pieces – "big pieces too" – but he had found one of them in his porridge.

The dead man was exhumed, and his stomach examined – by Bernard Spilsbury – for signs of poisoning with pow- dered glass. Spilsbury concluded that Edith's account was pure imagination.

Nevertheless, when the trial opened on 6 December 1922, Edith Thompson stood beside her lover in the dock. The jury heard how, in the summer of the previous, year – 1921 – the love affair had started on holiday on the Isle of Wight. The Thompsons had gone there with Edith's younger sister Avis Graydon, and her boyfriend Freddy Bywaters, who was a friend of her brothers. Edith had known him since he was a schoolboy (even now he was only eighteen).

Edith had married Percy Thompson when she was twenty- two, in 1915; her husband, a shipping clerk was two years her senior. Percy had joined the London Scottish Regiment, and his wife, who was a romantic young woman, inclined to hysteria, had taken to her bed. However, Thompson proved to have heart trouble, and was soon invalided out. Thompson seems to have been dull but reliable, and his pay was poor; in fact, Edith contributed more to the family budget with her pay as the manageress of a millinery firm in the City, for which she received the generous (for 1922) salary of £6 a week.

It seems that the lovers were first attracted to one another on the Isle of Wight holiday, and when Bywaters kissed Edith, she made no protest. But Thompson noticed nothing of the flirtation – he probably regarded Bywaters as little more than a child – and liked the young man enough to suggest that he come and lodge

In the 1920s many major criminals in London tended to be men renowned for their sheer masculine toughness rather than as businessmen-gangsters. East End villains such as Jew Jack "The Chopper King", Wassle Newman, Jimmy Spinks and Dodger Mullins (who was later to become something of a mentor to the Krays) were legendary for their displays of brute force. Newman was reputed to toughen his fists by tossing bricks in the air and punching them as they came down; but he was no master of organized crime. He simply enjoyed being a bully, and would go into pubs and take away the customers' beer, daring them to protest. Mullins was notorious for his perfunctory views on the fairer sex, and once disposed of a girlfriend he had tired of by pushing her out of a moving car. She broke her back. Spinks was a bully like Newman; when actually asked to pay for some fish and chips he was guzzling, he tossed the cat belonging to the shop's owners into the chip-fryer. One Glasgow "hard man", Jimmy "Razzle Dazzle" Dalziel, was so afraid of having his masculinity questioned that he would always dance with a member of his gang, the "Parlour Boys", rather than be seen being sentimental with a woman.

with them. Freddy accepted the suggestion, and a week later told Edith he was in love with her. They sealed their love with a kiss – but, at this stage, went no further.

Two months later – in August – Percy Thompson realized that he had made a mistake in inviting Bywaters to live with them. The young man was unmistakably sweet on Edith, and she encouraged him by allowing him to fetch and carry for her. In fact, this was what led to the quarrel that caused Freddy Bywaters to leave their home. One warm afternoon, as they sat in the garden waiting for the arrival of Avis Graydon, Edith, who was sewing, asked for a pin. Bywaters rushed in to get one. Percy Thompson was in a grumpy mood, and made some sarcastic remark about her desire to have people at her beck and call. The two began to bicker. Later, at tea, (Avis was late) Thompson continued to be grumpy, and made some critical remarks about Edith's family. In the garden, Freddy heard a crash as a chair overturned, and a gasp of pain from Edith as she was thrown

across the room. Bywaters made the mistake of interfering, and
was told to pack his bags and get out.

How the love affair continued is not clear – except that the
lovers now had to meet secretly. Neither is it known when
she cast aside her inhibitions and became the young man's
mistress. But from 9 September, Bywaters was away at sea,
and "Peidi" wrote to him at every opportunity ("darling your
old pal is getting quite a sport. On Saturday I was first in the Egg
and Spoon race and first in the 100-yard Flat race and third in the
50-yards last race . . .") When he returned, they began to meet
secretly again. Percy Thompson, now thoroughly suspicious,
waited at the station one day, and saw Edith get off the train
with Bywaters. He waited until later, at home, to upbraid her,
sneering that Bywaters had seen him at the station and "run
away". When Edith reported this aspersion to her lover, he lost
no time in calling at the house and insisting that he had not run
away – he had simply not seen Thompson. When Bywaters
told Percy Thompson that he was making Edith's life hell, the
husband replied with asperity: "I've got her and I'll keep her."

In November Bywaters went back to sea in the *Morea*, and
there were more letters. Thompson wanted his wife to have
a baby; she refused angrily. Then she suddenly decided she
preferred domestic peace, and told her lover that she had given
way and "surrendered to him unconditionally" – a phrase that
sounds as if it was intended to arouse jealousy. Now the letters
begin to contain daydreams of getting rid of her husband. How
about poisoned chocolates? Or hyoscine, the drug Crippen had
used? She might poison him with gas if they had gas in the
house . . . But perhaps a ground electric light bulb would serve
just as well? Or an overdose of opium? It was soon after this
that she told her lover that she had tried powdered glass three
times, but that she had decided to give up these attempts at
murder after her husband found a large piece of glass in his
porridge; further attempts could wait until Bywaters returned.
She reassured Bywaters that if Percy died, there would be no
suspicion because of his bad heart.

The *Morea* was away on a long voyage – to Australia – so Edith
had plenty of time to daydream. But finally – on 23 September,
1922 – the long wait was over. They met at a restaurant opposite
her office in Aldersgate Street. On Saturday morning she got
time off from work and they spent the morning in the park.
They even seem to have found an opportunity to make love,
for she writes tenderly about "what happened last night".

She was remorseful about going to the theatre with her

In 1918, as we shall see, New Orleans had its own series of "Ripper murders": an individual who became known. as "the Mad Axe Man" broke into houses and attacked sleepers with a hatchet; he also cut their throats with a razor. He was never caught; but, like the Ripper murders, this series of crimes suddenly ceased. The Axe Man crimes simply fail to fit the pattern of murder as it had been known up till then. He was not even a "degenerate" - at least, there were no sexual attacks on the victims. A new age of murder had begun.

This is apparent even to the most casual student of crime. The Crippen murder is basically the "old fashioned" type of crime; it might have been dramatised by an Elizabethan playwright. It is essentially a drama of good against evil, of a fairly decent human under the strain of temptation, giving way to "diabolic impulses" - like Macbeth. This element can be found in most classic murder cases - the Red Barn murder, Lizzie Borden, Crippen, William Herbert Wallace. The Victorians found it necessary to apply the same explanation to the strange crimes of Jack the Ripper who killed and disembowelled five prostitutes in 1888; the favourite theory was that he was some sort of religious maniac - perhaps also a surgeon - driven mad by brooding on sin and prostitution. Now, more than a century later, we can see that he was an ordinary sadist, a man who - probably when drunk - had an overwhelming urge to cut open women. And our knowledge of modern murderers of this type - we now call them "serial killers" - enables us to say with a fair degree of confidence that he was a member of the working class, not some unbalanced doctor or lawyer (or member of the royal family, as a recent theory has it).

husband, and advised her lover to "do something to make **199** you forget" – perhaps take Avis out. "I'll be hurt I know, but I want you to hurt me – I do really . . ."

In fact, Bywaters spent the evening with her parents in Upper Norwood. Then, with a sheath knife in his pocket, he had made his way to Ilford to meet them on their return from the theatre . . .

This, then, was the evidence presented before Mr Justice Shearman, who was clearly horrified by the letters and all they implied. "Right-minded persons will be filled with disgust", he told the jury. The Solicitor General, Sir Thomas Inskip, who presented the case for the prosecution, found it an easy task to convince the jury that Edith Thompson was a wicked and abandoned woman who had planned the murder of her husband. The letters – presented by the prosecution in telling but misleading extracts – left no doubt of it. Edith spoke in her own defence, alleging that that she was deliberately misleading her lover into thinking she wanted to kill her husband when her real motive was to keep his love. (She might have been more honest if she had said "keep him interested".)

After a hostile summing-up from the judge, the jury took only two hours to find both defendants guilty. When Mr Justice Shearman read aloud the death sentence, Edith cried: "I am not guilty. Oh God, I am not guilty." The date of the execution was set for 6 January, 1923. Three days before this, Bywaters told his mother that although *he* was guilty and deserved to hang, Edith had no idea he intended to attack her husband that night. But a last minute appeal – based on this "confession" – to the Home Secretary was rejected only hours before the execution. Both were hanged at precisely 9 a.m., she in Holloway, he in Pentonville. Edith Thompson was in such a state of collapse that she had to be carried to the scaffold.

Was she guilty? Certainly not of planning the events of the night of 4 October. But although the sixty-two letters fail to prove that she really intended her husband to die, they leave no doubt that it was she who put the idea of killing Percy Thompson into her lover's head. Her letters about ground glass and poison, whether fantasy or not, undoubtedly convinced Frederick Bywaters that Percy Thompson had to die. Whether or not that constitutes guilt must be left to the judgement of the reader.

# chapter five

# EARLY 20TH CENTURY CRIMES OF PASSION

*Crimes of passion murders are committed all over the world, even following the same pattern, without there being a connection between the cases except in the fact that they are similar in genre. In the early twentieth century the American equivalent of the Bywaters and Thompson murder (see page 000) was the Hall-Mills case; it became the great American cause célèbre of the 1920s. And another case, although murder is not a humorous subject, aroused universal hilarity due to the fact that the wife's lover lived in various attics throughout their fifteen-year love affair.*

## The Hall-Mills Murders

On 16 September 1922, a courting couple taking a stroll near Brunswick, New Jersey, came upon two corpses in a country lane. They proved to be those of the local minister Edward Wheeler Hall, who was forty-one, and of one of his choir singers, Mrs Eleanor Mills, thirty-four. Scattered around the bodies were various torn letters, and the minister's calling card was propped against one of his feet. Both had been shot dead; the woman's throat had been cut from ear to ear, and her tongue and vocal cords removed. The letters proved to be love letters from Mrs Mills to the Reverend Hall, and proved conclusively that she had been his mistress for some time.

Clearly, this was a *crime passionnel*, and all the evidence pointed towards the minister's wife Frances, seven years his senior, and her two brothers Willie and Henry – the latter was an expert shot. But quarrels between two lots of country police about their jurisdiction, and incredible official bungling, finally led a Grand Jury to decide that there was insufficient evidence to charge anyone with the murders.

Four years later, the case was reopened when the husband of a parlourmaid in the minister's household tried to get his marriage annulled, and made some amazing accusations. Arthur Riehl stated that the parlourmaid, Louise Geist, had learned that the minister and his mistress had planned to elope, and had passed on this information to Mrs Hall. On the night of the murder, Mrs Hall, her brother Willie, and Louise Geist drove out to the lovers' lane where the couple planned to meet, and killed the two of them. Louise received $5,000 for her part in the crime and for her silence. The newspapers made the accusation into front-page headlines, and Mrs Hall and her brothers were arrested.

Some of the most telling evidence against them came from a bizarre lady who became known as the Pig Woman; she was Mrs Jane Gibson, who ran a pig farm near De Russey's Lane, the scene of the murder, and who claimed that at 10.30 on the night of 14 September 1922 she had passed close to the crab apple tree under which the bodies were later found, and heard a quarrel, followed by shots. But the Pig Woman's mother, who was also in court, insisted that her daughter was a pathological liar. During the trial, the Pig Woman collapsed – she proved to be suffering from cancer – and had to give her evidence from a hospital bed in the courtroom.

But the most impressive evidence concerned the visiting card propped by the dead man's foot. It had been in a safe in the State Prosecutor's office since the dead after the murder. And when examined in the Middlesex County fingerprint laboratory, it had been found to contain a fingerprint. Lieutenant Fred Drewen mounted the stand and testified that he had taken the fingerprints of Willie Stevens, and that the print on the visiting card was that of Stevens's left index finger. Next, the head of the Bureau of Records of the Newark Police Department, Edward H. Schwartz, testified that he had examined the card and found that the fingerprint on it was that of Willie Stevens. Finally, Joseph Faurot, who had ended as New York's Deputy Police Commissioner, mounted the stand. He not only testified that the fingerprint was that of Willie Stevens, but produced transparencies of the accused man's fingerprints, which he projected on a screen, explaining to the jury his reasons for having no doubt. In an English or French court of law, that would have settled the case; unless Willie Stevens could explain how his fingerprints came to be on the minister's calling card, the jury would have concluded that it was he who had placed the card against the dead man's foot.

Fortunately for the defendants, there was a dramatic interruption; Alexander Simpson, the prosecutor, announced that the Pig Woman was at death's door, and about to sink into a coma. So Faurot stood down to make room for the Pig Woman's doctor, and the judge announced that the trial would be adjourned for the time being.

Back on the stand a few days later, Schwartz and Faurot again insisted that the fingerprint on the card was that of Willie Stevens, although they agreed that being exposed to the weather for thirty-six hours might have impaired the print.

When the maid, Louise Geist, appeared on the stand, she testified that, on the morning after the murder, Willie had told her that "something terrible happened last night". And another witness, Marie Demarest, told how a private detective hired by Mrs Hall had tried to bribe her to suppress part of her testimony.

Things looked black for the defendants. Yet, incredibly, the defence made no real attempt to discredit the most serious piece of evidence: the calling card. Robert J. McCarter told the jury: "I charge with all the solemnity that is involved in it that the card is a fraud." But he made no attempt to explain how a fraudulent fingerprint could be fabricated, or how, if the card itself was a fraud, Willie Stevens had been induced to put his fingerprint on it. The jury was apparently incurious about this vital point. On 3 December 1926, after deliberating for five hours, they returned a verdict of not guilty. James Mills, the sexton and husband of the murdered woman, remarked that he was not surprised, since money could buy anything . . .

At this distance in time, the solution to this "unsolved" murder case seems obvious. The defence was correct about one thing: Frances Hall had no idea that Eleanor Mills was her husband's mistress. When she found out – probably from overhearing a telephone conversation about an elopement – she summoned her brothers, and they hurried off to administer summary justice. Mrs Hall may have been doubly enraged because she genuinely liked Eleanor Mills and had always treated her with kindness. If the Pig Woman's testimony is correct, Hall was shot first, above the ear, while Eleanor ran away; they found her with the aid of a torch, dragged her back and shot her beside her lover. Then the infuriated wife slit her throat and removed the vocal cords that had been responsible for the sweet voice that had seduced her husband.

Then why was she acquitted, when all the evidence pointed to her guilt? The answer may lie in the flamboyant manner of the prosecuting counsel, a native of Jersey City, who had referred to the residents of Somerset County, where the trial took place, as country bumpkins. During the trial, his extrovert city manners evidently grated on the jury. It seems probable that the verdict was a gesture of defiance and contempt towards State Senator Alexander Simpson rather than an affirmation of belief in the innocence of Mrs Hall and her brothers.

# The Walburger Case

This case adds a touch of humour to crime as the murderer takes on the ingenious disguise of a ghost.

As early as 1908, Bert Walburger, an overweight Minneapolis

---

In March 1948, James Camb, a deck steward on a liner, was tried for the murder of an attractive passenger, actress Gay Gibson. The unusual feature of the case was that Gay Gibson's body was never recovered. Her cabin on the liner Durban Castle had been found empty on the morning of 18 October, 1947, and it was at first assumed that she had fallen overboard. Then a watchman stated that in the early hours of the morning, someone had pushed the bell in her cabin, and that when he went to answer it, James Camb had opened the door.

Questioned by the police, Camb stated that he had been invited to Gay Gibson's cabin, and that she had received him wearing only a dressing gown. He claimed that, in the act of sexual intercourse, she had been foaming at the mouth and then died. When the watchman had knocked at the door, he had panicked and pushed her body out of the porthole.

The fact that urine stains on the bedsheets suggested strangulation, and the girl's pyjamas were missing (suggesting that she had been wearing them when pushed out of the porthole) led the jury to find Camb guilty; he was sentenced to life imprisonment.

cabinet-maker, suspected that his wife Dotty was having an affair with a sixteen year old employee of a paint and varnish company named Gus Huberman. This seemed to suggest that the rather plain young woman was sex starved – or starved for romance – for Huberman was slight and pale, with a receding chin. Or perhaps the youth aroused her maternal instinct, for she had recently lost her own eight year old son, and Huberman was an orphan. A private detective hired by the jealous husband rushed back one day to report that Huberman and Dotty Walburger had taken a train to Chicago. Attempts to track them down were a failure, but Dotty soon returned of own accord; she admitted her infidelity and asked for a divorce. Her husband refused, on the grounds that his alimony would benefit "that shrimp".

Three years later, in 1911, Walburger decided that his rival had left town, and dismissed the private detective. In fact, Gus Huberman was by then spending most of his nights in the bed of their deceased son Raymond, and his days in the bed of Dotty Walburger. Eventually, he moved into the attic room in the Walburger's house, rendered confident by the knowledge that Walburger was too corpulent to climb the ladder and scramble through the trapdoor.

One day, Bert Walburger looked up from the garden, and saw Gus Huberman's face looking down at him. Dotty told him he was imagining things, and he reluctantly decided he must be suffering from overwork. During the day, Gus would make love to Dotty and help her with the housework. He was a combination of pet, houseboy and stallion. Meanwhile, Bert Walburger's business had become so prosperous that he now owned a factory that employed fifteen hundred people; Gus later claimed that his advice, passed on to Bert via his wife, had saved the business on a number of critical occasions.

Up in his attic, Gus listened in to the life that went on below. Admittedly, Sundays in summer were too hot, and on winter nights, he had to struggle to avoid coughs and sneezes, and had to learn to move as silently as a mouse. Yet life was smooth and pleasant enough, and he was neither sex starved nor underfed.

Bert's increasing prosperity led them to change house a number of times; when that happened, Dotty had to smuggle Gus into the attic again. There he spent his days reading Dickens, Mark Twain and any old magazines Dotty could provide. She also provided him with pocket money, but he had little opportunity to spend it.

During World War I, Gus announced that he was going to

fight for his country; Dotty's tears and pleas dissuaded him – temporarily. Finally, patriotism triumphed, and he went and enlisted. The sergeant's jibes about his size sent him scurrying back to his attic within hours. Now he was a deserter, he made doubly sure that no one suspected his presence.

Soon after that, Bert decided to retire, and the Walburgers moved out to Los Angeles. Gus went on ahead, and hung around until they arrived. He was trailing them as they went house-hunting in Los Angeles. Dotty rejected several houses because they had no attic. Finally, the Walburgers found a suitable place, and Gus moved into his fifth attic in fourteen years.

The end came some months later, on 29 August, 1922. Neighbours heard shots, and a woman screaming. They rang the police, who had to break into the house through the bolted front door. Bert Walburger was lying dead on the floor, shot through the head with a .25, a lady-size gun. Dotty Walburger was found locked in the closet in her locked bedroom. She told how she was getting undressed in the clothes closet when she heard shots; then the closet door was locked behind her. That was all she could tell them . . .

At first, nothing seemed to be missing. Then Dotty recalled her husband's diamond studded watch, and the large bank roll he habitually carried around. This must obviously have been the burglar objective. The investigation soon reached a dead end. The house proved to be full of fingerprints that the police were unable to identify, but whoever the burglar was, he had no criminal record.

A year later, the diamond-studded watch turned up – in the waistcoat pocket of an accountant named Sol Shephard. He was Mrs Walburger's accountant, and he said she had given him the watch. Dotty confirmed this – she had found the watch under a mat, and had only failed to notify the police because she imagined they were no longer interested.

A neighbour now came forward to offer evidence that seemed to incriminate Mrs Walburger – he told how, soon after the murder, she had asked him to destroy a small revolver by filing it into small pieces. He had dumped these into a tar sump. An enterprising newspaper succeeded in recovering the pieces. Then another neighbour of the Walburgers described how Dotty had asked *him* to dispose of yet another revolver soon after the murder. This was also finally located. It began to look as if Dotty Huberman *could* have killed her husband, then, with a certain amount of ingenuity, locked herself in the closet.

Mrs Walburger was questioned for days. But eventually, the police had to release her. However, before they did this, Mrs Walburger asked to see her accountant, Mr Sol Shepherd . . .

Eight years later, in 1930, Mr Shepherd went to the police and told them that his conscience was troubling him. When he had spoken to Mrs Walburger, she had told him that her dissolute younger brother was living in the attic of her home. Would he please go there, scratch on the wall, and take him food and water? Sol Shepherd did as she asked, and was confronted by a small man with a receding chin, who admitted that he had been living in various attics for years. But he admitted he was tired of his situation, and was anxious to leave. Besides, if the police found him now, it would incriminate Mrs Walburger. So Shepherd drove Gus Huberman to the main highway to San Francisco, and Gus finally detached himself from his mistress of fifteen years.

The police searched Dotty Walburger's former home – she had moved by now to a smaller residence – and found that the attic showed signs of long-time habitation. Soon after that, Gus Huberman was arrested. He was now married, and was working as the caretaker of an apartment building.

Back at the police station, Huberman admitted shooting Bert Walburger. But, he said, it had been an accident. Ever since the Walburger home had been burgled, he had kept a revolver close to hand. That night in August, he had heard the Walburgers returning from an evening out, then quarrelling. Bert had slapped his wife so hard she fell down. So he, Gus, had hastened downstairs, to find Bert Walburger standing over his prostrate wife. When Bert saw his rival, he exploded: "You little rat! What are you doing here?" There was a scuffle, and the gun had gone off. When the struggle was over, Bert Walburger lay dead, and Mrs Walburger was wailing: "Gee this is terrible!" Then Gus saw the answer: lock Dotty in her closet, then lock the bedroom door and retreat to his own attic . . .

The five week trial of Gus Huberman caused a sensation; the story of the "Phantom Lover in the Attic" gripped the imagination of America. But a moving speech from Gus's attorney, Earl Wakeman, ensured the sympathy of the jury for the poor orphan. They decided that he was guilty only of manslaughter, and Gus received a sentence of three years. The truth was, nobody had the heart to see him executed. And since the death of Bert Walburger had taken place eight years earlier, a statute of limitations meant that he was free. He went back to his wife and their apartment building.

Dotty Walburger was tried separately. But when the jury failed to reach an agreement, the DA decided he couldn't face it all over again, and begged to be excused. Mrs Walburger also walked free. She retired to a small apartment, and lived there peacefully until her death.

# Death at the Savoy

In September 1923, after a passionate appeal by the famous advocate Marshall Hall, a British jury acquitted a Frenchwoman who had shot her Egyptian husband to death. It appears to demonstrate that even the British are capable of recognizing that the perpetrator of a *crime passionel* may not be legally guilty. However, this was a case in which the killer hardly deserved clemency.

Madame Fahmy was thirty-three years old, and in the previous year she had married Prince Ali Kemal Fahmy Bey, a handsome and wealthy Egyptian playboy who was ten years her junior. He had fallen violently in love with Marguerite Laurent shortly after she had divorced her previous husband. The prince pursued her to Deauville, where she became his mistress. In December 1922 she became a Moslem, and they were married. But the marriage was unhappy. Madame Fahmy might look slender and vulnerable, but she had a violent temper, and was unaccustomed to being bossed around. Prince Fahmy, on the other hand, had an oriental prejudice in favour of obedient females. The two often clashed violently, and on one occasion he locked her in her cabin for twenty-four hours. "With women", he said, "one must act with energy and be severe". The prince also had a male secretary, Said Ernani, with whom he was rumoured to have a homosexual relationship.

On 9 July, 1923, the Fahmy's were staying at London's Savoy Hotel, and having a disagreement about some minor operation which she needed; she wanted to go to Paris and he wanted her to have it in London. At dinner there was a violent disagreement, and the princess was heard to say (in French – she spoke no English): "You shut up or I'll smash this bottle over your head." When the bandleader asked her if there was any tune she would like to hear, she replied: "I don't want any music – my husband threatened to kill me tonight." The maestro bowed politely and said: "I hope you will still be here tomorrow, madame." Later, her husband asked her to dance but she refused; clearly, Madame Fahmy was by no means under the thumb of her husband.

At about 1.30 that following morning, a porter was passing their suite when the prince came out in his pyjamas. "Look what she has done", he said, indicating a red scratch on his cheek. Madame Fahmy, still in evening dress, came out of the room, and said something the porter did not understand. He warned them that they might wake the other guests, and they went back into the room. As the porter turned away, a little dog ran out, and the prince bent down and whistled for it, snapping his fingers. A few moments later, three shots rang out. The porter ran back to the open door and saw Madame Fahmy throwing down a pistol, and her husband lying on the floor and bleeding from the head. A few hours later the prince died in hospital, and Madame Fahmy was arrested. Her trial opened less than two weeks later, on 23 July, 1923.

One thing that seems perfectly clear is that if the prince treated his wife badly, she was able to give as good as she got. But her advocate, Edward Marshall Hall, based his defence on the notion of a poor, oppressed woman who had made the mistake of marrying a despotic oriental of perverted sexual tastes, who often beat and kicked her. In fact, the secretary denied that his master had ever kicked her, although he admitted that the prince had once hit his wife so violently that he had dislocated her jaw.

The manager of the Savoy, giving evidence, described how Madame Fahmy had said to him, in French: "I lost my head." Marshall Hall suggested that a better translation of "J'ai perdu la tete" would be: "I was frightened out of my wits." The manager agreed.

The firearms expert, Robert Churchill, testified that although the pistol with which Fahmy was shot was an automatic, the trigger had to be pulled for each shot.

The jury was sent out while Marshall Hall asked the judge to rule against the prosecution, who wanted to question Madame Fahmy about her relations with other men, to prove she was an immoral woman. This, Marshall Hall said, would prejudice the jury against her. He made no attempt to deny that the allegations were true. Nevertheless, the judge ruled in his favour.

In a dramatic final speech, Marshall Hall described Madame Fahmy, crouching like a terrified animal, with the gun in her hands, and then the weapon exploding – to her horror and

consternation. He enacted the scene, pointing the gun at the
jury, then dropping it dramatically. "Members of the Jury, I want
you to open the doors so this Western woman can go out . . ."
he declaimed, in a flagrant appeal to racial prejudice. But they
were convinced, and took a little over an hour to acquit her.

That dramatic final scene, of course, did not and could not
have taken place. A few moments before his death, Prince
Fahmy was whistling for a little dog; the porter had only walked
a few yards when the shots rang out – three of them. The firing
of the gun was obviously no accident – she pressed the trigger
three times. But a sentimental British jury preferred to believe
that a pretty Frenchwoman killed her husband when she was in
a state of terror. (Marshall Hall made doubly sure of an acquittal
by hinting that the quarrel was really about the prince's desire
for anal sex, which his wife had refused.) So Madame Fahmy
walked free, and went on to become a film star, playing the part
of an Egyptian wife.

In the previous year, a British jury had sentenced an obviously
innocent woman – Edith Thompson – to hang; now another jury
acquitted a woman who was obviously guilty. C'est la vie.

# Ruth Snyder

The Snyder and Grey case was responsible for one of the most
macabre images of the 1920s – the photograph of Ruth Snyder
at the moment she was electrocuted, taken by a reporter with a
camera strapped to his ankle.

Ruth's crime – planning the death of her husband – had a pre-
cedent in the previous decade. In 1919, a Cleveland housewife
had hired two Italian thugs to murder her husband, publisher
Daniel D. Kaber, who was confined to his bed following a stroke.
Kaber's father was convinced that his daughter-in-law Eva was
responsible, but there was no evidence against her. He hired
Pinkerton detectives, who were able to prove that Eva had hired
two "hit men" named Pisselli and Calla for $5,000. Eva Kaber and
her two accomplices were all sentenced to life imprisonment.

A fourteen-year-old Swedish girl named Ruth Brown (her
father had anglicized his name from Sorensen) undoubtedly
read about the case, for Mrs Kaber was living in New York
when she was arrested by a detective named Arthur Carey,

and the story made headlines. Photographs show a remarkable resemblance between Eva Kaber and Ruth Brown – or Ruth Snyder, as she became. And when Ruth Snyder made up her mind that her own husband had to die, she decided on a less obvious method than hiring two thugs.

Ruth, born in 1895, was brought up in conditions of considerable poverty on 125th Street and Morningside, on the West side. She became a telephone operator when she was thirteen, then a stenographer. Life continued to be hard.

In 1914, she was still a telephone operator. One day she mis-routed a call, and was irritably upbraided by the man on the other end. She apologized so charmingly that he rang back and said he was sorry; they conversed, and he introduced himself as Albert Schneider, the art editor of *Motor Boat*, a Hearst publication; he told her that if she wanted a better job, he could probably provide one. Ruth took him up on the offer, and went to work as a secretary for *Motor Boat* in September. Schneider found the blue-eyed blonde delicious, and before Christmas, had proposed. It seems to have been the diamond that she found in a box of chocolates that led her to accept. They were married in the following July, when she was twenty and her husband thirty-three.

It was not a happy marriage. Their temperaments were unsympathetic. Schneider (he was to change his name to Snyder

---

Even in France, *crime passionel* does not always result in acquittal.

In 1951, Leone Bouvier, a peasant girl of St-Macaire-en-Mauges, met a car mechanic named Emile Clenet at a dance, and soon became his mistress. An unattractive girl, who had been brought up in extreme poverty, she craved affection – a characteristic of which several unscrupulous males had already taken advantage. They began meeting regularly on Sundays in a hotel bedroom. When she became pregnant, Clenet told her to procure an abortion; she did, but it made her ill and cost her her factory job. When Clenet then refused to see her again, she purchased a pistol. Seeing Clenet emerging from a cinema, she persuaded him to take her to a carnival, where he admitted to her that he intended to emigrate to North Africa. That night, in the midst of a farewell embrace, she shot him through the head, then went to join her sister in a convent.

Tried in December 1953, it took a jury only a quarter of an hour to find her guilty of murder. She was sentenced to life imprisonment.

a few years later in deference to the anti-German feeling caused
by the war) was a calm, efficient man of somewhat dominant
character – he had been known to overturn a table and stalk out
of a restaurant when the waiter displeased him – who needed a
good hausfrau; Ruth, whose life had been starved of excitement,
wanted to dance, to visit restaurants and holiday resorts, and
to play bridge. She found life as a housewife in Queens, Long
Island, a bore, and she enlivened it with bridge and luncheon
parties. In 1918 she gave birth to a daughter, Lorraine, but it
failed to improve her marriage; Albert Snyder made it clear that
he found fatherhood tiresome.

For the next seven years they continued to quarrel and lead
virtually separate lives – Snyder usually came home late, then
read the paper until bedtime. Ruth moved her mother in with
them to act as baby-sitter, and continued to do as she liked; what
this was, we can only guess from the fact that a notebook found
in her home contained the names of twenty-eight men.

These names included that of Henry Judd Grey, a rather quiet
little corset salesman who wore thick tortoise-shell spectacles.
Ruth had been introduced to him in a cheap Swedish diner
in New York in June 1925. A few weeks later, after a quarrel
with her husband, she returned from vacation on Shelter
Island with her daughter, and went to dine with Judd Grey.
After the meal, they called in at Grey's office, where Ruth
complained of her sunburned shoulders. Grey immediately
produced a remedy called camphor ice, which he rubbed on
her shoulders. Ruth burst into tears, explaining that she was
unaccustomed to such courtly behaviour. Judd kissed her. Then
he offered her a corselet as a gift and, with an audacity probably
due to drink, offered to fit it there and then. Whether their
lovemaking continued on the office floor, or in some nearby
hotel, is unknown; what is certain is that Ruth began spending
nights with him in hotels, and that her husband accepted her
explanation that she was staying with a friend. He even made
no objection when she invented a friend in Albany and went off
there for several days.

They seem to have been an odd pair. Grey was of English
puritan stock, and he was puritanical by nature, as well as mild
and gentle. He is certainly one of the most unlikely murderers in
criminal history. Ruth was undoubtedly the more dominant of
the two. But then, Grey seemed to enjoy being dominated – he
liked to embrace her ankles, and called her "Momsie". And the
more they made love, the more he wanted her. In fact, he was
already married, to a girl who would have suited Albert Snyder

down to the ground, a "home girl" whose major virtue was that she was "a careful and exceptionally exact housekeeper". Unfortunately, Isabel Gray and Albert Snyder never seem to have met.

Grey's salary was considerably smaller than that of Albert Snyder, and his new role as a lover demanded more money than he earned. Ruth seems to have lent – or given – him a number of sums, including a cheque for $200.

It is not clear why Ruth Snyder decided to kill her husband rather than simply running away with Judd Grey. But it is on record that, soon after Ruth became Grey's mistress, Albert Snyder narrowly escaped death on a number of occasions. One evening, when he was tinkering underneath the car, the jack slipped and he was almost crushed to death. Possibly this was an accident – an accident that made Ruth realize how convenient it would have been if Albert *had* been crushed. Not long after this, Snyder was running the car engine in the garage when Ruth brought him a glass of whiskey. It made him oddly dizzy, so that he hardly noticed when the garage door closed. He was almost unconscious from carbon monoxide fumes when he succeeded in staggering outside.

Yet although Albert Snyder told his brother that he thought his wife had tried to kill him, he nevertheless accepted her suggestion that he should insure his life. Perhaps he thought that no harm would come to him for the sake of a mere $1,000. In fact, the thousand dollar policy which he signed in triplicate was actually three policies, whose total amounted to more than $100,000. It was Ruth who paid the premiums.

A few months later, in July 1926, Albert Snyder awoke from a doze on the settee gasping for air; the room was full of coal gas. Ruth explained that she must have accidentally stepped on the tube connecting the gas cock to the fire, and pulled it off. In the following January she gave Albert a medicine to cure hiccups; it was not Alka-Seltzer but bichloride of mercury, and made him seriously ill.

When Ruth first raised the subject of killing her husband, Grey was deeply shocked. But as time went by, he became accustomed to it. To begin with, he thought it was idle talk. But when she announced, in September 1926, that she had definitely decided to kill Albert, Grey told her she ought to have her head examined. Still, he was interested enough to ask her how she intended to do it, and listened with fascination to her plan to knock her husband unconscious with a sleeping powder, then turn on the gas. In the following month, when she asked him to help her in killing her husband, he blenched and told her she was foolish to entertain such ideas. But when she emphasized how much she hated having sex with her husband, and how often he demanded his marital rights, he began to waver.

It seems absurd that, after so much planning, the murder itself was almost criminally incompetent. Grey, who had been drinking heavily to give himself courage, entered the house late on the evening of 20 March, 1927, and hid himself to await their return from a party. Ruth's mother was away, and Grey concealed himself in her bedroom. There he drank more whiskey.

At 2 a.m. the Snyders returned, together with eight-year-old Lorraine, who had also been to the party. Ruth was sober, but she had made sure that her husband had drunk more than enough. By 2.30, Snyder was asleep, and Ruth had sneaked out of her twin bed to summon her lover. Judd entered their bedroom carrying a sash weight, and took an almighty swing at the head of the sleeping man. In his excitement he missed, grazing Snyder's skull, and the intended victim was shocked awake. Grey hit him again, then staggered as Snyder punched him – Snyder, the boating fantatic, was far bigger than Grey. They struggled, and as Grey tried to free his necktie from Snyder's powerful grip, he dropped the sashweight. "Momsie, help me!" he gasped, and Ruth found the sash weight and hit her husband on the back of the head. Albert Snyder went limp.

The lovers now stuffed chloroform-soaked rags into Snyder's mouth and nostrils, then wound picture-wire around his throat so that it cut in deeply. Already, they were overdoing it – no burglar would have gone to so much trouble after knocking his victim unconscious. They then disarranged the furniture to lend weight to the burglar story, and pulled open the drawers. Grey changed into one of his victim's shirts – his own was bloodstained – and finally left, after tying her hands and ankles and binding a gag around her mouth. He declined her request to knock her unconscious, which proved to be another major mistake.

Lorraine Snyder was awakened by a tapping on her bedroom door, and opened it to find her mother lying on the floor, her wrists and ankles still bound. Ruth told her to summon the neighbours, and the child ran across the street to awaken Mr and Mrs Mulhauser. The latter found that Ruth had untied her hands, but not her ankles. Among the police who were summoned was Detective Arthur Carey, who had arrested Mrs Kaber seven years earlier. And Carey, like the young doctor who had preceded him, instantly smelt a rat. Ruth claimed that she had been attacked by a big man with a moustache, but failed to explain how she saw him in the dark. The doctor had already observed that she was unbruised and showed no other sign of rough handling. Carey decided that no professional burglar (or burglars) would have knocked Snyder unconscious, then chloroformed him and strangled him with picture wire; this was obviously the work of someone who wished him dead. And surely Ruth would have untied her own ankles after she had freed her hands, not waited for the Mulhauers to arrive? The sheer disorder of the house also suggested that the "burglary" had been staged by enthusiastic amateurs. A gun left on the bed also aroused Carey's suspicions – surely burglars would not have left it behind when Ruth might have freed herself and pursued them with a volley of shots? Finally, the bloodstained sash weight was found in the tool chest; why should a burglar go to the trouble of concealing it when he could simply drop it on the floor?

As the interrogation continued, Ruth was left in no doubt that the police knew she was lying. She stubbornly denied this, and also denied – what was equally obvious – that she must have had an accomplice. With typical incompetence, Grey had left behind a tie pin with his initials; Ruth explained that J.G. stood for Jessie Guishard, her husband's previous fiancée, who had died, and to begin with, the police believed her. But when they found the notebook containing the names of twenty-eight men, and found that of Judd Grey among them, they lost no time jumping to the correct conclusion. And when the cancelled cheque for $200 was found – made out to Judd Grey – Ruth finally began to look worried. But still she persisted in her story about the rough man with the black moustache.

After more than twelve hours of questioning, she was removed to the police station, and there she was told that Judd Grey had confessed. It was untrue – he had not even been found – but it convinced her. Believing herself betrayed, she felt outraged. So when Police Commissioner McLaughlin stated: "Grey helped to kill your husband, didn't he?", she answered defiantly: "Yes."

The rest was predictable. Grey was arrested at half past midnight in the Onondaga Hotel, Syracuse. He had already told a friend that he had been in Ruth's house when two burglars had broken in and attacked Ruth and her husband; he said he had hidden in a closet until they had gone. The friend had obligingly disposed of some bloodstained clothes. Now Grey told the police that he had not even been in the

Snyders' house that night. But when the police told him they had found the train ticket that proved he had travelled from Syracuse to Long Island, he admitted it quietly. By now, Ruth Snyder's confession was in all the headlines. Grey went on to tell the whole story, omitting no detail.

The trial lasted from 18 April, 1927, to 9 May. Ruth Snyder's defence blamed Judd Grey; Judd Grey's defence blamed Ruth Snyder. Ruth insisted that Grey had overpowered her and killed her husband; Grey was more chivalrous, but there was no doubt that he blamed his mistress. The jury reached a unanimous verdict of guilty – no other was possible – and both were sentenced to death.

Grey went to his death calmly and philosophically on 12 January, 1928. Ruth died hard; a few days before her execution she began to scream for hours every night. Like Edith Thompson, she had to be half-carried to her death. A reporter on the New York *Daily News* had a camera strapped to his ankle, with a shutter release in his pocket. As all eyes were fixed on the straining body, hurled against the straps by the powerful current, he stepped into the aisle and raised his trouser leg. The picture was published the following morning over the whole front page of the *Daily News*; it was subsequently syndicated all over the world.

# The Ruxton Case

The commonest motive for the *crime passionel* is jealousy. But most such murders are committed in hot blood, and in about one third of all such cases, the murderer commits suicide. This explains why so few jealousy-murders are to be found in books such as this; the details are usually so commonplace that there is virtually no story.

The Ruxton case is one of the most striking exceptions. 29 September, 1935, was a cool autumn day; a young lady had paused in her afternoon walk to lean on the parapet of a bridge across a pretty stream called the Gardenholme Linn. As she stared at the narrow, rocky stream, she noticed some kind of bundle that had jammed against a boulder. Something that looked unpleasantly like a human arm was sticking out of it.

The police were on the scene by mid-afternoon, and had

soon discovered two human heads on the bank of the Linn, as well as four bundles, each containing human remains – thigh bones, legs, pieces of flesh, and an armless torso. One piece of newspaper wrapped round two upper arms proved to be the *Sunday Graphic* for 15 September 1935.

When, the following day, Professor John Glaister – author of a classic *Medical Jurisprudence and Toxicology* – arrived with his colleague Dr Gilbert Millar, he quickly realized that this killing was not the work of some terrified amateur; he had taken care to cover his tracks. He had not only dismembered the bodies, but removed the skin from the heads, to make the faces unrecognizable, and cut off the fingertips to make fingerprint identification impossible. He had made only one mistake: instead of tossing the remains into the River Annan, a few hundred yards downstream, he had tossed them into its tributary, the Linn, which had been swollen with heavy rains at the time. If the rain had continued, the parcels would have ended up in the Solway Firth. But there were a few days of fine weather; the stream dwindled to its usual trickle, and the parcels caught in the rocks.

The remains were sent to the Anatomy Department of the University of Edinburgh, and there treated with ether to prevent further decomposition and destroy maggots; then they were "pickled" in a formalin solution. Glaister and Millar found themselves confronted with a human jigsaw puzzle of seventy pieces.

The first task was to sort the pieces into two separate bodies, and this was made easier by the fact that one was six inches shorter than the other. And when it was finally done, Glaister and his team found that they had one almost complete body, the taller one, and one body minus a trunk. There was also an item that caused much bafflement – an enormous single eye, which certainly did not belong to either of the bodies; by some odd chance, this eye, probably from an animal, had also found its way into the Linn.

What could be deduced about the murderer? First, that he was almost certainly a medical man. He had used a knife, not a saw, to dismember the body, and a human body is almost impossible to dismember with a knife without detailed knowledge of the joints. He had also removed the teeth, recognizing that they could lead to identification by a dentist.

Fortunately, the murderer had either lost his nerve or been interrupted, for he had left some of the hair on the smaller body – which, at first, Glaister thought to be that of a man. And when more parcels were found in the river, Glaister found that he had a pair of hands that still had fingertips. After soaking them in hot water, he was able to get an excellent set of fingerprints. And the discovery that the assorted pieces of flesh included three breasts also made it clear that both bodies were of women.

The next problem was the age of the bodies Glaister determined this by means of the skull sutures. Sutures are "joining lines" in the skull, and they seal themselves over the years; they are usually closed completely by the age of forty. In one of the two skulls, the smaller of the two, the sutures were unclosed; in the other, they were almost closed. This indicated that one body was that of a woman of about forty; the other was certainly under thirty. X-rays of the jaw-bone of the younger woman showed that the wisdom teeth had still not pushed through, which meant she was probably in her early twenties. The cartilage, the soft material of which bones are originally made, gradually changes into "caps", called "epiphyses", and the age can also be estimated from how far this change has taken place. The epiphyses of the smaller body confirmed that this was a girl of twenty or so; the other was of a woman approaching middle-age.

As to the cause of death, this was fairly clear. The taller woman had five stab wounds in the chest, several broken bones, and many bruises. The hyoid bone in the neck was broken, indicating strangulation before the other injuries had been inflicted. The swollen and bruised tongue confirmed this inference. Glaister reasoned that a murderer who strangled and beat his victim before stabbing her would probably be in the grip of jealous rage. As to the other body, the signs were that she had been battered with some blunt instrument. It hardly needed a Sherlock Holmes to infer that she had been killed as an afterthought, probably to keep her silent. The fact that the murderer had taken less trouble to conceal her identity pointed to the same conclusion.

Meanwhile, the police were working on their own clues. The *Sunday Graphic* was a special local edition, printed for the Morecambe and Lancaster area. And the clothes in which some of the remains had been wrapped were also distinctive: the head of the younger woman had been wrapped in a pair of child's rompers, and another bundle had been wrapped in a blouse with a patch under the arm . . .

And in Lancaster, a Persian doctor named Buck Ruxton had already attracted the suspicions of the local police. Five days before the remains were found in the Linn, Ruxton – a small, rather good-looking man with a wildly excitable manner – had called on the police and mentioned that his wife had deserted him. The police were investigating the murder of a lady called Mrs Smalley, whose body had been found a year earlier, and in the course of routine investigations, had questioned a domestic in Ruxton's household; he wanted to protest about this harassment. And when he spoke of his wife's disappearance, they were not in the least surprised; they knew that the relations between the two were stormy. Two years before, Mrs Isabella Ruxton had come to the police station to protest that her husband was beating her, and Ruxton had made wild accusations of infidelity against her; however, he had calmed down, and twenty-four hours later the two were apparently again on the best of terms.

The parents of Mrs Ruxton's maid, Mary Rogerson, were not only surprised but incredulous when Ruxton came and told them that their daughter had got herself pregnant by the laundry boy, and that his wife had taken her away for an abortion. Nothing was less likely; Mary was a plain girl, with a cast in one eye, who loved her home and her parents, and spent all her spare time with them; she was as unlikely to get herself pregnant as to rob a bank. In spite of Ruxton's feverish protests, they reported it to the police. On the evening of 9 October 1935, ten days after the remains had been found in the Linn, Ruxton came to the police and burst into tears. People were saying that he had murdered his wife and thrown her into the Linn; they must help him find her. They soothed him and sent him away. But, in fact, Ruxton had been the chief suspect since earlier that day. The Scottish police had been to see the Rogersons, and had shown them the patched blouse. As soon as they saw it, they knew their daughter was dead; Mary had bought it at a jumble sale and patched it under the arm. They were unable to identify the rompers, but suggested that the police show them to Mrs Holme, with whom Mary and the three Ruxton children had spent a holiday earlier that year. And Mrs Holme recognized the rompers as a pair she had given to Mary for the children.

The police spoke to the Ruxton's charlady, Mrs Oxley. She told them that on the day Mrs Ruxton and Mary Rogerson had disappeared, Sunday 15 September 1935, Ruxton had arrived early at her house and explained that it was unnecessary for her to come to work that day – he was taking the children to Morecambe, and his wife had gone to Edinburgh. The following morning, she found the Ruxton's house – at 2 Dalton Square – in a state of chaos, with carpets removed, the bath full of yellow

stains, and a pile of burnt material in the yard. A neighbour told
the police that Ruxton had persuaded her to come and clean up
his house to prepare it for the decorators, claiming that he had
cut his hand badly on a tin of peaches. She and her husband had
obligingly scrubbed out the house. And Ruxton had given them
some bloodstained carpets and a blue suit that was also stained
with blood.

On 12 October, the police questioned Ruxton all night, and at
7.20 the next morning he was charged with the murder of Mary
Rogerson.

In spite of Ruxton's attempts to cover his tracks, and to
persuade various witnesses to offer him false alibis, the truth
about the murders soon became plain. Ruxton was pathologically jealous, although there was no evidence that his "wife" –
they were in fact unmarried – had ever been unfaithful. A week
before the murder, Mrs Ruxton had gone to Edinburgh, where
she had a sister, with a family named Edmondson, who were
close friends of the Ruxtons. The Edmondsons and Mrs Ruxton
had all booked into separate rooms; nevertheless, Ruxton was
convinced that she had spent the night in the bed of Robert
Edmondson, an assistant solicitor in the Town Hall. Ruxton had
driven to Edinburgh to spy on them. The following Saturday,
Isabella Ruxton had gone to spend the afternoon and evening
with two of her sisters in Blackpool. Convinced that she was
in a hotel room with a man, Ruxton had worked himself into a
jealous frenzy, and when she came back far later than expected,
he began to beat her – probably in an attempt to make her confess
her infidelities – then throttled her unconscious and stabbed her.
Mary Rogerson had probably heard the screams and come in to
see what was happening; Ruxton believed she was his wife's
confidant in her infidelities, and killed her too. He had spent
the next day dismembering the bodies and packing them in
straw; that night, he made his first trip north to dispose of the
bodies . . .

Ruxton's counsel, Norman Birkett, must have known that his
client did not stand a ghost of a chance. His line of defence was
that the bodies found in the Linn were not those of Isabella
Ruxton and Mary Rogerson, but of some other persons. But
when the medical experts – Glaister, Millar, and Professor
Sydney Smith – gave their evidence, it was obvious that the
identity of the bodies had been established beyond all possible
doubt. One photograph, which has subsequently been used in
every account of the case, superimposed the larger of the two
skulls on a photograph of Mrs Ruxton. She had a rather long,

horsy face, and it was obvious that the two fitted together with gruesome exactitude. Ruxton seemed determined to trap himself in a web of lies and evasions. The result was a unanimous verdict of guilty, arrived at in only one hour. He was hanged at Strangeways jail, Manchester, on 12 May 1936.

Yet examination of the evidence – and of Glaister's famous book *Medico–legal Aspects of the Ruxton Case* (1937) – makes it clear that Ruxton came very close indeed to getting away with murder. If he had taken the trouble to remove Mary Rogerson's fingertips, and destroyed the telltale breast tissue as well as the trunk (which was never found), the evidence against him would have remained purely circumstantial; and since British juries are unwilling to convict on circumstantial evidence, he might well have been given the benefit of the doubt. Glaister's forensic skill and Ruxton's failure of nerve played an equal part in bringing him to the gallows.

# chapter six

# COLD-BLOODED CRIMES OF PASSION

*What brings a person to commit murder – high emotion, unrequited love, monetary gain? Certainly in the case of Albert Guay, who had a bomb planted on a plane which not only killed his wife but twenty-two other people as well; or when you kill someone that you don't really even love, as in the case of Ruth Ellis, just because they were refusing to speak to you, the answer is sheer cold-bloodedness. The reasoning behind these sort of crimes of passion surely cannot be explained in any other terms.*

## The Guay Case

If there was a prize for the most cold-blooded of all crimes of passion, it would probably go to Albert Guay.

On 9 September, 1949, a Quebec Airways Dakota DC-3 on a flight from Montreal to Seven Islands exploded in mid-air, only minutes after take-off. The plane dived into inaccessible forest near Sault-au-Cochon, forty miles northeast of Quebec. All twenty-three passengers were killed. Since witnesses noticed that the engines were still running as it crashed, engine failure was clearly not the cause of the disaster. But there was scorched metal in the luggage compartment, suggesting an explosion. Chemical analysis revealed minute traces of dynamite.

A careful check of every item of freight against the company's list revealed that only one seemed to be missing, a "religious statuette" weighing twenty-six pounds. But there was no record of its sender; all the reception could remember about the person who delivered it was that it was a woman dressed in black. An appeal through the news media failed to trace her. But ten days later, a taxi driver came forward to say that he had picked up a woman of this description on the day of the explosion. And he could also remember the address from which he had picked her up. This proved to be the home of a woman named Marie Pitre. But when the police tried to call on her, they learned that she was in hospital, recovering from the effects of an overdose of sleeping tablets.

As soon as she was able to give an interview, Marie Pitre told them how she had come to take the parcel to the airport. For many years she had been the mistress of a Quebec jeweller named Joseph Albert Guay, who was married. He had, she said, virtually blackmailed her into taking the statue to the airport by offering to cancel some of her promissory notes that he held. Their love affair had been over ever since he met an attractive nineteen year old night club cigarette girl named Marie-Ange Robitaille, who preferred to be called Mary Angel.

Then Marie Pitre dropped her bombshell. "I didn't know his wife would be on that flight." And she went on to describe how, some weeks before, Guay had telephoned her and asked her to purchase ten pounds of dynamite, which he needed for landscape gardening.

Assuming that it was this dynamite that had blown up the Dakota, how had it been detonated? It would need a timing mechanism. And Marie, they discovered, had a brother named Genereux Ruest who was an expert clock repairer . . . In fact, Ruest, who was a cripple, admitted that he had made the timing mechanism; Guay, he said, had told him that he needed it for exploding the dynamite to blow some rocks out of the ground.

Albert Guay, a thin-faced man with a pencil-line moustache, was arrested, and the newspapers headlined the "love bomb murder" – since it was by now plain that he had decided to kill his wife Rita in order to marry the pretty waitress Mary Angel. The crime caused such indignation that police had to hold back crowds who wanted to lynch the jeweller on the spot.

At the trial, Guay's defence lawyer had an impossible task; he was found guilty and sentenced to death. He met the hangman on 10 January, 1951. Eighteen months later, Marie Pitre and her brother also went to the gallows – new evidence had revealed that they had willingly participated in the murder plot that had killed twenty-two other people besides the intended victim.

# Ruth Ellis

On the evening of Easter Sunday, 10 April, 1955, two men emerged from the Magdala public house in Hampstead, and walked towards the grey-green Vanguard parked outside. They were David Blakely, twenty-five, the manager of a small engineering firm in Penn, and a car salesman, Clive Gunnell, thirty. Both were carrying quarts of light ale, for they were about to return to a party which they had left to buy more beer. As Blakely fumbled for his keys, a small peroxide blonde woman approached him, calling out: "David". Blakely failed to hear her. Moments later she stood beside him, took a revolver from her handbag, and pointed it at him. Blakely gave a cry of alarm and ran towards the back of the car. Two shots hit him in the back. He started to run uphill, and another shot hit him. Even as he lay on the pavement, with Clive Gunnell bending over him, the woman went on firing over Gunnell's shoulder; one shot hit a female pedestrian in the thumb. When the hammer clicked on an empty chamber, the woman turned and said unemotionally: "Go and call the police." A man strode out of the pub. "I *am* a police officer." He took the revolver away from her. David Blakely was dead when the ambulance arrived.

The killer was twenty-eight-year-old Ruth Ellis, and she and David Blakely had been lovers for two years, ever since they met at a London club. Blakely was something of a playboy; he had a well paid job, an inheritance of £7,000 (a considerable sum in 1953) and an allowance from his stepfather. His passion in life was racing cars.

Their relationship had been stormy; both were inclined to be jealous and possessive. Both were also emotionally unstable. Ruth hungered for constant flattery and attention; Blakely was immature, and inclined to become so rude when drunk that he drove away many regular customers at the Little Club, of which Ruth was the manageress. Eventually, the proprietor fired Ruth, largely because of her relationship with Blakely. A businessman named Desmond Cussen took her – and her two small children – into his flat in Devonshire Place and financed her; he was so devoted to her that he even allowed her to continue to sleep with Blakely.

Ruth's intensely possessive attitude to Blakely was due partly to insecurity. Born into a relatively poor family in Rhyl, North Wales, (her father was a musician), Ruth Neilson had left school at fifteen and worked as a machinist in a factory and a Woolworth's shopgirl. At seventeen she had become a photographer's assistant, and soon fell in love with a French Canadian soldier named Clare. She learned she was pregnant soon after Christmas 1944. Clare had promised to marry her, but a letter to his C.O. revealed that he already had a wife and children in Canada. Ruth got herself a job as a cashier, and a daughter was born in 1944. Clare paid maintainence, but it stopped when he returned to Canada.

She became a photographer's model and often posed in the nude. In a Mayfair club she met vice-boss Morris Conley, who was soon sleeping with her, and persuaded her to work for him as a hostess in the Court Club. She did not *have* to sleep with customers, but it helped her take-home pay. In 1950 she became pregnant again; she had an abortion. In November that year she married a recently divorced dentist, George Ellis – another customer – who was an alcoholic. He was forty-one, she twenty-four. A daughter was born in 1951, but by then her husband's alcoholism had been intensified by endless quarrels, often ending in violence, and they separated. She returned to being a club hostess for Maurice Conley, and in 1953, he made her manageress of the Little Club in Brompton Road, Knightsbridge. She received £25 a week and a rent-free flat. One client gave her £400 for going on holiday with him.

Her first meeting with the weakly handsome David Blakely was not a success – she remarked afterwards "I hope I never see that little shit again." But although Ruth had a violent temper she knew – as a hostess – how to keep it. Blakely had just become engaged to an heiress, but he was an incorrigible philanderer. Since Ruth made a habit of being available to customers of her choice, it was not too difficult to persuade her to let him sleep with her. He understood that he was not her "lover" – merely a customer who was being allowed to spend nights in her bed, as many others did. And, according to Ruth Ellis, she was not particularly in love with him either. Nevertheless, they seem to have found one another exciting in bed, and Blakely was soon sleeping in her flat five nights a week. They became lovers almost as a matter of habit. It was also a matter of vanity; Ruth liked the idea of having an affair with this ex-public schoolboy with his private income and racing car, and he liked the idea of having a sexy blonde mistress whose bed was right above the club.

In February 1954, she had an abortion – this time Blakely's baby. But while Blakely was away racing at Le Mans, she slept with her devoted admirer Desmond Cussen. He lent her money

– she was insatiable where cash was concerned – and pressed her to marry him. Ruth was not interested – not because she preferred Blakely, for both of them slept with other people, but because she was not deeply attracted to Cussen. She may also have preferred Cussen as an adoring swain rather than a husband who might take her for granted. Cussen even arranged to send her son Andy to a private school.

Ruth and Blakely quarrelled after she noticed love-scratches on his back. He was the one who made it up, and the affair continued. Both of them were now drinking much more heavily. He often hit her when he lost his temper, on one occasion knocking her down the stairs. One night, she went back home with a man who had picked her up, and took off all her clothes to reveal bruises all over her body. Profits at the Club were sagging, and when Conley finally fired her at the end of 1954, she moved in with Desmond Cussen. But she often spent the night in a hotel with Blakely.

It was clear to their friends that the couple were bad for one another. Blakely was aggressive when drunk, and he was drunk much of the time. Ruth was less aggressive but gave as good as she got. They often quarrelled, but always made up in bed. Even when she knew he was having an affair with a married woman in Penn, she continued to let him sleep with her. Towards the end of January 1955, they went on a nine day drinking spree that ended with quarrels and hysteria. On another occasion Ruth hid his car keys, and when Clive Gunnell and another friend arrived to pick him up, Ruth had a black eye and many bruises. There was another hysterical scene when Blakely found his car keys and tried to drive off. Yet after more bitter recriminations, he sent her red carnations with a note: "Sorry darling. I love you. David." When she decided to leave Cussen's flat, the faithful admirer lent her the money to rent a new one in Kensington. When Blakely told her he had broken off his affair with the married woman, she allowed him to stay there with her. She then persuaded Cussen to take her down to a pub in Penn, and found Blakely in there with the woman. Back in Kensington, after another violent quarrel, he hit her in the stomach and caused a miscarriage.

In spite of this, they spent the night before Good Friday, 1955, in her flat. Ruth had become extremely sexually demanding, and Blakely was taking amyl nitrite, a sexual stimulant. He left the flat early because he found her son Andy (now ten) too noisy. Later that day he told friends – a married couple named Findlater – that he couldn't stand it any longer, and had to get away from her. Carole Findlater, who had once been Blakely's girlfriend, was glad to hear it; she disliked Ruth intensely. She persuaded Blakely to come home for lunch, and that night he stood Ruth up and went out with them. Late at night, Ruth repeatedly rang the Findlaters demanding to talk to him. When they refused – or hung up when they recognized her voice – she drove around to their flat and smashed in all the windows of Blakely's car. The police arrived, and Ruth was finally driven back home by Desmond Cussen.

The following day – Saturday – was spent unsuccessfully pursuing Blakely – Ruth was now convinced he was making love to the nursemaid of the Findlaters. Until late that night she hung around opposite the Findlaters' flat. She went home in the early hours of the morning, and telephoned the Findlaters; again she failed to speak to Blakely.

On Sunday, there was another party at the Findlaters, after a lunchtime drink at the Magdala public house. At 9 that evening, Carole Findlater ran out of cigarettes, and asked Blakely to go and get her some. Blakely decided they also needed more beer, and asked Clive Gunnell to go with him to the Magdala public house . . .

According to Ruth Ellis – speaking shortly before her execution – she had been pouring out her fury to Desmond Cussen when he had handed her a loaded revolver. He had then driven her to woodland where she practised shooting. And later, she alleged, he drove her to the Magdala public house. She arrived minutes before David Blakely came out with Clive Gunnel. Soon after that, David Blakely lay dead on the pavement, and Ruth Ellis was taken into custody.

On Monday 20 June, 1955, Ruth Ellis stood in the dock at the Old Bailey. And when she told the prosecuting Q.C, Christmas Humphreys, that she had intended to kill Blakely, the judge warned the jury that only one verdict was possible: murder. They took only fourteen minutes to arrive at the guilty verdict.

The campaign for the abolition of capital punishment was then in full swing, and many petitions for her reprieve were sent to the Home Secretary, one with 50,000 signatures. But the bank manager's wife who had been wounded in the hand by Ruth Ellis wrote a letter to a newspaper pointing out that if Ruth was reprieved, "other vindictive and jealous young women" might begin gunning down their boyfriends. She had actually witnessed the murder, and obviously felt that a woman who could shoot someone with such deliberate intent deserved to die.

The knowledge that her reprieve had been turned down did not seem to bother Ruth Ellis; she wrote to one friend that being hanged would be no worse than having a tooth out. On 13 July, 1955, she drank a hot brandy, then walked firmly the few steps to the execution shed. She was the last woman to be hanged in England – ten years later, in 1965, capital punishment was abolished.

Clive Gunnell had a nervous breakdown after witnessing his friend being shot at close range. He told the present author that he rejected the idea that Ruth killed David Blakely because she was so much in love with him. He felt she was an exhibitionist who wanted to "become known", and that the murder was a theatrical performance as much as a *crime passionel*. Years of drunken parties and prostitution (for she was basically a high class call girl) had led to states of depression and boredom when she needed emotional stimulants. She killed Blakely because she was infuriated at his refusal to speak to her or see her after their last lovemaking session on Good Friday; there may also have been an element of self-disgust in her decision to make the break final by killing him. Her death, Gunnell argued, was a spectacular form of suicide.

# The De Kaplany Case

What is the most horrific crime of passion on record? There is a body of opinion in favour of a French case of 1958, which the press labelled "the demon lovers". Dr Yves Evenou was to all appearances a happily married man, who sometimes referred to his wife Marie-Claire as an angel. But Evenou harboured peculiar sexual tastes of which his wife knew nothing. In 1953, when a dressmaker named Simone Deschamps came to his surgery, Evenou divined instantly that this rather plain forty-three year old woman was a masochist, and therefore his ideal sex partner. They became lovers, and she submitted to sexual demands that included flagellation and semi-public strip-tease. In 1958, Evenou decided his wife had to die, and that the crime should be performed by his mistress – in the nude. By now, Simone Deschamps had moved into a flat directly underneath that occupied by the Evenous. On the evening of the murder, Evenou telephoned her, and she mounted the stairs wearing only a coat and shoes. In his flat she removed these. He then led her to the bed where his wife – a semi-invalid – lay half drugged. Evenou pulled back the bedclothes and ordered his mistress to strike. But Simone's hands were weak, and the first blow only awakened Marie-Claire. Evenou held her down while Simone completed the butchery, stabbing her eleven times. The murder of Marie-Claire Evenou was less an attempt to dispose of an unwanted wife than an act of sexual perversion by two lovers who had tried everything.

There was hardly any attempt to cover up the crime, and the lovers were arrested almost immediately. Evenou died before the trial – a life of excess had drained his vitality. Simone Deschamps escaped the death penalty, but received life imprisonment with hard labour.

But even the crime of Simone Deschamps sounds humane in comparison with the murder committed by the Hungarian doctor Geza de Kaplany. He had fled from communist persecution in Hungary, and took up practice in San Jose, California, in 1962, as an anaesthesiologist in a hospital. Kaplany was good looking in a cold, thin-lipped way. He soon fell violently in love with a beauty queen who was more than ten years his junior, and married her in 1962. But only a few days after he and Hajna moved into their apartment, he became impotent with his wife.

---

**The Denise Labbé case is perhaps one of the most sinister crimes of passion on record. Twenty-year-old Denise, a secretary, enjoyed mixing – and sleeping – with students at Rennes, and had a baby daughter, Catherine, by one of them. Then she met officer cadet Jacques Algarron, a brilliant mathematician who believed ardently in Nietzsche's theory of the superman. He decided that he and Denise were a "super-couple", and that to prove that she was above conventional morality, she should kill her daughter. She was so besotted with him that she agreed. Delays brought threats to break off the affair. Eventually, she tried to throw Catherine from a high window, but found she could not bring herself to do it. Then she pushed her into the canal, but relented, and summoned help. A second attempt at drowning was frustrated when neighbours heard the child's cries and pulled her out of the river. On 8 November, 1954, Denise Labbé finally drowned Catherine in a stone wash basin. Friends were suspicious, and Denise was questioned by police. Finally, she confessed, implicating her lover. "It was a ritual murder". She was sentenced to life imprisonment, Algarron to twenty years hard labour.**

He convinced himself that all the men in the apartment building were pursuing her, and that she was encouraging them. This, at all events, is the excuse he gave for what followed.

Kaplany bought himself a record player, and on the morning of 28 August, 1962, neighbours became indignant at the tremendous volume at which Kaplany was playing his new toy. They could also hear a woman's piercing screams above the music. Finally, the police arrived, and pounded on the door until it opened. Kaplany stood there in bloodstained underwear, and wearing rubber gloves. On the bed lay Hajna de Kaplany, so mutilated that the police were sickened. Kaplany had tied her hands and feet to the bedposts, then made razor cuts all over her body, into which he poured hydrochloric, sulphuric and nitric acid. He mutilated her face, her genitals, her breasts. His aim, he explained later, was not to kill her but to make sure that she ceased to be attractive to males.

Hajna died twenty-four hours later in hospital, while her mother knelt beside the bed and prayed – not for her to live, but to die.

At the trial, Kaplany became hysterical as he viewed the photographs of his wife's mutilated body. He was found guilty and sentenced to life imprisonment.

In fact, Kaplany was released after only eleven years, even before he was due for parole. Then he was virtually smuggled out of the country, to take up duties in Taiwan as a "cardiac specialist" – a position for which he was unqualified. The parole board never explained its strange decision – it may have been due to the feeling that his life would have been in danger if he had been released in the normal way.

This seems highly probable, since his crime was probably the most sadistic in American criminal history.

# • chapter seven •

# LATE 20TH CENTURY CRIMES OF PASSION

*E*ven *in the late twentieth century crimes of passion still occur, with the methods of murder similar to those used in the early twentieth century, or even back to the eighteenth century. The methods used being a gun, knife, or bludgeon. Even in this knowledgable and relaxed age (as opposed to the Victorian era), people are still overtaken by emotions that they cannot control and that cause them to murder.*

## The Red Mini Murder

At about 10 p.m. Thursday 2 March, 1967, a red Morris Mini crashed into a beech tree at Rummerhedge Wood, near Henley-on-Thames, west of London. Police Constable Sherlock arrived in his patrol car, to find three men at the scene of the accident. They explained that the two victims of the crash had already been taken to hospital by ambulance – an unconscious woman and a dazed man. They were merely witnesses who had arrived after the crash. One of them explained that when they had arrived, a man had already been there, bending over the woman, who was stretched out on the ground. The man had told them that he was going to his car to get a blanket – the witnesses had passed a dark Cortina parked around the bend – but a few moments later, they heard him drive off.

Sherlock decided that the accident could not have been serious, since the car was not badly damaged, and the windscreen

was unbroken. But he noted the large quantity of blood on the **231**
driver's side, and inferred that the driver had been badly cut.

PC Sherlock went home, and telephoned the Battle Hospital
in Reading – to learn, to his surprise, that the woman, a Mrs June
Serina Cook, was dead. He immediately drove to the hospital
and saw the dead woman. June Cook's head was bandaged,
and the surgeon explained that she had severe head injuries,
and that he had had to perform a tracheotomy to allow her to
breathe.

Sherlock also interviewed Raymond Sidney Cook, the husband of the dead woman, who had been in the car with her.
He smelt of alcohol and seemed to be in shock. His replies to
questions were incoherent mumbles. But he accepted Sherlock's
offer to drive him home – to Spencer's Wood, near Reading –
and Sherlock was surprised that he was able to give precise
instructions about the route, although he relapsed into mumbles
when asked about the accident.

The Cooks had apparently lived next door to June Cook's
parents, and Sherlock also went to interview them. He learned
that June Cook was a schoolteacher who was nine years older
than her thirty-two-year-old husband. June's parents had given
them the house next door. But they seemed to disapprove of
their son-in-law, and told Sherlock that the Cooks had been
quarrelling recently.

Next, the indefatigable Sherlock went back and looked again
at the scene of the accident. He had already noticed that there
were no skid marks. Yet there were pieces of bark on the ground
which the Mini had knocked off the tree. Had it been driven into
the tree fairly slowly, to give the impression of an accident? He
had noted earlier that when he had reversed the car, there was
no need to adjust the rear view mirror. Yet the dead woman
was six inches shorter than he was, and it was her blood that
stained the driver's seat . . .

The next day Sherlock went to look at the Mini in the garage
to which it had been towed. It had now been cleaned out, but
he noticed there were bloodstains *on the outside* of the car. It was
just possible that they had got there when the ambulance men
moved the body. But why was there also hair soaked in blood
near the *rear* wheel?

He talked again to Cook, who was now able to describe
how, as his wife was driving, a car had dazzled them with its
headlights. The next thing he knew was waking up dazed . . .

Sherlock had requested the aid of a Scene of Crimes officer, and
when Sergeant McMiken arrived, he took him to Rummerhedge

Wood. As he was setting up his camera, McMiken noticed something that had escaped Sherlock – a dark stain on the road seventy five yards from the scene of the accident; it looked like dried blood. All this made it clear that Cook's story of the accident could not be true.

The pathologist who examined Mrs Cook's body agreed when he was told that the windscreen was undamaged; he had assumed – from her broken neck – that she had been thrown through the windscreen. He also noted that Mrs Cook's bloodstream indicated that, like her husband, she had been drinking heavily. This was confirmed by Raymond Cook, who was now well enough to elaborate his story (although he still spoke very slowly, as if weighing every word). He explained that he and his wife always went out for dinner on a Thursday. On this particular evening, both had drunk a large amount at the George Hotel in Pangbourne. On the way home, he had felt faint, and his wife had taken over the driving. Soon after that, the oncoming car had dazzled them both . . .

But June Cook's parents were able to add an interesting piece of information to the jigsaw puzzle. Raymond Cook had been having an affair with a young blonde named Kim – they thought her surname was Mule – a nurse at the Borocourt Mental Hospital.

Detective Inspector Insel, who now took charge of the investigation, decided that the most important question was the identity of the man who had driven off in the dark Cortina. Luck was on his side. When newspapers published the story, a house painter named Angus Macdonald came forward to say that he had seen the Cortina on the evening of the accident. He did not know the identity of the male driver, but he *did* happen to know the identity of the attractive blonde who was in the car with him. It was Kim Newell, Raymond Cook's girlfriend, who happened to live next door to MacDonald's mother. MacDonald had even been curious enough to take the car's number – 7711 FM.

This was a major stroke of luck. The Cortina proved to belong to a heavy plant hire company in Wrexham, and when the police arrived, a man named Eric Jones was just getting into the car. Jones insisted that he had been nowhere near Reading or Rummerhedge Wood on 2 March, and gave an elaborate alibi. The police appeared to accept this; but their investigation into Jones's background revealed that he had also had an affair with Kim Newell before she met Raymond Cook. At a second interview, Jones changed his story about being nowhere near Reading on the day of the accident; he now admitted that he had been to see Kim Newell; she wanted to consult him about an abortion.

The father of the unborn child, apparently, was Raymond Cook. And Cook's background made it clear that he had a motive for killing his wife. She held the purse strings, and had some £10,000 in the bank, as well as owning various properties that provided an income in rent. At one point, Cook had left her to go and live with Kim Newell, and his wife had changed her will, leaving her money to the children, and also cancelled their joint bank account, containing £3,000. She had told the local vicar that her husband had agreed to return to her if she made some financial provision for him. And he had, in fact, returned in January 1967, two months before the accident.

The Home Office pathologist who examined Mrs Cook's body suggested that her neck had been broken by a heavy blow while she was kneeling on the ground, possibly with a second person holding her head.

On 17 March, the police felt they had enough evidence to charge Cook with his wife's murder. Soon after that, some new and important information came to light. A local dairyman went to the police to report a conversation between his wife and Kim's sister Janett; Kim Newell had told her sister that Eric Jones had murdered June Cook with a car jack. Her motive in making this disclosure was that she was afraid that Jones might also kill her, since she knew the truth . . .

A story of brutal and deliberate murder now emerged. Kim Newell had left her job, and was being supported by Raymond Cook. But Cook needed money; that was the only reason that he had returned to his wife. His solution to the problem of two "wives" was to plan the murder of the woman who held the purse strings – as soon as she had changed her will back in his favour. Eric Jones, Kim's ex-lover, had been drawn into the plot (although it is not clear what precisely he gained from his involvement in the murder). Their first plan involved driving the car into the river, but that was abandoned. On the night of the murder, Cook had been delayed – he was supposed to show Jones the site chosen for the murder. Instead, Kim Newell had to do it.

Later that evening, as the Cooks drove back from dinner, Jones thumbed a lift, claiming that his car had broken down. From the back seat he struck June Cook – who was in the passenger seat – a violent blow on the head; but it only stunned her. She was dragged from the car and beaten to death with the car jack by Jones, while her husband held her head. Then the car was driven into the tree, and June was placed in the driver's seat.

The full story of the murder was told to the police by Kim Newell when she was arrested. As a result, she stood beside Raymond Cook and Eric Jones in the dock, although a charge of murder against her was dropped in favour of a charge of being an accessory before the fact. All three were sentenced to life imprisonment.


# The Jean Harris Case

This book has so far contained no example of the commonest type of crime of passion – the murder of a husband (or lover) – by a rejected wife or mistress. In 1981, just such a case made headlines in America, and even in Europe; the reason was that the victim was something of a celebrity, and that the homicidal lady was also the highly respectable headmistress of an expensive girls' school in Virginia. The *New York Times* referred to the trial as "one of the most sensational ever".

Dr Herman Tarnower had become wealthy as a result of a simple invention, the "Scarsdale medical diet"; his book about it had been on the best-sellers lists for a long time. (Scarsdale is an expensive dormitory suburb of New York.) When Jean Harris met Dr Tarnower in 1966, she was forty-two; the doctor was fifty-six. The son of poor Jewish immigrants who had settled in Brooklyn, the intensely ambitious doctor had "played life to win". He had had a long succession of attractive blonde mistresses, and had ruthlessly terminated relationships when he was tired of them. He also ran the Scarsdale Medical Center, with the aid of his latest mistress, Lynne Tryforos, who, at thirty-seven, was twenty-two years his junior.

Jean Harris's life had also been a success story. She had majored in economics at the exclusive Smith College for girls, married a childhood sweetheart at twenty-three, and separated from him nineteen years later when she felt she had outgrown him. That was in 1965, a year before she met Tarnower. By then she had become an administrator in Springside School in Philadelphia.

She had been introduced to Tarnower at a dinner party, and these two highly intelligent people had found one another fascinating. Soon Tarnower was proposing marriage. In fact, he had never been married, and had just broken his promise to marry another woman. Jean Harris and "Hy" Tarnower travelled widely and often spent weekends together in the Hotel Pierre in New York. The idea of marriage was tactfully shelved, for she realized that he valued his freedom. In 1971 she improved her professional position by moving to Conneticut as headmistress of a private school, and in 1977, she moved again to the Madeira School in Virginia.

Even as early as 1972 she was aware that there were other women in Tarnower's life – in particular the twenty-nine year-old divorcee Lynne Tryforos, whose letters often followed them around the world. Mrs Harris regarded Lynne Tryforos as "a vicious adulteress and psychotic". But the adulteress had the advantage of being at Tarnower's side most of the time. In January 1980, Tarnower took Jean Harris to Miami for the New Year, but on New Years Day, her holiday was spoiled when she saw a message in the personal column on front of the *New York Times*; it read: "Hy T. Love always. Lynne."

The week of 7 March, 1980, had been a time of emotional stress; she had decided to expel four seniors when drugs were found in the dormitory. After that, she wrote Tarnower a ten page letter, which she sent by recorded delivery – because he claimed that some of her previous letters had failed to reach him. One writer on the case has spoken of its "insults hurled at Lynne Tryforos, its paranoid obsession with financial minutiae and its pitiable, distasteful grovelling." It was the letter of a woman who hated herself for her weakness, and hated – as well as adored – her lover. After sending it – on 10 March – she finalized her will, then rang Tarnower to tell him she was driving from Virginia to his home in Westchester. "Suit yourself" he said resignedly. He did not realize that she had recently bought a .32 revolver.

That evening, Tarnower gave a dinner party at which Lynne Tryforos was one of the guests. There was a conversation about wives murdering their husbands, and Tarnower remarked: "That is one of the advantages of being a bachelor – that could never happen to me." The party was over by 9; the guests – including Lynne – departed, and Tarnower went to bed early, as was his wont.

Jean Harris arrived at 10.30, and went in through the garage. She almost certainly expected to find her rival in Tarnower's bed, and was prepared to kill them both. In fact, Tarnower was alone, and that should have defused her murderous intentions. Unfortunately, Tarnower had made a mistake that cost him his life – he had forgotten to conceal his other mistress's night clothes and hair curlers. As the light came on, Tarnower woke up and said: "Jesus Christ, Jean, it's the middle of the night." He watched resignedly as Jean Harris stormed around the bedroom and threw the nightgown and curlers out of the window. When she went into hysterics he applied the recognized remedy and slapped her face; she stopped screaming. But the sight of the nightclothes had revived her jealous fury; she opened her handbag and took out the gun. As Tarnower grabbed it, it went off and shattered his hand. Still holding the gun, Tarnower picked up the telephone and pressed the button that would connect him with his housekeepers, the van der Vrekens. That was his second mistake – he should have thrown the gun out of the window first. Jean Harris lunged for it, and as they struggled, she pulled the trigger three times. Tarnower slumped between the twin beds, dying.

When a police patrolman arrived minutes later, summoned by the van der Vrekens, he saw a car with Virginia license plates making a U-turn. As he jumped out, a woman in a bloodstained white blouse told him: "Someone's been shot." She then went back into the house, and followed the patrolman up to the bedroom. As the patrolman tried to revive the dying man, Jean Harris sat on one of the twin beds and asked: "Hy, why didn't you kill me?".

Her story was that she had driven up to Westchester intending to kill herself – in fact, she had placed the gun to her head before Tarnower wrested it from her. When she had asked him to kill her, he had said: "Get out of here, you're crazy!" The gun had gone off accidentally as they struggled, then jammed. But even after Tarnower had collapsed, she had tried to kill herself – she went into the bathroom and banged it on the bath to try to unjam it.

Jean Harris was arrested and fingerprinted, then taken to court in White Plains. There she was granted bail. Instead of returning to Virginia, she then admitted herself to a local hospital "for rest and recuperation".

Tarnower's death gave his book a new lease of life; to the delight of his publishers, *The Scarsdale Medical Diet* rocketed up the best-seller charts.

Jean Harris's defence at her trial – which began on 21 November before Judge Russell B. Leggett – was that her only intention in going to see Tarnower was to commit suicide. But the fact that Tarnower had been shot four times undermined her insistence that the gun had gone off accidentally in the course of the struggle. And if she had intended to give herself up, as she alleged, why had she tried to escape, and only made a U-turn when she saw the police car with its flashing red light? It seemed clear that she was hoping to escape unrecognized, and that she only changed her mind and decided to "come clean" when she saw there was no hope of keeping her presence a secret. It seemed equally obvious that she had then decided on the suicide defence.

Jurors were impressed by her calm, quiet demeanour. But all that changed as they listened to the letter she had sent to her lover by recorded delivery, with its hysterical accusations. It made it very plain that she had gone to see Tarnower with murder in mind. Jean Harris was clearly a highly controlled woman who would tell whatever lies might influence the jury. In fact, it took the jury eight days to reach their verdict. But on 29 March, 1981, she was sentenced to fifteen years to life – a verdict that means that she could have no hope of parole before 1996.

The evidence presented in court made it clear that Tarnower was a lifelong seducer who took pleasure in having mistresses shuttling in and out of his bed – he is quoting as saying: "I don't love anyone and I don't need anyone" – and that he had undoubtedly treated Jean Harris very badly indeed. But the guilty verdict was a proof that her plea of being under intolerable emotional pressure failed to convince a jury who recognized her as a highly controlled woman who killed out of a desire for revenge.

# The Pam Smart Case

In March 1991, a murder case involving a pretty twenty-three-year-old widow created the same kind of sensation as the Jean Harris trial ten years earlier. Pam Smart was accused of persuading her sixteen-year-old schoolboy lover to murder her husband so that she could claim his insurance money and – sooner or later – marry her lover.

Pamela Wojas was born in Miami, Florida, in August 1967. In 1980, alarmed by Miami's soaring crime rate, the Wojases moved to Windham, New Hampshire. Her father was an airport worker who had worked his way up to airline pilot. As a highschool student, Pam (or Pame, as she preferred to spell it) got herself noticed a great deal as a girl who liked to be noticed. She also acquired a reputation for promiscuity, and the nickname "Seka", which referred to a pornographic movie star.

On New Years Eve 1985, Pam attended a party at the home of a young man called Greg Smart, who had a reputation as the local stud – at one party, he was said to have "scored" with three girls in the course of the evening, none of them knowing about the others. These two intensely egotistical young people saw one another as a natural challenge; but Pam was the more smitten of the two. When Pam returned to the University of Florida, in Tallahassee, Greg seemed to have no regrets at seeing her go. But during the summer vacation, they saw a great deal of one another. And in 1987, Greg startled his friends by announcing that he was moving to Florida to be near Pam. She found herself a job as a disc jockey with a small local radio station, and Greg helped her select the records. Soon they were living together. In January 1988, when Pam was twenty and Greg twenty-two, they decided to get married. It was then that Greg realized that he would need to find himself a good job if he intended to offer Pam the kind of middle class comforts to which they were both accustomed. He decided to become an insurance salesman; Pam hoped to be a TV reporter.

The problem was that two such dominant personalities were bound to quarrel. Pam was determined to "be on top"; Greg had no intention of letting her. When they were bickering one evening in a restaurant, he squirted a mouthfull of beer in her face. The bouncer threw him out, but eventually let him back on a promise of good behaviour. Ten minutes later, they began to bicker again, and he squirted more beer in her face. This time the bouncer threw him out for good.

Back in New Hampshire, the Smarts moved into Summerhill Condominiums, in the small community of Derry, and Greg quickly became a promising insurance salesman, while Pam took a step towards realizing her TV ambitions by becoming the director of the media center at School Administrative Unit 21 in Hampton. Her job was to "generate positive publicity". The couple married in May 1989. Their condominium cost $750 a month, and they ran two cars. In their first year of married life, Greg earned $42,000, and Pam more than $29,000. They dined often with Greg's parents, and went to a restaurant twice a week. Married life looked promising.

But they continued to have pesonality clashes. When Pam "bitched" too much, Greg was still inclined to squirt beer in her face, and on one occasion when he came in drunk in the early

hours of the morning, she left him to go home to mother. But **239**
the quarrel was soon made up. At School Unit 21, Pam Smart
had many admirers. One fifteen year old called Billy Flynn
turned to a friend after she had been introduced to his class
and murmured: "I'm in love." And another student, fifteen
year old Cecelia Pierce, also developed a crush on the young
publicity director. Both teenagers had a chance to get to know
Pam better when they collaborated with her in a competition to
make a video commercial to advertise the nutritive qualities of
orange juice. Billy Flynn was the cameraman. He also devised
some of the music – thumping electronic rap. Pam enjoyed being
group leader, and she accepted Cecelia's adoration as casually
as she accepted Billy's obvious devotion. Billy was not happy at
home – his father, an alcoholic, had showed him little affection,
but when he was killed in a crash caused by his drunkenness,
Billy was shattered.

Just before Christmas 1989 – when the Smarts had been
married a little over six months – Greg came home at 6 a.m.
claiming that he had spent the night at the home of a friend.
He finally admitted that he had spent the night with another
woman. Pam was outraged. She was also upset by Greg's
heavy drinking – on one occasion she arrived at the home of
her in-law's in her night dress, saying that Greg had tried to
strangle her.

It was not in her nature to take this kind of thing lying down.
The obvious revenge was infidelity. But with whom? Billy Flynn
was the obvious choice. One day she asked him: "Do you ever
think of me when I'm not around?" "Sure" said Billy. "I think
of you all the time." Soon after this, they drove to Billy Flynn's
house when no one else was home. They went up to his bedroom
to play records, and Billy locked the door. "Aren't you going
to kiss me?" asked Pam. "Yeah." "Or do I have to come over
there and rape you?" Tentatively, they exchanged their first kiss.
Pam seems to have felt instinctively that it was better to move
slowly.

In mid-February 1989, when Greg was on a skiing holiday,
Pam invited Billy and Cecelia to her condominum. After they
had listened to records for a while, Pam and Billy went upstairs;
he stripped naked, and she went into the bathroom and put on a
filmy nightdress. She came out and danced for him, then the two
had sex. Billy assured her that it was not his first experience, but
it was untrue. After that they made love at every opportunity; on
one occasion when they were both naked on the grass beside a
parking lot, a car pulled in and they both had to make a run for

it; Billy hurt his knee. On another occasion a man caught them having sex in the back of a car, and yelled indignantly.

It was also at about this time that Pam told Billy that if they were to be together forever, they would have to kill Greg. At first he thought it was a joke; but the persistence with which she returned to the idea made it clear that she was serious. Her plan was that Billy should go to their home and kill Greg while she was at a school meeting, to establish an alibi.

Oddly enough, Cecelia was also told about the plan. She pooh-poohed the idea. "He's never going to do it." Bill, she said, was too gentle by nature. She later explained that she did not take the plot seriously. But Pam was deadly serious – as Cecelia realized on 2 May, 1990 . . .

At about 10.20 on the previous evening, neighbours who lived near the Smart's condominium in Derry were electrified by a series of piercing screams. As they peered out of their windows they heard a woman call: "Help! My husband, my husband . . ." The neighbours next door preferred to lie low and ignored her as she banged on the door; it was a young married woman who lived two doors away who let her in. When two men finally looked into Pam Smart's house, they saw Greg Smart lying face down on the floor, with blood running from his nose. The police arrived soon after. It took them only moments to determine that Greg was dead. The post mortem revealed that he had been shot in the top of the head.

Pam seemed shattered; various neighbours tried to comfort her. But the detective who interviewed her that evening felt she seemed oddly calm for a woman who had just lost her newly wedded spouse. Friends were also inclined to wonder why she did not cry more. But they accepted Pam's suggestion that God was giving her the strength to bear the shock.

Apparently the murder had been committed by a burglar, or burglars. The house was in wild disarray. Greg's wallet was empty, but a diamond ring lay beneath him. Various items – such as a TV and video – had been placed near the doors as if for quick removal; it looked as if the burglars had been interrupted, or had simply panicked.

When marijuana was found in Greg Smart's pickup truck, neighbours evolved a new theory – that he had been killed by drug traffickers to whom he owed money. More than a month passed by with no leads. Then, in the second week of June, the whole case broke open.

On the evening of Saturday 9 June, a youth named Ralph Welch listened with incredulity as two of his closest friends,

Pete Randall and JR Lattime, described how, together with **241**
Billy Flynn, they had murdered Greg Smart. Ralph had heard
rumours of the killing that afternoon from another youth. It
seemed that the deal to murder Greg Smart had been discussed
around the area for at least a month before it happened. Billy's
affair with Pam was also common knowledge. In this small
community, most of the boys had known one another since
childhood, and secrets were seldom kept for long. When Ralph
confronted JR and Pete with questions about the murder, they
at first denied it, then told him the whole story. Ralph Welch
was horrified, and told them that he could not keep silent. The
three argued about it for a long time. The following day, more
bickering turned to blows, after which Ralph went to JR's parents
and told them that their son had been involved in the murder of
Greg Smart, and that Billy Smart had killed Greg with a gun
belonging to JR's father Vance.

Around midday on Sunday, Vance and Diane Lattime, dazed
but determined to get to the truth, called at the police station
and told them the whole story. Meanwhile, JR and Pete called
on Billy Flynn, who had spent the night with Pam, and told
him that all hell was about to break. Pam and her lover were
incredulous that they could have been so stupid as to tell Ralph
Welch about the murder. Later that day, the three boys fled in
the car belonging to Pete's mother. "He's my kid", said Mrs
Randall, "I'd do anything I could to help him." But the flight was
of short duration. In Connecticut, they called on Pete Randall's
grandparents and explained they were in trouble and had to lie
low for a while. Pete's grandfather called Pete's father, and Pete
was summarily ordered to return home or face arrest. So the boys
climbed back into the car and drove back to Derry. The following
day, they were arrested.

Pam Smart was reacting more calmly. She was certain that
her lover would protect her, and she was right. But she was
unaware that there was a weak link in the chain: Cecelia Pierce.
When the police heard rumours that Cecelia had known about
the murder before it happened, they took her in for questioning.
She flatly denied everything – until a detective told her firmly
that if she was later proved to be lying, she would be charged
with obstructing an investigation. Cecelia decided to cooperate.
The plan the police suggested was that she should telephone
Pam Smart, and try to get her to say something incriminating.
And the conversation would be recorded . . .

But Pam was not ready to incriminate herself. When Cecelia
rang her at work and asked if Pam wanted her to continue

denying that she and Billy had been lovers, Pam replied: "But we weren't." *"What?"* "We weren't." But in subsequent conversations – the police made sure Cecelia persisted – she made a number of comments that later formed an important part of the case against her.

One of her problems was to let Billy and his friends know she was not abandoning them; she shocked and startled some of her friends by saying that she would like to visit her husband's killers in jail, because, after all, they were only kids. She also sent Billy's mother a tape of heavy metal music that Billy had assembled for her (including a song called "Hot for Teacher"), with a note asking her to pass it on to him. When the police came to question her – ostensibly because she had known the accused boys well – she tried to convince them that they were not guilty. She even repeated some of the remarks she had made on the telephone to Cecelia the day before, giving them a turn that underlined her innocence – and also making it clear that she suspected the phone had been tapped.

On Wednesday 1 August, 1990 – three months after the murder – Officer Dan Palletier called on Pam at work. "Well, Pam, I have some good news and some bad news. The good news is that we've solved the murder of your husband. The bad news is that you're under arrest."

Her indictment on a murder charge made headlines. The newspapers found the story of her affair with a fifteen-year-old irresistable. They were equally fascinated by rumours that Cecelia had provided the information that led to her arrest in a series of taped phone conversations. Pam Smart proved to have many friends, who attended the pre-trial hearings wearing yellow ribbons: ribbons normally worn as a reminder of hostages in the Middle East. These were worn, they said, for "our hostage in the state of New Hampshire."

On 22 January, 1991, Pam Smart's supporters were dealt a heavy blow. Pete Randall agreed to a deal with the prosecution in which he would testify against Pam in exchange for a more lenient sentence. JR and Billy Flynn decided to follow suit.

Jury selection began on 19 February. On 5 March, the prosecution began to tell the story of the murder. Later in the day, Pete Randall took the stand, and described in a flat voice how, on May, 1990, he had gone to pick up the car belonging to JR's grandmother, "in order to go to Derry to kill Greg Smart."

Three days later, Billy Flynn described, equally factually, how he had first kissed Pam, and how they had first made love. (Resulting headlines were: "Smart killer recounts sex romp" and "Teacher seduced me with striptease".) He went on to describe how he and the other two boys had driven up to the empty house, and entered by an unlocked door in the basement. When Greg Smart finally came home, Billy Flynn grabbed him and began to hit him; Pete Randall threatened Greg with a knife and made him get down on his knees. Greg asked about his dog, and was told it was safe. When Pete asked for the diamond wedding ring, Greg refused. "My wife would kill me." He pleaded for his life, and the boys were moved – so much so that Pete Randall, who was supposed to slit Greg Smart's throat, could no longer bring himself to do it; he signalled to Billy Flynn, who took his revolver out, held it a few inches above the kneeling man's skull. He described how he had said "God forgive me" before he squeezed the trigger. As Pete Randall let go of Greg Smart's hair, Smart slumped on to the carpet. As he described the scene, Billy Flynn cried uncontrollably.

When Cecelia Pierce took the stand, she described how she had walked into the bedroom and found Pam and Billy naked on the floor, with Pam on top. One reporter murmured: "Why doesn't that surprise me?" In fact, Cecelia's testimony proved less crucial than the state had originally hoped. It had emerged that she had agreed to help the boys find a gun to kill Greg Smart, which made her virtually an accomplice. Her testimony was therefore bound to be suspect. The evidence of the tapes nevertheless left most jurors with no doubt that Pam Smart was guilty.

When Pam Smart took the stand, she conceded that she and Billy Flynn had been lovers, although she gave the date of their first sex act as mid-March rather than mid-February; in that time, Billy Flynn had become sixteen, and Pam could not be charged with having sex with a minor. She also insisted that she had wanted to end the affair, and had done so a month before her husband's murder. But Billy had been in her home just before the break, and had been in the basement by himself. The implication was that he had left the door open so he could break in and murder Greg Smart.

As to the incriminating tape conversations, Pam explained that she had believed that Cecelia knew more about the murder than she was telling, and was simply trying to get her to confess by pretending to know more about it than she really did . . .

The trial was shown live on television, and had more viewers than popular soap operas. Pam's cool demeanour in court led one reporter to dub her "the ice princess". One newspaper took a poll of readers on whether she was guilty; the vote was more than five to one that she was.

On 22 March, 1991, the jury was out for thirteen hours; when they filed in, none of them looked at Pam Smart – a sign that they had voted for a guilty verdict. In fact, they had found her guilty on three counts: conspiracy to commit murder, accomplice to murder, and tampering with a witness. (She had asked a boy to give false evidence implying that Cecelia was a liar.) The verdicts were unanimous. Judge Grey sentenced her to life imprisonment without possibility of parole. Pam commented about her lover: "I can't believe Billy. First he took Greg's life. Now he's taking mine."

But for their plea bargaining, the three youths would also have received the same sentence. In fact, the two active participants in the murder – Billy Flynn and Pete Randall – each received forty years, with twelve years deferred for good behaviour – a minimum of twenty-eight years each. JR Lattime received thirty years with twelve deferred.

Like all crimes of passion, the evidence in the Pam Smart case offers us an illusion of understanding what really happened. Yet most of the important questions remain unanswered. If Pam Smart wanted to go and live with Billy Flynn, why did she not simply leave her husband? Why did she want him killed? Was it because she was comfortable in her home and wanted to live there without him (Billy Flynn even testified that she had warned him not to get blood on the settee), or because she wanted the $140,000 insurance money?

Yet even if the answer to these questions is yes, it still leaves the riddle of why an apparently normal twenty-one-year-old should decide to have her husband murdered. What made her hate him so much? Was it his confession of infidelity? Or his habit of spitting beer into her face?

But then, it must be admitted that we are confronted with the same question in virtually every case in this book, no matter how straightforward the motivation appears. Why did Ruth Snyder decide that her husband had to die? Why did Ruth Ellis decide to kill a man with whom she was not really in love? Why did Eric Jones decide to risk his neck by becoming an accomplice in the Minicar murder? Unless every "passion killer" could be persuaded to give a completely frank account of his or her motivations, such questions must remain unanswered.

Equally puzzling is the motivation that led three normal teenagers to commit murder – particularly when two of them were uninvolved with the Smarts. Was it simply the boredom that

accounts for so much teenage crime in most wealthy societies? **245**
Or a desire to impress one another with their toughness? Or was
it simply a lack of imagination that meant that killing a human
being was for them as unreal as a television serial? If the latter,
then was a life sentence, in fact, the correct verdict?

When Pam Smart began her life sentence, a FRIENDS of
Pamela Smart newsletter continued to plead her total innocence.
But a final comment in Stephen Sawicki's book Teach me to Kill
seems to summarize the general feeling about the case: ". . .
most people would agree that the boys who killed on the night
of 1 May most likely would never have murdered anyone had
Billy Flynn not met up with one Pam Smart . . ."

# UNSOLVED CRIMES

# chapter one

# 19TH CENTURY UNSOLVED MURDERS

*A*n enormous percentage of murders – perhaps as many as one third – remain unsolved. This is particularly true in the late twentieth century, when "serial killers" strike at random – for example, in America in the 1980s, the uncaught "Green River Killer" of Seattle killed at least forty women, eight times as many as London's Jack the Ripper, who killed five prostitutes in 1888. So it is understandable that we look back on the nineteenth century with nostalgia, and find a certain quaint charm even in its murder cases. In fact, considering the undeveloped state of nineteenth-century crime detection, remarkably few of its famous murder cases remained unsolved.

One of the few that defied the skills of the New York police force was the case of the death of a salesgirl, which so intrigued Edgar Allen Poe that he used it as the basis for his story "The Mystery of Marie Roget".

If the death of "Marie Roget" is now no longer quite a mystery, the classic Victorian poisoning drama, the death of Charles Bravo, is as baffling as in 1876.

And another, the case of Lizzie Borden, is the most intriguing American murder mystery that took place almost a quarter of a century later, in 1892, and is regarded by most aficionados of crime as a fitting climax to the homicides of the age of gaslight.

# The Case of Mary Rogers

Mary Cecilia Rogers was born in New York in 1820; her mother, who became a widow when the child was five, supported herself by running a boarding-house in Nassau Street. Mary grew up into a tall, very beautiful young woman with jet-black hair. This led a cigar-store owner named John Anderson, whose shop was on Broadway, to offer her a job as a salesgirl. In 1840 this was regarded as an imaginative piece of business enterprise, for New York was even more "Victorian" than London, and young unmarried girls did not exhibit themselves behind shop counters, particularly in shops frequented exclusively by young men. Mary's mother objected to the idea, but her daughter's enthusiasm finally won her over. She drew many new customers to the shop, although – as Thomas Duke is careful to note in his *Celebrated Criminal Cases of America* (1910) – "the girl's conduct was apparently a model of modest decorum, and while she was lavish in her smiles, she did not hesitate to repel all undue advances".

She had been working in the store for about ten months when one day in January 1841 she failed to appear. Her mother had no idea where she was, and according to Duke, "Mr Anderson was unable to account for her absence". The police searched for her and the newspapers reported her disappearance. Six days later she reappeared, looking tired and rather ill, and explained that she had been visiting relatives in the country. Her mother and her employer apparently corroborated the story. But when a rumour began to circulate that she had been seen during her absence with a tall, handsome naval officer Mary abruptly gave up her job – only a few days after returning – and was no longer seen on Broadway. A month later she announced her engagement to one of her mother's boarders, a clerk called Daniel Payne.

Five months later, on Sunday, 25 July 1841, Mary knocked on her fiancé's door at 10 a.m. and announced that she was going to see her aunt in Bleecker Street; Payne said that he would call for her that evening. Payne also spent the day away from home, but when a violent thunderstorm came on towards evening he decided not to call for Mary, but to let her stay the night with her aunt. Mrs Rogers apparently approved. But when Mary failed to return home the following day she began to worry. When Payne returned from work and learned that Mary was still away, he rushed to see the aunt in Bleecker Street – a Mrs Downing – and was even more alarmed when she told him that she had not seen Mary in the past forty-eight hours.

It was two days later on Wednesday morning that three men in a sailing-boat saw a body in the water off Castle Point, Hoboken. It was Mary, and according to the *New York Tribune* "it was obvious that she had been horribly outraged and murdered". She was fully clothed, although her clothes were torn, and the petticoat was missing. A piece of lace from the bottom of the dress was embedded so deeply in the throat that it had almost disappeared. An autopsy performed almost immediately led to the conclusion that she had been "brutally violated". Oddly enough, Daniel Payne did not go to view the corpse, although he had earlier searched for her all over New York, including Hoboken. But after being interrogated by the police, Payne was released.

A week passed without any fresh clues, and a large reward was offered. Then the coroner received a letter from some anonymous man – who said he had not come forward before from "motives of perhaps criminal prudence" – and who claimed to have seen Mary Rogers on the Sunday afternoon of her disappearance. She had, the writer said, stepped out of a boat with six rough-looking characters, and gone with them into the woods, laughing merrily and apparently under no kind of constraint. Soon afterwards a boat with three well-dressed men had come ashore, and one of these accosted two men walking on the beach and asked if they had seen a young woman and six men recently. They said they had, and that she had appeared to go with them willingly. At this the trio turned their boat and headed back for New York.

In fact, the two men came forward and corroborated this story. But although they both knew Mary Rogers by sight, neither of them could swear that the girl they had seen was definitely Mary.

The next important piece of information came from a

stagecoach-driver named Adams, who said he had seen Mary arrive on the Hoboken ferry with a well-dressed man of dark complexion, and that they had gone to a roadhouse called "Nick Mullen's". This tavern was kept by a Mrs Loss, who told the police that the couple had "taken refreshment" there, then gone off into the woods. Some time later she had heard a scream from the woods; but since the place "was a resort of questionable characters" she had thought no more of it.

Two months after the murder, on 25 September, children playing in the woods found the missing petticoat in a thicket; they also found a white silk scarf, a parasol and a handkerchief marked "M.R." Daniel Payne was to commit suicide in this spot soon after.

A gambler named Joseph Morse, who lived in Nassau Street, was arrested and apparently charged with the murder; there was evidence that he had been seen with Mary Rogers on the evening she disappeared. The following day, he had fled from New York. But Morse was released when he was able to prove that he had been at Staten Island with another young lady on the Sunday afternoon. One odd story in the *Tribune* declared that Morse believed that the young lady *was* Mary Rogers, and that when he heard of the disappearance he assumed she had committed suicide because of the way he had treated her – he had tried to seduce her in his room. He was relieved to learn that the girl with whom he had spent the afternoon was still alive.

In the following year, 1842, Poe's "Mystery of Marie Roget" was published in three parts in *Snowden's Ladies' Companion*. But for anyone looking for a solution of the Mary Rogers mystery, it should be treated with extreme caution. Poe argues that Mary Rogers was not murdered by a gang but by a single individual. His original view seems to have been that the motive was rape; later he heard the rumour that Mary had died as a result of an abortion, and made a few hasty alterations in his story to accommodate this notion. He argues that the signs of a struggle in the woods, and the battered state of her face, indicate that she was killed by an individual – a gang would have been able to overpower her easily. He also speaks of a strip from the girl's skirt that had been wound around the waist to afford a kind of handle for carrying the body; but the evidence of two witnesses who dragged the body out of the water makes no mention of this "handle". In spite of this, there can be no doubt that Poe's objections to the gang theory carry a great deal of weight.

What was not known to Poe in 1842 is that Mary's employer, John Anderson, had been questioned by the police as a suspect; like all the others, he was released. But fifty years later – in December 1891 – new evidence was to emerge. By that time Anderson had been dead ten years; he became a millionaire, and died in Paris. Apparently he had told friends that he had experienced "many unhappy days and nights in regard to her" (Mary Rogers), and had been in touch with her spirit. His heirs contested his estate, and in 1891 his daughter tried to break her father's will on the grounds that when he signed it he was mentally incompetent. The case was settled out of court, and the records destroyed. But a lawyer named Samuel Copp Worthen, who had been closely associated with Anderson's daughter Laura Appleton, knew that his firm had kept a copy of the testimony in the Supreme Court of New York in 1891, and he made it his business to read it. He finally revealed what he had learned in the periodical *American Literature* in 1948. It revealed that Anderson had been questioned by the police about the death of Mary Rogers, and that this had preyed on his mind, so that he later declined to stand as a candidate for mayor of New York, in case someone revealed his secret.

The most significant part of the testimony was the assertion that Anderson had admitted to paying for an abortion for Mary Rogers and had got "in some trouble over it". But he had insisted that he had not "had anything, directly, himself to do with her problems".

This would obviously explain Mary's week-long disappearance from the cigar store, and the fact that she looked tired and ill when she returned. It probably also explains why she decided to leave the store a week later – not because of gossip about the naval officer, but because she needed more time to convalesce.

Worthen's theory is that in the six months after leaving the cigar store Mary again got herself pregnant, and once more appealed to Anderson for help. When she left home that Sunday morning she intended to go to Hoboken for an abortion. (In fact, there was a story that Mrs Loss, the tavern-owner, had admitted on her deathbed that Mary Rogers had died during an abortion; there is no hard evidence for this confession, but it *is* known that the District Attorney was inclined to the abortion theory of Mary's death.) She died during the abortion, and her body was dumped in the river to protect the abortionist – the dark-skinned man with whom she was seen on the ferry – and Mrs Loss's family.

How does this theory fit the known facts? The answer is: very well indeed, particularly if we make the natural assumption that the father of the second unborn child was Daniel Payne – for it seems unlikely that Mary agreed to marry him, then continued her affair with her former lover. (Nothing is known about this former lover, but Anderson is obviously a suspect.) We must assume, then, that Payne knew perfectly well that Mary was on her way to Hoboken to have an illegal operation. We may also probably assume that the pregnancy was still in its early stages, and that Mary anticipated very little trouble – after all, she had recovered from the earlier abortion in a week, though it still left her feeling ill. Mary's mother was probably also in the secret. Duke comments: "It was generally believed at the time that the murdered girl's mother knew more about her daughter's mysterious admirer than she chose to tell."

What of the evidence about the gang? It is possible, of course, that a young girl was actually seen entering the woods with a gang of men, and that this was nothing to do with Mary Rogers. But it is far more probable that the anonymous letter claiming that Mary had entered the woods with six ruffians was sent by Mrs Loss or one of her friends – it came from Hoboken. Then all she had to do was to persuade two of her relatives or friends to claim that they were the men on the beach, and that they had seen Mary enter the woods and seen the boat with three men that landed shortly afterwards . . . The result would be a perfect red herring, directing the attention of the police away from her own abortion parlour.

What of the petticoat found later in the woods? This, significantly enough, was found by Mrs Loss's children. We may assume that the petticoat, the umbrella and the handkerchief were left behind in Mrs Loss's roadhouse when Mary's body was dragged to the water in the middle of the night, and were later planted in the woods, in a place where the bushes were broken, to suggest evidence of a struggle.

And what of the evidence that Mary had been raped? This, apparently, was the coroner's report; we do not know whether she was examined by a doctor or if so what the doctor concluded. What we *do* know is that Mary's body was already decomposing, and that because of the hot July weather it was buried within a few hours of being taken out of the water; so any inquest would have been performed in haste. In 1841 the science of legal medicine was in its infancy, and it is doubtful whether anyone took a vaginal swab and examined it under a microscope for spermatozoa. What was probably taken for evidence of rape was actually evidence of an abortion that had gone wrong.

Duke reports that Daniel Payne committed suicide "at the same spot in the woods where his sweetheart was probably slain". Other writers on the case have questioned this (notably Charles E. Pearce in *Unsolved Murder Mysteries*, 1924). But Payne's suicide would certainly be consistent with the theory that he was the father of the unborn child.

It is a disappointing – if obvious – solution to one of the great "murder mysteries", that Mary Rogers died in the course of an abortion. Why is it not more generally known? Partly because Poe himself obscured the truth. In the 1850 edition of Poe's works published the year after his death "Marie Roget" appeared with a footnote that stated:

> It may not be improper to record . . . that the confessions of *two* persons (one of them the Madame Dulac of the narrative [Mrs Loss]) made at different periods long subsequent to the publication confessed, in full, not only the general conclusion but absolutely *all* the chief hypothetical details by which the conclusion was attained.

But this is obviously impossible. Mrs Loss only seems to have confessed that Mary had died in the course of an abortion in her tavern. Poe's theory was that she was murdered by a man "in a passion" who then dragged her body to the seashore. The likely truth seems to be that she died of an air embolism, and that the abortionist, with the aid of Mrs Loss, made the

> In a magazine called *The Unexplained* (No. 152) Grahame Fuller
> and Ian Knight suggest that Poe himself may have been the killer
> of Mary Rogers. A witness said he had seen her with a tall,
> well-dressed man of swarthy complexion on the afternoon she
> died; Poe ws of olive complexion, and was always well-dressed.
> But he was only five feet eight inches tall. Poe's biographers all
> insist on his gentleness and courtesy. On the whole, the notion
> of Poe as a demonic killer, writing "Marie Roget" to boast about
> his crime, must be relegated to the realm of fantasy.

death look like murder by tying a strip of cloth round her
throat; the two of them then probably carried it to the water.
Poe's "Marie Roget", far from being an amazingly accurate
reconstruction of the murder, is simply a bad guess. Poe may
not have been a murderer, but he was undoubtedly a liar.

# The Bravo Case

It happened in the Priory, Balham, south London, where
Charles Bravo, a thirty-year-old barrister, lived with his
newly-married wife Florence. She was an attractive girl, who
had been a widow for four years when Bravo married her in
December 1875. Her first husband, Captain Alexander Lewis
Ricardo, of the Grenadier Guards, had died of alcoholism,
leaving Florence a welcome – and, she thought, well-earned
– £40,000.

When Charles Bravo proposed to her, he was aware that
she was the mistress of a middle-aged doctor called James
Manby Gully, who had tended her when her first marriage
was breaking up. Charles's sexual past had not been entirely
blameless, so the lovers agreed to put all thoughts of jealousy
from their minds. Charles was undoubtedly in love with her,
and just as undoubtedly attracted by her money.

As she soon discovered, he could be overbearing and

bad-tempered; but Florence wasn't the type to be bullied. She had a mind of her own – and a tendency to drink rather too heavily. She ran the Priory – an imposing Gothic pile – with the help of a widow named Mrs Cox. To begin with, the marriage seemed happy – even though Florence had two miscarriages in four months, and Bravo suffered from fits of retrospective fury about Gully, and once even struck her.

On Friday, 21 April 1876, Charles Bravo ate a good supper

---

A dummy hanging by a noose at the Long Beach Amusement Park in California formed part of a "fun house" exhibit in the centre for over five years.

It was such a convincing piece that it was often used as a prop for films which were being shot in the Park. During the filming of an episode of *The Six Million Dollar Man*, one of the film cameramen became dissatisfied with the way in which the right arm was hanging from the body of the dummy and was attempting to adjust it in order to make it look real when the whole arm fell off. On closer examination a protruding bone was noted and he identified the dummy as a human but in not the and when sprayed as he an with had had been bought by the amusement park from a local wax museum.

of whiting, roast lamb, and anchovy eggs on toast, washing it down with burgundy. Florence and Mrs Cox drank most of two bottles of sherry between them. At ten that night, loud groans came from Bravo's bedroom; he had been seized with severe abdominal pains, and began vomiting. He vomited for three days, until he died.

Sir William Gull, Queen Victoria's physician (who was suspected by some twentieth-century criminologists of being Jack the Ripper), saw him before he died, and gave his opinion that Bravo was suffering from some irritant poison. A post-mortem confirmed this – there were signs of antimony poisoning. At this point Mrs Cox declared that Bravo had told her: "I have taken poison. Don't tell Florence."

An open verdict was returned at the inquest. But the newspapers smelled scandal, and openly hinted that Florence had killed her husband. Another inquest was held, prompted by Charles's brother Joseph, who was out to get a verdict of wilful murder – which would lead to Florence's arrest.

This time, the Dr Gully scandal came into open court – doing Gully a great deal of professional damage. Added to this a dismissed servant of the Bravos' testified that he had once bought tartar emetic for the doctor. But again, the jury decided that there was not enough evidence to charge anyone – although they agreed that it *was* a case of murder. So Florence was exculpated, and she died of alcoholism two years later in Southsea.

Ever since then, students of crime have argued about the case. The most popular theory, obviously, is that Florence did it. An inquest on the body of her first husband – conducted after the Bravo inquest – showed traces of antimony in *his* organs. However, Ricardo had by then been separated from Florence for months.

It seems possible that his violent attacks of vomiting were not due to alcoholism, but to slow poisoning with antimony. But why should Florence kill her husband? Possibly because he insisted on his marital rights, and she was terrified of further miscarriages; possibly because she came to realize that he was interested only in her money.

In *How Charles Bravo Died*, author Yseult Bridges suggests that Bravo accidentally took the poison with which he had been dosing Florence. Crime novelist Agatha Christie

It is tempting to speculate how many of the great mysteries of the past might have been solved if the police had been able to use modern methods. The Ripper murders would fairly certainly remain unsolved; in the few parallel modern cases I can think of the murderer has either remained uncaught, or was caught by chance. But some of the domestic mysteries would almost certainly not remain mysteries - a fingerprint on a bottle would have been enough. One of the great Victorian *causes célèbres,* the Pook case, would have been solved within hours if there had been tests for human blood in 1871. The victim, a servant girl named Jane Clouson, was found lying in a lovers' lane at Eltham, south London, her face and head horribly lacerated. She died shortly afterwards without speaking. The constable found a lathing hammer near the scene of the crime - a cross between a hammer and a chopper. This had made more than a dozen wounds, through one of which the girl's brain was protruding. It was discovered that she was two months pregnant. The young man who was believed to be responsible was Edmund Pook, the son of a Greenwich printer, in whose house Jane Clouson had been a servant for two years. Shortly before her seventeenth birthday, the girl had been dismissed through the agency of Pook's mother, who felt the girl was too familiar with her son.

Edmund Pook proved to be a spoiled, swaggering, altogether unpleasant young man. He flatly denied any intimacy with Jane Clouson, and said she was dirty. But he was unable to explain bloodstains on the cuff of his shirt, or on his clothes.

Fifty years later, it would have been a simple matter to test his later assertion that the blood was his own - he was subject to epileptic fits and nosebleeds. It is possible, of course, that his blood and Jane Clouson's were of the same group, but then, he certainly left fingerprints on the hammer.

> Gaslit London was a grim city in which mothers with babies at their breast slept out on the freezing pavements, a city of disease, violence and corruption. It comes to life in the pages of that curious work called *My Secret Life* by an unknown Victorian whom we know only as Walter. Walter often wandered around the slum streets, seeking satisfaction of his peculiar desires. He might have a sudden impulse to have sex with a pregnant woman, or with a young virgin, or even a child. On one occasion he picked up a woman and a ten-year-old girl, went back to a cold, dismal room with them, and spent the night possessing them both. Moreover, it was not the first time the child had been made to give herself to a man for money. Again and again, Walter describes possessing young girls for a shilling.

believed that Dr Gully did it, or helped Florence to do it. Many other writers believe Mrs Cox was the culprit. Bravo disliked her, and is known to have wanted to get rid of her. The Priory has now been turned into working-class flats, and has a reputation for being haunted; but no one has ever produced a satisfactory explanation of the mystery of Bravo's death.

# Lizzie Borden

At 11.15, on the morning of 4 August 1892 – the hottest day of the year – Lizzie Borden called the maid Bridget Sullivan and told her that someone had killed her father. The seventy-year-old banker was found on the divan in the parlour, his face unrecognizable; someone had struck him several blows with a hatchet. Borden's second wife, Abby, was believed to be out visiting a sick friend – according to Lizzie – but she was later found upstairs in the guest room, lying face downwards. She had also been killed with blows

from a hatchet – much heavier, more savage blows than those
that had killed Andrew Borden. Lizzie's story was that she
had been out in the barn, and had heard a cry from the house;
she rushed back to find her father dead.

It soon became clear that Lizzie had much to hide. Her
mother had died when she was two; two years later her father
remarried; Abby Gray was six years his junior, twenty-two
years older than Lizzie's sister Emma. Two days before the
murder, Lizzie had tried to buy prussic acid. Lizzie's father
and stepmother had been experiencing stomach pains for
some time before the murder. Lizzie hated her stepmother.

Moreover, medical evidence proved that Abby Borden had
died shortly after 9 a.m., while her husband was not killed
until about two hours later. It was just within the bounds of
possibility that an unknown assassin had entered the house
and murdered the couple – but not that he had remained
concealed for two hours, in a small house in which there were
two women. (Lizzie's sister was away staying with friends.)

Lizzie was arrested and tried. The evidence against her
was purely circumstantial; the prosecution merely attempted
to demonstrate that she was the likeliest person to have
committed the murders. But she was a respectable girl of
unblemished reputation, and the jury found her not guilty.
She lived on until 1927. During her lifetime it was impossible
for writers to speculate about whether she killed her father
and stepmother. But after her death, Edmund Pearson lost
no time in publishing his opinion that she was the killer.
(Even during her lifetime, the local newspaper in Fall River,
Massachusetts, printed sarcastic articles on the anniversary
of the murder – one of which concluded that the Bordens
had not been murdered at all, but had died of the heat.) His
*Trial of Lizzie Borden* in the Great American Trial series came
out in 1937, and the book is dedicated to the district attorney
who built up the case against Lizzie Borden. In 1959, a new
piece of evidence turned up. In a book called *Murder and
Mutiny*, published in 1959, E. R. Snow tells how he received
a letter from an elderly gentleman named Thomas Owens,
who had listened to a broadcast about the Borden case by
Snow. Owens had a strange story to tell. In 1896, four years
after the murder, Lizzie Borden went into the art gallery
and shop of Tilden-Thurber in Providence, Rhode Island,

and when she left, the assistant found that two expensive paintings on porcelain were missing. The following February, a lady went into the shop with one of the two paintings, and asked if a crack could be repaired. The manager was told, and he asked the lady where she had obtained the painting. "From Miss Lizzie Borden of Fall River." As a result of this, a headline "Lizzie Again" appeared in the *Providence Journal*, which stated that a warrant for her arrest had been issued for the theft of two paintings. What had happened, said Owens, was that the owners of the gallery had put a proposition to Lizzie: sign a confession to the murders, or we prosecute. Lizzie refused, and the item was published in the newspaper. This caused Lizzie to change her mind. After promises that the confession would not be used, Lizzie typed on a sheet of paper: "Unfair means force my signature here admitting the act of August 4, 1892, as mine alone, Lizbeth A Borden." The store decided to have the document photographed in case of accident, and Owens was asked to do it. He did; but he also made a second copy – or, he said, decided that the first copy was indistinct, and made another one for the store, without mentioning that he had the other. As the four principals in the episode died – there were two other men besides the store owners – he expected it to be publicized. And now, Owens was willing to sell the photograph of Lizzie's confessions for one hundred dollars. Snow persuaded him to take fifty, and printed the story in his book.

Another crime writer, Edward Radin, decided to look into the matter, and he soon established that Snow had been the victim of a swindler. It was Lizzie's signature, and the type face was that of a machine of the period, but the signature had been traced from Lizzie's will. It would be interesting to know whether Mr Snow demanded his fifty dollars back.

But obviously, the first part of the story was true. Lizzie *had* stolen the paintings, and the item really appeared in the *Providence Journal* in February 1897. Lizzie was a kleptomaniac. Although she had plenty of money (she left over a million dollars), she was a compulsive stealer. Oddly enough, she was also capable of great generosity.

Radin's book *Lizzie Borden, The Untold Story* asserts that Lizzie was innocent. The killer was Bridget Sullivan, the servant girl. It is known that Bridget was feeling ill on the

morning of 4 August; yet Mrs Borden had her cleaning all
the outside windows at 7.30 in the morning. Later that
morning, Bridget vomited. Certainly, she had a motive of
sorts – sheer resentment at her employer. Radin tells how he
was completely convinced by Pearson's view of the case until
he read the actual trial reports for himself and discovered that
Pearson had suppressed many pieces of evidence in Lizzie's
favour.

In 1964, Gerald Gross edited a volume of selections from
Edmund Pearson's articles on murder, and wrote a postscript
to Pearson's "final word" on the Borden case. Gross says,
very fairly, that Radin has distorted the evidence for Lizzie's
innocence as carefully as Pearson distorted that for her guilt,
and he points out that Pearson had to do a great deal of
omitting anyway, to pack the trial into one fair-sized volume.
But Gross's theory is that Lizzie killed her parents aided and
abetted by Bridget. There is a persistent story that Bridget
returned to Ireland after the trial, with a great deal of money
given to her by Lizzie. Radin points out, quite correctly, that
Bridget could certainly not be said to have testified in Lizzie's
favour at the trial; on the contrary, most of her evidence told
against her employer. If, however, she was an accomplice – or
an accessory after the fact – perhaps to helping Lizzie conceal
the murder weapon or the bloodstained dress (which Lizzie
burnt) – then Lizzie would certainly have a motive for giving
her money.

LIZZIE BORDEN.    EMMA BORDEN.    REV. MR. BUCK.    MRS. C. J. HOLMES.    MR. C. J. HOLMES.
THE PRISONER AND HER FRIENDS IN COURT.

Lizzie Borden in court.

　　In 1967 there appeared in America, Victoria Lincoln's *A Private Disgrace*. When Foster Damon – another expert on the Borden case – sent me a copy, he enclosed a card which said: "I think this is the final word on Lizzie." I am inclined to think he is right.

Victoria Lincoln was born in Fall River, so her insight into the town is obviously authentic. She was able to uncover some facts that suddenly make the whole case quite clear. There is only one point in Miss Lincoln's account that might be described as "speculation"; from accounts of the periodic fainting illness that Lizzie suffered from, she arrives at the conclusion that Lizzie suffered from epilepsy of the temporal lobe of the brain. Psychomotor epilepsy is distinguished by seizures of automatic activity. Miss Lincoln cites a case from a medical textbook in which a man woke from a seizure, to find that the boss had raised his salary, impressed by the lucid and forceful way in which the man had asked for a raise. Lizzie undoubtedly had strange attacks about four times a year, always at the time of her menstrual period. The evidence about these attacks points to psychomotor epilepsy. And Lizzie was menstruating at the time of the murders.

But Miss Lincoln's theory is not an attempt to prove that Lizzie committed the murders in a trance-like state. She intended to kill her stepmother – but by poison. She hated her and was violently jealous of her. A year before the murders, her stepmother's room had been broken into and robbed when Lizzie was in the house. The thief was supposed to have flitted in silently, without alerting Lizzie, Emma and the maid Bridget, broken into the room, taken money and jewellery, and flitted out via the cellar door. Andrew Borden soon asked the police to drop the investigation. He had a fairly shrewd idea of the identity of the thief.

Lizzie felt she had reason for hating her stepmother. First of all, it was a quarrel about a house. Mrs Borden's sister had not married so well, and she lived in half a house, the other half of which belonged to her mother. Her mother wanted to sell, but could hardly turn her own daughter out. So Andrew Borden came to the rescue, and quietly bought the whole house, giving half to the sister, and half to his own wife Abby. He did this with great secrecy, knowing the feelings of his children about their stepmother and her family, but

the news leaked. Lizzie was furious. She told her father
that charity should begin at home. She ceased to call Abby
"mother", and from then on, addressed her – when she had
to – as Mrs Borden. Andrew Borden tried to restore peace in
the home by giving Lizzie and her sister another house, which
had belonged to their grandfather. Lizzie was placated; but
she never forgave her stepmother, and continued to address
her as "Mrs Borden" after twenty-three years of calling her
"mother".

The trouble that led directly to the murder was an identical
situation, which took place five years later – just before the
murder. Uncle John Vinnicum Morse was a mid-westerner,
and he decided that he would like to move closer to his
brother-in-law's home (he was the brother of Borden's first
wife). Borden owned a farm at nearby Swansea, and Morse
asked if he could rent it. Borden said yes – and decided to
do again what he had already done over the business of his
sister-in-law's house – to transfer the farm to his wife's name.
Miss Lincoln dug up this curious transaction, the immediate
motive of the murder; Pearson and the other writers on the
case were unaware of it. Lizzie already disliked Uncle John
because he had aided and abetted her father in the previous
house transaction. So now he moved into their house again
as a guest, she felt distinctly edgy. Miss Lincoln does not
produce a convincing explanation why Borden decided to
transfer the farm to Abby; perhaps he wanted to give her
a present – he had recently bought back the other house
from his daughters for two thousand more than its value,
thus making them a present of a thousand dollars each. But
Borden was seventy; no doubt he wanted to leave his wife
well provided for in the event of his death. This was also why
Lizzie was so bitterly opposed to these property deals. And
it did not take long for the news about the Swansea property
to leak back to her. This is when she started trying to buy
poison. And although she was unsuccessful in her attempts
to buy prussic acid ("for cleaning a fur"), she presumably
bought *something*, for that evening Mr and Mrs Borden were
very sick indeed. Lizzie said she had been sick too, but we
have only her word for this.

There was another factor that has been largely ignored by
Pearson and Radin. Lizzie had a deep love of animals, and she

owned some pigeons, which lived in the barn roost. Borden kept everything locked up – he was capable of obsessive meanness – and when the barn was broken into twice by youths who wanted pigeon pie for supper, he chopped off the heads of all the pigeons with a hatchet. It was not exactly unkindness; in those days, America was still close to the pioneers, and most people killed their own chickens and butchered their own hogs. But he failed to calculate the effect on Lizzie.

This, in summary, is the new evidence dug up by Victoria Lincoln, and it certainly makes the case in every way more straightforward. The transfer of the deeds on the Swansea property was to take place on the day of the murder. Borden had thought up a stratagem to do this without arousing Lizzie's suspicions – a carriage would be sent to the door, and a note requesting that Mrs Borden visit a sick neighbour. The note arrived – or so Miss Lincoln believes – but by then, Mrs Borden was already dead, or about to die. She was working in the guest room, on all fours, when Lizzie came in behind her with the hatchet, and sliced into her skull with blow after blow. At this point, Miss Lincoln embarks on a speculation that I find difficult to accept. John Morse had left the house much earlier. He had no alibi for the time of the first murder, but an extremely detailed one for the second. Miss Lincoln believes that Morse went along to the house just to make sure that all went according to plan – after all, the affair of the farm was of immediate interest to him. He watched the boy deliver the note, and observed Lizzie's very abrupt manner as she took it, followed by her slamming of the door. Obviously, she was having one of her queer spells. Ever since Morse had been in the Bordens' house, there had been a brooding tension, and Mrs Borden probably suspected Lizzie of wanting to poison her. So Morse listened with more than usual attention to what followed, and rightly interpreted the heavy thud from the upstairs room – its window was wide open on the hot August morning – followed by a succession of squelching noises. Probably Mrs Borden groaned the first time – Bridget was out at the other side of the house cleaning windows, so she would not hear. And Morse, realizing what had happened, knew that an uncle from the mid-west would be a far more likely suspect for

a murder than the respectable daughter of the house. So he
hurried away and started establishing an alibi.

This *could* have happened, but there is no evidence that
it did. All that seems moderately certain is that, with the
stifling heat of the August morning, and the irritation of
her menstrual period, Lizzie had one of her queer spells,
and decided that she could not stand her stepmother a
moment longer. Miss Lincoln may well be right; it may
have been committed in a dream-like state, and the dream
may have involved the headless pigeons. Miss Lincoln could
be wrong in her diagnosis of psychomotor epilepsy; but it
is hard to doubt that all kinds of factors – the knowledge
of another property deal, her hatred of her stepmother and
determination to kill her, the heat, menstrual irritation –
suddenly decided her to use violence. Earlier writers on the
case were not aware of just *how much* violence and tension
there was in the air in the Borden house in the weeks before
the murder; it was a storm that had to break. Borden broke
his usual habit of reticence to tell a business associate that he
was having a lot of trouble at home at the moment.

What Lizzie did about her bloodstained dress after this
first murder is rather a mystery. Presumably she took it
off. At 10.45, Andrew Borden arrived home unexpectedly,
no doubt puzzled by his wife's non-appearance at the bank.
His daughter was on the point of leaving the house – to
establish an alibi. The doors were locked – as usual – and
Bridget had to let him in. Lizzie was heard to give a strange
laugh as her father came in. She told her father that Mrs
Borden had been called away to see a sick neighbour. Possibly
Andrew Borden accepted this story; possibly he supposed
Mrs Borden and Uncle John were now signing papers that
he had already signed. At all events, he went into the sitting
room and fell asleep. Bridget Sullivan testified that he was
carrying "something like a book". Miss Lincoln is inclined to
believe that this "something" wrapped in white paper was
the deeds to the Swansea property, and the agreement to
transfer it. Lizzie was later seen burning something in the
kitchen stove.

What happened next? Miss Lincoln believes that Lizzie
genuinely loved her father, but that seeing him asleep was
tempted to spare him the horror of seeing his wife's body,

and knowing that Lizzie was the killer. (For he *would* have known, just as he knew that Lizzie was the invisible thief of a year earlier.) Undoubtedly, he loved her, and he would cease to do so when the body was discovered. And so, according to Miss Lincoln, she regretfully raised the hatchet. . . .

I find this hard to accept. Andrew Borden was killed with nine blows, one of which sliced through his eye. Lizzie must have gone back upstairs to change her dress before the murder – unless she disposed of two bloodstained dresses – and then gone to get the hatchet from the basement. (It is true that she may have kept the dress in the basement too.) Two days before, her father had suffered from the same serious stomach complaint as her stepmother. She had made up her mind to kill him too. She did it less violently than in the case of her stepmother – nine blows instead of seventeen – but unflinchingly. Then she went to the barn and washed the hatchet, smashed off its bloodstained handle in a vice – which she burnt – and rubbed the blade in ashes. She removed the dress and folded it into a bundle. Or she may have simply hung it in her closet among her other dresses, as Miss Lincoln suggests, simply putting it inside another. By the time Bridget came in from cleaning the windows, and went to her room to lie down for a moment, Lizzie had changed and was ready to give the alarm.

There is some evidence for the epilepsy theory. Lizzie's mother suffered from severe migraines and sudden violent seizures of unmotivated rage. The evening before the murder, Lizzie called on a friend, Alice Russell, and said: "I'm afraid someone will do something. I don't know what but someone will do something." The heat wave had started the day before; she was experiencing the sense of brooding depression that Dostoievsky has described as preceding epileptic fits. "I feel depressed," she told Miss Russell, "I feel as if something was hanging over me that I can't shake off." Only that morning there had been a strange scene; her stepmother had approached a Doctor Bowen who lived opposite, and told him that her husband had received a letter threatening to poison him, and that they had been sick all the previous night. Doctor Bowen finally agreed to come to the house – and was met by a furious Andrew Borden, who told him to mind his own business and go away. And meanwhile the heat was tremendous, oppressive – it was one of the hottest days recorded in Fall River in living memory – and Lizzie's abdomen was aching in a way that indicated the approach of a menstrual period . . . She may well have foreboding.

No, forensic medicine would have made no difference to the Borden case. It might have established blood on the blade of the ash-coated hatchet, and drawn the net of circumstantial evidence a little tighter. And if someone had had Miss Lincoln's shrewdness, the forensic laboratories might have examined the *inside* of all Lizzie Borden's dresses for bloodstains that proved that a bloodstained dress had been hung up inside one of them. For what Lizzie did with the bloodstained dress between the day of the murder – Thursday – and Sunday morning, when she burnt it, is the chief unsolved mystery of the case. Emma and Alice Russell walked into the kitchen, and interrupted Lizzie, who was holding the Bedford cord dress. "I'm going to burn this old thing," said Lizzie. "It's all covered up with paint." Alice and Emma must have exchanged a horrified glance. It was their moment of decision. If they snatched it from Lizzie, or casually asked to look at it, it would undoubtedly send Lizzie to the scaffold. But what was the point? The Bordens were dead, and both Emma and her friend Alice knew about Lizzie's "queer spells". Alice merely said: "I wouldn't let anyone see you doing that if I were you," and then conveniently forgot the incident for four months. When Alice was questioned about Lizzie's dresses the next day, she went in to Lizzie and told her she really ought not to have burnt the dress. Lizzie simulated concern, and said: "Why did you let me do it?" Quite.

# chapter two

# EARLY 20TH CENTURY UNSOLVED MURDERS

*B*y the turn of the century, new methods of forensic analysis were turning crime detection into a science. There was the discovery of fingerprints, of blood groups, and of ballistics - methods of identifying which gun had fired a particular bullet. Ballistics played a part in the conviction of a villainous con-man named Samuel Herbert Dougal, who murdered his mistress Camille Holland in 1899 – after she ordered him to leave her home – and buried her body in the garden of Moat Farm, Essex. Dougal continued to live there for the next four years, forging cheques in the name of Miss Holland and seducing servant girls. When the police finally came to enquire about Miss Holland, he fled, but was captured in London. A decomposed female corpse was found in the garden of Moat Farm. It bore no distinguishing marks, but Camille Holland's shoemaker was able to identify the initialled boots found with the body. And the testimony of firearms expert Edward J. Churchill convinced a jury that Dougal had shot Miss Holland at a range of a few inches – he tested his theory by firing bullets at the skull of a sheep, and learned that the further away from the gun, the bigger the hole it made. Dougal confessed to the murder as he stood on the scaffold.

Churchill was also to play a central role in a case that is still regarded as one of the oddest unsolved mysteries of the twentieth century: the Luard mystery.

*But the Luard case seems typically British; it has the bland* **271**
*atmosphere of an Agatha Christie novel. Across the Atlantic,*
*murder was usually more violent and less mysterious. The unsolved*
*murder of Nora Fuller which occurred in San Francisco has the*
*dubious distinction of being one of the first recorded sex crimes of*
*the twentieth century. And the New Orleans Axeman as the classic*
*American murder mystery of the World War I period has something*
*in common with London's Jack the Ripper murders of 1888.*

# The Summer House Mystery

On 24 August 1908, fifty-eight-year-old Caroline Mary Luard,
attractive wife of seventy-year-old Major-General Charles
Edward Luard, was found shot dead in a summer-house close
to the Luards' rural residence, Ightham Knoll, near Sevenoaks
in Kent. The couple had left their house at 2.30 that afternoon.
General Luard's destination was Godden Green golf links,
three miles away, from which he wished to collect his golf
clubs in preparation for a weekend visit. His wife parted from
him after walking a short distance, her intention being to
proceed to the "Casa", an unoccupied woodland bungalow
surrounded by bracken, from which there was a pleasing
view of the countryside. Returning from the links, General
Luard refused a lift from a car-owning friend, the Reverend
R. B. Cotton. At home by 4.30, the General entertained a
Mrs Stuart to tea, expressing surprise that his wife had not
returned. By early evening he went to the Casa, and found
Mrs Luard prone on the verandah, two bullets in her head
and four valuable rings missing from her left hand. (During
the post-mortem it was established that the rings had been
removed some time after the shooting.)

Police fixed the murder time: Mrs Annie Wickham, wife
of a neighbour's coachman, had heard shots at 3.15, as
had Daniel Kettle, a farm labourer. There was an absence
of clues, although much talk of mysterious strangers seen
in the vicinity – not unlikely, for hop-picking Eastenders
were in Kent at this time enjoying their annual working
holiday; nor had the General's wife any enemies. At the

inquest General Luard was asked about firearms he kept at Ightham Knoll, and said he had not missed **any** revolver. The Reverend R. B. Cotton, questioned about his own mysterious stranger, mentioned a "sandy-haired tramp" he had seen emerge from the woods about the time of the murder. A juryman was assured that no certified lunatic had a grudge against Mrs Luard. Upon the adjournment of this inquest, General Luard himself became chief suspect and received many abusive letters.

The autopsy had disclosed that Caroline Luard had been shot twice with a .32 revolver. Luard himself had owned several revolvers of this calibre, and these were sent to Churchill – who ran a gun business in the Strand – for examination. Churchill fired test bullets from each of the guns, then examined them under a microscope. The difference in the rifle marks established that none of them had fired the murder bullet.

At the second inquest Mr Thomas Durrand, manager of a Sevenoaks brewery, spoke of seeing General Luard at 3.21 near Hall Farm, a quarter-hour's walk from the Casa. Ernest King, a labourer, testified that he saw General Luard walking towards Godden Green Golf Club at 3.25, twenty minutes' walk from the Casa, and Harry Kent, steward of the golf club, said he had seen General Luard on the eighteenth green at 3.30. All three witnesses spoke of the General's composure of manner. Servants at Ightham Knoll testified to the Luards' devotion, and General Luard himself, haggard and grief-stricken, presented a pitiful figure in the witness-box. This second inquest was adjourned, and General Luard, after putting up Ightham Knoll for sale, went to stay with his friend, Colonel Ward, MP. One morning he walked out and threw himself under a train near the local junction at West Farleigh. He had left Ward a letter saying he could not stand the strain of being under suspicion. To another friend he left a note:

> I have gone to her I loved. Goodbye. Something
> has snapped.
>
> Luard

Sixty years later, in 1959, when the present writer was compiling *An Encyclopaedia of Murder*, a correspondent sent me a copy of a paper on capital punishment by C. H. Norman, who had been at one time an official shorthand writer to the Court of Criminal Appeal. In this paper – which I included as an appendix in the *Encyclopaedia* – Norman stated his conviction that the killer of Mrs Luard was the "railway murderer" John Dickman, who was convicted in 1910 of murdering a wages clerk named Nisbet on a Newcastle train, and stealing £370. Nisbet was shot in the head five times. Sir S. Rowan-Hamilton, who edited the trial of Dickman for the *Notable British Trials* series, told Norman in a letter: "All the same Dickman was justly convicted, and it may interest you to know that he was with little doubt the murderer of Mrs Luard, for he had forged a cheque she had sent him in response to an advertisement in *The Times* (I believe) asking for help; she discovered it and wrote to him and met him outside the General's and her house and her body was found there. He was absent from Newcastle those exact days . . . I have seen replicas of the cheques."

Whether this is the true solution of the Luard mystery will never be known. The only conclusive piece of evidence would have been the gun with which Caroline Luard was shot. But the two guns used to kill Nisbet were never found; and if Dickman shot Caroline Luard, he undoubtedly took the same care to dispose of the .32 revolver that he used. Even as early as 1910, murderers who used guns were becoming aware of the danger posed by firearms experts.

# The Murder of Nora Fuller by a Degenerate

This, one of the first recorded sex crimes, is recounted in a typically leisurely manner by San Francisco police captain Thomas S. Duke in his classic *Celebrated Criminal Cases of America*, published in 1910.

Eleanor Parline, better known as Nora Fuller, was born in China in 1886.

In 1890 her father was an engineer on the Steamer Tai Wo. One night he was sitting asleep in a steamer chair on the deck of the vessel while at sea. Shortly after he was seen in this position his services were required in the engineroom, but when a helper was sent after him the chair was vacant, and Parline was never seen again. A year later Mrs. Parline married a man named W. W. Fuller, in San Francisco, but seven years later she obtained a divorce.

As she had four small children, Mrs. Fuller experienced much trouble in getting along. In 1902 she lived at 1747 Fulton Street. At that time Nora, who was then fifteen years of age, decided to quit school and seek employment.

On January 6 she wrote to a theatrical agency, and after stating that she had a fairly good soprano voice, asked for employment. Two days later the following advertisement appeared in the Chronicle and Examiner:

"Wanted – Young white girl to take care of baby; good home and good wages."

At the foot of the advertisement was a note directing anyone answering to address the communication in care of the paper the advertisement was

---

In their book *Perfect Murder*, Bernard Taylor and Stephen Knight conclude that there is no evidence whatever that Mrs Luard was murdered by railway-killer Dickman. Their view is that she was killed by some casual intruder intent on burglary. They point out that the month when she was killed was the middle of the hop-picking season, when hundreds of Londoners go to Kent for a paid holiday. Some East End crook who carried a gun (gun laws were far more lax in 1908) may have been on the lookout for somewhere to burgle, and been in the summer house when Mrs Luard came. The fact that her rings were removed and a pocket (probably containing her purse) was torn off adds some support to this theory.

found in. Nora Fuller answered it, and on Saturday, January 11, she received the following postal:

"Miss Fuller: In answer to yours in response to my advertisement, kindly call at the Popular restaurant, 55 Geary Street, and inquire for Mr. John Bennett, at 1 o'clock. If you can't come at 1, come at 6.

JOHN BENNETT."

Mrs. Fuller sent Nora to rendezvous, and the girl took the postal card with her. About one hour later Mrs. Fuller's telephone rang, and her twelve-year-old son answered.

A nervous, irritable voice, which sounded something like Nora's, told him that the speaker was at the home of Mr. Bennett, at 1500 Geary Street, and her employer wanted her to go to work at once.

The boy called out the message to his mother, who instructed him to tell Nora to come home and go to work Monday. The boy repeated the message, and the person at the other end said: "All right"; but before any more could be said by the boy the receiver at the other end was hung up. Nora Fuller never came home. A few days later the distracted mother notified the police.

F. W. Krone, proprietor of the Popular restaurant, was questioned and he stated that about 5:30 o'clock on the evening of January 11, a man who had been a patron of his place at different times during the past fifteen years, but whose name he had not up to that time heard, came to the counter and stated that he expected a young girl to inquire for John Bennett, and if she did to send her to the table where he was seated.

The girl did not appear, and Bennett, after waiting one-half hour, became restless and walked up and down the side-walk in front of the restaurant for several moments. He then disappeared.

This man was described as being about forty years of age, five feet nine inches high, weighing about 170 pounds, wearing a brown mustache, well dressed and refined appearing.

A waiter employed at the Popular restaurant, who frequently waited on "Bennett," stated that the much-wanted man was a great lover of porterhouse steaks, but the fact that he only ate the tenderloin part of the steak earned for him the sobriquet of "Tenderloin."

On January 16 lengthy articles were published in the papers in regard to the mysterious disappearance of the girl.

On January 8 a man giving the name of C. B. Hawkins called at Umbsen & Co.'s real estate office, and, addressing a clerk named C. S. Lahenier, inquired for particulars regarding a two-story frame building for rent at 2211 Sutter Street. The terms were satisfactory to Hawkins, but Lahenier asked the prospective tenant for references. He replied that he could give none, as he was a stranger in the city, but as he had a prepossessing appearance the clerk let him have the key after paying one month's rent in advance. The man then signed the name "C. B. Hawkins" to a contract.

He stated that he was then stopping at the Golden West Hotel with his wife. The description of Hawkins was identically the same as the description of Bennett.

On the following day the real estate firm sent E. F. Bertrand, a locksmith and "handy man" in their employ, to the Sutter Street house to clean it up.

Many days after this a collector for the firm named Fred Crawford reported that the house was still vacant – judging from outside appearances. He went to the Golden West Hotel to inquire for Hawkins, but he was not known there.

On February 8 the month's rent was up, and a collector and inspector named H. E. Dean was sent to the house.

Using a pass key he entered, but finding no furniture on the lower floor, he went upstairs, where he found the door to a back room closed. This he opened, but as the shade was down the room was in semi-darkness. He discerned a bright-colored garment on the floor, but as he seemed to know by intuition that something was wrong, he hurriedly left the building, and meeting Officer Gill requested him to accompany him back to the house. The officer entered the room, and upon raising the shade found the dead body of a young girl lying as if asleep in a bed. On the bed were two new sheets, which had never been laundered, a blanket and quilt. An old chair was the only other furniture in the house. Neither food nor dishes could be found. Nor was there any means of heating or lighting the house, as the gas was not connected.

The girl's clothing was in the bedroom, also her purse, which contained no money, but a card with the following inscription thereon:

"Mr. M. A. Severbrinik, of Port Arthur."

(It was subsequently learned that this man sailed for China on the Peking three hours before Nora Fuller left home on January 11.)

On the floor was the butt of a cigar, and on the mantelpiece in the front room was an almost empty whisky bottle. There were no toilet articles in the house except one towel.

Many letters were found addressed to Mrs. C. B. Hawkins, 2211 Sutter Street. They were from furniture houses and contained either advertisements or solicitations for trade. A circular letter addressed to Mrs. Hawkins and bearing a postmark of January 21, 11 p.m., or ten days after the disappearance of Nora Fuller, had been opened by someone and then placed in the girl's jacket, which was found in the room. Mrs. Fuller identified the clothing as belonging to her daughter, and subsequently identified the body as the remains of Nora. No trace was ever found of the postal card Nora received from Bennett.

Dr. Charles Morgan, the city toxicologist, examined the stomach and found no traces of drugs or poisons. Save for an apple, which the deceased had evidently eaten about one or two hours before death, the stomach was empty.

There was a slight congestion of the stomach, possibly due to partaking of some alcoholic drink when the stomach was not accustomed to it. Mrs. Fuller stated that Nora ate an apple shortly before she left home on January 11.

Dr. Bacigalupi, the autopsy surgeon, found two black marks on the throat, one on each side of the larynx, and as there was a slight congestion of the lungs, he concluded that death was due to strangulation. But the child had been otherwise assaulted and her body frightfully mutilated, evidently by a degenerate. Captain of Detectives John Seymour took charge of the case.

B. T. Schell, a salesman at J. C. Cavanaugh's furniture store, located at 848 Mission Street, stated that at 5 p.m., January 9, a man of the same description as "Hawkins" or "Bennett," and wearing a high silk hat, called and said that he wanted to furnish a room temporarily. He purchased two second-hand pillows, a pair of blankets, a comforter and top mattress. He insisted that the goods be delivered at night or not at all. This Schell promised to do. The customer then wanted to know what assurance he had that the salesman would not substitute another mattress, and Schell suggested that he put his initials on the mattress as a means of identification. Acting on this suggestion Hawkins used a large heavy pencil and wrote the letters "C. B. H." on the mattress. After leaving word to deliver the articles that night to 2211 Sutter Street the man departed.

Lawrence C. Gillen, the delivery boy for this firm, stated that he had to work overtime in order to take the articles to the Sutter Street house that night.

When he arrived the house was in darkness. He rang the bell and a man came to the door, and from what he could see with the lights from the street lamps he was of the same description as the man who made the purchases, and he wore a silk hat. Gillen asked him to light up so he could see, but he said, "Never mind, leave the things in the hall."

Richard Fitzgerald, a salesman employed at the Standard Furniture Company, 745 Mission Street, stated that a man of "Bennett's" description bought a bed and an old chair from him on January 10, and that he engaged an expressman, Tom Tobin, to deliver the same to 2211 Sutter Street.

Tobin stated that this man was present when he arrived, and requested him to set up the bed in the room where it was found. This man he described as being of Bennett's appearance.

It is probable that the sheets, towel and pillow cases were purchased at Mrs. Mahoney's dry goods store, 92 Third Street, which was just around the corner from the Standard Furniture Company. These articles were carried away by the purchaser.

On the floor of the room where the girl's body was found was a small piece of the Denver Post of January 9, upon which was a mailing label addressed to the office of the Railroad Employees' Journal, 210 Parrott Building.

When this paper arrived at the Parrott building it was given by Exchange Editor Scott to a Mr. Hurlburt, a delegate from Denver to a railroadmen's convention then in session in the assemblyroom in the Parrott building. After glancing at it he threw it on a large table, and some other delegate picked it up and took it to Dennett's restaurant, where he left it on the dining table. The steward of the restaurant, Mr. Helbish, picked it up, and after taking it to the counter began to read it, believing it was the San Francisco Post. He laid it down, and Miss Drysdale, the cashier, glanced over it. She laid it down, and how it got to 2211 Sutter Street remains a mystery.

A seventeen-year-old girl named Madge Graham met Nora Fuller in June, 1901, and they became very friendly. Madge boarded at Nora's house

for a while until her guardian, Attorney Edward
Stearns, requested her to move away, because a
lawyer named Hugh Grant was a frequent visitor
at the Fuller home.

She claimed that Nora Fuller frequently spoke
to her of having a friend named Bennett, also
she believed that the advertisement was a trick
concocted by Nora and "Bennett" to deceive Mrs.
Fuller.

She furthermore stated that Nora often telephoned to some man, and that one day Nora
requested her to tell Mrs. Fuller that she and
Nora were going to the theater that night. Madge
did as requested, but stated that instead of going
with her, Nora went with some man. It was also
claimed that someone gave Nora complimentary
press tickets to the theaters.

A. Menke, who conducted a grocery at Golden
Gate and Central Avenues, stated that Nora Fuller
frequently used his telephone to call up someone at
a hotel, although she had a telephone in her own
home a few blocks away.

Theodore Kytka, the handwriting expert, made
an examination of the original slips filled out by
"Bennett" for his advertisement for a young girl,
and also the signature of "C. B. Hawkins" to the
contract when they rented the house, and found
both were written by the same person.

On February 19 the Coroner's jury rendered the
following verdict:

"That the said Nora Fuller, aged fifteen, nativ-
ity China, residence 1747 Fulton Street, came to
her death at 2211 Sutter Street in the City and
County of San Francisco, through asphyxiation
by strangling on a day subsequent to January
11 and before February 4, 1902, at the hands of
parties unknown. Furthermore we believe that she
died within twenty-four hours after 12 m., January
11. In view of the heinousness of the crime, we
recommend that the Governor offer a reward of

$5,000 for the discovery and apprehension of the criminal.

"ACHILLE ROSS, Foreman."

Believing that the person who committed this crime might have changed his address and sent a written notification to that effect to the postal authorities, Theodore Kytka examined 32,000 notifications of changes of address. Of this number he found three signatures that bore considerable resemblance to the Bennett–Hawkins style of penmanship, and one of these three was almost identically the same.

This proved to be the signature of a man in Kansas City, Mo., and Captain Seymour went east to make a personal investigation. It was found, however, that the man had nothing to do with the crime.

On January 16, five days after the disappearance of Nora Fuller, but three weeks before her fate was known, the papers of San Francisco gave considerable space to the mysterious case. Two days later a gentleman connected with a local paper notified the police department that a clerk in their employ named Charles B. Hadley had disappeared. It was afterward said that he was short in his accounts with his employers.

Detective Charles Cody was detailed to locate the man, and he found that he had lived at 647 Ellis Street with a girl born and raised in San Francisco, who had assumed the name of Ollie Blasier, because of her infatuation for a notorious character known as "Kid" Blasier.

No trace of Hadley was found. Finally the body of Nora Fuller was discovered, and photographs of the signature of "C. B. Hawkins" on the contract with Umbsen & Co., and the "C. B. H." on the mattress, were published in all the papers.

The Blasier woman had a photograph of Hadley in her room, upon the back of which he had written his name, "C. B. Hadley." Seeing the great similarity in the handwriting she delivered this to Detective Cody, who in turn delivered it to Theodore Kytka for investigation.

Kytka determined at once that the person who wrote "C. B. Hadley" on the photograph also wrote "C. B. H." on the mattress, and "C. B. Hawkins" on the contract.

While Hadley had the same general physique as "Hawkins," it was known that he was always clean shaven. Miss Blasier stated, however, that she had seen Hadley wear a false brown mustache about the house, and it was subsequently learned that he purchased one at a Japanese store on Larkin Street.

In addition to this, Chief of Police Langley, of Victoria, B.C., made an affidavit to the effect that a Mr. Marsden, a storekeeper in Victoria, B.C., had stated that he had been a companion of Hadley's, and that while out on a "lark" he had seen Hadley wear a false mustache. Miss Blasier made a further statement as follows:

"I now recall that after the disappearance of Nora Fuller, Hadley made a practice of getting up early in the morning and taking the morning paper to the toilet to read.

"On the day of his final disappearance he followed this practice, and after he left the house I found the morning paper in the toilet, and I noticed a long article about the disappearance of Nora Fuller. It was evident that his mind was greatly disturbed on this morning.

"The next day I was making up my laundry, and at the very bottom of the pile of soiled clothing I found some of his garments which had blood on them. I burned them and also his plug hat.

"It is well known that Hadley is partial to porterhouse steaks and that he eats only the tenderloin.

"On the evening of January 16, Hadley telephoned to me that he would not be home. I confess that I suspect he committed this murder."

Theodore Kytka obtained Hadley's photograph

and altered it by giving him the appearance of wearing a mustache and plug hat. This was shown to different persons who had dealings with "Hawkins," with the following results:

Tobin, the expressman, said it looked very much like him; Lahenier, the real estate man, said it bore a marked resemblance. Ray Zertanna, who had seen Nora in the park with a man, stated that the picture was a good likeness of this man. Schell, who suggested that "Hawkins" place his initials on the mattress, said it was an exact likeness of Hawkins. Fred Krone, the restaurant man, who had the conversation with "Bennett" on the evening Nora left home, said it was not a likeness of Bennett.

Hadley left his money in a certain bank in the city, where it remains even now.

An investigation was then made as to his past, and it developed that he was an habitue of the tenderloin district, and that he was on the road to degeneracy. His true name was Charlie Start, and his respected mother resided in Chicago.

On May 6, 1889, Superintendent of Police Brackett, of Minneapolis, issued a circular letter offering $100 reward for the arrest of Charles Start for embezzlement.

About two years before the murder of Nora Fuller, Hadley enticed a fifteen-year-old girl into a room and outraged her. He then purchased diamonds and jewelry from a certain large jewelry store in San Francisco and gave them to the girl, who is now a respectable married woman residing in the neighborhood of San Francisco.

The country was flooded with circulars accusing Hadley of this murder and calling for his apprehension, but he was never located.

Many believe that he committed suicide.

On the morning of 24 May 1918, an Italian cobbler named Jake Maggio was awakened by a groaning sound coming from the next room, where his brother Joe slept with his wife. As he entered the room, he saw a woman lying on the floor, her head almost severed from her body; Joe lay in bed groaning. Nearby lay a bloodstained axe and a cut-throat razor, which had been used to slash Joe's throat. He died soon after.

By the time the police arrived, Jake and his second brother Andrew had found how the intruder entered – through a panel chiselled out of the back door. Jake and Andrew were arrested as suspects, but soon released.

On the pavement two streets away someone had chalked on the pavement: "Mrs Maggio is going to sit up tonight, just like Mrs Toney". It reminded the police that seven years earlier there had been four axe murders of Italian grocers, including a Mrs Tony Schiambra. They had been attributed to the criminal organization "the Black Hand", which was rife in New Orleans.

Five weeks after the Maggio killings, a bread delivery man found a back door with a panel chiselled out. When he knocked the door was opened by a man covered in blood. He was a Pole named Besumer, and inside lay a woman who was known as his wife. She was still alive, and told of being struck by a big white man wielding a hatchet. She died later, and Besumer was charged with her murder. But that night the axeman struck again – a young married man, Edward Schneider, returned home to find his pregnant wife lying in bed covered in blood. Rushed to hospital, she survived, and gave birth a week later. The attacker seemed to have entered by an open window.

Five days later, a barber named Romano became the next victim. His niece heard noises in his bedroom, and went in to find him being attacked by a big man wearing a black slouch hat. As she screamed the man "vanished as if he had wings". A panel had been chipped out of the door.

New Orleans was in a panic reminiscent of that which had swept London in the days of Jack the Ripper. There were several false alarms, and one man found an axe and chisel outside his back door. On 30 August 1918 a man named Nick Asunto heard a noise, and went to investigate; he saw a heavily-built man with an axe, who fled as he shouted. All New Orleans began taking elaborate precautions against the Axeman.

For the time being, the attacks ceased, and the ending of the war in 1918 gave people other things to think about. But in March 1919, a grocer named Jordano heard screams from a house across the street, and found another grocer, Charles Cortimiglia, unconscious on the floor, while his wife – a dead baby in her arms – sat on the floor with blood streaming from her head. She said she had awakened to see a man attacking her husband with an axe, and when she snatched up her baby, he killed the child with a blow, then struck her . . . The door panel had been chiselled out. Yet when Mrs Cortimiglia began to recover, she accused Jordano, the man who had found her, of being the killer, and although her husband (now also recovering) insisted that this was untrue, Jordano and his son were arrested.

Three days after the attack, the local newspaper received a letter signed "The Axeman", datelined "From Hell" (as in the case of a Jack the Ripper letter), and declaring that he would be coming to New Orleans next Tuesday at 12.15, but would spare any house playing jazz music. The following Tuesday, the streets of New Orleans rocked with jazz, and the Axeman failed to appear . . . Someone even wrote a "Mysterious Axeman Jazz".

Besumer, who had been in custody since his arrest, was tried and acquitted. But the Jordanos, to everyone's amazement, were found guilty, although Charles Cortimiglia repeated that they were innocent.

And the attacks went on – although there was to be only one further death. On 10 August 1919 a grocer named Steve Boca woke to find a shadowy figure holding an axe beside the bed. When he woke again, he was bleeding from a skull wound. He managed to stagger down to the home of a friend, Frank Genusa, and the frantic police arrested Genusa – then shamefacedly released him.

On 2 September a druggist named Carlson heard scratching noises from the back door, and fired his revolver through the panel. The intruder fled, leaving behind a chisel. The next day, neighbours found nineteen-year-old Sarah Lauman unconscious; she had been attacked with an axe and three teeth knocked out. She could remember nothing when she recovered.

The last attack was on a grocer named Mike Pepitone. His wife – in a separate bedroom – heard sounds of a struggle, and entered his room in time to see a man vanishing. Her husband had been killed with an axe blow so violent that it splattered blood up the wall. Again, a chiselled door panel revealed how the axeman had gained entry.

Then the murders ceased. The Jordanos were finally released when Mrs Cortimiglia confessed that she had lied because she hated them. Now, she said, her husband had left her, and she had smallpox – Saint Joseph had appeared to her and told her to confess. The Jordanos were released.

But Mrs Pepitone, widow of the last victim, was to enter the story again. On 7 December 1920, in Los Angeles, she had shot and killed a man named Joseph Mumfre, from New Orleans, in the street. She claimed he was the Axeman. She was sentenced to ten years in prison, but released after three.

Was Mumfre the Axeman? He could well have been. He had been released from prison just before the 1911 murders, then sent back for the next seven years. Released again just before the first of the 1918 murders, he had been back in prison during the "lull" between August 1918 and March 1919, when they began again. He left New Orleans shortly after the murder of Mike Pepitone.

What was his motive? Almost certainly, he was a sadist who wanted to attack women, not men. Joe Maggio was left alive; his wife was killed. Besumer was only knocked unconscious; his attractive wife died of her injuries. Many of the later victims were women, and it seems likely that he attacked the men when in search of women victims.

Why Italian grocers? In fact, many of the victims were not Italians. *But all kept small shops.* And a small shop is a place where an attractive wife can be seen serving behind the counter. Mrs Pepitone never revealed how she tracked down Mumfre, but it seems likely that he was a customer, and she recognized him and followed his trail to Los Angeles.

## • chapter three •

# AMERICAN MYSTERIES

*It would be a mistake to assume that America has had no classic unsolved murders in the Agatha Christie tradition. In fact, the famous Elwell case has been described as one of the classic murder mysteries of the century.*

*Another remarkable unsolved mystery has found a place in most books on the "Jazz Age"; in fact, the strange death of Starr Faithfull has become one of the recurring symbols of the Prohibition era. Violence, as once remarked by the American senator H. Rap Brown, is as American as cherry pie and this comment is certainly exemplified by some of America's most famous murder mysteries, such as the Axeman of New Orleans (see page 36) and the Evangelista murders. But perhaps the nearest equivalent to London's Jack the Ripper murders is the strange case of Cleveland's "Mad Butcher", where the bodies were violently mutilated by decapitation.*

## The Murder of Joseph Elwell

Joseph Bowne Elwell was found dead by his housekeeper Marie Larsen at 8.25 on the morning of 11 June 1920. He was slumped in an expensive upholstered chair in his living room with a bullet hole in the centre of his forehead, about two inches above the bridge of his nose. Blood flowed down his face and stained an open letter on his knee. Where the bullet had left the back of his head it had blown a roughly cross-shaped hole measuring nine inches across. Much of the contents of his skull were sprayed against the wall behind or lying precariously on his shoulders. Despite the huge loss of brain tissue, Elwell was still alive; his eyelids flickered spasmically as Mrs Larsen watched.

Exactly what happened next, the details of how he reached hospital and died at approximately 10 a.m., is a matter of claim and counter-claim. The reason that many people have differing accounts, and indeed the reason that anyone bothered to find them out, was that Joseph Elwell was a very well-known man in 1920. He frequented the same expensive New York clubs as Scott and Zelda Fitzgerald, relishing being part of that dazzling social set. Some people believe that Fitzgerald's Jay Gatsby was in part based upon Joseph Elwell.

Yet he was born to relatively poor parents. From an early age Joseph showed an incredible skill in bridge, indeed in all card games where skill was an element. He joined the Brooklyn's Irving Republican Club in order to sharpen his talent for bridge with many different partners. Soon he gained such a reputation that he began giving bridge lessons to the daughters of wealthy families. He was not a bridge teacher as such; he managed to give an impression that each paid assignment he received was taken on "as a special favour". He married a plump and reasonably well-off young lady named Helen Hanford, gaining in the process a skilled business manager. He was approached by a publisher to add to the then growing avalanche of bridge text books. His was easily the most successful. It was in fact written by Helen, using example hands and notes jotted down by the Great Man. Advanced manuals and commentaries upon tournament bridge hands followed, each selling very well.

Bridge was not Elwell's only pre-occupation at this time. Throughout his life Elwell's need to sleep with many women was enormous. Soon after his marriage he began failing to come home. The situation became more extreme when Helen had a child. Soon he began ringing if he *would* be home for dinner. Helen was not entirely the mistreated little woman however – from the outraged and jealous letters that Elwell would fire off occasionally to his wife's male acquaintances it would seem that she managed to adapt to the situation.

The Elwells' public affairs were in contrast rosy. Joseph became bridge tutor to the Vanderbilt family, renowned multi-millionaires. He was a close friend of Walter Lewisohn, the millionaire New York socialite. He even gave bridge lessons to King Edward VII.

His relationship with his wife inevitably grew distant however, with Joseph permanently on the look-out for any grounds for divorce and putting a great deal of his earnings into his parents' names in order to avoid having to pay it to Helen in alimony. When they eventually separated Helen got a meagre payment, and that only on the condition that she renounced any claim to money Joseph was making on real estate deals.

Indeed as Joseph's fortune increased so the range of his business dealings widened. He invested in race horses and Palm Beach luxury property, making money every time. He lost the investments he made in Tsarist Russia in 1917 with the Revolution, and responded by joining and sponsoring the American Protective League, a group whose espoused aim was to root out spies but who in fact just harassed anyone living in America who was not American.

His liaisons with many women continued, made more convenient by the fact that all the servants at his West Seventieth Street apartment lived off premises. All seemed to be ideal for Joseph Bowne Elwell until someone shot him between 7.25 and 8.35 a.m. that hot June morning.

It is possible to be this exact with respect to the time of the shooting due to a strange circumstance. At 6.30 that morning Jost Otten, Elwell's milkman, delivered a pint of milk and some cream. In order to place them against Elwell's door it was necessary to open the large double doors leading to the small hall of the apartment building. This presented no problem, as they were unlocked. Likewise the postman has no difficulty getting to Elwell's postbox on the internal door at 7.25 a.m. However, when Marie Larsen arrives at 8.35 a.m. the double doors are locked. It is clear that Elwell was alive to receive his post – one of the letters was open on his knee. This leads to the conclusion that the killer had a key. All the locks on the apartment had been changed recently due to a burglary attempt – the killer acquired a key soon before the murder. The likelihood seems to be that Elwell knew his killer.

Further evidence for this is presented by what he was *not* wearing when found. Nearly everyone who knew Elwell thought he had even white teeth and attractive shiny hair. In fact he was close to completely bald, and with only three teeth in his head. His expensive wig and tailored dentures remained upstairs in his bedroom. It is unlikely he would have entertained any of his lady friends without them.

The events of the preceding evening are reasonably clear. Elwell was out on the town with Walter Lewisohn and some friends, including Viola Kraus, Lewisohn's sister-in-law, allegedly one of Elwell's mistresses. These friends left Elwell to find his own way home when he declined a taxi ride with them. This was the last certain sighting of him before Marie Larsen found him the next morning.

The word "certain" is used advisedly, as Elwell's noto-riety coupled with the detective fiction style of his death led to a hurricane of conflicting stories regarding virtually every aspect of the known facts. As mentioned above, even the manner of his transferral to hospital is hotly debated. The newspapers tried to implicate all Elwell's friends in turn through snide innuendo, while also speculating about Elwell's ties to bootlegging and spying. So many people were intrigued by the case, and so many people took it upon themselves to investigate it that it became clear that the killer's total evasion of justice can be attributed almost entirely to too much speculation and almost no real investigation.

To present the facts without a gloss of idle rumination is thus made quite difficult. The objective details of the crime scene are among the few facts undisputed . . .

In the room where Elwell was discovered two cigarette butts were found. One of them was on the table next to Elwell's chair – a cigarette made especially to order. It had been left to burn completely. It had been lit at the wrong end i.e. the end with the manufacturers logo impressed into the paper. The other cigarette was of an over-the-counter variety. The police felt this to be such a vital clue that they refused to divulge the actual make. This cigarette had been extinguished on the mantelpiece and still showed signs of saliva on the end when Marie Larsen discovered it. For the saliva to remain partially unevaporated in the 70°F heat meant that the smoker must have drooled a great deal. In his book *The Slaying of Joseph Bowne Elwell* Jonathan Goodman asserts that the second butt was in fact left by an investigating officer, explaining their reticence to elucidate on its origins.

Upstairs the police found a great deal of lingerie in the spare bedroom. Although the newspapers got a lot of mileage out of this discovery it seems in retrospect to be quite unimportant.

The autopsy showed that the bullet entered Elwell's forehead at an upwards angle – perhaps meaning that it was fired from the hip. Another, more melodramatic interpretation of this fact has Elwell's head bent slightly back to look into the eyes of his killer. Around the entrance wound were many small gunpowder marks – as distinct from gunpowder burns. This meant that the shot must have been fired from between three feet and five inches from Elwell's head. Any closer and Elwell's face would have been burnt by powder from the gun's barrel. This fact tends to make suicide unlikely, as few suicides shoot themselves at a distance, thus risking a painful but not fatal winging shot. The lack of the weapon tends to further invalidate suicide as an explanation.

Those are the main details – Elwell was shot within the time space of one cigarette from a point lower than his seated head and from less than three feet away. Inevitably however these facts are not enough, the imagination demands some violent and passionate motive. Passion is of course the most proffered explanation, a wronged woman, or a brother or father. Some theories go further – linking this possible motive to possible murderers. For instance Viola Kraus, Walter Lewisohn's sister-in-law and supposed lover of Elwell, met her divorced husband the night before the murders. In fact, the divorce had only just gone through that day. Viola was dancing with Elwell. Did her husband see red and kill Elwell the next morning?

Another theory has Viola herself as killer. Elwell had been belatedly discussing divorce with Helen in the weeks leading up to his death. Did Viola take this as a tacit sign that he wished to marry her when their joint divorces cleared? Did she, when she found he simply wanted more freedom to see many other women, kill him in a fit of jilted rage?

Jonathan Goodman, in *The Slaying of Joseph Bowne Elwell*, puts forward a masterfully imagined theory. Based upon the fact that Walter Lewisohn went mad two years after Elwell's killing, some say for love of a dancer Leonora Hughes, Goodman argues that Lewisohn saw Elwell's (alleged) rejection of Viola as positive proof that he was after Ms Hughes. In order to avoid this situation Lewisohn has Elwell killed by a friend – the owner of the building that Elwell leased. This neatly explains the key problem as the owner would have up-to-date keys for his own building. The theory is supported by the fact that the alleged killer received a sinecure in Lewisohn's establishment after the killing.

Most intriguing of all however is a small point that Goodman raises merely in passing. Marie Larsen was a strict Swedish Lutheran. In her opinion all suicides went to hell. Is it not possible that she removed the gun from the scene in order to save Elwell's loved ones the terrible conclusion that Joseph was in the fire for eternity?

Admittedly all these theories are at best unprovable. It is only natural that many explanations have been presented for a set of circumstances that are, at the end of the day, insoluble.

# The Starr Faithfull Case

In the early morning sunshine of 8 June 1931, a beachcomber strolling along the sands at Long Beach, on the south shore of Long Island, found the body of a pretty girl. He dragged it clear of the tideline and summoned the police. They quickly identified the girl as Starr Faithfull, the twenty-five-year-old stepdaughter of Stanley Faithfull, a retired manufacturing chemist of Greenwich Village. He had reported Starr missing two days earlier.

An autopsy revealed that the girl had died by drowning

about forty-eight hours earlier, and had eaten a large meal not long before she died. There was no alcohol in her system, but traces of the drug veronal. She was clad only in an expensive silk dress, and traces of sand in her lungs indicated that she had been alive as she lay in the water. There were fingertip-shaped bruises on her upper arms, and indications of rape. All this suggested that Starr had been murdered by whoever had shaken her by the arms: that he had raped her – perhaps on the beach – and then held her head under the water. On the other hand, she may have consented to intercourse in a drugged trance, then have collapsed by the edge of the sea and drowned as the tide came in.

Starr was undoubtedly beautiful, and the fact that she was an heiress and the product of a Boston finishing school led the press to devote much breathless attention to the case. As reporters looked into her background, it became still more interesting. Far from being a prim young lady who had had the misfortune to be assaulted, it transpired that Starr had been sexually experienced for more than half of her brief life. At the age of eleven, it seemed, she had been seduced by

---

The first "Locked Room Mystery" was Poe's "*Murder in the Rue Morgue*". The first locked room novel seems to have been John Ratcliffe's *Nena Sahib*. This inspired a real murder. In 1881, the wife and five children of a Berlin carter named Fritz Conrad were found hanging from hooks in a locked room. It looked as if Frau Conrad, depressed by poverty, had killed her children and committed suicide. Police Commissioner Hollman was suspicious, and when he found out that Conrad was infatuated with a young girl student, he searched the apartment for love letters. He found none, but came upon a copy of *Nena Sahib* and read Ratcliffe's account of a "perfect murder", in which the killer drilled a tiny hole in the door, passed a thread through it, and used this to draw the bolt after the murder; he then sealed up the hole with wax. Hollman examined Conrad's door, and found a similar hole, filled in with sealing wax, to which threads of horsehair still adhered. Confronted with this evidence, Conrad confessed to murdering his wife and children, and was sentenced to death.

a middle-aged Boston business man who was the father of schoolfriends; he had drugged her with ether and raped her. This information came from her stepfather, Stanley Faithfull, whom Starr's mother had married some ten years earlier. This relationship had continued down the years.

It also seemed that Starr had been feverishly in love with an English ship's surgeon, Dr George Jameson-Carr, who did not return her feelings. On 29 May, a week before her death, Starr had been attempting to force her drunken attentions on Dr Jameson-Carr, aboard the *Franconia*. He had persuaded her to leave, but she had hidden among the passengers; when found later, she had to be transferred to a tug and taken ashore.

It emerged that Starr had fairly serious mental problems, and had been under psychiatric treatment for years. She was not normally a heavy drinker, but was inclined to get drunk at parties. She had been on two trips to England, where she had mixed with the "bright young things", and she longed to return to Europe; unfortunately, her stepfather was not wealthy – although comfortably-off – and there was no prospect of another trip in the immediate future. So Starr spent a great deal of time hanging around the New York docks, often going aboard liners for farewell parties – which is how she became acquainted with Dr Jameson-Carr. To try to prevent her drinking bootleg gin made of raw alcohol, her stepfather used to pack her a flask of Martini.

Was it possible that Starr had gone aboard a liner and then jumped over the side when it was off Long Island? Otherwise, it was difficult to explain what she was doing on Long Island, twenty miles or so from home. Or had she been pushed overboard? If so, was it by the rapist?

A second autopsy dampened these speculations when the doctor who performed it announced that, in his opinion, she had not been raped, but had submitted voluntarily to sexual intercourse. The missing underclothes certainly suggested that she had been naked at some point.

Starr's diaries increased the lurid speculation, for they revealed that she had had many lovers, one of whom was someone called A.J.P. She seemed to be fond of him but also afraid of him. One entry read: "Spent night A.J.P. Providence. Oh Horror, Horror, Horror!!!" The indications

were that, for all her craving for affection, Starr was not **295**
overly fond of the physical side of sex. This seemed to
be confirmed by a new item of scandal unearthed by the
investigators. A year before her death, a policeman had
burst into a room of a New York hotel where a girl had
been screaming. He found Starr naked and bruised, while
a furious young man, dressed only in his undershirt, was
glaring at her. She was drunk, and there was half a bottle of
gin on the table. The man identified himself as an ex-soldier
named Joseph Collins, produced his discharge papers, and
was allowed to go. Starr, who was very drunk, was taken
to the Bellevue Hospital suffering from "acute alcoholism"
and "contusions to face, jaw and upper lip". The implication
seemed to be that she had taken Collins to the room for
sex, then changed her mind, and the frustrated man had
attacked her.

Her mental problems obviously stemmed from her early
seduction by the Boston business man. Reporters soon
unearthed the fact that, as a child, Starr and her sister
Tucker had played with the children of Andrew J. Peters,
former Congressman and Mayor of Boston, who was a distant
relative of Mrs Faithfull. This could obviously be the "A.J.P."
of her diary. If Peters *was* her seducer, he had certainly paid
for it, for the investigation revealed that Mrs Faithfull had
signed a document aquitting someone of all responsibility for
damage done to Starr, in exchange for a large sum of money,
probably $80,000. (Stanley Faithfull alleged it was $20,000, but
his lawyer indicated that the sum was much greater.)

The story was kept alive by a new sensation at the cremato-
rium. The cremation of the body was interrupted by officials
from the District Attorney's office, who announced that it
could not go ahead until there was a third inquest. After this
inquest, District Attorney Elvin Edwards announced that he
knew the identity of the two men who killed Starr Faithfull by
holding her head underwater, and that he would be making
an arrest within thirty-six hours. When the arrest failed to
materialize, he acknowledged that "the lead was false".

At this point, Dr Jameson-Carr returned from Europe and
created another sensation by revealing that, in the days
between being thrown off the *Franconia* and her death, Starr
had written him three letters, and these made it abundantly

clear that she had intended to commit suicide. The first declared that she meant to "end my worthless, disorderly bore of an existence – before I ruin anyone else's life as well." "I take dope to forget, and drink to try and like people." The third letter, posted shortly before she left home for the last time, said that she intended to be successful this time (it emerged that she had made an earlier suicide attempt in London), and described how she intended to eat a large final meal, with plenty of alcohol (she was always worried about gaining weight), then kill herself. "I am going to enjoy my last cigarettes. I won't worry because men flirt with me in the streets – I shall encourage them – I don't care who they are. I'm afraid I've always been a rotten 'sleeper'; it's the preliminaries that count with me."

That seemed to settle the matter; Starr *must* have committed suicide. But why at Long Beach? Why wearing only a dress? Why by lying down in the water – as the sand in her lungs suggested – rather than jumping off a bridge or a quay?

In 1948, Morris Markey, a journalist who had worked on the case and become a friend of the Faithfulls, unveiled his own theory on the case. Starr, he believed, *had* left home determined to commit suicide, and had eaten her final meal as planned, although without much alcohol. Then she had picked up a man and gone to the beach with him. As on the previous occasion with the ex-soldier, she had declined sexual intercourse at the last minute, and the man had handled her roughly and raped her. Then, afraid of going to jail, he had drowned her, and walked away through the shallows to avoid leaving footprints.

The theory seems far-fetched – that she was murdered when she set out to commit suicide – yet it covers all the facts, and explains the puzzle of the male semen inside her.

A modern criminologist might suggest another solution: that Starr had taken a large dose of veronal and lay down on the beach to wait for the tide to come in; some passing beachcomber had found her – either before or after death – and had intercourse with her. The bruises on her arms could have been caused as her body was pounded by waves – a body will bruise for some time after death. If this theory is correct, then Starr committed suicide as she intended.

On the whole, these theories are probably as close as

Tucker Faithfull, Starr's chain-smoking younger sister, became a celebrity after Starr's death, with offers of nightclub engagements and movie parts. She loved the limelight, but two weeks after her sister's death, startled reporters with a sudden outburst: "I'm not sorry she's dead. Everybody's happier. She made life miserable."

The weekend Starr died, Tucker was spending a dirty weekend with a lover named Jones; she had pawned her fake leopardskin coat to pay her train fare, and had to borrow $5 to get home when Jones declined to give it to her.

She married a lawyer in 1937.

anyone will ever come to solving the mystery of the death of Starr Faithfull.

# The Evangelista Murders

On the morning of 3 July 1929 Vincent Elias, a dealer in real estate, called at the house of Benjamino Evangelista. Evangelista, or Benny Evangelist as he preferred to be known, was a repair and building contractor who lived in one of the poorer districts of Detroit. Elias arrived at Evangelista's three-storey house at about 10.30, and finding that his knocking brought no reply he decided to enter and investigate. Seeing that the foyer was empty Elias opened the door of Evangelista's office and walked into a scene that resembled an abattoir. Evangelista was slumped in his chair, surrounded and covered with blood. On the floor next to his body was his head, cleanly removed. The visitor fled to summon the police.

Soon patrolmen Costage and Lawrence arrived at the scene, and they continued the grisly investigation. Among the gore in Evangelista's office were two unused swords, a false beard and wig, and a notched staff. Also, on the floor near the severed head were photographs of a child in a coffin. Bloody footprints led to the stairs.

In the upstairs bedroom the shocked patrolmen found Evangelista's wife and youngest child, a baby. The mother had been almost beheaded, and her arm nearly severed, while the baby had been killed by multiple head wounds. In the adjoining room were the elder children's beds, two daughters of four and six, both decapitated, with some attempt to detach the arm of one of them. Finally the eldest daughter, an eight-year-old, was lying in the doorway to the landing, also hacked to death. Unlike Evangelista, who was fully clothed, the upstairs victims were in their night attire. Only the eldest daughter seemed to have had time to react to the murderer, having put on her bathrobe and made for her mother's bedroom.

Another bloody footprint descended the stairs, and a fingerprint of a left thumb, also in blood, was left on the latch of the outer door. What other evidence was left pointing to the identity of the killer will never be known, as the Detroit police failed to properly document or preserve any other physical evidence. Within hours the Evangelista home was packed with police and journalists, attracted not only by the gruesome and terrible aspect of the murders, but also by what the police discovered in the Evangelista cellar.

"Benny Evangelist", apart from being a building contractor, was a local faith healer. People paid high prices to receive cures from the "wise man". Despite this fundamentally unchristian sideline, the whole Evangelista family regularly attended the local Catholic church and seemed at least averagely devout. Both the police and the local people were thus surprised to find that Benny seemed to be the head of a pagan cult. His cellar was decorated like a temple, with the walls and ceiling draped with green cloth and an altar at one end. Above the altar were hung models of hellish demons, made from papier mache with dog hair glued onto them. An outward-facing sign in the basement window read "The Great Celestial Planet Exhibition". Among the papers removed by the police from Evangelista's office was a "Bible" of this cult titled *The Oldest History of the World, Discovered By Occult Science In Detroit, Michigan*. It was to run to four volumes, but only the first volume seems to have reached print. The book was a long and bloody story of prehistoric humanity, not unlike the Old Testament in style. There were many episodes of occult magic and royal intrigue. The principal character of the *History* is the Prophet Meil. Possibly Evangelista identified himself with Meil, as the staff found in his office was very similar to the one that the Prophet is described as carrying. The cultists who believed the details of the *History* called themselves The Great Union Federation of America.

The preface describes how the book came to be written: that it took exactly twenty years to write, from 2 February 1906 to 2 February 1926, and that the story came to the author in visions every night between midnight and 3 a.m. It was during this period, the police were later to establish, that the murders took place.

Also found among Evangelista's belongings were many items of female underwear, each labeled with the owner's name. Carried away, perhaps, by the occult atmosphere of the investigation, the police concluded that they were used for psychometry, the art of locating people through psychic impressions gained from their belongings.

Although their crime-scene investigations had been worse than useless, the Detroit police tried hard to find witnesses or dig up connections. The investigation reached the conclusion that the last person to see Evangelista alive was a local called Umberto Tecchio. Together with a friend, Tecchio had visited Evangelista at his house the evening before the murder to deliver the final payment on a house. However there was no mention of a completed sale in any of Evangelista's papers. Suspecting that Tecchio had been cheated by Evangelista and had wreaked bloody revenge, the police searched Tecchio's rooming house. In the barn below the house police found a dull axe, a sharp banana knife and a newly cleaned pair of shoes.

This evidence seemed hopeful, so the police next questioned Tecchio's room mate Angelo Depoli. He was uncommunicative and surly to such an extent that the police bad-temperedly set immigration on him. As it turned out Depoli was an illegal immigrant, and was deported. With him went any hope of establishing Tecchio's movements on the night of the murder.

Umberto Tecchio was certainly a violent man. His first wife had divorced him for knifing her brother to death. When she gained possession of the house and lived there with her new husband, Tecchio threatened to blow them up. Several days later the new husband was shot dead on the steps of his house. The police, apparently for reasons of leniency, ruled it a suicide. Also, just after the murders, police received a tip that a newspaper boy had seen Tecchio standing on the porch of Evangelista's house smoking a cigarette at 5 a.m. on the morning after the murders. Officers sent to find the newspaper boy were told he was dead.

There were other possibilities for violence revealed by police researching Evangelista's background. He had moved from Naples to live with his brother in Pennsylvania. His brother had eventually thrown him out of the house for his occult interests. Before moving to Michigan, Evangelista had lived in York, Pennsylvania, an area renowned for its occult sub-community. While living there he was friendly with Aurelius Angelino, a chief cultist, who was put in a mental asylum for killing two of his family and wounding the others with an axe in an attempt to dispose of them all. Police seemed so taken with this connection that they exhumed Evangelista in order to check his fingerprints. Exactly how he could have beheaded himself after killing his family was never fully explained by the police.

In the absence of any meaningful connections with York cultists, police researched the other possible source of suspects: Evangelista's reputed connection with the Black Hand, an extortion organization. Local sources reported that Evangelista delivered threats for the Black Hand. A retribution killing had taken place across the street from Evangelista's house early in 1926. At the time the police had known who the gunman was, but despairing of ever convicting him, they allowed him to flee to avoid further violence. The gunman's name was Louis Evangelist. Feeling that Evangelista may have had some connection with this killing police tracked down Evangelist to a railroad track-laying gang near Pittsburgh, but he seemed to know nothing of the subsequent murders.

Evangelista *had* received a death threat from the Black Hand; it was found among his papers dated roughly a year before the killings. There was also an unposted letter by Evangelista saying that a job had been bungled before and that a certain unnamed threat might have to be removed. Intriguing though these things are they provide no real evidence or even solid theory.

The murder investigation foundered, and remained unsolved on the Detroit police files. However information about the murders kept surfacing, a piece at a time.

A Mrs Emmanuel Maiccucci came forward to say that the Evangelistas had owned two machetes that had been missing from the scene. Mrs Maiccucci was the wife of Umberto Tecchio who had divorced him for the murder of her brother. She said that while she had been married to Tecchio he had taken her to Evangelista to cure an illness. She had noticed the machetes during her cure.

A young man came forward to say that he had been the newspaper boy who had seen Tecchio on the Evangelistas' porch. He told police that after he had realized what had gone on that night he had avoided the house for years, never passing it and too afraid to come forward.

Tecchio's fellow guests at the rooming house said that they were not sure whether Tecchio had come home at all on the night of the murders.

The reason for the sudden increase in information was simple: Tecchio had died. Whatever conclusions the police came to it was clear that many people in the local neighbourhood had been too afraid of Tecchio to reveal all that they knew. The existence of the newspaper boy had been hidden by the whole community. Some local people must have thought that Tecchio was the murderer.

However, the murders remain unsolved. There is no doubt that this has a lot to do with the incredible incompetence of the Detroit police. They deported their most valuable witness and when they later came to test the fingerprint on the latch against Tecchio's prints many policemen came to the conclusion that the mark had been made by an investigating officer.

The theories about the motive and murderer are varied and in some cases quite plausible. The photographs of the child in a coffin suggest to some people that Evangelista had failed to cure someone and that, in pagan tradition, he was put to death for the death of his patient. Another theory points out that Aurelius Angelino, the York cultist, had escaped from his asylum at the time of the murders, and that he, like the person who left the thumbprint on the latch, was left-handed. The main police theories, concerning the Black Hand and Umberto Tecchio, are to some degree tenable, but really do not justify such cold-blooded and wholesale violence.

In the end the cult connections are the most gripping if not the most plausible source of explanations. Was Evangelista's cult connected to a more widespread network of believers? The title "The Great Union Federation of America" tends to suggest it was. Did Evangelista somehow compromise or annoy a nationwide group of cultists and was ritualistically punished for it? It seems that the facts are destined to remain unknown.

# The Cleveland Torso Killer

On a warm September afternoon in 1935, two boys on their way home from school walked along a dusty, sooty gully called Kingsbury Run, in the heart of Cleveland, Ohio. On a weed-covered slope known as Jackass Hill, one challenged the other to a race, and they hurtled sixty feet down the slope to the bottom. Sixteen-year-old James Wagner was the winner, and as he halted, panting, he noticed something white in the bushes a few yards away. A closer look revealed that it was a naked body, and fhat it was headless.

The police who arrived soon after found the body of a young white male clad only in black socks; the genitals had also been removed. It lay on its back, with the legs stretched out and the arms placed neatly by the sides, as if laid out for a funeral. Thirty feet away, the policemen found another body, lying in the same position; it was of an older man, and had also been decapitated and emasculated.

Hair sticking out of the ground revealed one of the heads a few yards away, and the second was found nearby. The genitals were also found lying nearby, as if thrown away by the killer.

One curious feature of the case was that there was no blood on the ground or on the bodies, which were quite clean. It looked as if they had been killed and beheaded elsewhere, then carefully washed when they had ceased to bleed.

Medical examination made the case more baffling than ever. The older corpse was badly decomposed, and the skin discoloured; the pathologists discovered that this was due to some chemical substance, as if the killer had tried to preserve the body. The older victim had been dead about two weeks. The younger man had only been dead three days. His fingerprints enabled the police to identify him as twenty-eight-year-old Edward Andrassy, who had a minor police record for carrying concealed weapons. He lived near Kingsbury Run and had a reputation as a drunken brawler.

But the most chilling discovery was that Andrassy had been killed by decapitation. Rope marks on his wrists revealed that he had been tied and had struggled violently. The killer had apparently cut off his head with a knife. The skill with which the operation had been performed suggested a butcher – or possibly a surgeon.

It proved impossible to identify the older man. But the identification of Andrassy led the police to hope that it should not be too difficult to trace his killer. He had spent his nights gambling and drinking in a slum part of town and was known as a pimp. But further investigation also revealed that he had male lovers. Lead after lead looked marvellously promising. The husband of a married woman with whom he had had an affair had sworn to kill him. But the man was able to prove his innocence. So were various shady characters who might have borne a grudge. Lengthy police investigation led to a dead end – as it did in another ten cases of the killer who became known as "the Mad Butcher of Kingsbury Run".

Four months later, on a raw January Sunday, the howling of a dog finally led a black woman resident of East Twentieth Street – not far from Kingsbury Run – to go and investigate. She found the chained animal trying to get at a basket near a factory wall. Minutes later, she told a neighbour that the basket contained "hams". But the neighbour soon recognized the "hams" as parts of a human arm. A burlap bag proved to contain the lower half of a female torso. The head was missing, as were the left arm and lower parts of both legs. But fingerprints again enabled the police to trace the victim, who had a record for soliciting. She proved to be a forty-one-year-old prostitute named Florence Polillo, a squat, double-chinned woman who was well known in the bars of the neighbourhood.

Again, there were plenty of leads, and again, all of them petered out. Two weeks later, the left arm and lower legs were found in a vacant lot. The head was never recovered.

The murder of Flo Polillo raised an unwelcome question. The first two murders had convinced the police that they were looking for a homosexual sadist; this latest crime made it look as if this killer was quite simply a sadist – like Peter Kurten, the Dusseldorf killer, executed in 1931; he had killed men, women and children indifferently, and he was not remotely homosexual. And now the pathologist recalled that, a year before the first double murder, the torso of an unknown woman had been found on the edge of Lake Erie. It began to look as if the Mad Butcher was quite simply a sadist.

At least the Cleveland public felt they had one thing in their favour. Since the double killing, the famous Eliot Ness had been appointed Cleveland's Director of Public Safety. Ness and his "Untouchables" had cleared up Chicago's Prohibition rackets, then, in 1934, Ness had moved to Cleveland to fight its gangsters. With Ness in charge, the Head Hunter of Kingsbury Run – another press sobriquet – would find himself becoming the hunted.

But it was soon clear to Ness that hunting a sadistic pervert is nothing like hunting professional gangsters. The killer struck at random, and unless he was careless enough to leave behind a clue – like a fingerprint – then the only hope of catching him was in the act. And Ness soon became convinced that the Mad Butcher took great pleasure in feeling that he was several steps ahead of the police.

The Head Hunter waited until the summer before killing again, then lived up to his name by leaving the head of a young man, wrapped in a pair of trousers, under a bridge in Kingsbury Run; again, two boys found it on 22 June 1936. The body was found a quarter of a mile away, and it was obvious from the blood that he had died where he lay. And medical evidence showed that he had died from decapitation – it was not clear how the killer had prevented him from

struggling while he did it. The victim was about twenty-five,
and heavily tattooed. His fingerprints were not in police files. Three weeks later, a young female hiker discovered another decapitated body in a gully; the head lay nearby. The decomposition made it clear that this man had been killed before the previously-discovered victim.

The last "Butchery" of 1936 was of another man of about thirty, found in Kingsbury Run; the body had been amputated in two, and emasculated. A hat found nearby led to a partial identification: a housewife recalled giving it to a young tramp. Not far away there was a "hobo camp" where down-and-outs slept; this was obviously where the Butcher had found his latest victim.

The fact that Cleveland had been the scene of a Republican Convention and was now the site of a "Great Expo", led to even more frantic police activity and much press criticism. The murders were reported all over the world and, in Nazi Germany and Fascist Italy, were cited as proof of the decadence of the New World.

As month after month went by with no further grisly discoveries, Clevelanders hoped they had heard the last of the Mad Butcher. But in February 1937, that hope was dashed when the killer left the body of a young woman in a chopped-up pile on the shores of Lake Erie. She was never identified. The eighth victim, a young negress, *was* identified from her teeth as Mrs Rose Wallace, forty; only the skeleton remained, and it looked as if she may have been killed in the previous year.

Victim No. nine was male and had been dismembered; when he was fished out of the river, the head was missing, and was never found. This time the killer had gone even further in his mutilations – like Jack the Ripper. It was impossible to identify the victim. Two men seen in a boat were thought to be the Butcher with an accomplice, but this suggestion that there might be two Butchers led nowhere.

The Butcher now seems to have taken a rest until nine months later. Then the lower part of a leg was pulled out of the river. Three weeks later, two burlap bags in the river proved to contain more body-fragments, which enabled the pathologist to announce that the victim was female, a brunette of about twenty-five. She was never identified.

The killer was to strike twice more. More than a year after the last discovery, in August 1938, the dismembered torso of a woman was found on a dump on the lakefront, and a search of the area revealed the bones of a second victim, a male. A quilt in which the remains of this twelfth victim were wrapped was identified as having been given to a junk man. Neither body could be identified.

One thing was now obvious: the Butcher was selecting his victims from vagrants and down-and-outs. Ness decided to take the only kind of action that seemed left to him: two days after the last find, police raided the "shantytown" near Kingsbury Run, arrested hundreds of vagrants, and burned it down. Whether or not by coincidence, the murders now ceased.

The suspects. Two of the most efficient of the manhunters, Detectives Merylo and Zalewski, had spent a great deal of time searching for the killer's "laboratory". At one point they thought they had found it – but, like all leads, this one faded away.

Next the investigators discovered that Flo Polillo and Rose Wallace – Victim No. eight – had frequented the same saloon, and that Andrassy – No. two – had been a "regular" there too. They also learned of a middle-aged man called Frank who carried knives and threatened people with them when drunk. When they learned that this man – Frank Dolezal – had also been living with Flo Polillo, they felt they had finally identified the killer. Dolezal was arrested, and police discovered a brown substance like dried blood in the cracks of his bathroom floor. Knives with dried bloodstains on them provided further incriminating evidence. Under intensive questioning, Dolezal – a bleary-eyed, unkempt man – confessed to the murder of Flo Polillo. Newspapers announced the capture of the Butcher. Then things began to go wrong. The "dried blood" in the bathroom proved not to be blood after all. Dolezal's "confession" proved to be full of errors about the corpse and method of disposal. And when, in August 1939, Dolezal hanged himself in jail, the autopsy revealed that he had two cracked ribs, and suggested that his confession had been obtained by force.

Yet Ness himself claimed that he knew the solution to the murders. He reasoned that the killer was a man who had a

house of his own in which to dismember the bodies, and a car
in which to transport them. So he was not a down-and-out.
The skill of the mutilations suggested medical training. The
fact that some of the victims had been strong men suggested
that the Butcher had to be big and powerful – a conclusion
supported by a size twelve footprint near one of the bodies.

Ness set three of his top agents, Virginia Allen, Barney
Davis and Jim Manski, to make enquiries among the upper
levels of Cleveland society. Virginia was a sophisticated girl
with contacts among Cleveland socialites. And it was she who
learned about a man who sounded like the ideal suspect.
Ness was to call him "Gaylord Sundheim" – a big man
from a well-to-do family, who had a history of psychiatric
problems. He had also studied medicine. When the three
"Untouchables" called on him, he leered sarcastically at
Virginia and closed the door in their faces. Ness invited
him – pressingly – to lunch, and he came under protest.
When Ness finally told him he suspected him of being the
Butcher – hoping that shock tactics might trigger a confession
– "Sundheim" sneered: "Prove it".

Soon after this, "Sundheim" had himself committed to a
mental institution. Ness knew *he* was now "untouchable", for
even if Ness could prove his guilt, he could plead insanity.

During the next two years Ness received a series of
jeering postcards, some signed "Your paranoid nemesis".
They ceased abruptly when "Sundheim" died in the mental
institution.

Was "Sundheim" the Butcher? Probably. But not certainly.
In Pittsburgh in 1940, three decapitated bodies were found
in old boxcars (railway coaches). Members of Ness's team
went to investigate, but no clue to the treble murder was
ever discovered. The case remains unsolved.

**Who Killed Kennedy?**

At 12.30 p.m. on 2 November 1963, President John F. Kennedy was travelling through Dallas, Texas, in the back of an open limousine, with his wife beside him and Governor John B. Connally and Connally's wife in front of them. As the motorcade passed the Texas School Book Depository in Dealey Plaza, shots rang out and the President clutched his neck with both hands and slumped in his seat. A second bullet caused his head to "explode". Connally was also struck by a bullet. Jackie Kennedy cried: "They've killed my husband . . . I have his brains in my hand!"

The Secret Service ordered the car to drive at top speed to the Parkland Memorial Hospital. But despite all efforts to save him, the President died shortly afterwards. A bullet that later became known as Exhibit 399 was found on the stretcher.

The police had pinpointed the Book Depository as the source of the shots. Near a window on the sixth floor, they found three empty cartridge cases. A few minutes after the shooting, a motorcycle policeman was talking to the superintendent of the building when a man named Lee Harvey Oswald walked out of the elevator on the second floor. The policeman asked the superintendent: "Do you know this man?", and the superintendent said: "Yes, he works here." Oswald was allowed to walk out of the building.

Half an hour or so after the assassination, Oswald was walking down the street when police officer J. D. Tippit, driving a patrol car, called him over. Oswald spoke to him calmly then began to walk away. Tippit jumped from the car and ran after him; Oswald turned, pulled out a revolver, and shot Tippit dead, moving close to him to fire the final shot.

An hour later a ticket seller at the Texas Theater saw Oswald walk in without buying a ticket; she called the police. As they approached Oswald he pointed his gun and pulled the trigger; it misfired. Moments later he was in custody. Soon after, news bulletins announced the arrest of a suspect.

Oswald was an ex-marine who had defected to the USSR

and married a Russian girl. Refused a residence permit he had returned to the USA in June 1962. In March 1963 he had purchased a rifle with a telescopic sight from a mail order firm – his original intention was to assassinate a retired army general. He had moved to Dallas after further unsuccessful attempts to emigrate to Russia and Cuba, and had found a job in the Book Depository. It seems that when he learned from newspaper reports that the President would be visiting Dallas, and saw that the route passed below the Book Depository, he made plans to kill Kennedy.

The rifle with the telescopic sight was found on the sixth floor of the Book Depository, and one of Oswald's palm prints was found on it. He denied killing the President and Officer Tippit, and answered questions "arrogantly".

At 11.20 on Saturday, 24 November 1963, Oswald was being taken from the Dallas Police Headquarters to a car waiting outside, and crowds of photographers – including television crews – were taking pictures, when a man stepped forward, jammed a revolver against Oswald's chest, and pulled the trigger. The man was grabbed by a policeman as Oswald collapsed. Newsmen yelled to ask his name, and the man shouted back: "I'm Jack Ruby – you know me."

Oswald was rushed to Parkland Hospital and operated on by the same surgeon who had tried to save Kennedy's life. But by 1.07 he was pronounced dead.

Ruby was a Dallas nightclub owner who had many friends in the police force – as well as gangland connections. Witnesses reported that he had been behaving oddly since Kennedy's assassination, and his charlady mentioned that he had been talking to himself on the morning he killed Oswald. Tried for murder in 1964, Ruby was sentenced to death, but died of cancer in 1967, before the sentence could be carried out.

To large numbers of Americans, it seemed too convenient that Kennedy's assassin had been killed within two days, and that Oswald's killer had had so little trouble in shooting him. There was soon talk of conspiracy. This began when a film taken by a local business man, Abraham Zapruder, was examined frame by frame, and seemed to show that the first shot caused Kennedy's head to jerk *backwards* – although the Book Depository was behind him. This led to the belief that there was a second gunman *ahead* of the President, on a grassy knoll, and that Oswald had, in fact, shot Kennedy, but had probably missed. (In the Marine Corps, Oswald's appalling marksmanship had been a joke.) The Zapruder film seemed to indicate that at least four shots, not three, had been fired. Examination of the wounds suggested that Connally had been hit by the same bullet that passed through Kennedy's neck.

A woman named Julia Mercer testified that she was driving through Dealey Plaza an hour and a half before the assassination when she saw a green truck parked with two tyres on the kerb. A man she later identified as Oswald got out with a rifle and went towards the grassy knoll. She looked back at the driver, and later identified him as Jack Ruby.

Another popular conspiracy theory was that Vice President Lyndon Johnson – who had won Texas for the Democrats by a narrow majority – had planned the assassination in order to become president. A libellous play called *Macbird*, based on this theory, had a long run on Broadway.

FBI Director J. Edgar Hoover was another candidate for the role of paymaster of the assassin. He disliked Kennedy, and disliked his brother Robert – the Attorney General – even more. Robert Kennedy was speaking of an all-out war on the Mafia with his own Justice Department, challenging Hoover's long-established supremacy.

Another conspiracy theory declared that the CIA was responsible – Kennedy's own intelligence agency – because there was a feeling of anger about the incompetence of the Bay of Pigs invasion of Cuba. Many theories include heavy involvement with Cuban anti-Castro exiles – Oswald himself had attempted to join an anti-Castro group in Miami a few months before the assassination. One view holds that he was trying to infiltrate the group for his Communist masters, another that he joined the assassination conspiracy on behalf of Cuban exiles who felt betrayed by Kennedy.

One of the members of an anti-Castro group was an ultra-conservative named David Ferrie, a completely hairless character (he suffered from a disease called alopecia) who glued bits of orange hair to his head and eyebrows. Ferrie called himself "Dr" as well as "Bishop", and had lost his job as an airline pilot because of his sexual preference for boys.

His hatred of Kennedy was almost pathological. He had been
a boyhood friend of Oswald, and was seen with him shortly
before the assassination.

In the mid-1960s, the New Orleans District Attorney Jim
Garrison alleged that Ferrie, Oswald and a business man
called Clay Shaw had been behind the assassination. But a
few days after Garrison announced his findings to the press,
Ferrie's naked body was found in his apartment, together
with two suicide notes. Cause of death was listed as a brain
haemorrhage, possibly brought on by an unknown poison.
The same day, Ferrie's close anti-Castro associate Eladio del
Valle was murdered in Miami, shot through the heart – his
killer was never found. The only man to go on trial was Clay
Shaw, but the evidence against him was negligible, and he
was found not guilty.

Perhaps more convincing than any of these theories is
the argument that Kennedy was murdered by the Mafia,
on whom he – via his brother Robert – had declared war.
In the 1950s, Robert Kennedy had served on a senate committee whose aim was to expose Mafia involvement with
the Teamsters' Union, headed by Jimmy Hoffa. Kennedy's
father Joe Kennedy is alleged to have been in partnership with
gangster Frank Costello in the bootleg era. Sam Giancana, the
Chicago mob boss, was actually sharing a bedfellow, Judith
Exner, with the President, who was a notorious womanizer.
It was alleged that Kennedy was supplied with ladyfriends by
Frank Sinatra, a friend of Giancana and other Mafia figures,
and that Kennedy's affair with Marilyn Monroe originated in
his Sinatra connection. The aim of Giancana may have been to
exert pressure on the Kennedy brothers to soften their stance
towards the mob. Giancana also believed that he was basically
responsible for Kennedy's election as President, since he had
"delivered" a vital Chicago vote in the 1960 election – a vote
without which Kennedy's bid for the presidency would have
been stillborn. Carlos Marcello, a New Orleans Mafia boss
who was also being hounded by Robert Kennedy, is reported
to have said that Robert Kennedy would be "taken care of"
by the killing of his brother the President. "When attacked
by a dog, it is no good cutting off the tail. Cut off the head
and the dog is out of business."

Significantly, Jack Ruby was born in Chicago, and as a

teenager worked for Al Capone as a delivery boy. There is some evidence that it was the Chicago "mob" that placed Ruby in Dallas – his task being to run a restaurant as a front for Syndicate business. A 1956 FBI report mentioned him as a mob contact. Just before the assassination, Ruby was in deep financial trouble, owing the government $60,000 in taxes. Then he suddenly told his lawyer that his problems had been miraculously solved. At about this time, he is known to have had many meetings with old mob acquaintances.

Shortly after Ruby's trial in 1964, Chief Justice Earl Warren, president of the Warren Commission charged with investigating the Kennedy assassination, and Congressman Gerald Ford – the future President – went to Dallas to interview Ruby. Ruby told them that he would have to be taken to Washington before he could answer their questions freely. "I want to tell the truth, and I can't tell it here." He said later: "I have been used as a scapegoat."

When the Warren Report on the assassination was published in 1979, it concluded that all the evidence suggested that Oswald had acted alone in killing Kennedy. It could very well be that this simple solution is indeed the final truth. But, three decades after the assassination, there are certainly very few people who would accept that conclusion.

# chapter four

# BRITISH ENIGMAS

*T*o return to Britain after studying American homicide is like returning to the country after a month in a busy metropolis. The scale of events is somehow smaller. Having said that, it must be admitted that the scale of incompetence in some classic English mysteries is awe-inspiring. For example, in the case that has become known as the Croydon poisonings, one simple blunder on the part of the pathologist guaranteed that a murderer – or murderess – would never be brought to justice.

It must be admitted that most British murders of the twentieth century lack the element of mystery – there is not a single one, with the exception of the Luard case (see page 23), in which the motive is not crudely obvious. The Wallace case, which took place in Liverpool in 1931, is the exception. And in spite of recent evidence which seems to point towards a solution, it retains the tantalizing quality of one of the great unsolved mysteries.

A unique case is the Harry Whitecliffe mystery because it does not reside in the question "Who killed so-and-so", but in the precise identity of a man who is alleged to be a mass murderer.

**The Case of the Croydon Poisonings**

The London suburb of Croydon has always been a quiet and respectable area – one in which the scandals tend to be of the domestic rather than criminal variety. Yet, in the early months of 1929, this peaceful back-water was discovered to be the scene of what was to become one of the most notorious cases of mass poisoning in British legal history.

In April 1928, Edmund Creighton Duff was living with his wife Grace and their three children at 16 South Park Road, Croydon. At fifty-nine, Duff, a retired British Resident in the civil service of Northern Nigeria and veteran of the Boer War, was supplementing his modest pension by working at a City firm of paper manufacturers and indulging in the odd financial investment. He was a jovial and well-liked man – nicknamed "Major Duff" by his friends – who gave the impression of exceptional fitness and robust constitution.

Thus, while enjoying a spring fishing trip, he was disturbed to find he was running a fever. He returned home early and complained of it to his wife, but she paid it little heed; he had a tendency to overreact on the rare occasions he felt under the weather. Despite the fever he ate a supper of chicken and vegetables and washed it down with bottled beer. Shortly afterwards he complained of severe stomachache and on his way to bed of leg cramps. During the night his condition worsened and a physician, Dr John Binning, was called to attend him.

Binning diagnosed colic, but as Duff worsened he realized it was something far more dangerous. He and his partner, Dr Robert Elwell, fought hard to keep their patient alive, but at 11.20 p.m. on the evening after his return from his fishing trip Edmund Duff died in agony.

The two doctors were at a loss to explain their patient's death and so were legally unable to sign the death certificate; in such circumstances an inquest is automatically carried out. Despite the fact that Duff had exhibited all the major symptoms of arsenic poisoning, neither doctor was inclined to follow this suggestion to its logical conclusion. They were both friends of the Duffs – Dr Elwell especially, who liked to half-jokingly flirt with Grace Duff – and understandably dismissed the possibility of murder.

The pathologist who performed the autopsy, Dr Robert Bronte, reported to the coroner's inquest that the body showed no sign of the ingestion of arsenic. He attributed the death to a heart attack brought on by sunstroke sustained on the fishing trip. In the light of subsequent events this autopsy report was rather amazing to say the least; Dr Bronte had made a misjudgment of staggering proportions. If he had conducted the autopsy more thoroughly a murder enquiry would have ensued and, quite possibly, two lives would have been saved.

Duff's funeral was, of course, attended by his wife's family; her mother, the rather imperious Mrs Violet Emilia Sidney, her younger sister Miss Vera Sidney – unmarried and at forty, a boisterous good-natured woman and the apple of her mother's eye – and her brother Thomas Sidney, a professional entertainer.

Although not noticeably well-to-do the Sidneys were an upper class family and highly respected in the local community. They were a close-knit, not to say clannish family, and Edmund had always been treated as a bit of an outsider. In fact, there had been some friction between Edmund Duff and the Sidneys. Mrs Sidney had felt Duff to be rather too lower class and underpaid for her daughter – especially after he lost £5,000 of Grace's money on a bad investment. The abrasively humorous Tom Sidney considered Edmund too stuffy and often made jokes at his expense. It was also suggested, after the discovery of the murders, that Duff had had an affair with Tom's attractive American wife, Margaret. Even so, the idea of any foul-play involved in his death had, as yet, occurred to nobody.

On 11 February 1929, almost a year after the death, Vera Sidney – Grace's younger sister – complained of feeling off-colour. This in itself was unusual since she generally refused to "give in" to sicknesses and thought little of those that did. In fact she was not the only person in Violet Sidney's house who felt ill that day. The maid, Kate Noakes, and the family cat were also ill. The connecting factor was the soup all three had eaten at lunchtime.

Vera rallied a couple of days later, as did the maid and

cat, but then made the mistake of taking the soup again for lunch, this time joined by her Aunt Gwen. Both became ill, but only Vera was seriously affected. Again doctors Binning and Elwell were called. This time they were unwilling to take any chances and brought in a stomach specialist. He diagnosed intestinal influenza.

Vera died in great pain on 15 February, four days after she was first taken ill. Again, the possibility of murder was still not considered by the family physicians despite the fact that she had displayed virtually the same symptoms of arsenic poisoning as had Edmund Duff.

Violet Sidney was shattered by her daughter's death and her family feared that the old lady might die of the shock. Doctor Elwell prescribed her a strengthening tonic to be taking before meals and she started to slowly recover. Then, on 5 March 1929, she took her tonic, ate her lunch and became very ill. In her lucid moments she insisted that she had been poisoned. The tonic had tasted oddly gritty and bitter and she was convinced that something had been added to it. The already weakened, seventy-year-old lady died within hours, once again displaying the symptoms of arsenic poisoning.

This time even Elwell and Binning could not ignore the evidence and refused to sign the death certificate. Even so, Violet Sidney had been laid to rest by the time the Home Office decided to make enquiries; so she had to be disinterred, along with her daughter and later her son-in-law, to be re-examined. This time the autopsies were carried out by Dr Bernard Spilsbury, a brilliant pathologist who did much to advance the field of forensic science. His more expert examination found the bodies to contain up to five grains of arsenic each; more than enough to cause death. At last the murders were out.

The poisonings received much media coverage and people up and down the country followed the reports of the three inquests with avid interest. It seemed clear to most observers that a member of the family or somebody close to it was probably responsible. The chances of an outsider, for whatever reason, being able to administer poison surreptitiously was next to nil.

Edmund Duff, it was reported, had quite probably been

poisoned on his return from the fishing trip; most likely administered in his bottled beer. Vera had almost certainly been fed the arsenic in her soup; Violet Sidney never partook of soup and the maid had ineffectively been told she could not have any (let alone give it to the cat). Finally forensic examination indeed found heavy traces of arsenic in Violet's tonic bottle. The likeliest source of the arsenic was deduced to be weedkiller, freely available and present in the houses of all the male participants.

Police conducted a large and exhaustive investigation and the Coroner's Court questioned all possible suspects with great care, but in the end the case came to nothing. The evidence was too scanty to implicate any one person or persons of committing the murders and no solid motive could be attached to any of them. In the end, the three people considered most likely to have been the murderer were Tom Sidney, Grace Duff and, rather weirdly, Violet Sidney, the poisoned mother.

Violet was accused by some of hating Edmund Duff and of somehow getting into his pantry and doctoring a bottle of his beer. Then a year later, mad with guilt, she was said to have poisoned her much loved daughter to punish herself. Finally she committed suicide, revealing as she died that the poison had been in her tonic.

It is probably quite safe to reject this theory completely. Violet was not fond of Duff, but had never shown any sign of virulently hating him. All agreed that her shock and grief over the death of Vera were genuine and finally she had seemed both amazed and affronted when proclaiming that she had been poisoned.

Tom Sidney had some financial motive for killing his sister and mother; he stood to gain about £8,000 (about £180,000 in 1992 currency) from their wills, but at the time of the murders he was doing quite well himself and his finances were on a comfortable upturn. An anonymous letter was sent to the coroner at the time of the inquests claiming that Duff was seeing Tom's wife, but no other evidence was ever found to suggest that he had a reason to kill his stuffy brother-in-law.

The most likely candidate, in fact, was Grace Duff. Outwardly a bright and cheerful woman, she was known by close acquaintances to have dark mood swings and to have resented her husband's overly brutal amorous advances (she complained that he left her covered in bruises). Edmund had been away working in Africa for much of their married life and his retirement and permanent return might have upset the balance of her life. She was highly protective of her children and Edmund's dodgy financial deals threatened the future of the whole family. She may have wanted him out of the way so that she might marry Dr Elwell, her flirtatious family physician. It is even possible that she killed him for sleeping with her brother's wife.

Her financial state was improved by her husband's death; in fact she gained enough from his life insurance to buy the house they had previously only rented. Even so, she was still far from being comfortably off; £8,000 might have seemed very tempting and having committed one murder others might have seemed less difficult.

Tom Sidney claimed to have no doubt that Grace was the murderer, and apparently neither did Scotland Yard. He later said that the police suggested that he move as far from Grace as possible, so he took his family to the USA. But we only have his word that this was the case; in the States he was also somewhat safer from British justice if new evidence was uncovered. It had also come to light that Violet's estranged husband, the father of Grace, Tom and Vera, had had an illegitimate son who was said to have resented his father's previous family. There is still no definite proof to connect Grace with the poisonings and in the end she remains merely the most likely of several suspects.

---

The first inquest on Edmund Duff, performed immdiately after his death by Dr Patrick Bronte, found that he died of natural causes. When Sir Bernard Spilsbury performed a second inquest, he found that Bronte had left most of the intestines unexamined, and that he had accidentally put back into Duff's body some of the organs from a woman on whom he had been performing an inquest the same day.

# The Wallace Case

William Herbert Wallace seemed to be a completely ordinary little man. The critic James Agate once said of him: "That man was born middle-aged". But the appearance of ordinariness concealed a certain sadness and unfulfilment. Wallace was born in Keswick in the Lake District in 1878, the child of lower middle class parents. But he had an intellectual turn of mind, and when he discovered the *Meditations* of the Roman emperor Marcus Aurelius, decided that he was by nature a stoic – that is, one who doesn't expect much out of life, but who thinks it can be improved by hard work and discipline. Like H. G. Wells's Kipps or Mr Polly – of whom he constantly reminds us – he became a draper's assistant, and found the life just as boring as they did. His quest for adventure took him to India – but still as a draper's assistant – then to Shanghai; he found both places a great disappointment, and inevitably caught a bad dose of dysentery, which further undermined his already delicate constitution. So with his Marcus Aurelius in his pocket he returned to England. He became a Liberal election agent in Yorkshire, and on a holiday in Harrogate, met a mild-looking, dark haired young lady named Julia Thorp. She was undoubtedly cleverer than Wallace; she was well-read, spoke French, played the piano and made excellent sketches. They talked about Marcus Aurelius and other intellectual matters and, in a rather leisurely manner, decided they liked one another enough to get married. They married in 1913 and lived in Harrogate. But in the following year, the outbreak of war cost Wallace his job – political agents were not needed during a war. Fortunately, it also caused many job vacancies, and Wallace soon found employment as an insurance agent in Liverpool, working for the Prudential. They moved into a rather dreary little terrace house in a cul-de-sac called Wolverton Crescent, in the Anfield district. And for the next seventeen years, they lived a life of peaceful and rather penurious dullness. Wallace pottered about in a chemical laboratory in his home, and even gave occasional lectures on it at the technical college. He also joined a chess club that met regularly in the City Café in North John Street.

Julia read library books and sang at the piano. They had no children and, apparently, no real friends. And although life on less than £4 a week was hardly idyllic, they seemed happy enough.

The evening of 19 January 1931 was chilly and damp, but by seven o'clock, a few members had already arrived at the chess club in the City Café. Shortly after 7.15, the telephone rang. Samuel Beattie, captain of the club, answered it. A man's voice asked for Wallace. Beattie said that Wallace would be in later to play a match, and suggested he ring back. "No, I'm too busy – I have my girl's twenty-first birthday on." The man said his name was Qualtrough, and asked if Beattie could give him a message. Beattie wrote it down. It asked Wallace to go to Qualtrough's home at 25 Menlove Gardens East the following evening at 7.30. It was, said Qualtrough, a matter of business.

Wallace slipped quietly into the club some time before eight. Beattie gave him the message, and Wallace made a note of the address in his diary.

The following evening, Wallace arrived home shortly after six, had "high tea" – a substantial meal – and left the house at a quarter-to-seven. He instructed his wife to bolt the back door after him – that was their usual practice. Julia Wallace, who was suffering from a heavy cold, nevertheless went with him to the back gate and watched him leave. Wallace walked to a tramcar, asked the conductor if it went to Menlove Gardens East, and climbed aboard. The conductor advised him to change trams at Penny Lane, and told Wallace where to get off. The conductor of the second tram advised him to get off at Menlove Gardens West.

Wallace now spent a frustrating half hour or so trying to find Menlove Gardens East. Apparently it did not exist; although there *was* a Menlove Gardens North and a Menlove Gardens West. Wallace decided to call at 25 Menlove Gardens West, just in case Beattie had taken down the address wrongly; but the householder there said he had never heard of a Mr Qualtrough. Wallace tried calling at the house of his superintendent at the Prudential, a Mr Joseph Crew, who lived in nearby Green Lane, but found no one at home. He asked a policeman the way, and remarked on the time: "It's not eight o"clock yet." The policeman said: "It's a quarter to."

A case that would have taxed the ingenuity of Sherlock Holmes took place in Montana in September 1901. The body of an old man named Dotson was found in his cabin, near Helmsville, with a bullet in the heart. On the opposite wall, a gun had been rigged up in a wooden frame, with the muzzle pointing at the dead man. A string ran from the dead man's head, through a metal ring in the wall, to the trigger of the gun. It looked like a clear case of suicide. A note beside the body seemed to confirm this. It read: 'It warnt my son Clint done that Cullinane murder. Clint tried to save me. I done it.' It was signed Oliver Dotson, and friends verified that it was in his handwriting.

The 'Cullinane murder' had taken place on August 5, 1899. A prospector named Gene Cullinane had been found-shot dead in his cabin, not far from Dotson's place. A few days later, sheriff's officers arrested Clint Dotson, and two other men named Oliver Benson and Ellis Persinger. Benson and Persinger admitted robbing Gene Cullinane, but alleged that it was Clint Dotson who had shot the prospector twice in the heart. Benson and Persinger were sentenced to ten years in prison; Clint Dotson received life.

Now it looked as if Dotson might have been innocent after all. He had what amounted to a double alibi. He was behind bars at the time of his father's death, so there could be no question that he might have forced his father to sign a false confession. Old Man Dotson seemed to be offering his son a kind of posthumous alibi for the time of the murder...

He called in a general shop, then in a newsagent's, where he borrowed a city directory, which seemed to prove beyond all doubt that Menlove Gardens East did not exist. He even asked the proprietress to look in her accounts book to make sure that there was no such place as Menlove Gardens East. People were to remark later that Wallace seemed determined to make people remember him. Finally, even the pertinacious Wallace gave up, and returned home.

He arrived back at 8.45, and inserted his key into the front door. To his surprise, it seemed to be locked on the inside. He tried the back door; that was also locked. Receiving no reply to his knock, he called on his next-door neighbours, the Johnstons, looking deeply concerned, and asked them if they had heard anything unusual – only a thin partition wall separated them from the Wallaces. They said no. John Johnston suggested that perhaps Wallace should try his own back door key, but advised him to try the front door again. And this time, to Wallace's apparent surprise, it opened. Wallace entered the house, and the Johnstons waited politely. A few moments later, Wallace rushed out, looking shocked. "Come and see – she's been killed." They followed him through to the sitting room or parlour, which was at the back of the house. Julia Wallace was lying on the floor, face downward, and the gash in the back of her head made it clear that she had been the victim of an attack. The floor was spattered with blood. Wallace seemed curiously calm as he lit a gas mantle, walking around the body to do so, then suggested that they should look in the kitchen to see if anything had been taken. There was a lid on the kitchen floor, which Wallace said had been wrenched from a cabinet. He took down the cash box from a shelf, looked inside, and told the Johnstons that he thought about £4 had been taken. Then, at Johnston's suggestion, Wallace went upstairs to see if anything was missing, and came down almost immediately saying: "There's £5 in a jar they haven't taken." At this point, Johnston left to fetch the police. Wallace had a momentary breakdown, putting his hands to his head and sobbing, but quickly recovered himself. Mrs Johnston and Wallace then returned to the sitting room, where Wallace commented: "They've finished her – look at the brains." And indeed, Julia Wallace's brains were oozing onto the floor. Then

Wallace said with surprise: "Why, whatever was she doing with her mackintosh and my mackintosh?" There was, in fact, a mackintosh under the body, which Wallace shortly identified as his own.

There was a knock at the door; it proved to be a policeman. Wallace told him about his fruitless search for Qualtrough, then accompanied him upstairs. Constable Williams felt that Wallace seemed "extraordinarily cool and calm". The bedroom seemed to have been disturbed, with pillows lying near the fireplace, but the drawers of the dressing table were closed.

Another policeman arrived; then, just before ten o"clock, Professor J. E. W. MacFall, the professor of forensic medicine at Liverpool University. MacFall concluded that Mrs Wallace had died of a violent blow, or blows, to the back left hand side of the skull, and deduced that she had been sitting in an armchair, leaning forward as if talking to somebody, when the blow had been struck. She had fallen to the floor, and the attacker had rained about eleven more blows on her. He also reached the interesting conclusion that Mrs Wallace had died about four hours earlier – that is, at six o'clock.

This, it later proved, was impossible, for the fourteen-year-old milk boy, Alan Close, was to testify that he had delivered a can of milk at 6.25, and that it had been taken in by Mrs Wallace, who advised him to hurry home because he had a cough.

But MacFall had planted suspicion of Wallace in the minds of the police. Two weeks later, on 2 February 1931, Wallace was charged with his wife's murder. He became very pale and replied: "What can I say to this charge, of which I am absolutely innocent?"

His trial began on 22 April, before Mr Justice Wright. The prosecution case was that Wallace had concocted an elaborate plan to murder his wife, and had phoned the café to make the appointment with Qualtrough on the evening before the murder. The endless and elaborate enquiries about Menlove Gardens East were intended to provide him with a perfect alibi; but Mrs Wallace was already lying dead in her sitting room when William Herbert Wallace left the house. In the closing speech for the crown, Mr E. G. Hemmerde made much of the "inherent improbabilities" in Wallace's story:

that surely an insurance agent would not spend his evening on such a wild goose chase, that he would have hurried back home the moment he knew that a Menlove Gardens East did not exist. He also made much of Wallace's apparent calmness immediately after the discovery of the body, and mentioned in passing the possibility that Wallace had stripped naked and then put on his mackintosh, and battered his wife to death, before leaving the house to look for Qualtrough.

The judge's summing up was favourable to Wallace, and there was some surprise when, after only an hour, the jury returned a verdict of guilty. Wallace was shattered, he had been confident of acquittal. But he appealed against the verdict, and in the following month, the Court of Criminal Appeal quashed it, and Wallace was freed.

He was taken back at his old job. But most of his colleagues had doubts about his innocence. He was given a job in the office. He moved house to Meadowside Road in Bromsborough, a Liverpool suburb. And on 26 February 1933 – less than two years after his ordeal – he died in hospital of cancer of the liver. Ever since that date, writers on crime have disputed his guilt or innocence.

The main problem, of course, is that of motive. Wallace was a lifelong keeper of diaries, and his diaries make it clear that his married life was peaceful and serene. There was no suggestion of another woman, or that he was tired of his wife. His diaries after his trial continue to protest his innocence, with entries like: "Julia, Julia my dear, why were you taken from me?" The crime writer Nigel Morland, who examined the case at length in *Background to Murder* and who was convinced of Wallace's guilt, has to fall back on generalizations like: "The human heart is always a vast mystery."

Yseult Bridges, who also wrote about the case, became convinced of Wallace's guilt when she read a series of "ghosted" articles about his life which appeared in *John Bull* in 1932. There Wallace remarks that he had matched his brains against some of the greatest chess players in the world. Yseult Bridges comments that "he was never more than a third rate player in an obscure little club", and concludes that Wallace was a pathological liar. But another writer, Jonathan Goodman, looked more closely into the matter,

and concludes (in *The Killing of Julia Wallace*) that Wallace
was telling the truth after all; in the 1920s he *had* played
in "simultaneous exhibition matches" against world-famous
players like Capablanca – and been thoroughly beaten.

Kenneth Gunnell, a parliamentary candidate from Redruth,
Cornwall, independently discovered that Wallace was telling
the truth about his chess opponents, and so began to study
the case in detail. He made one odd discovery. Amy Wallace,
the wife of Wallace's elder brother Joseph, was a tough and
dominant lady, and Gunnell found out that in Malaya – where
she had lived in the 1920s – Amy had been a member of
a flagellation sect, and indulged in beating black boys. He
noted that after his acquittal, Wallace sometimes acted like a
man with something on his mind – not murder, perhaps, but
some guilty secret. Could it be that Amy Wallace was Herbert
Wallace's mistress, and that *she* murdered Julia? Mr Gunnell
even speculated that the murder weapon was the metal handle of a riding whip. Unfortunately, Mr Gunnell's stimulating
theory remained unpublished. Yet when I read the typescript
of his book, I found myself ultimately unconvinced. Although
my view of Wallace was rather negative – he seemed to me
a cold-hearted egoist who had married Julia for her money
(which he used to pay his debts), then treated her purely as
a piece of domestic furniture – it seemed clear that he was
simply not the type to indulge in affairs with highly dominant
women; Amy Wallace probably terrified him.

In 1960 I collaborated with Patricia Pitman on *An Encyclopaedia
of Murder*. Mrs Pitman was convinced of Wallace's guilt,
I – in spite of misgivings about his character – of his
innocence. He simply had no reason to kill Julia. Two
or three years later, she surprised me by telling me that
she was now convinced of Wallace's innocence. It seemed
that she had been talking to one of Britain's leading crime
experts, J. H. H. Gaute, a director of Harraps publishers,
and he had told her the real identity of the murderer. I
hastened to contact Joe Gaute, with whom I had had much
friendly correspondence about murder. It was from him that
I first heard the name of the man he was certain was the
killer of Julia Wallace: Gordon Parry. Wallace himself, it
seemed, had believed that Parry murdered his wife, and
after his retirement had made a public statement to the

effect that he had had an alarm button installed inside his front door.

After the murder, Wallace had been asked by the police what callers might have been admitted to the house by his wife; he named fifteen people (including his sister-in-law Amy). Asked if he suspected any of them Wallace hesitated, then admitted that he was suspicious of a young man named Gordon Parry. This man had called at his house on business, and was trusted by Julia. But he had a criminal record. And he knew where Wallace kept his collection money. At the time of the murder, Parry was heavily in debt. Questioned by the police, Parry alleged that he had been with "friends" on the evening of the murder, and the friends corroborated this; however, two years later, Parry admitted that it had been "a mistake".

Crime writer Jonathan Goodman, who was writing a book on the Wallace case, tracked down Parry's father through the Liverpool town clerk, and from him obtained Gordon Parry's address in Camberwell, South London. Together with another crime expert, Richard Whittington-Egan, Goodman went to call on him.

Parry, a powerfully built little man with sleeked-back grey hair and a military moustache, received them with the "bogus bonhomie of a car salesman", and talked to them on his doorstep. They decided that "his manner masks . . . considerable firmness, even ruthlessness. He would be a nasty man to cross." Parry hinted that he could reveal much about Wallace, and described him as "a very strange man" and "sexually odd". He seemed to know what had become of everybody involved in the case, as if he had been carefully following its aftermath over the years. And when he finally dismissed Goodman and Whittington-Egan, they both had the feeling that he was thinking that he had fooled better people than they were . . . In his book *The Killing of Julia Wallace*, Goodman refers to Parry as "Mr X", and it is fairly clear that he regards him as the chief suspect.

In 1980, a news editor in Liverpool's Radio City, Roger Dilkes, became interested in the Wallace case, and started researching it for a programme. He contacted Jonathan Goodman, who at first was understandably cagey about revealing Parry's identity, in case he found himself involved in a libel suit. But through Wallace's solicitor, Hector Munro, Dilkes tracked down Parry's identity. At the time of the murder, Parry was twenty-two. The son of well-to parents, he had worked for the Prudential for a while, but had failed to pay in various premiums he had received – his parents had paid the money. Parry had been charged at various times with theft, embezzlement and indecent assault – at his trial a medical expert had described him as "a sexual pervert".

Dilkes persisted, but when he finally tracked down Parry to North Wales, he discovered that he had died a few weeks before, in April 1980. Nevertheless, he continued with his investigation. Who were the "friends" who had given Parry his alibi for the night of the murder? The answer that emerged was that it was not friends but *a* friend – a Miss Lily Lloyd, to whom Parry was engaged. And from Jonathan Goodman he learned that when Parry had jilted her two years later, Miss Lloyd had gone to Wallace's solicitor and offered to swear an *affidavit* saying that the alibi she had given Parry for the night of the crime was untrue. Dilkes then managed to track down Miss Lloyd, who had played a piano in a cinema in the 1930s. If the police had taken the trouble to check *her* alibi, they would have learned that she could not have been with Parry at the time of the murder – she was working in the cinema.

Finally, Dilkes uncovered the clinching piece of evidence. At the time of the murder, a young garage mechanic named John Parkes had been working near Parry's home. He knew Parry as a "wide boy" – in fact, had been to school with him. On the night of the murder, Parry had called at the garage in an agitated state, and washed down his car with a high pressure hose. Parkes saw a glove in the car, and pulled it out to prevent it getting wet. It was soaked with wet blood.

Dilkes had finally tracked down the murderer of Julia Wallace, but half a century too late.

# The Harry Whitecliffe Mystery

According to a book published in France in 1978, one of England's most extraordinary mass murderers committed suicide in a Berlin jail in the middle of the jazz era. His name was Harry Whitecliffe, and he murdered at least forty women. Then why is his name not more widely known – at least to students of crime? Because when he was arrested he was masquerading under the name Lovach Blume, and his suicide concealed his true identity from the authorities.

The full story can be found in a volume called *Nouvelles Histoires Magiques – New Tales of Magic* – by Louis Pauwels and Guy Breton, published by Editions J"ai Lu. In spite of the title – which sounds like fiction – it is in fact a series of studies in the paranormal and bizarre; there are chapters on Nostradamus, Rasputin and Eusapia Palladino, and accounts of such well-known mysteries as the devil's footprints in Devon.

According to the chapter "The Two Faces of Harry Whitecliffe", there appeared in London in the early Twenties a collection of essays so promising that it sold out in a few days; it consisted of a series of marvellous pastiches of Oscar Wilde. But its author, Harry Whitecliffe, apparently preferred to shun publicity; he remained obstinately hidden. Would-be interviewers returned empty-handed. Then, just as people were beginning to suggest that Whitecliffe was a pseudonym for some well-known writer – Bernard Shaw, perhaps, or the young T. S. Eliot – Whitecliffe finally consented to appear. He was a handsome young man of twenty-three, likeable, eccentric and fond of sport. He was also generous; he was said to have ended one convivial evening by casually giving a pretty female beggar £500. He professed to adore flowers, but only provided their stems were not more than twenty centimetres long. He was the kind of person the English love, and was soon a celebrity.

Meanwhile he continued to write: essays, poetry and plays. One of his comedies, *Similia*, had four hundred consecutive performances in London before touring England. It made him a fortune, which he quickly scattered among his friends. By the beginning of 1923 he was one of the "kings of London society".

Then, in September of that year, he vanished. He sold all his possessions, and gave his publisher carte blanche to handle his work. But before the end of the year he reappeared in Dresden. The theatre then presented *Similia* with enormous success, the author himself translating it from English into German. It went on to appear in many theatres along the Rhine. He founded a press for publishing modern poetry, and works on modern painting – Dorian Verlag – whose editions are now worth a fortune.

But he was still something of a man of mystery. Every morning he galloped along the banks of the river Elbe until nine o'clock; at ten he went to his office, eating lunch there. At six in the evening, he went to art exhibitions or literary salons, and met friends. At nine, he returned home and no one knew what he did for the rest of the evening. And no one liked to ask him.

, One reason for this regular life was that he was in love – the girl was called Wally von Hammerstein, daughter of aristocratic parents, who were favourably impressed with the young writer. Their engagement was to be announced on 4 October 1924.

But on the previous day Whitecliffe disappeared again. He failed to arrive at his office, and vanished from his flat. The frantic Wally searched Dresden, without success. The police were alerted – discreetly – and pursued diligent inquiries. Their theory was that he had committed suicide. Wally believed he had either met with an accident or been the victim of a crime – he often carried large sums of money. As the weeks dragged by her desperation turned to misery; she talked about entering a convent.

Then she received a letter. It had been found in the cell of a condemned man who had committed suicide in Berlin – he had succeeded in opening his veins with the buckle of his belt. The inscription on the envelope said: "I beg you, monsieur le procureur of the Reich, to forward this letter to its destination without opening it." It was signed: Lovach Blume.

Blume was apparently one of the most horrible of murderers, worse than Jack the Ripper or Peter Kürten, the Düsseldorf sadist. He had admitted to the court that tried

him: "Every ten days I have to kill. I am driven by an irresist-
ible urge, so that until I have killed, I suffer atrociously. But
as I disembowel my victims I feel an indescribable pleasure."
Asked about his past, he declared: "I am a corpse. Why bother
about the past of a corpse?"

Blume's victims were prostitutes and homeless girls picked
up on the Berlin streets. He would take them to a hotel, and
kill them as soon as they were undressed. Then, with a knife
like a Malaysian "kris", with an ivory handle, he would
perform horrible mutilations, so awful that even doctors
found the sight unbearable. These murders continued over
a period of six months, during which the slum quarters of
Berlin lived in fear.

Blume was finally arrested by accident, in September 1924.
The police thought he was engaged in drug trafficking, and
knocked on the door of a hotel room minutes after Blume
had entered with a prostitute. Blume had just committed his
thirty-first murder in Berlin; he was standing naked by the
window, and the woman's body lay at his feet.

He made no resistance, and admitted freely to his crimes
– he could only recall twenty-seven. He declared that he
had no fear of death – particularly the way executions were
performed in Germany (by decapitation), which he greatly
preferred to the English custom of hanging.

This was the man who had committed suicide in his prison
cell, and who addressed a long letter to his fiancée, Wally
von Hammerstein. He told her that he was certain the devil
existed, because he had met him. He was, he explained, a
kind of Jekyll-and-Hyde, an intelligent, talented man who
suddenly became cruel and bloodthirsty. He thought of
himself as being like victims of demoniacal possession. He
had left London after committing nine murders, when he
suspected that Scotland Yard was on his trail. His love for
Wally was genuine, he told her, and had caused him to "die
a little". He had hoped once that she might be able to save
him from his demons, but it had proved a vain hope.

Wally fainted as she read the letter. And in 1925 she entered
a nunnery and took the name Marie de Douleurs. There she
prays for the salvation of a tortured soul. . . .

This is the story, as told by Louis Pauwels – a writer who
became famous for his collaboration with Jacques Bergier on

a book called *The Morning of the Magicians*. Critics pointed out that that book was full of factual errors, and a number of these can also be found in his article on Whitecliffe. For example, if the date of Blume's arrest is correct – 25 September 1924 – then it took place before Whitecliffe vanished from Dresden, on 3 October 1924 . . . But this, presumably, is a slip of the pen.

But who was Harry Whitecliffe? According to Pauwels, he told the Berlin court that his father was German, his mother Danish, and that he was brought up in Australia by an uncle who was a butcher. His uncle lived in Sydney. But in a "conversation" between Pauwels and his fellow-author at the end of one chapter, Pauwels states that Whitecliffe was the son of a great English family. But apart from the three magistrates who opened the suicide letter – ignoring Blume's last wishes – only Wally and her parents knew Whitecliffe's true identity. The judges are dead, so are Wally's parents. Wally is a seventy-five-year-old nun who until now has never told anyone of this drama of her youth. We are left to assume that she has now told the story to Pauwels.

This extraordinary tale aroused the curiosity of a well-known French authoress, Françoise d"Eaubonne, who felt that Whitecliffe deserved a book to himself. But her letters to the two authors – Pauwels and Breton – went unanswered. She therefore contacted the British Society of Theatre Research, and so entered into a correspondence with the theatre historian John Kennedy Melling. Melling had never heard of Whitecliffe, or of a play called *Similia*. He decided to begin his researches by contacting Scotland Yard, to ask whether they have any record of an unknown sex killer of the early 1920s. Their reply was negative; there was no series of Ripper-type murders of prostitutes in the early 1920s. He next applied to J. H. H. Gaute, the possessor of the largest crime library in the British Isles; Gaute could also find no trace of such a series of sex crimes in the 1920s. Theatrical reference books contained no mention of Harry Whitecliffe, or of his successful comedy *Similia*. It began to look – as incredible as it sounds – as if Pauwels had simply invented the whole story.

Thelma Holland, Oscar Wilde's daughter-in-law, could find no trace of a volume of parodies of Wilde among the comprehensive collection of her late husband, Vyvyan

Holland. But she had a suggestion to make – to address inquiries to the Mitchell Library in Sydney. As an Australian, she felt it was probably Melling's best chance of tracking down Harry Whitecliffe.

Incredibly, this long shot brought positive results: not about Harry Whitecliffe, but about a German murderer called Blume – not Lovach, but Wilhelm Blume. The *Argus* newspaper for 8 August 1922 contained a story headed "Cultured Murderer", and sub-titled: "Literary Man's Series of Crimes". It was datelined Berlin, 7 August.

> Wilhelm Blume, a man of wide culture and considerable literary gifts, whose translations of English plays have been produced in Dresden with great success, has confessed to a series of cold-blooded murders, one of which was perpetrated at the Hotel Adlon, the best known Berlin hotel.

The most significant item in the newspaper report is that Blume had founded a publishing house called Dorian Press (Verlag) in Dresden. This is obviously the same Blume who – according to Pauwels – committed suicide in Berlin.

But Wilhelm Blume was not a sex killer. His victims had been postmen, and the motive had been robbery. In Germany postal orders were paid to consignees in their own homes, so postmen often carried fairly large sums of money. Blume had sent himself postal orders, then killed the postmen and robbed them – the exact number is not stated in the *Argus* article. The first time he did this he was interrupted by his landlady while he was strangling the postman with a noose; and he cut her throat. Then he moved on to Dresden, where in due course he attempted to rob another postman. Armed with two revolvers, he waited for the postman in the porch of a house. But the tenant of the house arrived so promptly that he had to flee, shooting one of the policemen. Then his revolvers both misfired, and he was caught. Apparently he attempted to commit suicide in prison, but failed. He confessed – as the *Argus* states – to several murders, and was presumably executed later in 1922 (although the *Argus* carries no further record).

It seems plain, then, that the question "Who was Harry

Whitecliffe?" should be reworded "Who was Wilhelm Blume?"
For Blume and Whitecliffe were obviously the same person.

From the information we possess, we can make a tentative reconstruction of the story of Blume–Whitecliffe. He sounds like a typical example of a certain type of killer who is also a confidence man – other examples are Landru, Petiot, the "acid bath murderer" Haigh, and the sex killer Neville Heath. It is an essential part of such a man's personality that he is a fantasist, and that he likes to pose as a success, and to talk casually about past triumphs. (Neville Heath called himself "Group Captain Rupert Brooke".) They usually start off as petty swindlers, then gradually become more ambitious and graduate to murder. This is what Blume seems to have done. In the chaos of postwar Berlin he made a quick fortune by murdering and robbing postmen. Perhaps his last coup made him a fortune beyond his expectations, or perhaps the Berlin postal authorities were now on the alert for the killer. Blume decided it was time to make an attempt to live a respectable life, and to put his literary fantasies into operation. He moved to Dresden, calling himself Harry Whitecliffe, and set up Dorian Verlag. He became a successful translator of English plays, and may have helped to finance their production in Dresden and in theatres along the Rhine. Since he was posing as an upper class Englishman, and must have occasionally run into other Englishmen in Dresden, we may assume that his English was perfect, and that his story of being brought up in Australia was probably true. Since he also spoke perfect German, it is also a fair assumption that he was, as he told the court, the son of a German father and a Danish mother.

He fell in love with an upper class girl, and told her a romantic story that is typical of the inveterate daydreamer: that he was the son of a "great English family", that he had become an overnight literary success in London as a result of his pastiches of Oscar Wilde, but had at first preferred to shun the limelight (this is the true Walter Mitty touch) until increasing success made this impossible. His wealth is the result of a successful play, *Similia*. (The similarity of the title to *Salome* is obvious, and we may infer that Blume was an ardent admirer of Wilde.) But in order to avoid too much publicity – after all, victims of previous swindles might expose him – he lives the quiet, regular life of a crook in hiding.

And just as all seems to be going so well – just as success, respectability, a happy marriage, seem so close – he once again runs out of money. There is only one solution: a brief return to a life of crime. One or two robberies of postmen can replenish his bank account and secure his future . . . But this time it goes disastrously wrong. Harry Whitecliffe is exposed as the swindler and murderer Wilhelm Blume. He makes no attempt to deny it, and confesses to his previous murders; his world has now collapsed in ruins. He is sent back to Berlin, where the murders were committed, and he attempts suicide in his cell. Soon after, he dies by the guillotine. And in Dresden the true story of Wilhelm Blume is soon embroidered into a horrifying tale of a Jekyll-and-Hyde mass murderer, whose early career in London is confused with Jack the Ripper. . . .

Do any records of Wilhelm Blume still exist? It seems doubtful – the fire-bombing of Dresden destroyed most of the civic records, and the people who knew him more than sixty years ago must now all be dead. Yet Pauwels has obviously come across some garbled and wildly inaccurate account of Blume's career as Harry Whitecliffe. It would be interesting to know where he obtained his information; but neither Françoise d"Eaubonne nor John Kennedy Melling have been successful in persuading him to answer letters.

# chapter five

# HOLLYWOOD SCANDALS

*O*ne of the first great successes to come out of the west coast village called Hollywood was The Life of an American Fireman (made in 1902 – The Great Train Robbery came the following year). The excited patrons saw a house on fire, a man being rescued from an upstairs window, then a woman and a child, coughing and staggering as they are overcome with smoke. The firemen dash through the streets on their horse-drawn wagons. As the mother and child collapse, unconscious, a fireman bursts in through the door. He carries the unconscious mother to a ladder that appears at the window; she wakes and begs him to save her baby. He carries her down, then goes back into the burning building, and gets the child. Mother and child are united as the house blazes. There wasn't a dry eye in the cinema. It had only lasted a few minutes, but people felt as if they'd been through a crisis together; they smiled through their tears at their next door neighbour. What a noble, interesting thing life is, after all! And the cinema could suddenly bring it home to you . . . It deserves to be classified with the novel as one of the greatest imaginative advances in human history.

Then there was Chaplin, the comic but game little tramp, always in trouble, always fighting against the odds, always looking shyly and adoringly at the pretty girl in the spring dress – and often getting her in the end. People could certainly identify with him. Chaplin records his amazement when he left Hollywood, where he'd been churning out two-reelers for years, to visit England and other *towns in the United States, to realize that he was world famous. It wasn't just because Chaplin was a great performer. It was because he came from Hollywood – a word that was acquiring a dubious quality called "glamour". Hollywood was a magic land, a kind of fairyland on earth.*

*Many of its inhabitants held the same view, though for different reasons. It was soon clear that there was as much money in movies as in oil. Even the most successful actors and comedians could only play in one theatre at a time; but a movie could be shown in a hundred vaudeville theatres and Nickelodeons all over the country. One of the earliest successes,* Rescued by Rover *(made in England), cost seven pounds thirteen shillings and ninepence to produce (in 1905). The prints – 400 of them – sold for a little over £10 each, so the producer, Hepworth, multiplied his investment by five hundred or so.* The Dream of a Rarebit Fiend *cost $350 to make, and made $30,000. When the full length "drama" came in, around 1915, a movie might cost $50,000 and make a million. Producers found themselves unimaginably rich, rich on the scale of an eastern potentate. Their way of spending their money was to shower it on stars, directors and sets. In 1905, $10 a week was regarded as a reasonable wage for an actor; by 1920, a star could receive $100,000 for a movie that took ten weeks to make. Hollywood had the glamour of immense riches.*

*It was the Arbuckle case of 1921 that shocked the general public into realizing that many of its celluloid heroines and saints were nymphomaniacs and sinners. The studios had always done their best to hush up divorces and similar scandals. But now the jolly, fat-boy of the screen, who looked so completely amiable (as, indeed, he was), was suddenly associated with a rape ending in death. The lid was off Hollywood, and the stench was like a graveyard. In her best known photograph, Virginia Rappe looked so sweet and wholesome, the kind of girl every decent American boy wanted to marry. The thought of the manner of her death aroused a kind of morbid fascination; the grinning Fatty Arbuckle became a real life Dracula or Jack the Ripper. He was acquitted, and the jury foreman at his last trial said: "We feel a great injustice has been done him." Arbuckle chortled with delight; the studio bosses announced more Arbuckle pictures. They had simply failed to understand that once an idol has been de-glamorized, there can be no come-back. Possibly Arbuckle might have made a new career as an actor in horror movies, to fit his new image; but no one thought of that. He died of a heart attack in 1933, a tired and disappointed man.*

# The Murder of William Desmond Taylor

And in the year after the Arbuckle scandal, while the fat clown was still on trial, another scandal struck Hollywood like an earth tremor. The victim was the suave, handsome British film director William Desmond Taylor. Taylor was a cultured man who was enthusiastic about the works of Freud. No doubt he found himself in agreement with Freud's thesis that the libido is the basic animal drive, for he himself had an insatiable sexual appetite. And as the $100,000 a year chief-director of Lasky Studios (later Paramount), he had no difficulty in keeping himself supplied with a stream of young girls, all of whom wanted to marry him. Taylor had no intention of marrying anyone for a long time; he was enjoying life too much. Then, on 21 February 1922, it came to a sudden end. His valet, Peavy, returning to Taylor's expensive Westlake Park home at 7.30 in the morning, found

Hollywood began as a ranch near the small town of Los Angeles in 1886. In 1913, a New York film company run by two men named Schmuel Gelbfisz and Jesse Lasky sent their new employee Cecil B. DeMille to Flagstaff, Arizona, looking for a place to make westerns. Flagstaff was too flat, so he got back on the train and went on to Los Angeles, where he rented a barn on the Hollywood ranch, and made a smash hit called *The Squaw Man*.

Schmel Gelbfisz was already calling himself Samuel Goldfish, but he then decided on a further change – to Samuel Goldwyn. Under that name he is known as the author of some famous remarks, such as "Include me out", and "My film *Hans Christian Andersen* is full of charmth and warmth". He always referred to the classic film made by his own studio as *Withering Heights*. When told that he could not make *The Well of Loneliness* because it was about lesbians, he said, "Ok, make 'em Austrians."

his master lying on his back, quite dead. The death was
assumed to be natural until Taylor was turned over, and
two bullet holes were seen. The police searching the house
found evidence of Taylor's incredible love-life, including a
note from a popular star of the day, Mary Miles Minter –
a Chaplin leading lady – which read "Dearest, I love you, I
love you, I love you" with a whole row of kisses. At Taylor's
funeral, she kissed the corpse on the lips. Like Arbuckle, she
was unaware of the attitude of the outside world to the idols
who inhabited their dream paradise. They were supposed to
live up to their screen image of purity and innocence. Miss
Minter's career came to an end with the scandal. So did that of
Mabel Normand, a comedienne who, next to Mary Pickford,
was Hollywood's most popular actress. Miss Normand had
spent an hour or so with Taylor the evening before his death,
although she had left early. She claimed to be his fiancée. But
police discovered that the angelic-looking Miss Normand had
been experimenting with drugs, and that Taylor had been
doing his best to track down whoever was supplying her.

In fact, the aftermath of Taylor's death was almost worse
than the murder itself. It emerged that Miss Minter was
not twenty, as she was supposed to be, but thirty. Peavy,
the valet, was very obviously homosexual, and for a while,
this seemed to supply a possible motive for the crime. For
Taylor's previous valet, a man named Sands, had been
forging cheques in Taylor's name while his master was in
Europe, and smashing his cars. Yet when he returned, Taylor
only fired him. Since then, Taylor had been burgled twice.
Was it possible that Sands was Taylor's lover, and had killed
him out of jealousy or revenge? This notion was exploded
when it was revealed that "Sands" was actually Taylor's
disreputable brother Denis, who had come to America with
him years before. Denis was never located.

In 1967, the famous director King Vidor decided to turn the
Taylor mystery into a film. What he learned about the power
of the studios and the corruption of the Los Angeles police
department shocked him. To begin with, Adolph Zukor and
other executives of Famous Players Lasky had descended on
Taylor's house immediately after the murder and destroyed
a quantity of letters and papers. But according to information
leaked to the press, the police had no difficulty finding out

that Taylor had been having affairs with half the celebrated beauties of Hollywood. They also found quantities of silk knickers in Taylor's bedroom – souvenirs, apparently, of his many conquests, as well as pornographic photographs showing Taylor in the act of lovemaking with various ladies, and a pink silk nightie monogrammed MMM.

Mary Miles Minter and Mabel Norman were naturally among the suspects. So was Mary's mother, Charlotte Shelby, a tough Hollywood Mom who may have been in love with Taylor herself. But she, apparently, had a good alibi.

When Vidor's biographer, Sidney Kirkpatrick, began gathering material for his book, he discovered that a whole year seemed to be missing from his papers: 1967. When he found the missing papers in a locked strongbox in the garage, he discovered that they concerned Vidor's investigations of the Taylor case. And when he read them, he saw why Vidor had decided to abandon the whole project.

It seemed that Vidor had soon discovered that Taylor was not what he pretended to be; the evidence indicated that the insatiable Don Juan was, in fact, a bisexual, with a distinct preference for men, and (quite possibly) for young boys, who were procured by his valet. And at least one Hollywood journalist was able to tell Vidor authoritatively that the killer was the mother of Mary Miles Minter, the ambitious and ruthless Charlotte Shelby who, like everyone else, was unaware of Taylor's true sexual inclinations. Charlotte was not only fixated on Taylor; she was also quite determined that her daughter – who was also her meal ticket – should not get involved with any man. It seems that on the evening in question, Mary was having a tête-a-tête with Taylor when Mabel Norman turned up; so Mary fled into hiding. Her mother became increasingly irritable, and finally went looking for her with a pistol. She saw Mabel Normand emerge from Taylor's house, then peered in through the window and saw her daughter coming out of hiding. This was too much and she stalked in and shot the dastardly seducer – in the back, having made him raise his arms.

So what about all the stories of underwear and pornographic pictures? These, apparently, were the work of the film studio, which promptly went into action to throw up a heavy smoke screen. Hollywood had enough scandals –

> Mabel Normand's career experienced a setback as a result of the William Desmond Taylor affair, but it was wrecked by a further scandal in 1924. She was visiting Chaplin's leading lady Edna Puviance and her oilman lover Cortland S. Dines; all got very drunk. When Edna's chauffeur came to pick her up, he and Dines got into an argument and the chauffeur shot Dines, slightly wounding him. (The chauffeur was obviously her lover.) At a hearing, it was revealed that the chauffeur was a convicted criminal and a drug addict. This, combined with the fact that the women were drunk on bootleg liquor (1924 was the middle of the Prohibition) and that everyone was rumoured to be naked, was the final nail in the coffin of Mabel's career.

Fatty Arbuckle had just been arrested – and they had no intention of this one reaching court. So the press was fed with scandalous stories about silk nighties. The careers of Mary Miles Minter and Mabel Normand were ruined, but the wicked Charlotte lived on and prospered.

According to Kirkpatrick, Vidor decided to give up the film because he didn't want to taint the lives of the stars concerned. He may also have been worried about libel. But surely the true answer is that even in 1967, a film about a Don Juan who turned out to be a homosexual pedophile was just not good Hollywood material. That particular can of worms was just a little too putrid.

# The Jean Harlow Mystery

In the early Thirties, some Hollywood producers decided they might as well cash in on the bad reputation of the movie capital. So while some studios were making fortunes with films like *Little Women* and *Rebecca of Sunnybrook Farm*, others introduced a new frankness to the screen. Mae West's line "Come up, see me sometime" became the great catch phrase of the day. Middle-aged men and women chuckled appreciatively when she sang: "I Like a Man Who Takes His Time". And the latest screen idol was a blonde newcomer called Harlean Carpenter, who chose the screen name Jean Harlow. Harlow replaced Clara Bow, the "It" girl, in the public's estimation; Clara Bow lost her reputation in 1930, when her ex-secretary testified in court that she was virtually a nymphomaniac, spending her large income on good-looking gigolos. Yet even Harlow – whose screen personality was nearly as uninhibited as Mae West's – felt the chilly breath of scandal when her husband, the director and movie-supervisor Paul Bern, was found shot dead under mysterious circumstances in September 1932. Amusingly enough, what alarmed the studios was not that the public might feel Harlow was as wicked as her screen parts, but that she might arouse pity – and contempt. She had been married to Bern – who was regarded as a Hollywood "genius" – for only two months, and reports said they were ideally happy. But police investigation revealed that, for many years before marrying Harlow, Bern had lived with another lovely blonde, Dorothy Millette. After a nervous breakdown, Dorothy had spent some time in a mental home, then continued to live in the Algonquin Hotel in New York, at Bern's expense. She killed herself the day after Paul's death – she was in San Francisco at the time. Was it she who had killed Bern? Bern was naked when he was found, and a woman's wet swimsuit had been found beside the swimming pool. Hollywood was afraid that Harlow might arouse pity as a woman who could not keep her husband – and that would ruin her screen image just as surely as the Taylor scandal had ruined Mabel Normand's.

There were whispers of an even more embarrassing nature. Jean Harlow told friends, in the strictest confidence, that Bern was impotent. On the night before his death, he had come into her bedroom wearing a huge artificial phallus, and had pranced around the room with it on, until the two of them, shrieking with laughter, tore it to pieces with scissors and flushed it down the lavatory.

In 1960, the Hollywood screenwriter Ben Hecht wrote an article in *Playboy* claiming that Bern *had* been murdered by another woman, probably Dorothy Millette. The studio had

On September 23, 1935, two decapitated bodies were found in the area of Kingsbury Run and East 45th Street, a slum area. Both had been mutilated with a knife; both were men - one, a 28-year-old medical orderly, the other, a 40-year-old vagrant, who was never identified. The fact that both victims were male suggested that the killer was homosexual, and a sadistic pervert. But when, four months later, the headless body of a 42-year-old prostitute was found not far from Kingsbury Run, the police became less sure that they were looking for a homosexual; the woman's body had been hacked as if in a frenzy, and the head was never found.

The man who was then in charge of Cleveland's Police department was Eliott Ness - hero of T.V. 's 'Untouchables'. Ness recognized that the usual methods of detection were of doubtful value here. But he realized that the mad killer was finding most of his victims among prostitutes and down-and-outs. The latter congregated in a shanty-town area in the centre of the city, near the market. One night in August, Ness raided the place, forced its inhabitants to leave, and burnt it down. This had the desired effect of depriving the killer of his victims; there were no more murders.

Ness also reasoned that the 'Mad Butcher' must be of a certain type. He must be big and powerful to overpower his victims. He must own a car, to transport the bodies. He must live alone, and in some quiet area - perhaps an unfrequented *cul de sac* - in order not to arouse the curiosity of his neighbours. And in order to fit this pattern, he must be rich, or at least well off.

Ness's team made painstaking enquiries in Cleveland society and, according to Oscar Fraley, chronicler of the 'Untouchables', soon found a suspect who fitted. He was physically huge, homosexual, sullen and paranoid, and well-to-do. Ness had the man brought in for questioning, and for months played a cat and mouse game with him. The man, confident he was cleverer than the police eventually admitted the murders.

forged the suicide note. Yet in retrospect, Hecht's version
seems unlikely. Why did Dorothy Millette have a nervous breakdown in the first place – was it because Bern was impotent? Why did she and Bern never live together again, although they remained fond of one another? (The tone of the letters exchanged between them makes it unlikely that she would kill him.) The note itself sounds too authentic to be a forgery. It said: "Unfortunately, this is the only way to make good the frightful wrong I have done you and to wipe out my abject humiliation. I love you"; a postscript added, "You understand last night was only a comedy". That has the ring of authenticity, and it fits the story of impotence and the dildo episode. The fact that Bern was naked when he was shot also suggests self-humiliation.

Four years later, in 1936, Jean Harlow also died, of a gall bladder infection. She was twenty-six. There were many American matrons who felt it was divine justice.

# The Death of Thelma Todd

In 1935, another Hollywood tragedy ended in murder – although it is still officially listed as suicide. Thelma Todd became Miss Massachusetts at the age of sixteen, and shortly thereafter, she threw up a job as a teacher to go to Hollywood. In 1926, when she was twenty-one, she appeared with fifteen other promising "starlets" in a film called *Fascinating Youth*, and her career was launched. Her real talent proved to be in comedy, and the beautiful and statuesque blonde appeared with Laurel and Hardy and the Marx Brothers. ("Madame, you're making history. Madame, you're making me, I wish you'd keep your hands to yourself.") She was a kind, good-natured, popular girl, with an odd touch of sadness, a feeling that life – or perhaps just her life – was unreal. In 1932 – when she was twenty-seven – she married an agent named Di Cicco, but two years later they were divorced. She had already decided to retire from films and go into the restaurant business in 1935 when Stanley Lupino and his daughter Ida decided to give a party for her. Di Cicco came to the restaurant and there was a quarrel. In the early hours of a Sunday morning in December 1935, she was driven to her home in Santa Monica. More than twenty-four hours later, she was found dead in her car, in the garage above the beach restaurant she owned. There was blood on her face, and she still wore the party clothes. She had died of carbon monoxide poisoning. The odd thing was that her evening slippers showed no sign of the wear they would have received climbing the rough concrete stairs – 270 of them – from the beach to the garage. All the evidence pointed to murder – particularly when it was discovered that she had been alive on the Sunday after the party, and had been seen in a car with a dark, foreign-looking man. It looked very much as if he had driven into the garage with her, knocked her unconscious, then turned on the exhaust and left her.

Again, the movie moguls went into a frantic scramble of panic. A scandal of this sort was the last thing the studio wanted. The police suddenly announced that, in spite of the blood on her face, they were treating Thelma Todd's death as a case of suicide. Even when they received a telegram from Ogden, Utah, saying that Thelma Todd's killer was in a hotel there, they did nothing about it. The case has remained as mysterious as when it happened.

By 1968, the golden days of Hollywood were only a distant memory, and a death that occurred in a Spanish-style hilltop home above Laurel Canyon may be regarded as a sad postscript to the history of the great years. Ramon Navarro, the handsome star of *Ben Hur* and *The Prisoner of Zenda*, was found, naked and beaten to death, on his bed, his hands tied behind him. The house was ransacked. Navarro's telephone bill revealed that a long call had been made to Chicago on 30 October, the evening of his death. It was easy to discover that the call had been made by a young man named Tom Ferguson. The police arrested Tom and his brother Paul, a male prostitute. When they discovered that seventy-year-old Navarro, the idol of American women, had been homosexual, they had solved the case. The Ferguson brothers admitted going to Navarro's house – at his request – and then tying him up and beating him to make him reveal

The robbery netted the brothers about $45. Both brothers
received life imprisonment.

# The Mystery Death of Marilyn Monroe

But by far the most famous of all Hollywood scandal stories
is the mystery surrounding the death of Marilyn Monroe.

The life of Hollywood's most famous "sex symbol" had
been a tale of hardship and misfortune. Norma Jeane Baker
(or Jean, as she sometimes spelt it) was born in Los Angeles
in 1926, the illegitimate daughter of Gladys Pearl Baker (née
Monroe), a film cutter at the Columbia and RKO studios, and
a fellow lodger called C. Stanley Gifford. There was a history
of mental instability and suicide in Gladys's family. For most
of Norma Jean's childhood, her mother was confined in
mental institutions, and from the age of five, the child spent
most of her life in foster homes – no less than twelve of them.
At the age of seven her mother had her back home to live,
but then had a nervous breakdown and was hospitalized
yet again. At the age of eight (other biographical sources
say eleven) she was persuaded to remove her dress by a
gentlemanly old boarder who caressed her genitals; finally,
troubled by his excitement, she put her clothes back on and
went to tell her foster mother, who told her angrily to shut
up. But she later admitted to a lover that the experience had
not been traumatic – in fact, that she had found it oddly
pleasant.

At sixteen, she married a twenty-one-year-old aircraft-
worker, Jim Dougherty, mainly to gain her independence,
but they had little in common; a year later, she made her
first suicide attempt. In the same year she became a paint
sprayer in a defence plant and was "discovered" by an army
photographer; her "pin-ups" achieved great success among
GIs, and the army medical corps voted her the girl they would

The police are continually being astonished by some of the strange forms of suicide they encounter. Wendel and Svensson's classic study *Crime Detection* has a description of a man who killed himself by placing the blade of a jack knife against his forehead, and then driving it in by beating his head against a tree; it also contains a photograph of the body of an old lady who carefully placed all her furniture in a pile in the middle of the room, lay down on it, and set it on fire.

Taylor's *Medical Jurisprudence* has an even stranger case of a man who burned himself to death by lying down on his mattress and setting it on fire; but as he burned to death, he periodically got up, and made notes about his sensations.

All healthy creatures loathe the thought of death; so we find such cases incomprehensible. We try to dismiss them by saying: 'They were insane' - and we are reassured by the usual coroner's verdict: 'Suicide while the balance of mind was disturbed.' Yet in recent years, criminologists have realized that this simplistic view is false, and that the truth about suicide brings us to the edge of some of the most disturbing and fascinating revelations in the whole field of criminology.

Expressed in crudely simple terms, you could say that most psychologists now accept that murder *is* a form of suicide. At first sight, this seems absurd. Take the case of a bank robber who shoots a policeman in the course of escape, or a rapist who strangles the girl to make sure she cannot identify him. Surely this is a matter of self-preservation rather than 'suicide'?

No. The impulse that makes a man *capable* of murder springs from his indifference to life: *to others' and to his own.*

most like to examine. During this period, she later confessed **347**
to Ted Jordan, an actor who became her lover, she often
went out to bars, became acquainted with men, and allowed
them to make love to her. It may be that her earlier sexual
encounter with the boarder had established a pattern – the
recognition that she could give men pleasure and excite their
tenderness by removing her dress. She always seems to have
been singularly frank about sex, describing it uninhibitedly
in four-letter words.

By 1946 she had been to a charm school and become a
successful model; soon afterwards she was signed on by
20th Century Fox at $125 a week, and her name changed
to Marilyn Monroe.

The two years she spent as a Fox starlet were not a success;
after two brief appearances she was dropped. Columbia
signed her up, and she received good reviews playing
the lead in a low budget musical, *Ladies of the Chorus*.
But Columbia also allowed her contract to expire. While
unemployed she posed for a nude calendar photograph, for
which she was paid $50; it went on to make three quarters
of a million dollars for the calendar company.

In the 1950s, she returned to Fox, and although she always
played the same dumb blonde, her popularity increased
slowly but surely. She herself was frank about the extent
to which her success was due to granting her sexual favours
to directors and agents: she commented: "I spent a lot
of time on my knees." But her sexual acquiescence was
also the secret of her immense success on the screen: it
was the combination of physical beauty and the hint of
submissiveness, of availability, that made her every man's
dream. It was also the basic cause of her downfall; every man
wanted her, and her desire to please meant that she often
said yes. The list of her lovers was immense, and one writer
estimates that she had as many as fourteen abortions.

Her marriage to baseball star Joe Di Maggio in 1954
confirmed her status as Hollywood's latest "sex goddess".
But he wanted a wife rather than a movie star, and they
divorced only nine months later.

Deciding that she wanted to be a "real actress" she went to
New York to study at the Actors Studio, where she met the
playwright Arthur Miller. Back at Fox, she was now the most

valuable property in Hollywood, and her salary reflected this. But she was also well known for her unpunctuality and unreliability. This was due mainly to her depressions, and their accompanying listlessness. Marriage to Arthur Miller in 1956 seemed to stabilize her, but after an affair with her co-star Yves Montand in 1960, they were divorced. After that she embarked on an affair with Frank Sinatra.

Miller had written a screenplay especially for her – *The Misfits*, a grim and depressing piece of work about drifters that contributed to the death of one of its male stars, Clark Gable, and which increased her tendency to depression. A month after the premiere she had a total breakdown and entered a psychiatric hospital. On the set of her final film, *Something's Got to Give*, her behaviour became increasingly erratic, until she was finally sacked.

No one, therefore, was greatly surprised when, on 5 August 1962, her housekeeper found her naked and lifeless body on her bed, apparently a victim of suicide (although there was no suicide note). The coroner's verdict was death by an overdose of barbiturates – Nembutal. Yet there were some odd discrepancies. Although there were huge quantities of barbiturates in her bloodstream and liver, there was no sign of it in her stomach – an impossibility unless she had injected it. But no sign of needle punctures was found at the autopsy, and there was no syringe in the room.

Persistent rumours began to circulate that her death was not suicide, but murder. It had been widely known among journalists that Marilyn had had an affair with President Kennedy – a notorious womanizer – but it was less well known that she had later had an affair with his brother Robert, the Attorney General. A detective named Fred Otash later revealed that he had bugged the telephone in Marilyn's home at the behest of Bobby Kennedy. Kennedy spoke openly to Marilyn about some rather dangerous secrets, such as his intention of having Fidel Castro assassinated. (Thirteen years later, it was revealed that President Kennedy had authorized the CIA to try and assassinate Castro.) Kennedy also told her that he intended to get "that son of a bitch Jimmy Hoffa" into jail no matter what it cost him – Hoffa was head of the Teamsters Union and a man with known links to organized crime. Marilyn kept notes of these conversations because

Kennedy was sometimes irritated by her failure to remember
things he had said to her.

According to a man named Bob Slatzer, who claimed that
he and Marilyn had been briefly married in 1946, Marilyn had
been hoping to marry Bobby Kennedy, who had promised to
divorce his wife. But Bobby Kennedy was warned off such
an idea by his brother, and he accordingly broke with her
not long before her death. She was bitter, and felt she had
been used; she tried to ring Kennedy in Washington many
times, without success. She hinted strongly to the actor Peter
Lawford that she was pregnant with Bobby Kennedy's child.
More dangerously, she told Slatzer that she was thinking of
calling a press conference to "blow the lid off the whole damn
thing". She repeated the same thing to Lawford, declaring
that she had been "used . . . thrown from one man to
another" (which obviously referred to the Kennedys) and
that she was "going public with everything". Since Lawford
was John Kennedy's brother-in-law, this was a sure way of
getting her message through to the President.

On the weekend she died, Robert Kennedy travelled to
San Francisco to address a law conference. In his Monroe
biography *Goddess*, Anthony Summers argues convincingly
that Robert Kennedy came over to see her that afternoon,
to explain that their affair had come to an end. In fact,
neighbours reported seeing Robert Kennedy arrive with
another man carrying a bag like a doctor's bag. Kennedy
himself is alleged to have testified in a secret deposition that
he had been there, and that the doctor had given Marilyn an
injection of a strong sedative to calm her nerves.

It later emerged that Marilyn's home had also been
"bugged" by an electronics expert named Bernard Spindel,
who was employed by Jimmy Hoffa. Spindel subsequently
went to prison, and alleged that he had also bugged the home
of Peter Lawford. Hoffa's intention was to get compromising
material about Robert Kennedy. Kennedy found out about the
tapes of his conversation with Marilyn, and offered Spindel
$25,000 for them, which Spindel refused.

That some kind of "cover up" had happened became clear
in the years following her death. Peter Lawford admitted that
she had telephoned him – sounding tired and slurry – to say
goodbye during that last evening, and that he had wanted to

But there is one aspect of 'victimology' that has so far been totally neglected by the criminologist: the quession of the 'born victim': the person who seems to be 'destined' for murder.

Anyone who has read a biographical sketch of President Kennedy - with his childhood illnesses, his accident proneness, his wartime misadventures - feels that this *was* the type of president to be killed by an assassin's bullet. The same applied to his brother Robert. On the other hand, Lyndon Johnson somehow didn't look accident prone; a kind of invulnerability was a chart of his total personality.

It would be easy for speculations of this kind to turn into absurd hypotheses and preposterous guesses. However, the psychologist Carl Jung developed a valuable concept called 'synchronicity' which could be defined as 'a coincidence that is not a coincidence

Since President Kennedy's death, many writers have pointed out the number of strange similarities between the assassinations of Lincoln and Kennedy; both were shot in the head from behind, both succeeded by a southerner called Johnson, both advised by their - secretaries against the visit that led to the assassination, and so on. There is also the extraordinary fact-that ever since Lincoln, who was elected in 1860, *all* presidents elected at 20-year inervals have been assassinated or died in office: Garfield, 1880, McKinley, 1900, Harding, 1920, Roosevelt, 1940, Kennedy, 1960.

rush over to see she was all right. He was dissuaded because it would compromise him. What seems clear is that before her death was announced, someone rushed to her house to remove compromising material, such as the red notebook recording Kennedy's conversations – most writers on the case believe this was done by CIA agents on the orders of Robert Kennedy. The housekeeper, Mrs Murray, told two conflicting stories about the time she found Marilyn's body – that it was at midnight, and that it was at 3.30 a.m.

Most of this evidence seems to suggest suicide – except for the absence of barbiturates in her stomach. Is it possible that she injected herself with the drug, and that the telltale syringe was removed by the "searchers"? This is unlikely, since she is known to have been a "pill popper" who never used a syringe. Another possibility emerges from remarks made by Lawford's ex-wife Deborah Gould; she claims she asked her husband how Marilyn died, and that he replied: "She took her last big enema." This suggests that she was sometimes in the habit of taking drugs anally – which has a far quicker effect than taking them orally, since the drugs enter the large intestine immediately.

But if Marilyn sometimes took drugs by enema, then it is also possible that she was killed by the same method. People to whom she talked on the afternoon of her death say she sounded slurred. A neighbour who sometimes lent her sleeping pills says she asked to borrow some that afternoon; but there had been pills in the house in the morning. If she had been "popping pills" all day, she may have lapsed into unconsciousness, and been vulnerable to attack.

If she *was* murdered, then the chief suspect is bound to be Bobby Kennedy himself. The private detective Fred Otash claims that Lawford burst into his office at 3 a.m., announcing that Marilyn Monroe was dead, and that Bobby Kennedy was there – adding that Kennedy and Marilyn had "got into a big fight that evening". Otash went on to allege that he was then hired by Lawford to go to Marilyn's home and remove any evidence of links with the Kennedys.

Norman Mailer, in his biography of Marilyn Monroe, denies that the Kennedys could have been implicated in her death, because it would have been stupid of them to risk everything. His theory is that disaffected members of the CIA, angry about the bungled assassination attempt on Castro, killed Marilyn to destroy the Kennedy Administration. They left the room looking as if she had committed suicide, but knew that the lack of barbiturates in her stomach would point to murder. The finger would then be pointed at the Kennedys.

Since Jimmy Hoffa knew of the existence of the compromising tapes, he also had a motive for killing Marilyn Monroe. Her death, and the subsequent revelation of her affairs with both Kennedy brothers, would trigger a scandal, and would probably prevent Kennedy from being re-elected in 1964. In fact, Spindel's home was raided in 1966, on the orders of the Manhattan District Attorney, Frank Hogan, and all his equipment seized. He believed that this was inspired by Robert Kennedy. And members of the DA's staff subsequently told a reporter that the tapes contained evidence that "Marilyn had been murdered and that Bobby Kennedy was involved "if only as a catalyst causing someone else to do it." This "someone else" was presumably Jimmy Hoffa.

But if Marilyn Monroe was murdered in order to ruin the Kennedys, then why did the scandal never explode as planned? Was it because the cover-up by the Kennedys was too efficient? (It is known that Marilyn's phone records for August were illegally seized from the General Telephone Company, presumably to hide the number of calls she made to Washington in her last days.) Even so, it is hard to believe that the Kennedys' many underworld enemies would have failed to make use of compromising material.

Milo Speriglio, a private detective hired by Robert Slatzer, has stated unequivocally: "Marilyn Monroe was politically assassinated" – for the sake of the tapes of sessions with Robert Kennedy, and the red notebook containing his "secrets". Speriglio later changed his opinion and came to believe that she was killed at the behest of Mafia boss Sam Giancana, who wanted her dead because she knew of his involvement in the plot to kill Castro.

One man who may know more of the truth than most is Marilyn's doctor, Ralph Greenson, to whom she talked confidentially on the afternoon before her death. Greenson says he cannot reveal what she said, but that it leads him to believe that her death was not suicide. Pressed for more

> Asked if it was true that she had nothing on when the famous calendar photograph was taken, Marilyn Monroe replied: "I had the radio on."

information, he said exasperatedly: "Listen . . . talk to Bobby Kennedy."

Most of those who might have been able to tell the truth about Marilyn Monroe's death died without revealing it: President Kennedy in 1963, Robert Kennedy in 1965, Jimmy Hoffa in 1975. (Hoffa simply vanished, and has never been found.) The final verdict must be that Marilyn Monroe *could* have committed suicide – she had reason to do so – but that much of the evidence points towards murder. On the other hand, if Lawford's remark that she used enemas to administer drugs is correct, then suicide remains the likeliest possibility after all.


# The Black Dahlia

No account of Los Angeles murder mysteries would be complete without a mention of the most gruesome riddle of all: the death of aspiring actress Elizabeth Short. Known as the Black Dahlia because of her preference for black underwear, "Beth" had spent much of her short life (she was twenty-two when she was murdered) wandering aimlessly – from Massachusetts to Florida, from Florida to California, then Chicago, then California again. Like Marilyn Monroe, she spent her life seeking security and affection.

In January 1947, her body was found in a vacant lot in Los Angeles, severed in half at the waist; medical examination revealed that she had been suspended upside down and tortured to death over many hours – the body was covered with cigarette burns and small cuts. The letters "BD" had been cut into her thigh.

The killer sent the police some of her personal possessions

– including her birth certificate and address book – together with a letter made up of words and letters clipped from newspapers. The horror of the crime made it headline news, and in due course, the police received twenty-eight confessions, all of which proved to be false. Two films have been made about the case, and a novel that suggests that she was involved in sadistic pornographic movies. But although more confessions have continued to pour in down the years, the case remains unsolved.

# chapter six

# OTHER UNSOLVED MURDERS

*I*n The Murderer's Who's Who *by J. H. H. Gaute and Robin Odell, there is only one entry for Australia under the heading "Unsolved murders", compared to five for America and thirteen for England. That one Australian entry concerns a rather commonplace gangland murder which has achieved a certain classic status largely because of the bizarre name under which it is usually classified: the Shark Arm Murder.*

*A death in Kenya, East Africa, in 1941, eclipsed even the war when the body of Lord Erroll was found murdered in a ditch. And in Britain, witchcraft involvement added to the mystery of who murdered Charles Walton. How did he come to have a pagan symbol cut into his neck and chest?*

## The Shark Arm Murder

On the morning of 18 April 1935, two Sydney fishermen finally subdued a fourteen foot tiger shark. The beast had been thrashing at the end of the line for most of the night, desperate to disentangle itself. The bait had been set out the

The only other Australian murder mystery to find its way into anthologies of true crime concerns the death of fourteen-year-old Shirley Collins. Pretty but extremely shy, Shirley was invited to her first party at Richmond, Melbourne, on 12 September 1953. She failed to arrive. Two days later, her naked body was found at Mount Martha, thirty-eight miles from Melbourne. Her head had been crushed by a heavy stone, and broken beer bottles with bloody fingerprints were found nearby. (They failed to identify her attacker.) Yet there had been no sexual assault. She must have been taken there by car – yet the idea of a forcible kidnapping had to be ruled out since the streets were crowded that Saturday evening. The boyfriend who had invited her to the party had a perfect alibi – he had waited for her on the station for an hour and a half, seen by many porters, then gone to the party. The idea that the extremely shy girl might accept a lift from a stranger also had to be ruled out. The biggest police operation in Melbourne's history failed to unearth a single clue as to why a girl who set out for Richmond would end up so far away, stripped and battered to death.

previous evening, and had soon attracted a small shark. This more suitable catch had itself then brought the attentions of a monster tiger shark. Soon only the head of the small shark remained and it was the interloper that struggled on the line.

The shark was put on display at the Coogee aquarium, where it proved to be a popular attraction. On 25 April – an Australian public holiday – people flocked to the aquarium to see the new exhibit. Since being caught the shark's health had deteriorated, requiring extra oxygen to be pumped into the water. To the crowd the shark seemed tired and listless, flicking itself up and down its small tank as if in a trance. Suddenly, as the crowd watched, it spiralled round itself three times, vomiting black, oily clouds into the water. As the foul mess cleared a human arm, trailing a length of rope tied around its wrist, floated to the surface.

When the police arrived they carefully filtered the rest of the shark's vomit for human body parts. The shark itself was killed and slit open, but nothing further was found. The least sinister explanation was the first to be considered: that the arm belonged to a suicide. Mysteriously the shark had failed to even semi-digest the arm. Indeed, it was in such good condition that police were able to scalpel off the fingerprints and check them against records. A good match was found, a man called James Smith.

Smith, variously described as a builder, an engineer, a road labourer and bookie, had a string of minor convictions. When the police contacted his wife they were told that he had disappeared on 8 April, saying that he was going fishing with a friend. Unfortunately he had neglected to name the friend. Mrs Smith identified the arm by a small tattoo just above the wrist, depicting two men boxing. She told police that her husband had committed suicide.

This conclusion was being reached at the same time by Dr Victor Çoppelson, an expert on shark bites who had been called in to examine the severing wound on Smith's arm. It was obvious to Coppelson, due to the clean appearance of the wound, that the arm had been cut off with a knife, not bitten or torn off by a shark. Someone had prepared the tiger shark's meal.

He also solved the mystery of why the arm was undigested. The shark had been sent into shock by its long struggle against the line; its digestive system had shut down. Coppelson also revealed that the arm had reached the tiger shark third-hand. Severed by an unknown human, the arm had been originally eaten by the smaller shark. In eating it, the tiger shark had also unwittingly eaten the arm.

The police were now investigating a murder. They immediately set about dragging the bay for the remainder of Smith's body. Meanwhile inquiries had turned up the nature of Smith's last job: he had been hired to guard and run a powerful motor launch called "Pathfinder". This gave police an insight into a possible motive for the murder . . .

In the 1930s Sydney was a violent city. There was a large criminal underworld controlling the flow of refined opium from the East to America. Ships sailing directly from the Far East to America's West Coast were thoroughly searched by coastguards. However, with ships from Australia the authorities were more lax. Thus, at Sydney, motor launches would transfer the opium from Far Eastern to America-bound ships under the cover of night. Many men made fortunes on this contraband trade. These men would hire poor labourers to run their launches, promising a small sum if they were ever imprisoned. Competition was fierce, leading in effect to a gang-war situation. Rivals' boats were sunk, and murder of the hired help was common.

Taking the next logical step, police traced "Pathfinder" and tried to contact its owner. They discovered that "Pathfinder" had been sunk at the beginning of April. Its owner was a Mr Reginald Holmes, a boat-builder and launch-proprietor who, it was rumoured, was an important figure on the narcotics scene. When interviewed Holmes seemed agitated, distancing himself from the crime by claiming that both he and Smith had been blackmailed by a rival launch-proprietor, Patrick Brady, ever since the sinking of "Pathfinder". The basis of this alleged blackmail was never made public, but seems likely to have centred around opium dealing. It was to see Brady, Holmes claimed, that Smith had set out on 8 April.

From this point the police's investigation becomes a catalogue of misjudgement. They took the precaution of arresting Brady on a trumped-up bureaucratic charge to prevent his flight. Holmes, for no explicable reason, was left without any police supervision. It seems clear that the Sydney police chronically underestimated the violence of its criminal element.

While searching Brady's beach-hut police noticed several mysterious absences. The mattress off the bed had gone, as had a tin trunk. Three mats and a coil of rope were missing from Brady's boat.

Police invited Sir Sydney Smith, the great forensic scientist, who was at the time attending a conference in the city, to suggest how the disposal of the body was achieved. He obliged with a neat and plausible model. The body had been dismembered on the mats and the mattress, and the resulting pieces stuffed into the trunk. The body could not be completely contained however and so the arm was tied to the trunk with rope and, with the bloody mats, thrown into the sea. The trunk sank to the bottom, but the arm worked loose, eventually to be eaten by the small shark.

Unfortunately the police would soon have more to explain.

Soon after Brady's arrest a motor launch was seen to be zig-zagging at a dangerous speed all around the bay. Policemen who tried to flag the boat down had to swerve to avoid being rammed. A long chase requiring half a dozen police boats eventually cornered the launch. At the controls was Reginald Holmes, smelling strongly of alcohol and bleeding heavily from a bullet wound in his head. He claimed that as he left his home that morning, a gunman had tried to kill him. Holmes had succeeded in escaping by fleeing in his launch. He had tried to escape the police because he thought they were gunmen too.

Whether the police believed Holmes's story, or whether they accepted the altogether more likely explanation that they had stumbled upon a failed suicide attempt, they seem to have had a grievous lack of foresight. Either situation would necessitate police surveillance, Holmes was after all their key witness against Brady who was their only suspect. During his stay in hospital Holmes told police that he was sure Brady had killed Smith. He said that Brady had told him as much, and warned him that if he told the police Brady or his friends would kill him. Amazingly, after he was discharged from hospital Holmes received no police protection.

On the morning of the inquest Holmes was found dead in his car, shot through the chest and groin. Deprived of their only witness, police were dealt another blow when the coroner refused to accept Smith's arm as a token of his death. Without a body murder is extremely difficult to prove. The Sydney police had no real evidence without Holmes; thus Brady was released. Two associates of Brady who were arrested for the murder of Holmes also walked free due to insufficient evidence.

Rumours persist that it was in fact Holmes who dismembered Jim Smith, afterwards paying Brady to take the prison sentence. All that is certain is that, through police incompetence, the case remains officially unsolved.

# The Death of Lord Erroll

During the early years of World War II, few murder cases excited much attention in Britain, which was preoccupied with the large scale tragedy set in motion by Hitler. But in Kenya, East Africa, even the war was eclipsed by a murder mystery that split the British expatriate community.

In that remote and idyllic part of the world, in which modern anthropology has placed the Garden of Eden, social life among British expatriates went on just as before the war – which meant a great deal of big game hunting, social activity, heavy drinking and adultery. One of the most prominently active in all these departments was a handsome – if slightly overweight – aristocrat named Josslyn Hay, who was the twenty-second Earl of Erroll, a Scottish title. Erroll had been expelled from Eton at seventeen, eloped with a married woman to Kenya, then deserted her for an heiress, who died in 1939 of alcoholism. Erroll was a notorious philanderer, and was believed to have slept with every attractive woman in the "Happy Valley" and for miles around.

In November 1940, two more Britons joined the expatriate community: Sir Henry – "Jock" – Delves Broughton, and his lovely young wife Diana. Broughton was thirty-five years her senior, a rather dour, unpopular man who had spent much of his inherited wealth on horses and bridge. In early life he had married well, but his wife's attempts to become a famous hostess had foundered on his unpopularity. When they divorced in 1939, he lost no time in proposing to the aristocratic Diana Caldwell, who rode to hounds, flew her own plane, and ran a Mayfair cocktail bar. He soothed any doubts she might have entertained by assuring her that if she fell in love with a younger man, he would not only grant her a divorce, but would provide her with an income of £5,000 a year.

Diana enjoyed the social life of the Muthaiga Country Club, where she and her husband lived before moving to a farm. But at a Club ball in November, while her husband was away inspecting a farm, she met Lord Erroll, who lost no time in making immoral proposals. After some slight initial resistance, she capitulated, and by the time Broughton returned, his wife was in love with the younger man. Unfortunately, Broughton no longer had the cash to make good his promise of a £5,000 a year allowance – and in any case, no desire to lose a second wife so late in life; he was neurotically afraid of loneliness.

In spite of his shock, Broughton seemed to be taking it very well. On 23 January 1941, he invited his wife, Lord Erroll, and a friend named June Carberry, to a "farewell dinner" at the Muthaiga Club, and toasted the "happy couple". Erroll and Diana left to go dancing, and Broughton's last words to Erroll were to ask him to make sure Diana was home by 3 a.m. In fact, Erroll brought her home by 2.30, accompanied her to the front door, then drove off.

Half an hour later, two blacks driving a milk truck were blinded by headlights blazing through the falling rain, and saw a car tilted over at an angle in a drainage trench. They peered in through the window and saw a man – a soldier – who was obviously dead.

The police were called, and at 8 that morning, a pathologist named Geoffrey Timms was passing by when he saw the "accident". He stopped and ordered the body to be taken out of the car – it had to be dragged out, since the foot was stuck under the accelerator. He then recognized the dead soldier as Lord Erroll. But it was not until the body was taken to the mortuary, and a wound in the left ear washed, that he realized that Erroll had been shot. A .32 bullet was found embedded in his brain.

By now, the car had been towed away, and the removal of the body meant that vital clues had probably been lost. Heavy rain in the night had washed away tyre marks or footprints.

The obvious suspect was Broughton. He claimed to have spent the night in bed, except for two occasions – at 2 o'clock and 3.30 – when he knocked on the bedroom door of June Carberry "to check that she was all right." Obviously, he could have left the house between these two visits, but there was absolutely no evidence that he had.

Superintendent Arthur Poppy, in charge of the case, knew Broughton, and thought that he was probably capable of the murder. When he heard that Broughton had been engaged in target practice at a nearby farm, he sent detectives to try and find samples of the bullets and spent cases; they found .32 bullets that matched the one found in Erroll's brain and another discovered in the car. Poppy's theory was that Broughton had sneaked out of the house while Erroll was saying goodbye to Diana, and hidden himself in his car. He had waited until Erroll slowed down, then shot him in the ear, hanging onto the safety straps – which were torn out – as the car crashed into the ditch. Then he had returned home and climbed in through a window.

On the morning after the murder, Broughton had set fire to the rubbish in the rubbish pit in his garden, sprinkling it with petrol; later, the remains of a golf stocking, with traces of what looked like blood, were found in the pit. Poppy also found a pair of burnt gym shoes, and theorized that Broughton had worn these to do the murder. He was inclined to believe that the crime was premeditated, since Broughton had reported the theft of two .32 Colt revolvers three days before Erroll's death.

Broughton was arrested on 10 March 1941, and his trial began on 26 May. But although the prosecution case looked watertight, it foundered on the fact that the gun that had killed Erroll had five right hand grooves and a black powder propellant, while the stolen Colts would have had six grooves. The bullets found at the firing range failed to strengthen the case, since the gun that fired them could not be produced. In any case, there was no definite evidence that Broughton had fired these bullets.

So on 1 July 1941, Sir Jock Delves Broughton was found not guilty, and celebrated his acquittal with a dinner at the Muthaiga Club (as a consequence of which he was deprived of his membership). And life stubbornly refused to return to normal. Ostracized by his neighbours, Broughton decided to go to Ceylon; reluctantly, Diana went with him. Later that year, when he rented Erroll's house, the "Djinn Palace", their relationship became increasingly strained, and she frequently accused him of Erroll's murder; finally they separated.

Broughton returned to England in 1942, and was immediately arrested by the Fraud Squad. In 1938, he had been the victim of two mysterious robberies, both of which had

brought him large – and much needed – sums in insurance
compensation. The "Broughton pearls" had been stolen from
Diana's car on the Côte d"Azur, and later that year, his home
had been burgled, and three valuable paintings stolen. Many
years later, Broughton's friend Hugh Dickinson was to admit
that he had carried out both thefts at Broughton's request.

The Fraud Squad failed to make the charges stick, and
Broughton was released for lack of evidence. But his son
Evelyn had by now discovered that Broughton had defrauded
the estate and cheated him out of the bulk of his inheritance.
Broughton's depression increased, and on 2 December 1942,
three months after his return to England, he committed
suicide at the Adelphi Hotel in Liverpool with a lethal dose
of Medinal.

When the author James Fox studied the case in order to
write a book, *White Mischief*, he learned that Broughton
had, in fact, confessed to killing Erroll. He had made his
confession to a horse dealer named Alan Horne. According
to Broughton, he had planned the murder of Erroll in association with a man he called "Derek", and he and "Derek"
had paid an African £1,000 to kill Erroll.

In 1979, June Carberry's daughter Juanita, who had been
fifteen at the time of the murder, admitted that Broughton
had confessed to her on the day after the murder. He told
her that after killing Joss Erroll, he had thrown the gun into
the Thika Falls – he was afraid that the police had seen him
do it. "I felt very protective of him after that," Juanita told
James Fox, adding that the murder had been a spontaneous
outburst of violence and misery because he could not bear to
lose Diana.

It seems, then, that the devious Sir Delves lied to the end.
The theft of the Colts seems to indicate that he planned the
murder. And the story about "Derek" proves that, even when
he had decided to "confess", his natural deviousness made
him incapable of telling the whole truth.

# Jack the Stripper

Since World War II, there have been only two unsolved murder cases in the United Kingdom which rate inclusion in most encyclopaedias of crime. The first, the "Thames Nude Murders", was a series of prostitute-killings in the mid-1960s, so called because the victims were left naked, most of them close to the river. The killer, who became known as Jack the Stripper, was apparently a deviant with a taste for oral sex. The last four victims had traces of spray paint on their bodies, indicating that they had been kept in or near a paint-spray shop. In early 1965, a solution of the case seemed imminent when the police identified the shop as one on an industrial estate in west London. It seemed almost certain that the killer was a van driver who worked at night, and who had access to the shop. The suspect, a forty-five-year-old man, committed suicide, leaving a note saying that he was "unable to stand the strain any longer." The identity of Jack the Stripper has never been revealed.

---

**Many husbands in the Happy Valley must have smiled grimly to hear of Joss Erroll's death. For all his charm, he was a thoroughly detestable individual: good-looking, arrogant, and a dedicated seducer of other men's wives. It gave him particular pleasure to seduce the wives of men who regarded him as a friend – one of his favourite remarks was "To hell with husbands" – and then to borrow money from the cuckolded spouse. He was a bully who treated his servants abominably. He loved humiliating women, and enjoyed the sense of power it gave him to know he had slept with every attractive woman in the "white highlands". He once shocked a friend by saying to a child in a hotel lobby, "Come to daddy", when the child's legal father was within earshot. He also liked to say that he divided women into three categories: "droopers, boopers and super-boopers". There was not a man in the Muthaiga Club who was not longing to see him get his comeuppance.**

# The Lower Quinton Witchcraft Murder

Charles Walton was practically retired from labouring by the spring of 1945. He had worked on the local farms all his life and now, in his seventy-fourth year, was afflicted with crippling rheumatism. Despite this he still insisted on doing some work around farmer Albert Potter's farm when the weather allowed him.

St Valentine's Day, 14 February 1945, was a clear and sunny day in Lower Quinton when Charles Walton took up his walking stick and made for Meon Hill on Potter's farm to do some hedge cutting. Walton lived with his niece Edith who had a war job in a nearby factory. When she got home at 6 o'clock that evening, her uncle had not returned. Normally he was back from work around 4. Edith was anxious, worried that he had fallen and, unable to stand up, was lying out in the open in the approaching darkness.

Co-opting a neighbour to help her search, Edith made for Potter's farm. Accompanied by the farmer, Edith and her neighbour hunted through the fields by torchlight. Their shouts brought no reply. Edith was beginning to fear for her uncle's life. Suddenly, in the beam of the torch, they saw a body. Charles Walton was pinned to the ground with his own pitchfork. Edith, stunned with shock, returned to her cottage escorted by the neighbour while Potter remained with the body.

Only when the police arrived with spotlights did it become clear how violently Walton had been butchered. His throat was slashed with his own hand scythe, which had been left jutting from the wound. His arms were criss-crossed with cuts where he had evidently tried to defend himself. The pitchfork that fixed him to the ground took two policemen to remove – Potter had tried and failed. Cut into the wrinkled skin of Walton's neck and chest was a cross.

Superintendent Robert Fabian, known as Fabian of the Yard, one of Britain's most celebrated detectives, took over the case after local police failed to uncover any leads. A tin watch had been removed from the corpse, and Fabian enlisted the help of the Royal Engineers equipped with mine detectors to search the surrounding countryside for it. Meanwhile constables took statements from the village's 493 inhabitants.

The crime should have been easy to solve. The murderer must have been someone with a grudge against Walton. In a small community, such a motive would be difficult to hide. This was the rational view. The terrible violence of the attack and the superstitious silence of the locals suggested a more ritualistic cause for Walton's death.

The pinning of a witch to the ground in order to destroy her power is a ritual dating from Anglo-Saxon times. The villagers tacitly implied that this is what happened to Walton. In 1875 a man called John Haywood had murdered an old lady named Ann Turner because he believed her to be a witch who was persecuting him. In his statement to the court he said that it was common knowledge that most of the misfortunes suffered by the local community were inflicted by a small coven of witches. He had merely taken his revenge. He had stabbed her with a pitchfork and cut a cross into her neck.

Fabian uncovered only one other lead. A villager had made a statement to the effect that a POW from the nearby camp was seen wiping blood from his hands in a ditch on the day of the killing. The camp inmates were all searched and an Italian was found to have bloodstains on his coat. He refused to answer questions. The coat was sent, along with other samples taken from villagers, to the forensic lab. The Royal Engineers were despatched to search the ditch. They found metal. It was not however the tin watch, but a rabbit snare. The blood on the coat also proved to be that of a rabbit. The POW had declined to talk because he was scared that he would be punished for poaching.

There the investigation ended – it remained one of Fabian's few total failures. But in their book *Perfect Murder*, Bernard Taylor and Stephen Knight claim to have learned the solution to the mystery. In "The Mysterious Death of Charles Walton", Knight alleges that Fabian was certain of the identity of the killer, but simply lacked the evidence to prosecute. The murderer, Knight says, was Farmer Potter himself. His motive had nothing to do with ridding the countryside of a witch, but was purely financial. Walton was an obsessive saver, and he had lent Potter a large sum when Potter was on the brink of ruin. The money became due; Potter was unable to pay it back, and on that St Valentine's Day, he chose a violent solution to his problem. Potter may not have intended to kill Charles Walton when he went to talk to him about the debt – or to ask for an extension. Perhaps Walton threatened him with court action, or flourished the receipt under his nose. Whatever the reason, Potter killed the frail old man, then mutilated the body to suggest a witchcraft connection.

Knight's evidence for this theory tends to centre upon Potter's conflicting statements to police and the ease with which he found Walton's body in the dark that February evening. His attempts to pull the pitchfork from Walton's chest were, according to the theory, attempts to cover his fingerprints from the time of the murder.

Whether or not Potter killed Walton, the aspect of the story that intrigues is the idea of a well hidden group of Satan worshippers at the heart of a seemingly tranquil English village life. Even if Potter did kill Charles Walton and mark the body with pagan symbolism, where did he learn the pagan symbolism? It would seem that the more comfortable, greed-based explanation of Charles Walton's murder merely leads to more questions.

# SERIAL KILLERS

# · chapter one ·

# AN ADDICTION TO MURDER

*T*he term serial killer was invented in the early 1980s by FBI
agent Robert Ressler, to describe someone who kills repeatedly
and obsessively.

In the past we called anyone who killed several people a "mass
murderer". But then, the mass murderer may be someone like the
unknown killer who slaughtered the Evangelista family in Detroit on
2 July, 1929, chopping off the heads of all six. Or like Charles Whitman,
the sniper who shot eighteen people from a tower on the campus of the
University of Texas in August 1966. These were clearly not serial killers
– which means one after another – because the murders all happened on
the same occasion. Neither was the French "Bluebeard" Landru, because
although he killed eleven women between 1914 and 1918, his crimes were
coldly and carefully planned, and the motive was purely financial. For,
as we shall see, the modern serial killer tends to choose his victims at
random, and the motive is usually sexual. Even more important is the
fact that he (or she) becomes addicted to murder, exactly as if it were
a drug.

# Eighteenth and Nineteenth Century Crimes

Now oddly enough, sex crime is a relatively modern phenomenon. In the eighteenth century, the usual motive for most crime was money, and throughout most of the nineteenth century, the majority of murders were committed in the course of robbery – with a few during domestic quarrels. It was only towards the end of the century that "sex crime", in our modern sense of the word (that is, murder for rape) began to appear. In the eighteen and nineteenth centuries, prostitutes were so cheap – and almost any lower class girl could be had for a few pence – that sex crime would have been pointless. But Victorian prudery gradually created a new attitude towards sex – as something rather wicked and forbidden. This was first reflected in the rise of pornography ("dirty books" were also an invention of the nineteenth century) which was often about rape or child-sex. And, inevitably, a time came when dreams of "the forbidden" turned into the real thing. In July 1867, a clerk named Frederick Baker persuaded eight year old Fanny Adams to go with him for a walk in the fields near Alton, Hampshire. Her dismembered body was found a few hours later in a hop garden. Baker had written in his diary: "Killed a young girl today. It was fine and hot." Baker was hanged at Winchester.

Two years later, in Boston, a bellringer named Thomas Piper began attacking and raping girls, battering them unconscious; in May 1875 he lured five year old Mabel Young into the belfry knocked her unconscious with a cricket bat, but was interrupted. The girl died in hospital and Piper was hanged after confessing to five sex murders and several rapes of children. Piper had some claim to be regarded as the first serial killer.

On the other hand, that dubious distinction might be claimd by a German murderess named Anna Zwanziger, a domestic servant who, in the first decade of the nineteenth century, developed a strange obsession with poisoning with arsenic. The wife of a judge named Glaser seems to have been her first victim in August 1808; the judge himself followed, probably because he resisted Anna's hints about marriage. Another judge named Grohmann died in May 1809. Weeks later she poisoned the wife of her latest employer, a magistrate named Gebhardt. When he dismissed her, most people in the house became violently ill, and it was discovered that someone had put arsenic in the salt cellars. Tests for arsenic had just been invented, and Anna was arrested in September 1809. Frau Glaser's body was exhumed and found to be full of arsenic. After being sentenced to death by beheading, Anna Zwanziger admitted that she frequently administered poison simply for her own entertainment. She is quoted as saying that "poison was her truest friend", and the German judge Feuerbach says that she trembled with rapture when she looked upon arsenic. This casual attitude towards her victims certainly entitles her to be labelled a serial killer rather than someone who murdered for profit.

Gesina Gottfried, another German, began by poisoning a brutal husband who beat her, then killed her second husband and his parents. In the course of her subsequent travels as a domestic servant she killed at least another half a dozen people. Her last intended victim, a man called Rumf, wondered about the white powder she had sprinkled on the leg of pork, and went to the police to get it analysed. When it was identified as arsenic, she confessed to her murders with a certain pride, and was executed in 1828. Like Anna Zwanziger, she had somehow become addicted to administering poison.

This is even more true of a Frenchwoman named Helene Jegado, a Breton peasant woman who went on a poisoning spree over a twenty year period, beginning around 1830. In one house where she worked, seven people died in agony, including her own sister; by 1851 the number of her victims had swelled to at least twenty-three, although a more probable estimate is sixty. Arrested for poisoning a fellow servant of whom she was jealous, she was executed in 1852.

A Dutch nurse named van der Linden – of whom, unfortunately, little is known – surpassed all three women by poisoning more than a hundred.

Here, then, we can see the true characteristics of the serial killer – a kind of obsessive *repetitiveness* that resembles a hiccup. What causes it? Some religiously-inclined people suggested that a demon had got into them (and many serial killers have, in fact, declared that they were possessed by the Devil). Whatever the answer, there seems to be no doubt that murder can become an addiction, and that most serial killers are, in some sense, "driven by a demon".

One of the oddest cases of "murder addiction" on record took place in the Lyon area of France in the mid-nineteenth century. In May 1861, an attractive twenty-seven year old servant girl named Marie Pichon was accosted by a peasant with a deformed upper lip, who asked her the way to the registry-office for servants. When the man learned that Marie was looking for work, he offered her a good job at a country house near Montlul. The girl agreed to accompany him there, and they travelled to Montlul by train. The peasant, who seemed a stolid but decent sort of man, told her that he was the gardener of a certain Madame Girard, and that another servant who was due to arrive the day before had fallen ill, so that Madame was in urgent need of a replacement.

At Montlul, the peasant took her box on his shoulder, and told her they would take a short cut across the fields. As night closed in, he stopped to take breath, and suggested that they should abandon her trunk until morning. Without waiting for her agreement, he dropped it in a ditch, then he plodded on into the darkness. The girl became increasingly nervous at his odd behaviour, and when they came to a hilltop, and there was still no sign of lights, she declared her unwillingness to go any further. The man then rounded on her suddenly and threw a noose round her neck. She pushed him and they both fell down. Marie was first on her feet, running into the darkness. She crashed through hedges, scratching herself and tearing her clothes, and frequently fell over. But eventually, the footsteps of her pursuer died away, and she almost collapsed with relief when she came to a house. Its owner, who was still unharnessing his horse after a journey, was startled by this bloodstained apparition, but he let her in, and sent for the local constable. Then she was taken to the police station, where she repeated her story. In spite of her exhaustion, she was taken back over the route she had traced with the murderous peasant. They eventually found the ditch where the man had dropped her trunk – but it had vanished.

The news caused a sensation in the Trevoux district – particularly when it was recollected that Marie Pichon was not the first girl to place her trust in a peasant with a deformed lip. Six years earlier, in 1855, a servant girl named Josephine Charloty had become suspicious as she plodded across the fields behind the squarely-built man who was carrying her trunk, and had finally fled and taken refuge in a farmhouse. Another girl, Victorine Perrin, had simply lost her trunk when the man had run off into the trees. In all, five girls had escape alive. But others had vanished and never been seen again. In February 1855, a few months before the escape of Josephine Charloty, hunters had found the battered corpse of a young woman hidden in a thicket; she was naked except for her bloodstained shoes and a piece of ribbon. The body was later identified as that of Marie Buday, who had left Lyon with a "countryman" a few days before she was found. Another girl, Marie Curt, had turned down the offer of a job from the man with the twisted lip, but recommended a friend named Olympe Alabert; Olympe had then vanished.

Now although the police had been aware that a peasant posing as a gardener was abducting and murdering girls, no one seems to have made a determined effort to find him. (The French police force was still in its infancy.) But the case of Marie Pichon was discussed all over the district. And three men in an inn at nearby Dayneux decided that the peasant with the deformed lip sounded like a local gardener known as Raymund, who lived nearby. Raymund kept himself to himself, spent a great deal of time in Lyon – where he was supposed to work as a porter – and had a lump on his upper lip. His real name, it seemed, was Martin Dumollard.

A local Justice of the Peace agreed that Dumollard certainly sounded as if he might be the wanted man, and issued a search warrant. This search was conducted by the magistrate himself, and it left no doubt that Dumollard was a major suspect. The house was found to contain many women's garments, and some of them were bloodstained. Dumollard was immediately arrested. He strenuously denied knowing anything about missing women, and went on denying it even when confronted by Marie Pichon herself, who identified him as her attacker.

Meanwhile, Dumollard's wife had decided to save her own neck by confessing. She admitted that her husband had brought home Marie Pichon's box, and that he had burned much of its contents in a wood – obviously concerned that if the police tracked him down the box would conclusively prove his guilt. The investigators went to the spot she indicated, and found buried ashes and fragments of books and clothes, which Marie Pichon identified.

Martin Dumollard continued to insist stolidly that he knew nothing about any crimes. But his wife Anne admitted that a woman's watch found in their house had been brought home one night four years earlier, with a quantity of bloodstained clothes. Dumollard had told her he had killed a girl in a wood at Mont Main, and was now going to bury her. He left the house with a spade . . .

A careful search of the wood revealed a depression that might be a grave. Two feet below the surface, the diggers found a female skeleton. The skull showed she had died from a violent blow on the head.

Dumollard continued to deny all knowledge of the crime. But his wife went on to describe another occasion when he had returned home and told her he had killed a girl. This body was also discovered buried in a wood, the Bois de Communes. The dry earth had preserved the flesh, and the position of the body made it clear that the girl had been buried alive and had suffocated while trying to claw her way out of the grave. She was identified as Marie Eulalie Bursod.

In the seven months that followed, it became clear that Martin Dumollard had killed at least six girls (clothes of ten were found in his home), and had unsuccessfully tried to lure another nine to their deaths. On 20 January, 1862, he and his wife were tried at the Assizes at Bourg (Ain), and he was found guilty and sentenced to death. Anne Dumollard was sentenced to twenty years imprisonment. He was guillotined on 20 March, 1862, and his head sent to be examined by phrenologists, who declared that, according to the shape of his skull, Dumollard should have been a man of the finest character.

Why did Dumollard kill? We do not know whether sex played any part in the crimes. But the notion that he murdered purely for profit seemed unlikely. The possessions of a servant girl would fetch very little money on the second-hand market, and it seems relatively certain that such girls would have very little money. So Dumollard's relative prosperity (his house was larger than that of most peasants) can hardly be explained by his crimes.

We know little of Dumollard's background except that his parents were tramps who wandered around Italy, and that his father was a murderer who was broken on the wheel. He was undoubtedly miserly, obsessed by money – his last words to his wife were to remind her that someone had failed to repay a debt – and it seems just possible that he killed the girls for their meagre possessions. But the likeliest explanation is that Dumollard became a "murder addict", and went on killing because it gave him pleasure to lure girls to their death. He has all the characteristics of the modern "serial killer".

# Jack the Ripper

Early in the morning of 31 August 1888, a carter named George Cross was walking along Bucks Row, Whitechapel – in London's East End – when he saw what he thought was a bundle of tarpaulin lying on the pavement. It proved to be a woman with her skirt above her waist. In the local mortuary, it was discovered that she had been disembowelled. Mary Ann Nicholls was almost certainly the first victim of the sadistic killer who became known as Jack the Ripper. (He provided himself with the nickname in a series of letters that he wrote to the Central News Agency.) Just over a week later, he killed and disembowelled a prostitute named Annie Chapman in a Whitechapel backyard. On the morning of 30 September, he was interrupted soon after he had cut the throat of a third victim – a woman called Elizabeth Stride – and immediately went and killed and then disembowelled another woman, Catherine Eddowes. On the morning of 9 November, he committed his last murder indoors, and spent hours dissecting the body of Mary Kelly by the light of a pile of rags burning in the grate. By this time Londoners were in a

> The Marquis de Sade, who gave his name to sadism, never actually killed anyone. He had a taste for whipping prostitutes on their bare behinds – for which he paid them well – but only harmed one of them inadvertently when he gave her an aphrodisiac called Spanish Fly which made her ill. It was his atheism and anticlerical views that first landed him in jail, and he was later imprisoned in an asylum for writing dirty books. Nowadays, in the company of Jean Genet and William Burroughs, he would simply be a respected writer.

state of hysteria, and the Chief of Police was forced to resign. But the Whitechapel murders were at an end.

All theories suggesting that the Ripper was a "gentleman" – an insane doctor, a cricket-playing lawyer, a member of the royal family – are almost certainly wide of the mark. The kind of frustration that produced the Ripper murders is characteristic of someone who lacks other means of self-expression, someone who is illiterate or only semi-literate. Such a suspect came to the attention of Daniel Farson after he had directed a television programme about Jack the Ripper.

He received a letter (signed G.W.B.) from a seventy-seven-year-old man in Melbourne, Australia, who claimed that his father had confessed to being the Ripper.

> My father was a terrible drunkard and night after night he would come home and kick my mother and us kids about, something cruelly. About the year 1902 I was taught boxing and after feeling proficient to hold my own I threatened my father that if he laid a hand on my mother or brothers I would thrash him. He never did after that, but we lived in the same house and never spoke to each other. Later, I emigrated to Australia . . . and my mother asked me to say goodbye to my father. It was then he told me his foul history and why he did these terrible murders, and advised me to change my name because he would confess before he died.

He goes on to explain: "He did not know what he was doing but his ambition was to get drunk and an urge to kill every prostitute that accosted him." Whether or not G.W.B.'s father – whose job was collecting horse-manure – was Jack the Ripper, he is certainly a far more likely suspect than a member of "Walter's" social class.

To us, it seems obvious that Jack the Ripper's murders were sex crimes (for example, the impulse that drove him to seek out another victim when he was interrupted while killing Elizabeth Stride). But it was by no means obvious to the Victorians, who preferred to think in terms of religious mania and "moral insanity". Sexual murders were a new phenomenon in the 1880s, and the average Victorian still found it puzzling that anyone should want to kill for the sake of sexual satisfaction.

The Whitechapel murders changed all this: they produced a deep disquiet, a morbid thrill of horror that made the name of Jack the Ripper a byword all over the world. It was an instinctive recognition that some strange and frightening change had taken place. In retrospect, we can see that the Ripper murders were a kind of watershed between the century of Victorian values and the age of violence that was to come.

Jack the Ripper, as depicted in a drawing in the "Illustrated Police News" of 1889.

# chapter two

# SERIAL MURDER IN EUROPE

*T**he age of sex crime began slowly. Until after World War I, sexual murder remained a rarity, an exception. In 1901, a carpenter named Ludwig Tessnow was arrested on the island of Rugen, off the Baltic coast, on suspicion of killing and mutilating two small boys; three years earlier he had escaped being charged with murdering two little girls by insisting that stains on his clothes were of wood dye, not blood. But by 1901, new techniques of forensic medicine were able to prove that the stains on his clothes were human blood, and that others were of sheep he had slaughtered and mutilated. Tessnow was executed.*

## The Gatting Mystery

Near Brisbane, Australia, in 1898, two girls named Norah and Ellen Murphy, together with their brother Michael, set out for a dance on Boxing Day, and failed to return home. Their bodies were found the next day in a paddock near Gatton; both girls had been raped and battered to death. Convicts were suspected of the crime but it was never solved.

Two years earlier, in 1896, another rape case had made headlines, but the girl had survived. Sixteen-year-old Mary Jane Hicks made the mistake of accepting a lift from a Sydney cabman, who tried to "take liberties" with her. A group of youths interrupted the attempted seduction and persuaded her to go with them. Three of them also tried to assault her, and her screams brought two would-be rescuers. But they were overwhelmed by a gang of eighteen hooligans – known as the "Waterloo Push" – who soon overpowered them. One of the rescuers ran to the nearest police station. But by the time mounted policemen arrived, the girl had been forcibly raped by a dozen gang members. Six hours later, several members of the gang were in custody. In New South Wales at that time, the penalty for rape was death. Eleven gang members and the cab driver, Charles Sweetman, were charged. Public indignation was tremendous, and nine of the eleven were found guilty and sentenced to death. Eventually, only four were hanged. The cabman Sweetman was sentenced to two floggings and fourteen years hard labour. The savagery of the sentences is an indication of the Victorian horror of sex crime – the feeling that it was something that had to be stopped at all costs. Even the later revelation that Mary had not been a virgin, and had not protested when the cabman tried to "take liberties", made no difference. "Victorian morality" took the sternest possible view of such matters.

# H. H. Holmes

The Chicago murderer H. H. Holmes – real name Herman Webster Mudgett – has some claim to be America's first serial killer. The son of a postmaster, Holmes became a doctor, then a swindler. After a chequered career as a con man, Mudgett moved to Chicago in 1886 – when he was twenty-six – and became the partner of a certain Mrs Holten, who needed an assistant in her drugstore. Mrs Holten mysteriously vanished, and Holmes – as he now called himself – took over the store. He did so well that he built himself a large house – it was later to become known as "Murder Castle" – full of hidden passageways and secret rooms; its innovations included chutes down to the basement, whose purpose – it was later realized – was to facilitate the conveyance of bodies to the furnace. During the World Fair of

1893, many out-of-town guests who came to stay in Holmes's "castle" disappeared. So did a whole succession of attractive secretaries and mistresses. Holmes was finally betrayed by the train robber Marion Hedgepeth, whom he had met in jail and promised a share in the loot – from a dishonest insurance scheme – in exchange for an introduction to a crooked lawyer. Holmes failed to keep his part of the bargain; Hedgepeth contacted the insurance company, and revealed that the "accidental" death of a man called Pitezel was actually murder. Holmes's insurance scheme also included killing off Pitezel's wife and five children to cover his tracks, and by the time the police had caught up with him, three of the children were dead, buried under the floorboards of houses rented by Holmes or incinerated in their stoves. The subsequent investigation revealed that Holmes had committed at least twenty-seven murders. He was hanged in May 1895.

# Bela Kiss

Holmes differs from more recent serial killers in that his motives were partly financial – although it seems clear that an intense sexual obsession also played its part in the murders. This is also true of Hungary's most notorious mass murderer, Bela Kiss.

In 1916, the Hungarian tax authorities noted that it had been a long time since rates had been paid on a house at 17 Rákóczi Street in the village of Cinkota, ten miles northwest of Budapest. It had been empty for two years, and since it seemed impossible to trace the owner, or the man who rented it, the district court of Pest-Pilis decided to sell it. A blacksmith named Istvan Molnar purchased it for a modest sum, and moved in with his wife and family. When tidying-up the workshop, Molnar came upon a number of sealed oildrums behind a mess of rusty pipes and corrugated iron. They had been solidly welded, and for a few days the blacksmith left them alone. Then his wife asked him what was in the drums – it might, for example, be petrol – and he settled down to removing the top of one of them with various tools. And when Molnar finally raised the lid, he clutched his stomach and rushed to the garden privy. His wife came in

to see what had upset him; when she peered into the drum
she screamed and fainted. It contained the naked body of a
woman, in a crouching position; the practically airless drum
had preserved it like canned meat.

Six more drums also proved to contain female corpses. Most
of the women were middle-aged; none had ever been beautiful.
And the police soon realized they had no way of identifying
them. They did not even know the name of the man who
placed them there. The previous tenant had gone off to the
war in 1914; he had spent little time in the house, and had
kept himself to himself, so nobody knew who he was. The
police found it difficult even to get a description. They merely
had seven unknown victims of an unknown murderer.

Professor Balazs Kenyeres, of the Police Medical Laboratory,
was of the opinion that the women had been dead for more
than two years. But at least he was able to take fingerprints;
by 1916, fingerprinting had percolated even to the highly
conservative Austro-Hungarian Empire. However, at this stage,
fingerprinting was unhelpful, since it only told them that the
women had no criminal records.

Some three weeks after the discovery, Detective Geza
Bialokurszky was placed in charge of the investigation; he
was one of the foremost investigators of the Budapest police.
He was, in fact, Sir Geza (*lovag*), for he was a nobleman whose
family had lost their estates. Now he settled down to the task
of identifying the female corpses. If Professor Kenyeres was
correct about time of death – and he might easily have been
wrong, since few pathologists are asked to determine the age
of a canned corpse – the women must have vanished in 1913
or thereabouts. The Missing Persons' Bureau provided him
with a list of about 400 women who had vanished between
1912 and 1914. Eventually, Bialokurszky narrowed these down
to fifteen. But these women seemed to have no traceable
relatives. Eventually, Bialokurszky found the last employer of
a thirty-six-year-old cook named Anna Novak, who had left her
job abruptly in 1911. Her employer was the widow of a Hussar
colonel, and she still had Anna's "servant's book", a kind of
identity card that contained a photograph, personal details, and
a list of previous employers, as well as their personal comments.
The widow assumed that she had simply found a better job or
had got married. She still had the woman's trunk in the attic.

This offered Bialokurszky the clue he needed so urgently: a sheet from a newspaper, *Pesti Hirlap*, with an advertisement marked in red pencil:

> Widower urgently seeks acquaintance of mature, warm-hearted spinster or widow to help assuage loneliness mutually. Send photo and details, Poste Restante Central P.O.Box 717. Marriage possible and even desirable.

Now, at last, fingerprinting came into its own. Back at headquarters, the trunk was examined, and a number of prints were found; these matched those of one of the victims. The post office was able to tell Bialokurszky that Box 717 had been rented by a man who had signed for his key in the name of Elemer Nagy, of 14 Kossuth Street, Pestszenterzsebet, a suburb of Budapest. This proved to be an empty plot. Next, the detective and his team studied the agony column of *Pesti Hirlap* for 1912 and 1913. They found more than twenty requests for "warm-hearted spinsters" which gave the address of Box 717. This was obviously how the unknown killer of Cinkota had contacted his victims. On one occasion he had paid for the advertisement by postal order, and the post office was able to trace it. (The Austro-Hungarian Empire at least had a super-efficient bureaucracy.) Elemer Nagy had given an address in Cinkota, where the bodies had been found, but it was not of the house in Rákóczi Street; in fact, it proved to be the address of the undertaker. The killer had a sense of humour.

Bialokurszky gave a press conference, and asked the newspapers to publish the signature of "Elemer Nagy". This quickly brought a letter from a domestic servant named Rosa Diosi, who was twenty-seven, and admitted that she had been the mistress of the man in question. His real name was Bela Kiss, and she had last heard from him in 1914, when he had written to her from a Serbian prisoner of war camp. Bialokurszky had not divulged that he was looking for the Cinkota mass murderer, and Rosa Diosi was shocked and incredulous when he told her. She had met Kiss in 1914; he had beautiful brown eyes, a silky moustache, and a deep, manly voice. Sexually, he had apparently been insatiable . . .

Other women contacted the police, and they had identical

stories to tell: answering the advertisement, meeting the handsome Kiss, and being quickly invited to become his mistress, with promises of marriage. They were also expected to hand over their life savings, and all had been invited to Cinkota. Some had not gone, some had declined to offer their savings – or had none to offer – and a few had disliked being rushed into sex. Kiss had wasted no further time on them, and simply vanished from their lives.

In July 1914, two years before the discovery of the bodies, Kiss had been conscripted into the Second Regiment of the Third Hungarian Infantry Battalion, and had taken part in the long offensive that led to the fall of Valjevo; but before that city had fallen in November, Kiss had been captured by the Serbs. No one was certain what had become of him after that. But the regiment was able to provide a photograph that showed the soldiers being inspected by the Archduke Joseph; Kiss's face was enlarged, and the detectives at last knew what their quarry looked like. They had also heard that his sexual appetite was awe-inspiring, and this led them to show the photograph in the red-light district around Conti and Magyar Street. Many prostitutes recognized him as a regular customer; all spoke warmly of his generosity and mentioned his sexual prowess. But a waiter who had often served Kiss noticed that the lady with whom he was dining usually paid the bill . . .

Now, at last, Bialokurszky was beginning to piece the story together. Pawn tickets found in the Cinkota house revealed that the motive behind the murders was the cash of the victims. But the ultimate motive had been sex, for Kiss promptly spent the cash in the brothels of Budapest and Vienna. The evidence showed that he was, quite literally, a satyr – a man with a raging and boundless appetite for sex. His profession – of plumber and tinsmith – did not enable him to indulge this appetite so he took to murder. He had received two legacies when he was twenty-three (about 1903) but soon spent them. After this, he had taken to seducing middle-aged women and "borrowing" their savings. One of these, a cook name Maria Toth, had become a nuisance, and he killed her. After this – like his French contemporary Landru – he had decided that killing women was the easiest way to make a living as well as indulge his sexual appetites. His favourite reading was true-crime books about con men and adventurers.

Bialokurszky's investigations suggested that there had been more then seven victims, and just before Christmas 1916, the garden in the house at Cinkota was dug up; it revealed five more bodies, all of middle-aged women, all naked.

But where was Kiss? The War Office thought that he had died of fever in Serbia. He had been in a field hospital, but when Bialokurszky tracked down one of its nurses, she remembered the deceased as a "nice boy" with fair hair and blue eyes, which seemed to suggest that Kiss had changed identity with another soldier, possibly someone called Mackavee; but the new "Mackavee" proved untraceable. And although sightings of Kiss were reported from Budapest in 1919 – and even New York as late as 1932 – he was never found.

# Fritz Haarmann

Where sex crime is concerned, World War I seems to have been a kind of watershed. Now, suddenly, the twentieth century entered the "age of sex crime". And – perhaps predictably – the country in which this first became apparent was Germany where, after 1918, the miseries and deprivations of inflation and food shortage made a maximum impact. Hanover in Saxony was one of the cities that was most badly hit. It was in Hanover that Haarmann committed one of the most amazing series of crimes in modern times.

---

Necrophile Ed Gein, on whom Thomas Harris based "Buffalo Bill" in *Silence of the Lambs*, used the skin of corpses to make himself waistcoats. This was not the first use of human skin for practical purposes. Concentration camp guard Irma Grese is said to have made lampshades of human skin. The skin of a victim of the guillotine was used to bind the second edition of Rousseau's *Social Contact* – the book that, more than any other, was responsible for the French Revolution. The skin of William Corder, who murdered Maria Marten in the Red Barn in 1827, was used for book binding in the following year.

---

Haarmann was born in Hanover on 25 October 1879; he was **387** the sixth child of an ill-assorted couple; a morose locomotive stoker known as "Sulky Olle" and his invalid wife, seven years his senior. Fritz was his mother's pet and hated his father. He liked playing with dolls, and disliked games. At sixteen he was sent to a military school (for NCOs) at New Breisach, but soon released when he showed signs of epileptic fits. He went to work in his father's cigar factory but was lazy and inefficient. He was soon accused of indecent behaviour with small children and sent to an asylum for observation; he escaped after six months. He then took to petty crime, as well as indecent assaults on minors. He also had a brief sexually normal period about 1900, when he seduced a girl to whom he was engaged and then deserted her to join the Jäger regiment. The baby was still-born. He served satisfactorily until 1903, then returned to Hanover, where his father tried to have him certified insane again – without success. He served several sentences in jail for burglary, pocket-picking and confidence trickery. His father tried getting him to do respectable work, setting him up as the keeper of a fish-and-chip shop. Fritz promptly stole all the money he could lay his hands on. In 1914 he was sentenced to five years in jail for theft from a warehouse. Released in 1918, he joined a smuggling ring, and soon became prosperous. With his headquarters at 27 Cellarstrasse, he conducted business as a smuggler, thief and police spy. (This latter activity guaranteed that his smuggling should not be too closely scrutinized.)

Many refugee trains came into Hanover; Haarmann picked up youths and offered them a night's lodging. One of the first of these was seventeen-year-old Friedel Rothe. The lad's worried parents found that he had been friendly with "detective" Haarmann; the police searched his room, but found nothing. (Haarmann later admitted that the boy's head lay wrapped in a newspaper behind his stove at the time.) But they caught Haarmann *in flagrante delicto* with another boy, and he received nine months in jail for indecency. Back in Hanover in September 1919, he changed his lodging to the Neuestrasse. He met another homosexual, Hans Grans, a pimp and petty thief, and the two formed an alliance. They used to meet in a café that catered for all kinds of perverts, the Café Kröpcke. Their method was always the same; the enticed a youth from the railway station back to Haarmann's room; Haarmann killed him (according to his own account, by biting his throat), and the boy's body was dismembered and sold as meat through Haarmann's usual channels for smuggled meat. His clothes were sold, and the useless (i.e. uneatable) portions were thrown into the Leine. At the trial, a list of twenty-eight victims was offered, their ages ranging between thirteen and twenty. One boy was killed only because Grans took a fancy to his trousers. Only one victim, a lad named Keimes, was found, strangled in the canal. There was a curious incident in connexion with this case; Haarmann called on the missing youth's parents as a "detective" and assured them he would restore their son in three days; he then went to the police and denounced Grans as the murderer! Grans was in prison at the time, so nothing came of the charge.

Haarmann had some narrow escapes; some of his meat was taken to the police because the buyer thought it was human flesh; the police analyst pronounced it pork! On another occasion, a neighbour stopped to talk to him on the stairs when some paper blew off the bucket he was carrying; it was revealed to contain blood. But Haarmann's trade as a meat smuggler kept him from suspicion.

In May 1924, a skull was discovered on the banks of the river, and some weeks later, another one. People continued to report the disappearance of their sons, and Haarmann was definitely suspected; but months went by, and Haarmann continued to kill. Two detectives from Berlin watched him, and he was arrested for indecency. His lodgings were searched and many articles of clothing taken away. His landlady's son was found to be wearing a coat belonging to one of the missing boys. And boys playing near the river discovered more bones, including a sack stuffed with them. A police pathologist declared they represented the remains of at least twenty-seven bodies.

Haarmann decided to confess. His trial began at the Hanover Assizes on 4 December 1924. It lasted fourteen days and 130 witnesses were called. The public prosecutor was Oberstaatsanwalt Dr Wilde, assisted by Dr Wagenschiefer; the defence was conducted by Justizrat Philipp Benfey and Rechtsanwalt Oz Lotzen. Haarmann was allowed remarkable freedom; he was usually gay and irresponsible, frequently interrupting the proceedings. At one point he demanded indignantly why there were so many women in court; the judge answered apologetically that he had no power to keep them out. When a woman witness was too

distraught to give her evidence about her son with clarity, **389**
Haarmann got bored and asked to be allowed to smoke a cigar;
permission was immediately granted.

He persisted to the end in his explanation of how he had
killed his victims – biting them through the throat. Some boys
he denied killing – for example, a boy named Hermann Wolf,
whose photograph showed an ugly and ill-dressed youth; like
Oscar Wilde, Haarmann declared that the boy was far too ugly
to interest him.

Haarmann was sentenced to death by decapitation; Grans to
twelve years in jail.

During the same period Karl Denke, landlord of a house in
Münsterberg, killed more than a dozen vagrants – male and
female – who called at his door, and ate portions of their
bodies, which he kept pickled in brine. Georg Grossmann, a
sadistic sexual degenerate, lived from 1914 to 1921 on the flesh
of victims he lured to his room in Berlin; police investigating
sounds of a struggle found the trussed-up carcase of a girl
on the bed, the cords tightened as if for butchering into neat
sections.

# Peter Kurten, the "Dusseldorf Vampire"

In the year 1913 another notorious sex killer committed his
first murder. On a summer morning, a ten-year-old girl named
Christine Klein was found murdered in her bed in a tavern in
Köln-Mülheim, on the Rhine. The tavern was kept by her father,
Peter Klein, and suspicion immediately fell on his brother Otto.
On the previous evening, Otto Klein had asked his brother for
a loan and been refused; in a violent rage, he had threatened
to do something his brother "would remember all his life". In
the room in which the child had been killed, the police found a
handkerchief with the initials "P.K.", and it seemed conceivable
that Otto Klein had borrowed it from his brother Peter. Suspicion
of Otto was deepened by the fact that the murder seemed

otherwise motiveless; the child had been throttled unconscious, then her throat had been cut with a sharp knife. There were signs of some sexual molestation, but not of rape, and again, it seemed possible that Otto Klein had penetrated the child's genitals with his fingers in order to provide an apparent motive. He was charged with Christine Klein's murder, but the jury, although partly convinced of his guilt, felt that the evidence was not sufficiently strong, and he was acquitted.

Sixteen years later, in Düsseldorf, a series of murders and sexual atrocities made the police aware that an extremely dangerous sexual pervert was roaming the streets. These began on 9 February 1929, when the body of an eight-year-old girl, Rosa Ohliger was found under a hedge. She had been stabbed thirteen times, and an attempt had been made to burn the body with petrol. The murderer had also stabbed her in the vagina – the weapon was later identified as a pair of scissors – and seminal stains on the knickers indicated that he had experienced emission.

Six days earlier, a woman named Kuhn had been overtaken by a man who grabbed her by the lapels and stabbed her repeatedly and rapidly. She fell down and screamed, and the man ran away. Frau Kuhn survived the attack with twenty-four stab wounds, but was in hospital for many months.

Five days after the murder of Rosa Ohliger, a forty-five-year-old mechanic named Scheer was found stabbed to death on a road in Flingern; he had twenty stab wounds, including several in the head.

Soon after this, two women were attacked by a man with a noose, and described the man as an idiot with a hare lip. An idiot named Stausberg was arrested, and confessed not only to the attacks but to the murders. He was confined in a mental home, and for the next six months, there were no more attacks. But in August, they began again. Two women and a man were stabbed as they walked home at night, none of them fatally. But on 24 August, two children were found dead on an allotment in Düsseldorf; both had been strangled, then had their throats cut. Gertrude Hamacher was five, Louise Lenzen fourteen. That same afternoon, a servant girl named Gertrude Schulte was accosted by a man who tried to persuade her to have sexual intercourse; when she said "I'd rather die", he answered: "Die then", and stabbed her. But she survived, and was able to give a good description of her assailant, who proved to be a pleasant-looking, nondescript man of about forty.

The murders and attacks went on, throwing the whole area into a panic comparable to that caused by Jack the Ripper. A servant girl named Ida Reuter was battered to death with a hammer and raped in September; in October, another servant, Elizabeth Dorrier, was battered to death. A woman out for a walk was asked by a man whether she was not afraid to be out alone, and knocked unconscious with a hammer; later the same evening, a prostitute was attacked with a hammer. On 7 November, five-year-old Gertrude Albermann disappeared; two days later, the Communist newspaper *Freedom* received a letter stating that the child's body would be found near a factory wall, and enclosing a map. It also described the whereabouts of another body in the Pappendelle meadows.

Albert Anastasia, the Mafia's "King of Brooklyn", was also known as "The Mad Hatter" or "The Executioner". A homicidal maniac with a violent temper, he liked killing for the sake of killing and ordered deaths on the slightest pretext. After reading in the newspaper that a local citizen had recognized the famous bank robber Willie Smith and turned him in to the police, Anastasia ordered that this conscientious citizen be immediately killed. "I hate a rat," he said, "no matter who he is." He liked to have murder victims hideously tortured before their death and when unable to participate himself he insisted that every detail of the torture be later recounted to him; he particularly relished it when they begged for mercy. He lived like an emperor near New York Harbour in New Jersey, in a vast house surrounded by a seven-foot barbed-wire fence, a pack of Dobermans and a permanent bodyguard. His money came from the waterfront rackets: extortion, theft, gambling, loan-sharking and kick-backs. The 40,000 longshoremen who worked in the port were all under his thumb. Also, his brother "Tough Tony" was president of the biggest union and he was thought to have the entire roll-call of local police and politicians on his payroll.

Gertrude Albermann's body was found where the letter had described, amidst bricks and rubble; she had been strangled and stabbed thirty-five times. A large party of men digging on the Rhine meadows eventually discovered the naked body of a servant girl, Maria Hahn, who had disappeared in the previous August; she had also been stabbed.

By the end of 1929, the "Düsseldorf murderer" was known all over the world, and the manhunt had reached enormous proportions. But the attacks had ceased.

The capture of the killer happened almost by chance. On 19 May 1930, a certain Frau Brugmann opened a letter that had been delivered to her accidentally; it was actually addressed to a Frau Bruckner, whose name had been misspelled. It was from a twenty-year-old domestic servant named Maria Budlick (or Butlies), and she described an alarming adventure she had met with two days earlier. Maria had travelled from Cologne to Düsseldorf in search of work, and on the train had fallen into conversation with Frau Bruckner, who had given the girl her address and offered to help her find accommodation. That same evening, Maria Budlick had been waiting at the Düsseldorf railway station, hoping to meet Frau Bruckner, when she was accosted by a man who offered to help her find a bed for the night. He led her through the crowded streets and into a park. The girl was becoming alarmed, and was relieved when a kindly-looking man intervened and asked her companion where he was taking her. Within a few moments, her former companion had slunk off, and the kindly man offered to take the girl back to his room in the Mettmänner Strasse. There she decided his intentions were also dishonourable, and asked to be taken to a hostel. The man agreed; but when they reached a lonely spot, he kissed her roughly and asked for sex. The frightened girl agreed; the man tugged down her knickers, and they had sex standing up. After this, the man led her back to the tram stop, and left her. She eventually found a lodging for the night with some other nuns, and the next day, wrote about her encounter to Frau Bruckner.

Frau Brugmann, who opened the letter, decided to take it to the police. And Chief Inspector Gennat, who was in charge of the murder case, sought out Maria Budlick, and asked her if she thought she could lead him to the address where the man had taken her. It seemed a remote chance that the man was the Düsseldorf murderer, but Gennat was desperate. Maria remembered that the street was called Mettmänner Strasse, but had no idea of the address. It took her a long time and considerable hesitation before she led Gennat into the hallway of No. 71, and said she thought this was the place. The landlady let her into the room, which was empty, and she recognized it as the one she had been in a week earlier. As they were going downstairs, she met the man who had raped her. He went pale when he saw her, and walked out of the house. But the landlady was able to tell her his name. It was Peter Kürten.

Kürten, it seemed, lived with his wife in a top room in the house. He was known to be frequently unfaithful to her. But neighbours seemed to feel that he was a pleasant, likeable man. Children took to him instinctively.

On 24 May 1930, a raw-boned middle-aged woman went to the police station and told them that her husband was the Düsseldorf murderer. Frau Kürten had been fetched home from work by detectives on the day Maria Budlick had been to the room in Mettmänner Strasse, but her husband was nowhere to be found. Frau Kürten knew that he had been in jail on many occasions, usually for burglary, sometimes for sexual offences. Now, she felt, he was likely to be imprisoned for a long time. The thought of a lonely and penniless old age made her desperate, and when her husband finally reappeared, she asked him frantically what he had been doing. When he told her that he was the Düsseldorf killer, she thought he was joking. But finally he convinced her. Her reaction was to suggest a suicide pact. But Kürten had a better idea. There was a large reward offered for the capture of the sadist; if his wife could claim that, she could have a comfortable old age. They argued for many hours; she still wanted to kill herself. But eventually, she was persuaded. And on the afternoon of the 24th, Kürten met his wife outside the St Rochus church, and four policemen rushed at him waving revolvers. Kürten smiled reassuringly and told them not to be afraid. Then he was taken into police custody.

In prison, Kürten spoke frankly about his career of murder with the police psychiatrist, Professor Karl Berg. He had been born in Köln-Mülheim in 1883, son of a drunkard who often forced his wife to have sexual intercourse in the same bedroom as the children; after an attempt to rape one of his daughters, the father was imprisoned, and Frau Kürten obtained a separation and married again. Even as a child Kürten was oversexed, and tried to have intercourse with the sister his father had attacked. At the age of eight he became friendly with a local dog-catcher, who taught him how to masturbate the dogs; the dog-catcher also ill-treated them in the child's presence. At the age of nine, Kürten pushed a schoolfellow off a raft, and when another boy dived in, managed to push his head under, so that both were drowned. At the age of thirteen he began to practise bestiality with sheep, pigs, and goats, but discovered that he had his most powerful sensation when he stabbed a sheep as he had intercourse, and began to do it with increasing frequency. At sixteen he stole money and ran away from home; soon after, he received the first of seventeen prison sentences that occupied twenty-four years of his life. And during long periods of solitary confinement for insubordination, he indulged in endless sadistic day-dreams, which "fixed" his tendency to associate sexual excitement with blood. In 1913, he had entered the tavern in Köln-Mülheim and murdered the ten-year-old girl as she lay in bed; he had experienced orgasm as he cut her throat. The handkerchief with initials P.K. belonged, of course, to Peter Kürten.

And so Kürten's career continued – periods in jail, and brief periods of freedom during which he committed sexual attacks on women, sometimes stabbing them, sometimes strangling them. If he experienced orgasm as he squeezed a girl's throat, he immediately became courteous and apologetic, explaining "That's what love's about." The psychiatrist Karl Berg was impressed by his intelligence and frankness, and later wrote a classic book on the case. Kürten told him candidly that he looked with longing at the white throat of the stenographer who took down his confession, and longed to strangle it. He also confided to Berg that his greatest wish was to hear his own blood gushing into the basket as his head was cut off. He ate an enormous last meal before he was guillotined on 2 July 1931.

# chapter three

# THE PSYCHOPATHIC KILLER

*In 1970, an American publisher brought out a volume called* Killer, A Journal of Murder, *and made the world suddenly aware of one of the most dangerous serial killers of the first half of the twentieth century. His name was Carl Panzram, and the book was his autobiography, written more than forty years earlier. It was regarded as too horrifying to publish at the time, but when it finally appeared, it was hailed as a revelation of the inner workings of the mind of a serial killer. However, Panzram belongs to a rare species that criminologists label "the resentment killer". Far more common – particularly in the last decades of the twentieth century – is the travelling serial killer, the man who moves restlessly from place to place. In a country as large as America, this makes him particularly difficult to catch, since communication between police forces in different states is often less efficient than it should be. Earle Nelson, the "Gorilla Murderer", is generally regarded as the first example of the "travelling serial killer".*

# Carl Panzram

Panzram was born in June 1891, on a small farm in Minnesota, in the American midwest. His father had deserted the family when Carl was a child, leaving his mother to care for a family of six. When Carl came home from school in the afternoon he was immediately put to working in the fields. "My portion of pay consisted of plenty of work and a sound beating every time I done anything that displeased anyone who was older and stronger . . ."

When he was eleven, Carl burgled the house of a well-to-do neighbour and was sent to reform school. He was a rebellious boy, and was often violently beaten. Because he was a highly "dominant" personality, the beatings only deepened the desire to avenge the injustice on "society". He would have agreed with the painter Gauguin who said: "Life being what it is, one dreams of revenge."

Travelling around the country on freight trains, the young Panzram was sexually violated by four hoboes. The experience suggested a new method of expressing his aggression. ". . . whenever I met [a hobo] who wasn't too rusty looking I would make him raise his hands and drop his pants. I wasn't very particular either. I rode them old and young, tall and short, white and black." When a brakesman caught Panzram and two other hoboes in a railway truck Panzram drew his revolver and raped the man, then forced the other two hoboes to do the same at gunpoint. It was his way of telling "authority" what he thought of it.

Panzram lived by burglary, mugging and robbing churches. He spent a great deal of time in prison, but became a skilled escapist. But he had his own peculiar sense of loyalty. After breaking jail in Salem, Oregon, he broke in again to try to rescue a safe blower named Cal Jordan; he was caught and got thirty days. "The thanks I got from old Cal was that he thought I was in love with him and he tried to mount me, but I wasn't broke to ride and he was, so I rode him. At that time he was about fifty years old and I was twenty or twenty-one, but I was strong and he was weak."

In various prisons, he became known as one of the toughest

troublemakers ever encountered. What drove him to his most violent frenzies was a sense of injustice. In Oregon he was offered a minimal sentence if he would reveal the whereabouts of the stolen goods; Panzram kept his side of the bargain but was sentenced to seven years. He managed to escape from his cell and wreck the jail, burning furniture and mattresses. They beat him up and sent him to the toughest prison in the state. There he promptly threw the contents of a chamberpot in a guard's face; he was beaten unconscious and chained to the door of a dark cell for thirty days, where he screamed defiance. He aided another prisoner to escape, and in the hunt the warden was shot dead. The new warden was tougher than ever. Panzram burned down the prison workshop and later a flax mill. Given a job in the kitchen, he went berserk with an axe. He incited the other prisoners to revolt, and the atmosphere became so tense that guards would not venture into the yard. Finally, the warden was dismissed.

The new warden, a man named Murphy, was an idealist who believed that prisoners would respond to kindness. When Panzram was caught trying to escape, Murphy sent for him and told him that, according to reports, he was "the meanest and most cowardly degenerate that they had ever seen." When Panzram agreed, Murphy astonished him by telling him that he would let him walk out of the jail if he would swear to return in time for supper. Panzram agreed – with no intention of keeping his word; but when supper time came, something made him go back. Gradually, Murphy increased his freedom, and that of the other prisoners. But one night Panzram got drunk with a pretty nurse and decided to abscond. Recaptured after a gun battle, he was thrown into the punishment cell, and Murphy's humanitarian regime came to an abrupt end.

This experience seems to have been something of a turning point. So far, Panzram had been against the world, but not against himself. His betrayal of Murphy's trust seems to have set up a reaction of self-hatred. He escaped from prison again, stole a yacht, and began his career of murder. He would offer sailors a job and take them to the stolen yacht; there he would rob them, commit sodomy, and throw their bodies into the sea. "They are there yet, ten of 'em." Then he went to West Africa to work for an oil company, where he soon lost his job for committing sodomy on the table waiter. The US Consul declined to help him and he sat down in a park "to think things over". "While I was sitting there, a little nigger boy about eleven or twelve years came bumming around. He was looking for something. He found it too. I took him out to a gravel pit a quarter of a mile from the main camp . . . I left him there, but first I committed sodomy on him and then killed him. His brains were coming out of his ears when I left him and he will never be any deader . . .

"Then I went to town, bought a ticket on the Belgian steamer to Lobito Bay down the coast. There I hired a canoe and six niggers and went out hunting in the bay and backwaters. I was looking for crocodiles. I found them, plenty. They were all hungry. I fed them. I shot all six of those niggers and dumped 'em in. The crocks done the rest. I stole their canoe and went back to town, tied the canoe to a dock, and that night someone stole the canoe from me."

Back in America he raped and killed three more boys, bringing his murders up to twenty. After five years of rape, robbery and arson, Panzram was caught as he robbed the express office in Larchmont, New York and sent to one of America's toughest prisons, Dannemora. "I hated everybody I saw." And again more defiance, more beatings. Like a stubborn child, he had decided to turn his life into a competition to see whether he could take more beatings than society could hand out. In Dannemora he leapt from a high gallery, fracturing a leg, and walked for the rest of his life with a limp. He spent his days brooding on schemes of revenge against the whole human race: how to blow up a railway tunnel with a train in it, how to poison a whole city by putting arsenic into the water supply, even how to cause a war between England and America by blowing up a British battleship in American waters.

It was during this period in jail that Panzram met a young Jewish guard named Henry Lesser. Lesser was a shy man who enjoyed prison work because it conferred automatic status, which eased his inferiority complex. Lesser was struck by Panzram's curious immobility, a quality of cold detachment. When he asked him: "What's your racket?" Panzram replied with a curious smile: "What I do is reform people." After brooding on this, Lesser went back to ask him how he did it; Panzram replied that the only way to reform people is to kill them. He described himself as "the man who goes around doing good". He meant that life is so vile that to kill someone is to do him a favour.

When a loosened bar was discovered in his cell, Panzram received yet another brutal beating – perhaps the hundredth of his life. In the basement of the jail he was subjected to a torture that in medieval times was known as the strappado. His hands were tied behind his back; then a rope was passed over a beam and he was heaved up by the wrists so that his shoulder sockets bore the full weight of his body. Twelve hours later, when the doctor checked his heart, Panzram shrieked and blasphemed, cursing his mother for bringing him into the world and declaring that he would kill every human being. He was allowed to lie on the floor of his cell all day, but when he cursed a guard, four guards knocked him unconscious with a blackjack and again suspended him from a beam. Lesser was so shocked by this treatment that he sent Panzram a dollar by a "trusty". At first, Panzram thought it was a joke. When he realized that it was a gesture of sympathy, his eyes filled with tears. He told Lesser that if he could get him paper and a pencil, he would write him his life story. This is how Panzram's autobiography came to be written.

When Lesser read the opening pages, he was struck by the remarkable literacy and keen intelligence. Panzram made no excuses for himself:

> If any man was a habitual criminal, I am one. In my life time I have broken every law that was ever made by God and man. If either had made any more, I should very cheerfully have broken them also. The mere fact that I have done these things is quite sufficient for the average person. Very few people even consider it worthwhile to wonder why I am what I am and do what I do. All that they think is necessary to do is to catch me, try me, convict me and send me to prison for a few years, make life miserable for me while in prison and turn me loose again . . . If someone had a young tiger cub in a cage and then mistreated it until it got savage and bloodthirsty and then turned it loose to prey on the rest of the world . . . there would be a hell of a roar . . . But if some people do the same thing to other people, then the world is

**400**

surprised, shocked and offended because they get
robbed, raped and killed. They done it to me and
then don't like it when I give them the same dose
they gave me.
(From *Killer, a Journal of Murder*, edited by Thomas
E. Gaddis and James O. Long, Macmillan, 1970.)

Panzram's confession is an attempt to justify himself to one other
human being. Where others were concerned, he remained as
savagely intractable as ever. At his trial he told the jury: "While
you were trying me here, I was trying all of you too. I've found
you guilty. Some of you, I've already executed. If I live, I'll
execute some more of you. I hate the whole human race." The
judge sentenced him to twenty-five years.

Transferred to Leavenworth penitentiary, Panzram murdered
the foreman of the working party with an iron bar and was
sentenced to death. Meanwhile, Lesser had been showing
the autobiography to various literary men, including H. L.
Mencken, who were impressed. But when Panzram heard
there was a movement to get him reprieved, he protested
violently: "I would not reform if the front gate was opened
right now and I was given a million dollars when I stepped
out. I have no desire to do good or become good." And in
a letter to Henry Lesser he showed a wry self-knowledge: "I
could not reform if I wanted to. It has taken me all my life so
far, thirty-eight years of it, to reach my present state of mind.
In that time I have acquired some habits. It took me a lifetime to
form these habits, and I believe it would take more than another
lifetime to break myself of these same habits even if I wanted
to . . ." ". . . what gets me is how in the heck any man of your
intelligence and ability, knowing as much about me as you do,
can still be friendly towards a thing like me when I even despise
and detest my own self." When he stepped onto the scaffold on
the morning of 11 September 1930, the hangman asked him if
he had anything to say. "Yes, hurry it up, you hoosier bastard.
I could hang a dozen men while you're fooling around."

# Earle Nelson

On 24 February 1926, a man named Richard Newman went to call on his aunt, who advertised rooms to let in San Francisco; he found the naked body of the sixty-year-old woman in an upstairs toilet. She had been strangled with her pearl necklace, then repeatedly raped. Clara Newman was the first of twenty-two victims of a man who became known as "the Gorilla Murderer". The killer made a habit of calling at houses with a "Room to Let" notice in the window; if the landlady was alone, he strangled and raped her. His victims included a fourteen-year-old girl and an eight-month-old baby. And as he travelled around from San Francisco to San Jose, from Portland, Oregon to Council Bluffs, Iowa, from Philadelphia to Buffalo, from Detroit to Chicago, the police found him as elusive as the French police had found Joseph Vacher thirty years earlier. Their problem was simply that the women who could identify "the Dark Strangler" (as the newspapers had christened him) were dead, and they had no idea of what he looked like. But when the Portland police had the idea of asking newspapers to publish descriptions of jewellery that had been stolen from some of the strangler's victims, three old ladies in a South Portland lodging-house recalled that they had bought a few items of jewellery from a pleasant young man who had stayed with them for a few days. They decided – purely as a precaution – to take it to the police. It proved to belong to a Seattle landlady, Mrs Florence Monks, who had been strangled and raped on 24 November 1926. And the old ladies were able to tell the police that the Dark Strangler was a short, blue-eyed young man with a round face and slightly simian mouth and jaw. He was quietly spoken, and claimed to be deeply religious.

> When the problem of serial murder was first publicized in the United States, various experts estimated that the number of victims amounted to between 3,000 and 5,000 a year. In the late 1980s, a more careful estimate by the National Center for the Analysis of Violent Crime (NCAVC) revealed that the actual figure was probably between 300 and 500 a year – frightening enough, but hardly on the same scale as the earlier "expert" estimate.

On 8 June 1927, the strangler crossed the Canadian border, and rented a room in Winnipeg from a Mrs Catherine Hill. He stayed for three nights. But on 9 June, a couple named Cowan, who lived in the house, reported that their fourteen-year-old daughter Lola had vanished. That same evening, a man named William Patterson returned home to find his wife absent. After making supper and putting the children to bed, he rang the police. Then he dropped on his knees beside the bed to pray; as he did so, he saw his wife's hand sticking out. Her naked body lay under the bed.

The Winnipeg police recognized the *modus operandi* of the Gorilla Murderer. A check on boarding-house landladies brought them to Mrs Hill's establishment. She assured them that she had taken in no suspicious characters recently – her last lodger had been a Roger Wilson, who had been carrying a Bible and been highly religious. When she told them that Roger Wilson was short, with piercing blue eyes and a dark complexion, they asked to see the room he had stayed in. They were greeted by the stench of decay. The body of Lola Cowan lay under the bed, mutilated as if by Jack the Ripper. The murderer had slept with it in his room for three days.

From the Patterson household, the strangler had taken some of the husband's clothes, leaving his own behind. But he changed these at a second-hand shop, leaving behind a fountain pen belonging to Patterson, and paying in $10 bills stolen from his house. So the police now not only had a good description of the killer, but the clothes he was wearing, including corduroy trousers and a plaid shirt.

The next sighting came from Regina, two hundred miles west; a landlady heard the screams of a pretty girl who worked for the telephone company, and interrupted the man who had been trying to throttle her; he ran away. The police guessed that he might be heading back towards the American border, which would take him across prairie country with few towns; there was a good chance that a lone hitch-hiker would be noticed. Descriptions of the wanted man were sent out to all police stations and post offices. Five days later, two constables saw a man wearing corduroys and a plaid shirt walking down a road near Killarney, twelve miles from the border. He gave his name as Virgil Wilson and said he was a farm-worker; he seemed quite unperturbed when the police told him they were looking for a mass murderer, and would have to take him in on suspicion. His behaviour was so unalarmed they were convinced he was innocent. But when they telephoned the Winnipeg chief of police, and described Virgil Wilson, he told them that the man was undoubtedly "Roger Wilson", the Dark Strangler. They hurried back to the jail – to find that their prisoner had picked the lock of his handcuffs and escaped.

Detectives were rushed to the town by aeroplane, and posses spread out over the area. "Wilson" had slept in a barn close to the jail, and the next morning broke into a house and stole a change of clothing. The first man he spoke to that morning noticed his dishevelled appearance and asked if he had spent the night in the open; the man admitted that he had. When told that police were on their way to Killarney by train to look for the strangler, he ran away towards the railway. At that moment, a police car appeared; after a short chase, the fugitive was captured.

He was identified as Earle Leonard Nelson, born in Philadelphia in 1897; his mother had died of venereal disease contracted from his father. At the age of ten, Nelson was knocked down by a streetcar and was unconscious with concussion for six days. From then on, he experienced violent periodic headaches. He began to make a habit of peering through the keyhole of his cousin Rachel's bedroom when she was getting undressed. At twenty-one, he was arrested for trying to rape a girl in a basement. Sent to a penal farm, he soon escaped, and was recaptured peering in through the window of his cousin as she undressed for bed. A marriage was unsuccessful; when his wife had a nervous breakdown, Nelson visited her in hospital and tried to rape her in bed. Nothing is known of Nelson's whereabouts for the next three years, until the evening in February 1926, when he knocked on the door of Mrs Clara Newman in San Francisco, and asked if he could see the room she had to let . . .

# Gordon Cummins, the "Blackout Ripper"

Sex crimes invariably increase during wartime. This is partly because the anarchic social atmosphere produces a loss of inhibition, partly because so many soldiers have been deprived of their usual sexual outlet. Nevertheless, the rate of sex crime in England during World War II remained low, while the murder rate actually fell. One of the few cases to excite widespread attention occurred during the "blackouts" of 1942. Between 9 and 15 February, four women were murdered in London. Evelyn Hamilton, a forty-year-old schoolteacher, was found strangled in an air raid shelter; Evelyn Oatley, an ex-revue actress, was found naked on her bed, her throat cut and her belly mutilated with a tin-opener; Margaret Lower was strangled with a silk stocking and mutilated with a razor blade, and Doris Jouannet was killed in an identical manner. The killer's bloody fingerprints were found on the tin-opener and on a mirror in Evelyn Oatley's flat. A few days later, a young airman dragged a woman into a doorway near Piccadilly and throttled her into unconsciousness, but a passer-by overheard the scuffle and went to investigate. The airman ran away, dropping his gas-mask case with his service number stencilled on it. Immediately afterwards, he accompanied a prostitute to her flat in Paddington and began to throttle her; her screams and struggles again frightened him away. From the gas-mask case the man was identified as twenty-eight-year-old Gordon Cummins, from north London, and he was arrested as soon as he returned to his billet. The fingerprint evidence identified him as the "blackout ripper", and he was hanged in June 1942. Sir Bernard Spilsbury, who had performed the post-mortem on Evelyn Oatley, also performed one on Cummins.

# Christie, the "Monster of Notting Hill"

John Reginald Halliday Christie, whose crimes created a sensation in post-war London, belonged to another typical class of serial killer: the necrophile. (Henry Lee Lucas and Jeffrey Dahmer are later examples.)

On 24 March 1953, a Jamaican tenant of 10 Rillington Place was sounding the walls in the kitchen on the ground floor, previously occupied by Christie. One wall sounded hollow and the Jamaican pulled off a corner of wallpaper. He discovered that the paper covered a cupboard, one corner of which was missing. He was able to peer into the cupboard with the help of a torch and saw the naked back of a woman. Hastily summoned policemen discovered that the cupboard contained three female bodies. The first was naked except for a brassière and suspender belt; the other two were wrapped in blankets and secured with electric wire. There was very little smell, which was due to atmospheric conditions causing dehydration. (Some of the more sensational accounts of the case state inaccurately that the tenant was led to the discovery by the smell of decomposition.) Floorboards in the front room appeared to have been disturbed, and they were taken up to reveal a fourth body, also wrapped in a blanket.

Christie had left on 20 March, sub-letting to a Mr and Mrs Reilly, who had paid him £7, 13s. in advance. The Reillys had been turned out almost immediately by the owner, a Jamaican, Charles Brown, since Christie had no right to sub-let, and had, in fact, left owing rent.

The back garden was dug up, and revealed human bones – the skeletons of two more bodies. A human femur was being used to prop up the fence.

It was now remembered that in 1949, two other bodies – those of Mrs Evans and her baby daughter Geraldine – had been discovered at the same address. Both had been strangled, and the husband, Timothy Evans, was hanged for the double murder. Evans was a near-mental defective, and it seemed conceivable that the murders for which he was hanged were the work of the man who had killed the women in the downstairs flat.

On 31 March, Christie was recognized by PC Ledger on the embankment near Putney Bridge and was taken to Putney Bridge Police Station. In the week since the discovery of the bodies, the hue and cry had been extraordinary, and newspapers ran pictures of the back garden of 10 Rillington Place and endless speculations about the murders and whether the murderer would commit another sex crime before his arrest. (Mr Alexie Surkov, the secretary of the Soviet league of writers, happened

---

The three doctors called in to pronounce upon Henri Desire Landru's mental condition were agreed upon one thing: the man, despite the ten women he was said to have murdered, was not mad. The first medical expert, Dr. Vallon, faced the crowded court at the lady-killer's trial and stated:

'I already had to examine the accused in 1904, when he was being charged with obtaining money by false pretences. I found him then in a state bordering on the psychopathic, but he was not mad. Perhaps he was on the borderline, but not beyond it. I find now that Landru is perfectly lucid, perfectly conscious of what he is doing. He is quick and alert in his mind. He is easy and facile in repartee. In short, he must be considered responsible for the acts of which he is accused.'

Landru - whose criminal and sexual career had been under police surveillance for some twenty years - was jubilant when he heard this. 'The crimes of which I am accused could only be explained by the most pronounced insanity.' he asserted. 'The doctors say I am sane - therefore I am innocent.'

Said to be 'completely lacking in moral responsibility', Landru displayed an ambivalent attitude towards women, whom he courted like any other men and later killed with a brutal lack of feeling that branded him as a monster without humanity or heart.

'Bluebeards' ? The original Bluebeard, the 15th century Marshal of France, Gilfe de Rais, who fought beside Joan of Arc, was not a killer of women, but of children. Noted because of his glossy blue-black beard, he was a sexual pervert, and also thought he could use the children's blood in the making of gold. But it was the French writer of fairy stories, Charles Perrault, who created the popular version of Bluebeard the lady-killer in the late seventeenth century. One of his more macabre stories tells how a young girl, Fatima, marries the rich landowner Bluebeard, and one day looks into a secret room - to find there the bodies of his previous wives. Although Perrault wrote the tale from the Gallic viewpoint, many countries have similar legends of wife-killers - Cornwall has a story of a giant called Bolster who killed his wives each year by throwing rocks at them. The folk- imagination understands these dark male compulsions to destroy women and also the woman's half-frightened, half-fascinated- attitude towards it.

to be in England at the time, and later commented with irony on the press furore.)

Christie made a statement admitting to the murders of the four women in the house. In it he claimed that his wife had been getting into an increasingly nervous condition because of attacks from the coloured people in the house, and that on the morning of 14 December 1952, he had been awakened by his wife's convulsive movements; she was having some kind of a fit; Christie "could not bear to see her", and strangled her with a stocking. His account of the other three murders – Rita Nelson, aged twenty-five, Kathleen Maloney, aged twenty-six, Hectorina McLennan, aged twenty-six, described quarrels with the women (who were prostitutes) during the course of which Christie strangled them. Later, he also confessed to the murders of the two women in the garden. One was an Austrian girl, Ruth Fuerst, whom Christie claimed he had murdered during sexual intercourse; and Muriel Eady, a fellow employee at the Ultra Radio factory in Park Royal where Christie had worked in late 1944.

A tobacco tin containing four lots of pubic hair was also found in the house.

There were many curious features in the murders. Carbon monoxide was found in the blood of the three women in the cupboard, although not in Mrs Christie's. The three had semen in the vagina; none was wearing knickers, but all had a piece of white material between the legs in the form of a diaper. This has never been satisfactorily explained.

Christie admitted at his trial that his method of murder had been to invite women to his house and to get them partly drunk. They were persuaded to sit in a deck-chair with a canopy, and a gas pipe was placed near the floor and turned on. When the girl lost consciousness from coal-gas poisoning, Christie would strangle her and then rape her. But since the women were prostitutes, it would hardly seem necessary to render them unconscious to have sexual intercourse. One theory to explain this has been advanced by Dr Francis Camps, the pathologist who examined the bodies. He suggests that Christie had reached a stage of sexual incapability where the woman needed to be unconscious before he could possess her. (In Halifax, as a young man, Christie had earned from some girl the derogatory nicknames, "Can't Do It Christie" and "Reggie-No-Dick".)

The body of Rita Nelson was found to be six months' pregnant.

Christie was tried only for the murder of his wife; his trial opened at the Central Committee Court on Monday 22 June 1953, before Mr Justice Finnemore; the Attorney-General, Sir Lionel Heald, led for the Crown; Mr Derek Curtis Bennett, QC defended.

Christie's case history, as it emerged at his trial, was as follows: He was fifty-five years-old at the time of his arrest. He was born in Chester Street, Boothstown, Yorkshire, in April 1898, son of Ernest Christie, a carpet designer. The father was a harsh man who treated his seven children with Victorian sternness and offered no affection. Christie was a weak child, myopic, introverted, and jeered at by his fellow pupils as a "cissy". He had many minor illnesses in his childhood – possibly to compensate for lack of attention. He was in trouble with the police for trivial offences, and was beaten by his father whenever this occurred.

At the age of fifteen (this would be in about 1913) he left school and got a post as a clerk to the Halifax Borough Police. Petty pilfering lost him the job. He then worked in his father's carpet factory; when he was dismissed from there for petty theft, his father threw him out of the house.

Christie was a chronic hypochondriac, a man who enjoyed being ill and talking about his past illnesses. (His first confession starts with an account of his poor health.) In 1915 he suffered from pneumonia. He then went to war, and was mustard-gassed and blown up. He claimed that he was blind for five months and lost his voice for three and a half years. The loss of voice was the psychological effect of hysteria, for there was no physical abnormality to account for it. His voice returned spontaneously at a time of emotional excitement.

Christie claimed that one of the most important events in his childhood was seeing his grandfather's body when he was eight.

In 1920, Christie met his wife Ethel, and they were married in the same year. They had no children. Christie claimed he had no sexual relations with his wife for about two years – which, if true, supports the view of his sexual inadequacy and the inferiority neurosis that afflicted his relations with women. In 1923, he quarrelled with his wife and they separated; he also lost his voice for three months. Details of the life of the Christies between the two wars are not available, except that he was knocked down by a car which did not stop, in 1934, and sustained injuries to the head, the knee and collar-bone. (Christie seems to have been one of those unfortunate people who are born unlucky.) And when he worked for the post office, it was found that he was stealing money and postal orders from letters; for this he received seven months in prison. His longest term of employment was with a transport firm; this lasted for five years.

Duncan Webb, who was not the most reliable of crime-writers, declared that Christie claimed to be a rich man when he married his wife, and that he joined the Conservative Association (presumably in Halifax) and tried to play the man about town. On separating from his wife in 1923, (after a second term in prison for false pretences), he came to London, and lodged in Brixton and Battersea. He struck a woman over the head with a cricket bat, and went to jail again. His wife was induced to visit him, and started to live with him again when he came out.

Jerry Thompson was a rapist. His one and only murder victim was found on the morning of June 17, 1935, in a ditch in the cemetery at Peoria, Illinois. She was a pretty girl, and her white dress had been pulled up under her armpits; her torn underwear lay nearby. The medical report revealed that she had been raped and strangled. She was identified as 19-year-old Mildred Hallmark, a waitress, who had vanished the evening before, shortly after leaving the cafeteria where she worked. When the police appealed for information, several girls came forward, and disclosed that they had also been raped. The attacker was a good-looking young man who had offered them a lift, then driven them to a quiet place and forced them to submit.

The police decided to make a general appeal through the newspapers, asking for all women who had been attacked to come forward, with a promise of complete anonymity. They hoped that one of these women might be able to give them some clue to the identity of the rapist. The response startled them. More than 50 women came forward, and it became clear that the police were looking for a serial rapist.

In many cases he had stopped beside a girl walking along a lonely street and dragged her into the car. If she resisted or - screamed, he silenced her with a violent punch dn the jaw or in the stomach. He would drive to a lonely place, undress the girl, and commit rape. Then he would take out a camera, and take photographs of her naked, sprawled in obscene positions. He would tell the girl that if she told the police her name would appear in the newspapers, and everyone would know what had happened to her. There are few girls who do not prefer privacy to revenge.

In 1939, Christie joined the War Reserve Police, and became known as an officious constable who enjoyed showing his authority and "running in" people for minor blackout offences. His wife often went to visit her family in Sheffield, and it was during one of her visits there that Christie brought Ruth Fuerst back to the house and strangled her. Although in his second confession he mentions strangling her during the act of intercourse, it is almost certain that he somehow persuaded her to inhale gas – perhaps from the square jar of Friar's Balsam, which he covered with a towel, claiming that it was a cure for nose and throat infections; while the victim's head was hidden under the towel, Christie inserted a tube leading from the gas tap. It may be that he only wanted to render the girl unconscious in order to have sexual intercourse, and decided to kill her later to cover up the assault. In his confession he told of hiding Ruth Fuerst's body under the floorboards when his wife returned with her brother. The next day, when they were out, he moved the body to the wash-house and later buried it in the back garden under cover of darkness.

At his trial, Christie declared that he was not sure whether Ruth Fuerst was his first victim. However, unless he had some other place in which to dispose of bodies, it seems probable that his "vagueness" was intended to impress the jury that his mind was wandering.

In December 1943, Christie was released from the War Reserve and went to work at Ultra Radio. Here he became friendly with Muriel Eady, who often came to visit the Christies. On one occasion she came alone when Christie's wife was on holiday, and complained of catarrh. She buried her face in Christie's jar of Friar's Balsam, and later ended, like Ruth Fuerst, buried in the tiny garden.

Whether the Evans Murders were committed by Christie or by Timothy Evans will now never be known, but it seems almost certain that Christie committed them. In his third confession from Brixton prison, he declares that in August 1949, Timothy Evans and his young wife (who lived above the Christies) quarrelled violently about a blonde woman. Christie claimed that he found Mrs Evans lying on the floor in front of the gas fire, having attempted suicide, and that he gave her a cup of tea. The next day he found her there once again, and she asked his help in killing herself, offering to let him have sexual intercourse. He strangled her with a stocking, and (in view of the later cases) probably had intercourse with her. When Timothy Evans came home, Christie told him that his wife had gassed herself and that no doubt Evans would be suspected of her murder. What happened then is not certain. It is possible that Evans then murdered the baby, Geraldine, who was later found with her mother in the wash house. Within a few days he sold his furniture and disappeared. But he then walked into the Merthyr Tydfil police station and claimed that he had killed his wife and put her body down a drain. The bodies were discovered in the wash house, and Evans was charged with murder. At one point, he claimed that Christie was the murderer, but when told that the child's body had also been found, he withdrew this allegation. Evans was of low mentality and illiterate; it is impossible to know what went on in his mind before his execution, or whether he murdered his daughter. What is most surprising is that he did not inform on Christie when he found that his wife was strangled; this makes it seem possible that he had murdered his daughter, and saw no point in involving Christie too.

In December 1952 came the murder of his wife. The motive for this is not clear, although it may well have been a desire to have the house to himself for further murders. Whether or not this was his intention, Christie killed again a few weeks later. Rita Nelson had last been seen alive on 2 January 1953. Hers was the second body in the cupboard. Christie claimed she had accosted him and demanded money, finally forcing herself into his house and starting a fight. What seems more likely is that she came back to the house by his invitation and was gassed as she sat in the deck-chair.

The next victim was Kathleen Maloney, last seen alive on 12 January 1953. Again, Christie claims she started a fight, but this seems unlikely.

Christie had no money at this time, and sold his furniture for £11 and his wife's wedding ring. He had written to his wife's bank in Sheffield, forging her signature, and asked for her money to be sent. (He had also sent a postcard to his wife's sister before Christmas claiming that she had rheumatism in her fingers and could not write.)

Some time in February, Christie claims that he met a couple who told him they had nowhere to stay. The man was out of

ON 2 JUNE 1985, a security guard at South City Lumber in San Francisco observed a young Asian walking out with a vice without stopping at the check-out desk. The guard alerted a policeman, who caught up with the man just as he was putting the vice into the boot of a car. As soon as he saw the policeman, the Asian ran away, and disappeared among the parked cars. An older, bearded man who was bending over the open boot explained that it was all a mistake, and offered to pay for the vice. The policeman insisted on making a routine search of the car, and in a green holdall, discovered a hand gun with a silencer. Since this was against the gun laws of California, the policeman told the bearded man that he would have to accompany him to the station. There, the man handed over his documentation, which gave his name as Robin Stapley, and then asked for a glass of water. When it was handed to him, he popped a small capsule into his mouth, and swallowed it down with the water. A moment later, he slumped forward dead. A check with the fingerprint records revealed that the name of the dead man was, in fact, Leonard Lake, and that he had a criminal record for burglary. Papers found in his wallet led the police to a small ranch at Wilseyville, Calaveras County, a hundred and fifty miles north east of San Francisco. There they discovered a bedroom equipped with chains, shackles, and hooks in the ceiling - it looked ominously like a torture chamber. And in an underground bunker with prison cells, they discovered video tapes that showed young women being sexually abused by Leonard Lake and by his partner, a young Chinaman called Charles Ng. In a trench nearby, police unearthed the remains of eight victims. Eventually, fragments of bone found on the property and photographed in the ranchhouse brought the total to twenty-four, including two small children. It eventually became clear that Lake and Ng had made a habit of luring men and women to the bungalow, and then murdering them work. They came and stayed with Christie for a few days, and then left. Later, the woman – Hectorina McLennan – returned alone, and was murdered by Christie around 3 March. After this, Christie claims he lost his memory and wandered around London (subsequent to 20 March, when he left Rillington Place) sleeping in a Rowton House part of the time. When caught, he was unshaven and shabby, with no money.

The defence was of insanity, but the jury rejected it, following several medical opinions that Christie was sane, and he was sentenced to death and executed on 15 July 1953.

---

**Henry Lee Lucas, the American serial killer, confessed to three hundred and sixty murders, but doubts have been expressed about this figure – although it is certain that his victims ran into dozens. But no one has doubted the record of another killer, Pedro Alonzo Lopez, the "Monster of the Andes", who confessed in 1980 to raping and murdering three hundred and sixty young girls, most of whom were under the age of twelve, in Columbia and Ecuador. He was sentenced to sixteen years in prison, the maximum under Ecuadorian law.**

# • chapter four •

# THE HIGH IQ KILLER

*F*rom Martin Dumollard onward, most serial killers have been curiously stupid – Carl Panzram was one of the few exceptions. But in the second half of the twentieth century, criminologists became aware of a new phenomenon – the "high IQ" killer. Dumollard killed for money; Earle Nelson and Christie killed for sex. But the "high IQ" killer cannot be classified so simply. He has often read books on criminology and psychology, and he may argue lucidly in favour of a life of crime. The "Moors murderer" Ian Brady was of this type; so was the Muswell Hill murderer Dennis Nilsen and the "Hillside Strangler" Kenneth Bianchi.

The emergence of the "high IQ" killer dates from the 1960s. But Brady and Manson were pre-dated by an American case that dates from the late 1950s.

## Melvin Rees

On Sunday, 11 January 1959 an old blue Chevrolet forced another car off a lonely country road in Virginia, and a tall, thin young man with staring eyes advanced on it waving a revolver. He ordered the Jackson family – consisting of Carrol

Jackson, his wife Mildred, and their two children, Susan, aged five, and a baby, Janet – into the boot of his car, and sped off. Carrol Jackson was later found dead in a ditch; underneath him lay Janet, who had also been shot. Two months later, the bodies of Mildred Jackson and Susan were uncovered in Maryland; Mildred Jackson had been strangled with a stocking and Susan battered to death.

Two years earlier, in June 1957, a man with staring eyes had approached a courting couple in a car – an army sergeant and a woman named Margaret Harold – and asked for a lift. On the way he pulled out a gun and demanded money; when Margaret Harold said: "Don't give it to him", he shot her in the back of the head. The sergeant flung open the door and ran. When police found the car, they also found the body of Margaret Harold lying across the front seat without her dress; a police spokesman described the killer as "a sexual degenerate". Near the scene of the crime the police discovered a deserted shack full of pornographic pictures.

Five months after the murders of the Jackson family, in May 1959, the police received an anonymous tip-off that the murderer was a jazz musician named Melvin Rees; but police were unable to trace Rees. Early the following year, a salesman named Glenn Moser went to the police, acknowledged that he was the author of the anonymous tip-off, and told them that he now had the suspect's address: Melvin Rees was working in a music shop in Memphis, Arkansas. Rees was arrested there, and soon after he was identified by the army sergeant as the man who had shot Margaret Harold. A search of the home of Rees's parents uncovered the revolver with which Carrol Jackson had been shot, and a diary describing the abduction of the Jacksons and their murder. "Caught on a lonely road . . . Drove to a select area and killed the husband and baby. Now the mother and daughter were all mine." He described forcing Mildred Jackson to perform oral sex, and then raping her repeatedly; the child was also apparently raped. (Full details have never been released.) He concluded: "I was her master." The diary also described the sex murders of four more girls in Maryland. Rees was executed in 1961.

Violent sex murders were common enough by the late 1950s. What makes this one unique for its period was Rees's "Sadeian" attitude of self-justification. On the night before the Jackson killings, Rees had been on a "benzedrine kick", and in the course of a rambling argument had told Moser: "You can't say it's wrong to kill. Only individual standards make it right or wrong." He had also explained that he wanted to experience everything: love, hate, life, death . . . When, after the murders, Moser asked him outright whether he was the killer, Rees disdained to lie; he simply refused to answer, leaving Moser to draw the self-evident conclusion. Rees was an "intellectual" who, like Moors murderer Ian Brady in the following decade, made the decision to rape and kill on the grounds that "everything is lawful". He may therefore be regarded as one of the first examples of the curious modern phenomenon, the "high IQ killer". His sexual fantasies involved sadism (Mildred Jackson's death had been long and agonising) and power. In that sense, his crimes anticipate those of the serial killer who was to emerge two decades later.

Unfortunately we know nothing of Rees's background, or what turned him into a serial killer. Yet on the basis of other cases, we can state with a fair degree of confidence that parental affection was lacking in childhood, and that he was a lonely introverted child who was not much liked by his schoolmates. It is difficult, if not impossible, to find a case of a serial killer of whom this is not true.

# Werner Boost, the Düsseldorf "Doubles Killer"

7 January, 1953 was a cold, snowy night in Düsseldorf, West Germany. Shortly before midnight, a fair-haired young man, who was bleeding from a head wound staggered into the police station and said that his friend had just been murdered. The "friend", it seemed, was a distinguished lawyer named Dr Lothar Servé. The officer on duty immediately telephoned Kriminal Hauptcommissar Mattias Eynck, chief of the North Rhineland murder squad, who hurried down to the station. The young man had identified himself as Adolf Hullecremer, a

nineteen-year-old student, and explained that he and Dr Servé had been sitting in the car "discussing business", and looking at the lights on the river, when both doors of the car had been jerked open by two men in handkerchief masks. One of the men began to swear, then shot Servé in the head. As Hullecremer begged for his life, the second man whispered that if he wished to stay alive, he should "sham dead". He then hit Hullecremer on the head with a pistol. As he lost consciousness, Hullecremer heard him say: "He won't wake again." When the men had gone, he made off as fast as he could.

After Hullecremer's head had been bandaged, he said he felt well enough to take the police and the doctor back to the car. It was parked in a grove of trees on the edge of the river, its engine still running. Across the rear seat lay the body of a man of about fifty, bleeding from a wound in the temple. The doctor pronounced him dead.

The motive was clearly robbery – the dead man's wallet was missing. Eynck concluded that the robbers were "stick-up men" who had chosen this spot because it was known as a "lovers' lane". The fact that the two men had been in the rear seat when attacked suggested a homosexual relationship.

Forensic examination revealed no fingerprints on the car, and falling snow had obliterated any footprints or other tyre tracks. The murder enquiry had reached an impasse when, a few weeks later, a tramp found a .32 calibre pistol – of Belgian make – in the woods, and forensic tests showed it to be the murder weapon. Photographs of its bullets were sent to all police stations, and the Magdeburg police – in former East Germany – contacted Eynck to say that the same gun had been used in a murder a few years earlier in a town called Hadersleben. Two East Germans attempting to flee to the former West had been shot with the same weapon. This seemed to suggest that the murderer was himself an East German refugee who had moved to Düsseldorf. But there the trail went cold – thousands of East Germans had fled the Communist regime to the large cities of West Germany since the war.

Almost three years later, in October 1955, Eynck found himself wondering whether the double killers had struck again. A young couple had vanished after an evening date. The man was twenty-six-year-old Friedhelm Behre, a baker, and his fiancée was twenty-three-year-old Thea Kurmann. They had

spent the evening of 31 October in a "bohemian" restaurant
called the Cafe Czikos, in the old quarter of Düsseldorf, and
had driven off soon after midnight in Behre's blue Ford. The
next day, worried relatives reported them missing. But there
was no sign of the couple or of the blue car. Four weeks later, a
contractor standing by a half-dredged gravel pit near Düsseldorf
was throwing stones at a metal object when he realized that it
was the top of a blue car. He called some of his men, and
they heaved it ashore. In the back seat lay two decomposing
corpses. They proved to be those of the missing couple, the
girl still dressed in her red satin evening dress, which had been
torn and pulled up.

The medical report revealed that Friedhelm Behre had been
shot through the head at close range. The girl had been
garrotted, possibly by a man's tie, after being raped. It looked
as if the killer had wrenched open the rear door as the couple
were petting, shot the man, then dragged the girl out. After
rape, her body was thrown into the back seat, and the car
driven to the gravel pit, where it was pushed into the water.

To Eynck, this sounded ominously like the Servé murder.
Again, there were no fingerprints – suggesting that the killer
had worn gloves. The bullet had disappeared. It had gone right
through the victim's skull, but it should have been somewhere in
the car. Its absence suggested that the murderer had removed it
to prevent the identification of the gun.

The murder caused panic among Düsseldorf's young lovers,
and over the Christmas period, the usual lay-bys were deserted.
Meanwhile, Chief-Inspector Botte, in charge of the investigation,
quickly found that he had run out of clues.

Three months later, on the morning of 8 February, 1956, a
businessman named Julius Dreyfuss reported that his Mercedes
car was missing – together with its chauffeur, a young man
named Peter Falkenberg. The chauffeur had failed to arrive
to pick up his employer. It seemed possible that Falkenberg
had driven away to sell the expensive car. But an hour or so
later, a woman reported that a black car was parked in front of
her house with its headlights on. It proved to be the missing
Mercedes. And there was a great deal of blood inside – both
in the front and the rear seats.

At about the same time, a woman had reported that her
daughter, twenty-three year old Hildegard Wassing, had failed

to return home after a date. A few days before, Hildegard and a friend had met a young man named Peter at a dance; he had told them he was a chauffeur. Hildegard had agreed to go out with him the following Tuesday, 7 February, and her brother had noticed that he was driving a black Mercedes. To Eynck, it sounded as if Peter Falkenberg and Hildegard Wassing had fallen victim to the "car murderer".

The next morning, a gardener was cycling to work near the small village of Lank-Ilverich, near Düsseldorf, when he saw the remains of a burning haystack some distance from the path. He strolled over to look – and then rushed for the nearest telephone as he saw the remains of two corpses among the burnt hay.

Eynck arrived soon after, and noticed the smell of petrol. Both bodies were badly charred, but rain had prevented the fire from totally incinerating them. Forensic examination revealed that the man – identified from dental charts as Peter Falkenberg – had been shot through the head. Hildegard Wassing had been raped and then strangled – the rope was still sunk in the burnt flesh.

Thousands of Düsseldorf residents were questioned, but once again, there were no obvious leads. The car killer was evidently a man who took great care to leave no clues. Then a detective named Bohm came upon a possible suspect. In the small town of Buderich, not far from the burnt haystack, he was told of a young man named Erich von der Leyen, who had once attacked some children with a manure fork, and was regarded as a "loner" by his neighbours. He was originally from East Germany, and now lived in lodgings in a place called Veert. Von der Leyen worked as a travelling salesman for agricultural machinery, so his log-book should have shown precisely where he was when the couple were murdered. But the entry for 7 February had been made later, and the travelling times for drives seemed implausible. Moreover, there were red spots on the front seat-covers. These were sent for forensic examination, and were reported to be human bloodstains. Erich von der Leyen was placed under arrest. Stains on his trousers also proved to be blood.

Von der Leyen insisted that he had no idea where the stains came from – the only way he could account for them was to recall that his girlfriend's dachsund had been in his car when it was on heat. That sounded unlikely. The police asked another

forensic expert to examine the bloodstains on the trousers, and **421**
see if he could determine their age. Under the microscope, he
saw epithelial cells – evidence that it *was* menstrual blood. The
stains on the car seat were re-tested, and the laboratory admitted
with embarrassment that these were also of menstrual blood –
and, moreover, from a dog. The police had to release von der
Leyen, and to apologize for the intense interrogations he had
endured.

Soon after this, on the evening of 6 June, 1956, a forest
ranger named Erich Spath was walking through woods near
Meererbusch, not far from the burnt haystack site, when he saw
a man lurking in the undergrowth, and peering from behind a
tree at a car in which a courting couple were petting. The man
was so absorbed that he did not hear the ranger. Then Spath
saw him draw a revolver from his pocket, and creep towards
the car.

Spath placed his rifle to his shoulder and crept up behind
the young man. "Drop it!" The man turned round, then threw
away his gun and ran. Spath chased him and soon caught up
with him, crouching in a hollow.

Half an hour later, the car with the courting couple – and
also containing the ranger and his captive – pulled up in front
of Düsseldorf's main police station. The suspect – who was dark
and good-looking – had accompanied them without protest and
without apparent concern, as if his conscience was clear. And
when they stood in the office of Kriminal Hauptkommissar
Mattias Eynck, Spath understood why. The young man –
who gave his name as Werner Boost – explained that he had
merely been doing a little target practice in the woods, and had
thought *he* was being attacked. He obviously felt that no one
could disprove his story and that therefore the police would be
unable to hold him.

"Is your gun licensed?" asked Eynck.

"Well . . . no. It's a war trophy . . ."

"In that case, I am charging you with possessing an illegal
weapon."

The gun was found in the undergrowth where Boost had
thrown it. Nearby was a motor cycle, which proved to have
been stolen. Boost was also charged with its theft. A magistrate
promptly sentenced him to six months in jail, which gave Eynck
the time he needed to investigate the suspect.

At first the trail seemed to be leading nowhere. The pistol had not been used in any known crime; Boost was, as he said, an electrical engineer who worked in a factory, and who was regarded as a highly intelligent and efficient worker; he had been married for six years, had two children, and was a good husband and provider. His wife, Hanna, told Eynck that he spent most of his evenings at home, working in his own laboratory or reading – he was an obsessive reader. Occasionally, she admitted, he became restless and went out until the early hours of the morning.

She led Eynck down to the basement laboratory. There he discovered various ingredients for explosives, as well as some deadly poison. He also found a quantity of morphine.

Back in the flat, Eynck noticed a letter postmarked Hadersleben. He recalled that the Belgian pistol, which had been found within a few hundred yards of Boost's flat, had been used in a double murder in Hadersleben, near Magdeburg. "Do you know someone in Hadersleben?" he asked. Hanna Boost told him that it was her home town, and that she had married her husband there.

"How did you both escape from East Germany?"

"Werner knew a safe route through the woods."

But she insisted that, as far as she knew, her husband had never owned a gun.

Now, at last, the case was beginning to look more promising. Back in his office, Eynck looked through the latest batch of information about Boost, which had come from a town called Helmstedt, which had been taken over by the Russians in 1945. And at about this period, there had been a great many murders – about fifty in all – of people trying to escape from the Russian to the British zone. Werner Boost had been in Helmstedt at the time. Then he had moved to Hadersleben, and the murders had ceased. But the two would-be emigrés had been shot in Hadersleben while trying to escape . . .

There was another interesting item – a notebook which had been found in the saddle of Boost's stolen motorcycle. And it contained an entry: "Sunday, 3 June. Lorbach in need of another shot. Must attend to it."

Eynck sent for Boost and questioned him about the item. Boost said smoothly:

"Frank Lorbach is a friend of mine, and we go shooting

together. On that day, he just couldn't hit the bull's eye, so **423** I made a note to give him another shot."

Eynck did not believe a word of it. He asked Boost about his days in Helmstedt, and whether he had ever helped refugees to escape. Boost admitted that he had, and said he was proud of it. "And did you ever shoot them?" Boost looked horrified. "Of course not!"

Eynck now sent out one of his detectives to try to locate Franz Lorbach. This was not difficult. Lorbach proved to be a man of twenty-three with dark curly hair, whose good looking face lacked the strength of Werner Boost's. He was a locksmith, and insisted that he only had the most casual acquaintance with Boost. Eynck knew that he was lying. He also noticed Lorbach's dilated pupils, and surmised that he was a drug addict, and that Boost was his supplier. He was certain that, when his craving became strong enough, Lorbach would talk. He held him in custody for questioning.

Meanwhile, Boost and Lorbach were placed in a police line-up, wearing handkerchief masks over the lower half of their faces. Adolf Hullecremer, the student who had been with Dr Servé when he was shot, was able to identify Boost as Serve's assailant. He said he recognized the eyes. But he failed to identify Lorbach.

After a day or two in custody, Lorbach began to show symptoms of withdrawal from drugs. And one day, as Eynck was questioning Boost again – and getting nowhere – he received a phone call saying that Lorbach wanted to talk to him.

Lorbach was pale, his eyes were watery, and his nose twitched like a rabbit's.

"I want to tell you the truth. Werner Boost is a monster. It *was* he who killed Dr Servé, and I was his accomplice . . ."

Lorbach admitted that it was a love of poaching that had drawn the two of them together in 1952. They often went shooting in the woods. But Boost seemed to have a maniacal hatred of courting couples. "These sex horrors are the curse of Germany." So they would often creep up on couples who were making love in cars and rob them. Then, he said, Boost had an idea for rendering them unconscious. He had concocted some mixture which he forced them to drink. Then he and Lorbach would rape the unconscious girls. "Some of them were very lovely. I feel ashamed – my wife is going to have a baby. But it was Boost who made me do it. I had to do it. He kept me supplied with morphine, which he obtained from the chemist who sold him chemicals."

He insisted that he had taken part only in the attack on Servé and Hullecremer. Boost had been indignant to see two men in a car together, and had ordered him to kill the young man. But Lorbach had not the stomach for it. Instead, he had whispered to him to pretend to be dead. Lorbach's failure to shoot Hullecremer enraged Boost – he made Lorbach kneel in the snow, and said: "I ought to kill you too . . ."

Lorbach led the police to a place at the edge of the forest, where Boost kept his loot concealed. In a buried chest, they found watches, rings and jewellery. There were also bottles of poison, some knives, and a roll of cord which proved to be identical to that which had been used to strangle Hildegard Wassing.

Lorbach also disclosed that Boost had ordered Lorbach to kill his wife, Hanna Boost, if he was arrested. There was a phial of cyanide hidden behind a pipe in his flat, and Lorbach was to slip it into her drink, so that she could not incriminate her husband. Eynck found the phial exactly where Lorbach had said it was.

Lorbach also confirmed that he and Boost had been involved in an earlier attempt at crime, a year before the murder of Dr Servé. The two men had placed a heavy plank studded with long nails across the road, to force motorists to stop. But the first car to come along had contained four men – too many for them to tackle – and it had driven on to the verge and around the plank. Two more cars also contained too many passengers. Then a security van came, and a man with a gun removed the plank. After that, police arrived – evidently alerted by one of the cars – and Boost and Lorbach had to flee. In fact, as long ago as 1953, Eynck had suspected that Dr Servé's murderer' was responsible for this earlier attempt.

Lorbach also detailed Boost's plans to rob a post office by knocking everyone unconscious with poison gas, and to kidnap and murder a child of a rich industrialist for ransom.

On 11 December, 1956, Boost was charged with the murders of Dr Servé, Friedhelm Behre, Thea Kurmann, Peter Falkenberg and Hildegard Wassing. But when Lorbach, the main prosecution witness, suffered a nervous breakdown due to drug problems, the trial had to be postponed. Meanwhile,

Boost was extradited to Magdeburg for questioning about the
murder of the couple at Hadersleben. But he stonewalled
his questioners as he had tried to stonewall the Düsseldorf
police, and was finally returned to Eynck's jurisdiction with
no additional charges against him.

Boost's trial began in the courthouse at Düsseldorf on 3
November, 1961, before Judge Hans Naecke, two associate
magistrates, Dr Warda and Dr Schmidt, and a six man jury. Boost
maintained his total innocence, and his lawyer, Dr Koehler, lost
no time in pointing out that the testimony of a drug addict like
Franz Lorbach was hardly reliable. Lorbach himself was a poor
witness, who mumbled and became confused. But he was able to
tell one story that strengthened the case against Boost. Lorbach
confessed that Boost had blackmailed him – by threatening
withdrawal of his drug supply – into taking part in another
attack on a couple. They had held up two lovers in the woods.
Boost had tried to kill the man, but the gun had misfired. The
girl had run away screaming, and Boost had ordered Lorbach
to catch her. Lorbach had done so – but then whispered to her
to lie low for a while. When he returned, Boost had knocked the
man unconscious – but Lorbach had warned him there was a
car coming, and they had roared away on Boost's motorbike.

Eynck told the court that he had traced this couple, and that
they had confirmed the story in every detail. They were not
married – at least not to one another – which is why they had
failed to report the incident. But Eynck was able to offer their
deposition in evidence.

Boost's lawyer counter-attacked by pointing out that there
had recently been a murder of a couple in a car near Cologne,
and that Boost was obviously not guilty of this crime.

After a month of listening to this and similar evidence, the
six jurors decided that the evidence that Boost had murdered
the two couples was insufficient. But they found him guilty of
murdering Dr Servé. He was sentenced to life imprisonment,
and Lorbach to three years, as his accomplice – much of which
he had already served. Boost's sentence was exactly the same
as if he had been found guilty on all charges.

# Lucian Staniak, the "Red Spider"

For criminologists, one of the most frustrating things about the Iron Curtain was that it was virtually impossible to learn whether its police were facing the same types of crimes as in the west. But in the late 1960s, accounts of the "Red Spider" case made it clear that communist regimes also spawned serial killers.

In July 1964, the communist regime in Poland was getting prepared to celebrate the twentieth anniversary of the liberation of Warsaw by Russian troops; a great parade was due to take place in Warsaw on the 22nd. On the 4 July the editor of *Przeglad Polityczny*, the Polish equivalent of *Pravda*, received an anonymous letter in spidery red handwriting: "There is no happiness without tears, no life without death. Beware! I am going to make you cry." Marian Starzynski thought the anonymous writer had him in mind, and requested police protection. But on the day of the big parade, a seventeen-year-old blonde, Danka Maciejowitz, failed to arrive home from a parade organized by the School of Choreography and Folklore in Olsztyn, one hundred and sixty miles north of Warsaw. The next day, a gardener in the Olsztyn Park of Polish Heroes discovered the girl's body in some shrubbery. She had been stripped naked and raped, and the lower part of her body was covered with Jack-the-Ripper-type mutilations. And the following day, the 24th, another red-ink letter was delivered to *Kulisy*, a Warsaw newspaper: "I picked a juicy flower in Olsztyn and I shall do it again somewhere else, for there is no holiday without a funeral."

The first group of organized serial killers in history were the Hindu "thugs" (pronounced "tugs"), from whom we derive our modern word "thug". When the British annexed India in the late eighteenth century the conquerors noted that the roads were infested with bands of robbers who strangled their victims. It became slowly apparent that the killing was, in fact, a religious ceremony, and that the Thugs killed people – often a whole caravan-load consisting of dozens – as a sacrifice to the black goddess Kali. The bodies were mutilated, then buried. In 1829, a British army captain, William Sleeman, organized the suppression of Thuggee, so that within twenty years it had virtually ceased to exist.

Analysis of the ink showed that it had been made by dissolving red art paint in turpentine.

On 16 January 1965, the Warsaw newspaper *Zycie Warsawy* published the picture of a pretty sixteen-year-old girl, Aniuta Kaliniak, who had been chosen to lead a parade of students in another celebration rally the following day. She left her home in Praga, an eastern suburb of Warsaw, and crossed the river Vistula to reach the parade. Later, she thumbed a lift from a lorry driver, who dropped her close to her home at a crossroads. (The fact that a sixteen-year-old girl would thumb a lift like this indicates that the level of sex crime in Poland must be a great deal lower than in England or the US.) The day after the parade, her body was found in a basement in a leather factory opposite her home. The killer had removed a grating to get in. The crime had obviously been carefully planned. He had waited in the shadows of the wall, and cut off her cry with a wire noose drooped over her head. In the basement, he had raped her, and left a six-inch spike sticking in her sexual organs (an echo of the Boston Strangler). While the search went on another red-ink letter advised the police where to look for her body.

Olsztyn and Warsaw are one hundred and sixty miles apart; this modern Ripper differed from his predecessor in not sticking to the same area. Moreover, like Klaus Gosmann, he was a man with a strong dramatic sense: the selection of national holidays for his crimes, the letter philosophising about life and death.

The Red Spider – as he had come to be known, from his spidery writing – chose All Saints day, 1 November, for his next murder, and Poznan, one hundred and twenty-four miles west of Warsaw, as the site. A young, blonde hotel receptionist Janka Popielski, was on her way to look for a lift to a nearby village, where she meant to meet her boyfriend. Since it was her holiday, the freight terminal was almost deserted. Her killer pressed a chloroform-soaked bandage over her nose and mouth. Then he removed her skirt, stockings and panties, and raped her behind a packing shed. After this, he killed her with a screwdriver. The mutilations were so thorough and revolting that the authorities suppressed all details. The Red Spider differed from many sex killers in apparently being totally uninterested in the upper half of his victims. Janka was stuffed into a packing case, where she was discovered an hour later. The police swooped on all trains and buses leaving Poznan, looking for a man with bloodstained clothes; but they failed to find one. The next day, the Poznan newspaper *Courier Zachodni* received one of the now-notorious letters in red ink, containing a quotation from Stefan Zeromsky's national epic *Popioly* (1928): "Only tears of sorrow can wash out the stain of shame; only pangs of suffering can blot out the fires of lust."

May Day, 1966, was both a communist and a national holiday. Marysia Galazka, seventeen, went out to look for her cat in the quiet suburb of Zoliborz, in northern Warsaw. When she did not return, her father went out to look for her. He found her lying in the typical rape position, with her entrails forming an abstract pattern over her thighs, in a tool shed behind the house. Medical evidence revealed that the killer had raped her before disembowelling her.

Major Ciznek, of the Warsaw Homicide Squad, was in charge of the case, and he made a series of deductions. The first was that the Red Spider was unlikely to confine himself to his well-publicized murders on national holidays. Such killers seek victims when their sexual desire is at maximum tension, not according to some preconceived timetable. Ciznek examined evidence of some fourteen other murders that had taken place since the first one in April 1964, one each in Lublin, Radom, Kielce, Lodz, Bialystock, Lomza, two in Bydgoszcz, five in the Poznan district. All places were easily reached by railway; the *modus operandi* was always the same. Every major district of Poland within two hundred and forty-eight miles of Warsaw was covered. Ciznek stuck pins in a map and examined the result. It looked as if Warsaw might be the home of the killer, since the murders took place all round it. But one thing was noticeable. The murders extended much farther south than north, and there were also more of them to the south. It rather looked as if the killer had gone to Bialystock, Lomza and Olsztyn as a token gesture of extending his boundaries. Assuming, then, that the killer lived somewhere south of Warsaw, where would this be most likely to be? There were five murders in the Poznan district, to the west of Warsaw. Poznan is, of course, easily reached from Warsaw. But where in the south could it be reached from just as easily? Cracow was an obvious choice. So was Katowice, twenty miles or so from Cracow. This town was also at the centre of a network of railway lines.

On Christmas Eve, 1966, Cracow was suddenly ruled out as a

Three service men getting on a train between Cracow **429**
and Warsaw looked into a reserved compartment and found the
half naked and mutilated corpse of a girl on the floor. The leather
miniskirt had been slashed to pieces; so had her abdomen and
thighs. The servicemen notified the guard, and a message was
quickly sent to Warsaw, who instructed the traindriver to go
straight through to Warsaw, non-stop, in case the killer managed
to escape at one of the intervening stations. A careful check of
passengers at Warsaw revealed no one stained with blood or
in any way suspicious. But the police were able to locate the
latest letter from the killer, dropped into the post slot of the
mail van on top of all the others. It merely said: "I have done
it again," and was addressed to *Zycie Warsawy*. It looked as if
the Red Spider had got off the train in Cracow, after killing the
girl, and dropped the letter into the slot.

The girl was identified as Janina Kozielska, of Cracow. And the
police recalled something else: another girl named Kozielska had
been murdered in Warsaw in 1964. This proved to be Janina's
sister Aniela. For Ciznek, this ruled out Cracow as the possible
home of the killer. For he would be likely to avoid his home
territory. Moreover, there surely had to be some connection
between the murders of two sisters . . . The compartment on
the Cracow-Warsaw train had been booked over the telephone
by a man who said his name was Stanislav Kozielski, and that
his wife would pick up the tickets. Janina had paid 1,422 zloty
for them – about twenty-five pounds. Janina had come to
the train alone and been shown to her compartment by the
ticket inspector. She said that her husband would be joining
her shortly. The inspector had also checked a man's ticket a
few moments later, but could not recall the man. It was fairly
clear, then, that the Red Spider knew the girl well enough to
persuade her to travel with him as his wife, and had probably
paid for the ticket. He had murdered her in ten minutes or so,
and then hurried off the train.

Ciznek questioned the dead girl's family. They could not suggest who might have killed their daughter, but they mentioned
that she sometimes worked as a model – as her sister had. She
worked at the School of Plastic Arts and at a club called The
Art Lovers Club.

Ciznek recollected that the red ink was made of artist's paint
dissolved in turpentine and water; this looked like a lead.

The Art Lovers Club proved to have one hundred and eighteen members. For an Iron Curtain country, its principles were remarkably liberal; many of its members painted abstract, tachiste and pop-art pictures. Most of them were respectable professional men – doctors, dentists, officials, newspapermen. And one of them came from Katowice. His name was Lucian Staniak, and he was a twenty-six-year-old translator who worked for the official Polish publishing house. Staniak's business caused him to travel a great deal – in fact, he had bought an *ulgowy bilet*, a train ticket that enabled him to travel anywhere in Poland.

Ciznek asked if he could see Staniak's locker. It confirmed his increasing hope that he had found the killer. It was full of knives – used for painting, the club manager explained. Staniak daubed the paint on with a knife blade. He liked to use red paint. And one of his paintings, called "The Circle of Life", showed a flower being eaten by a cow, the cow being eaten by a wolf, the wolf being shot by a hunter, the hunter being killed by a car driven by a woman, and the woman lying with her stomach ripped open in a field, with flowers sprouting from her body.

Ciznek now knew he had his man, and he telephoned the Katowice police. They went to Staniak's address at 117 Aleje Wyzwolenia, but found no one at home. In fact, Staniak was out committing another murder – his last. It was a mere month after the train murder – 31 January 1967 – but he was impatient at the total lack of publicity given to the previous murder. So he took Bozhena Raczkiewicz, an eighteen-year-old student from the Lodz Institute of Cinematographic Arts, to a shelter built at the railway station for the use of stranded overnight travellers, and there stunned her with a vodka bottle. In accordance with his method when in a hurry, he cut off her skirt and panties with his knife. He had killed her in a few minutes between 6 o'clock and 6.25. The neck of the broken bottle had a clear fingerprint on it.

Staniak was picked up at dawn the next day; he had spent the night getting drunk. His fingerprints matched those on the bottle. He was a good-looking young man of twenty-six. And when he realized that there was no chance of escape, he confessed fully to twenty murders. He told the police that his parents and sister had been crossing an icy road when they were hit by a skidding car, being driven too fast by the young wife of a Polish Air Force pilot. The girl had been acquitted of careless driving. Staniak had seen the picture of his first victim in a newspaper, and thought she looked like the wife of the pilot; this was his motive in killing her. He had decided against killing the wife of the pilot because it would be traced back to him.

Sentenced to death for six of the murders – the six described here – Staniak was later reprieved and sent to the Katowice asylum for the criminally insane.

The Soviet Union always played down its crime figures, insisting that crime was largely a problem for the wicked Capitalist west, although in the mid-1980s, the Tass News Agency admitted that a man would go on trial in the city of Vitebsk for the murder of thirty-three women. But in April 1992, in the new Russia, Andrei Chikatilo, a fifty-six-year-old teacher of literature, went on trial in Moscow for murdering fifty-three children – eleven boys and forty-two girls – at Rostov over a twelve-year period. Chikatilo admitted that he lured his victims into the woods, tied them to trees and stabbed them between the eyes, after which he sliced up the bodies and ate the flesh. After three months in prison in 1984 for theft of State property, he made up for lost time by killing eight people in one month. A convicted rapist was mistakenly executed for one of Chikatilo's crimes.

# chapter five

# THREE BRITISH CASES

Compared to America, or even Germany, France and Italy, Great Britain has had few cases of serial murder. In fact, compared to America, England's murder rate is absurdly low. Until well into the 1960s it was a mere 150 a year, compared to America's 10,000. (America's population is about three times that of England.) By the 1990s, England's murder rate has risen to around 700 a year; America's was 23,000. (Los Angeles alone has more murders per year than the whole of Great Britain.)

It seems odd, then, that in spite of its low murder rate, Britain has produced three of the most horrific cases of serial murder of the twentieth century.

The first of these has become known simply as the Moors Murder Case.

## The Moors Murder Case

Between July 1963 and October 1965, Ian Brady and his mistress Myra Hindley collaborated on five child murders. They were finally arrested because they tried to involve Myra's brother-in-law, David Smith, in one of the murders, and he went to the police.

In 1922 America produced a classic triangle case, with comic variations. On the night of August 22nd neighbours of the Oesterreich family in Los Angeles heard guinshots and screams. The police found Mrs. Walburga Oesterreich in hysterics, and her husband dead upon the floor. Questioned, she said they had returned from an evening out to find an intruder in the house. Her husband had grappled with him, and been shot.

Fred, a 60-year-old sewing-machine factory owner, proved to be a millionaire. While his wife was winding up his business affairs, the police became increasing sceptical of her story; finally, they arrested her on suspicion. Mrs. Oesterreich sent for her lawyer, and told him that her ne'er-do-well 'half brother' was living in the attic at her home; would he go along and legally evict him?

The lawyer duly went to the house, climbed the stairs, and tapped on a trapdoor in Walburga's bedroom ceiling. There was a short wait, then out stepped a small, shy-looking man, who identified himself as Otto Sanhuber. Inspired by the lawyer's friendly manner, Sanhuber poured out the true version of Fred Oesterreich's death and the incredible account of a 19-year-old love affair, in which he had lived in the attic of the Oesterreich's house, emerging to raid the icebox and make love to Walburga.

The story began in 1903, when Walburga was 36. Her 41-year-old husband was a drunk, and unpleasant with it. One day Otto - then a 17-year-old mechanic - called at the Oesterreich home to repair Walburga's sewing machine. They were attracted to each other, and he soon became her lover. Fred suspected that his wife was 'seeing someone', and had her followed by a private detective. Mrs. Oesterreich found out about this, and in a fury threatened to leave her husband - who quickly gave way and apologized. However, Walburga knew that her lover would have to stop his visits altogether. Either that, or he must move into the house for good.

The psychology of women who kill is one of the most fascinating subjects in the whole field of criminology, for, on the whole, women are not inclined to crimes of violence. At present, women form a negligible percentage of all criminals - well under 10%.

It *is* true that crimes of violence among adolescent girls - mostly from slum areas - more than doubled in the first three years of the 1970s, but there is no sign of a general rise. And, in spite of overcrowding in the big cities which always produces a rise in the crime rate - it seems unlikely that female crime will ever become a serious social problem.

The reason is obvious; woman's basic instinct is for a home and security, and someone who values security will think twice about doing anything to jeopardize it. Man, with his more restless desires, his wider sense of purpose, is more likely to take risks, including crime.

What about the women who do commit crimes - particularly the most serious crime of all, murder? The first noticeable thing in considering a cross-section of such women is that so many of them are sexually unattractive, often downright ugly. There *are* cases of pretty criminals - Marie de Brinvilliers, Ruth Ellis, Sharon Kinne - but they are rarities. Most murderesses are physically unattractive, highly dominant, and highly sexed. And this immediately explains why they take to crime, for *all* crime springs out of frustration - from the drunken husband who batters the baby to the company director who embezzles millions.

Ian Brady, who was twenty-seven at the time of his arrest, was a typical social misfit. The illegitimate son of a Glasgow waitress, he was brought up in a slum area of Clydeside. Until the age of eleven he seems to have been a good student; then he was sent to a "posh" school, together with a number of other re-housed slum boys, and began to develop a resentment towards the better-off pupils. From then on he took to petty crime; his first appearance in court was at the age of thirteen, on a charge of housebreaking. He had served four years on probation for more burglaries when he moved to Manchester to live with his mother and a new stepfather in 1954. As a result of another theft he was sentenced to a year in Borstal. Back in Manchester, he went back on the dole. It was a dull life in a small house, and he seems to have been glad to get a job as a stock clerk at Millwards, a chemical firm, when he was twenty-one.

It was at this point that he became fascinated by the Nazis and began collecting books about them. They fed his fantasies of power. So did his discovery of the ideas of the Marquis de Sade, with his philosophy of total selfishness and his daydreams of torture. It becomes clear in retrospect that Brady always had a streak of sadism. A childhood friend later described how he had dropped a cat into a deep hole in a graveyard and sealed it up with a stone. When the friend moved the stone to check on his story, the cat escaped.

For Brady, the Nazis represented salvation from mediocrity and boredom, while de Sade justified his feeling that most people are contemptible. Brady particularly liked the idea that society is corrupt, and that God is a lie invented by priests to keep the poor in a state of subjugation. Stifled by ennui, seething with resentment, Brady was like a bomb that is ready to explode by the time he was twenty-three.

It was at this time that a new typist came to work in the office. Eighteen-year-old Myra Hindley was a normal girl from a normal family background, a Catholic convert who loved animals and children, and favoured blonde hair-styles and bright lipstick. She had been engaged, but broken it off because she found the boy immature. Brady had the sullen look of a delinquent Elvis Presley, and within weeks, Myra was in love. Brady ignored her, probably regarding her as a typical working-class moron. Her diary records: "I hope he loves me and will marry me some day." When he burst into profanity after losing a bet she was deeply shocked. It was almost a year later, at the firm's Christmas party in 1961, that he offered to walk her home, and asked her out that evening. When he took her home, she declined to allow him into the house – she lived with her grandmother – but a week later, after another evening out, she surrendered her virginity on her gran's settee. After that, he spent every Saturday night with her.

Myra found her lover marvellously exciting and sophisticated. He wore black shirts, read "intellectual" books, and was learning German. He introduced her to German wine, and she travelled as a pillion passenger on his motorbike. He talked to her about the Nazis, and liked to call her Myra Hess (a combination of a famous pianist and Hitler's deputy). He also introduced her to the ideas of the Marquis de Sade, and set out converting her to atheism, pointing out the discrepancies in the gospels – it did not take long to demolish her faith. He also talked to her a great deal about his favourite novel, *Compulsion* by Meyer Levin, a fictionalized account of the Leopold and Loeb murder case.

It was in July 1963 – according to her later confession – that he first began to talk to her about committing "the perfect murder", and suggesting that she should help him. In her "confession" (to Chief Superintendent Peter Topping) she alleges that Brady blackmailed her by threatening to harm her grandmother, and by showing her some pornographic photographs of her that he had taken on an occasion when he had slipped a drug into her wine. The photographs certainly exist – thirty of them – some showing them engaged in sexual intercourse and wearing hoods. (These were taken with a time-lapse camera.) Emlyn Williams, who saw them, states that some show keen pleasure on their faces, which would seem to dispose of Myra's claim that they were taken when she was unconscious. Whether or not she was telling the truth about blackmail, it seems clear that Brady could have persuaded her to do anything anyway.

In her confession to Chief Inspector Peter Topping (published in 1989 in his book *Topping*), she described how, on 12 July 1963, she and Brady set out on their first "murder hunt". By now Myra Hindley owned a broken-down van. She was sent ahead in the van, with Brady following behind on his motorbike. Her job was to pick up a girl and offer her a lift. The first child they saw was Myra's next-door neighbour, so she drove past her. The second was sixteen-year-old Pauline Reade, who was on her way to a

dance. Myra offered her a lift, and she accepted. In the van,
Myra explained that she was on her way to Saddleworth Moor
to look for a glove she had lost at a picnic. If Pauline would like
to come and help her search, she would give her a pile of records
in the back of the van. Pauline was delighted to accept.

Once on the moor, Brady arrived on his motorbike, and was
introduced as Myra's boyfriend. Then Brady and Pauline went
off to look for the glove. (Since it was July it was still daylight.)
By the time Brady returned to the car, it was dark. He led Myra to
the spot where Pauline Reade's body was lying. Her throat had
been cut, and her clothes were in disarray; Myra accepted that
Brady had raped her. That, after all, had been the whole point
of the murder. Together they buried the body, using a spade
they had brought with them. Brady told her that at one point
Pauline was struggling so much that he had thought of calling
for her to hold the girl's hands – clearly, he had no doubt that
she would co-operate. On the way home, they passed Pauline's
mother and brother, apparently searching for her. Back at home,
Brady burned his bloodstained shoes and trousers.

In an open letter to the press in January 1990, Brady was to
contradict Myra Hindley's account; he insisted that injuries to
the nose and forehead of Pauline Reade had been inflicted by
her, and that she had also committed some form of lesbian
assault on Pauline Reade. According to Brady, Myra participated
actively and willingly in the murders.

Five months later, Brady was ready for another murder. On
Saturday 23 November, 1963 they hired a car – the van had been
sold – and drove to nearby Ashton market. There, according
to Myra, Brady got into conversation with a twelve-year-old
boy, John Kilbride, and told him that, "If Jack would help
them look for a missing glove, he would give him a bottle of
sherry he had won in the raffle". Because Myra was present,
John Kilbride accompanied them without suspicion. They
drove up to Saddleworth Moor, and the boy unsuspectingly
accompanied Brady into the darkness. Myra Hindley claims
that she drove around for a while, and that when she came
back and flashed her lights, Brady came out of the darkness
and told her that he had already buried the body. He also
mentioned taking the boy's trousers down and giving him a
slap on the buttocks. In fact, Myra said, she was fairly certain
that he had raped John Kilbride. He had explained that he had

strangled him because the knife he had was too blunt to cut his throat.

In June the following year – in 1964 – Brady told her he was "ready to do another one". (Like all serial killers he had a "cooling-off period" – in this case about six months.) According to Myra, he told her that committing a murder gave him a feeling of power. By now they had their own car, a Mini. On 16 June, 1964 she stopped her car and asked a twelve-year-old boy, Keith Bennett, if he would help her load some boxes from an off-licence; like John Kilbride, Keith Bennett climbed in unsuspectingly. The murder was almost a carbon copy of the previous one; Keith Bennett was strangled and buried on Saddleworth Moor. Brady admitted this time that he had raped him, and added: "What does it matter?" Keith Bennett's body has never been found.

On Boxing Day, 1965, Brady and Hindley picked up a ten-year-old girl, Lesley Ann Downey, at a fairground at Ancoats. Myra Hindley had taken her grandmother to visit an uncle. They took the child back to the house, and Brady switched on a tape recorder. Myra claims she was in the kitchen with the dogs when she heard the child screaming. Brady was ordering her to take

---

No criminologist has so far succeeded in explaining why so many serial killers have emerged in the second half of the twentieth century. One thing seems clear: that in the past, such crimes were almost invariably committed by tyrants like Ivan the Terrible, or wealthy perverts like the French child murderer Gilles de Rais. The explanation that suggests itself is that the advance of civilisation has raised the general level of comfort so that large numbers of people have a security that was almost-unknown in the ancient world. Millions of people are now able to enjoy the kind of leisure that would have been envied by Greek tyrants or Roman emperors. The trouble is that leisure and comfort also produce boredom, a desire for sensation, and this seems to explain why an increasing number of criminals have come to behave like Ivan the Terrible or Gilles de Rais.

off her coat and squeezing her by the back of the neck. Then Lesley's hands were tied with a handkerchief and Brady set up the camera and a bright light. The child was ordered to undress, and Brady then made her assume various pornographic poses while he filmed her. At this point, Myra claims she was ordered to go and run a bath; she stayed in the bathroom until the water became cold. When she went back into the bedroom, Lesley had been strangled, and there was blood on her thighs – from which Myra realized that she had been raped. At 8 o'clock that evening they took the body up to Saddleworth Moor and buried it.

In his open letter to the press in January 1990, Ian Brady denied that Myra had played no active part in the murder of Lesley Ann Downey. "She insisted upon killing Lesley Ann Downey with her own hands, using a two-foot length of silk cord, which she later used to enjoy toying with in public, in the secret knowledge of what it had been used for."

In October 1965, Brady decided it was time for another murder. He had also decided that he needed another partner in crime, and that Myra's seventeen-year-old brother-in-law, David Smith, was the obvious choice. Smith had already been in trouble with the law. He seemed unable to hold down a job. His wife was pregnant for the second time, and they had just been given an eviction notice. So Smith listened with interest when Brady suggested a hold-up at an Electricity Board showroom. On 6 October Smith came to the house hoping to borrow some money, but they were all broke. Brady suggested: "We'll have to roll a queer." An hour later, Brady picked up a seventeen-year-old homosexual, Edward Evans, and invited him back to the house in Hattersley. Back at the flat, Myra went off to fetch David Smith. They had only just returned when there was a crash from the living room. Brady was rolling on the floor, grappling with Evans. Then he seized an axe and struck him repeatedly: "Everywhere was one complete pool of blood." When Evans lay still, Brady strangled him. Then he handed the bloodstained hatchet to Smith, saying "Feel the weight of that". His motive was obviously to get Smith's fingerprints on the haft. Together, they mopped up the blood and wrapped up the body in polythene. Then Smith went home, promising to return the next day to help dispose of the body. But Brady had miscalculated. Smith might feel in theory that "people are like maggots, small, blind and worthless", but the

440 fact of murder was too much for him. When he arrived home he was violently sick and told his wife what had happened. Together they decided to phone the police, creeping downstairs armed with a screwdriver and carving-knife in case Brady was waiting for them. The following morning, a man dressed as a baker's roundsman knocked at Brady's door, and when Myra opened it, identified himself as a police officer. Evans's body was found in the spare bedroom. Forensic examination revealed dog hair on his underclothes – the hair of Myra Hindley's dog – indicating that he and Brady had engaged in sex, probably while Myra was fetching David Smith.

Hidden in the spine of a prayer book police found a cloakroom ticket, which led them to Manchester Central Station. In two suitcases they discovered pornographic photos, tapes and books on sex and torture; the photographs included those of Lesley Ann Downey, with a tape recording of her voice pleading for mercy. A twelve-year-old girl, Patricia Hodges, who had occasionally accompanied Brady and Hindley to the moors, took the police to Hollin Brown Knoll, and there the body of Lesley Ann Downey was dug up. John Kilbride's grave was located through a photograph that showed Hindley crouching on it with a dog. Pauline Reade's body was not found until 1987, as a result of Myra Hindley's confession to Topping. Brady helped in the search on the moor and as we know, the body of Keith Bennett has never been recovered.

Brady's defence was that Evans had been killed unintentionally, in the course of a struggle, when he and Smith tried to rob him. Lesley Ann Downey, he claimed, had been brought to the house by Smith to pose for pornographic pictures, for which she had been paid ten shillings. (His original story was that she had been brought to the house by two men.) After the session, she left the house with Smith. He flatly denied knowing anything about any of the other murders, but the tape recording of Lesley Ann Downey's screams and pleas for mercy made it clear that Brady and Hindley

When Moors Murdered Myra Hindley – who participated with Ian Brady in murdering children – heard that her dog had died in police custody, she remarked: "They're just a lot of bloody murderers".

# The Yorkshire Ripper

During the second half of the 1970s, the killer who became known as the Yorkshire Ripper caused the same kind of fear among prostitutes in the north of England as his namesake in the Whitechapel of 1888.

His reign of terror began in Leeds on a freezing October morning in 1975, when a milkman discovered the corpse of a woman on a recreation ground; her trousers had been pulled down below her knees, and her bra was around her throat. The whole of the front of the body was covered with blood; pathologists later established that she had been stabbed fourteen times. Before that, she had been knocked unconscious by a tremendous blow that had shattered the back of her skull. She was identified as a twenty-eight-year-old prostitute, Wilma McCann, who had left her four children alone to go on a pub crawl. Her killer seemed to have stabbed and slashed her in a frenzy.

Three months later, on 20 January, 1976, a man on his way to work noticed a prostrate figure lying in a narrow alleyway in Leeds, covered with a coat. Like Wilma McCann, Emily Jackson had been half-stripped, and stabbed repeatedly in the stomach and breasts. She had also been knocked unconscious by a tremendous blow from behind. When the police established that the forty-two year old woman was the wife of a roofing contractor, and that she lived in the respectable suburb of Churwell, they assumed that the killer had selected her at random and crept up behind her with some blunt instrument. Further investigation revealed the surprising fact that this apparently normal housewife supplemented her income with prostitution, and that she had had sexual intercourse shortly before death – not necessarily with her killer. The pattern that was emerging was like that of the Jack the Ripper case: a sadistic maniac who preyed on prostitutes.

Just as in Whitechapel in 1888, there was panic among the prostitutes of Leeds, particularly in Chapeltown, the red light area where Emily Jackson had been picked up. But as no further "Ripper" murders occurred in 1976, the panic subsided. It began all over again more than a year later, on 5 February, 1977, when a twenty-eight year old woman named Irene Richardson left her room in Chapeltown looking for customers, and encountered a man who carried a concealed hammer and a knife. Irene Richardson had been struck down from behind within half an hour of leaving her room; then her attacker had pulled off her skirt and tights, and stabbed her repeatedly. The wounds indicated that, like Jack the Ripper, he seemed to be gripped by some awful compulsion to expose the victim's intestines.

Now the murders followed with a grim repetitiveness that indicated that the serial killer was totally in the grip of his obsession. During the next three and a half years, the man whom the press christened the Yorkshire Ripper, murdered ten more women, bringing his total to thirteen, and severely injured three more. Most of the victims were prostitutes, but two were young girls walking home late at night, and one of them a civil servant. With one exception, the method was always the same – several violent blows to the skull, which often had the effect of shattering it into many pieces, then stab wounds in the breast and stomach. In many cases, the victim's intestines spilled out. The exception was a civil servant named Marguerite Walls, who was strangled with a piece of rope on 20 August, 1979, after being knocked unconscious from behind.

One victim who recovered – forty-two-year-old Maureen Long – was able to describe her attacker. On 27 July, 1977, she had been walking home through central Bradford after an evening of heavy drinking when a man in a white car offered her a lift. As she stepped out of the car near her front door, the man struck her a savage blow on the head, then stabbed her several times. But before he could be certain she was dead, a light went on in a nearby gypsy caravan, and he drove away. She recovered after a brain operation, and described her attacker as a young man with long blond hair – a detail that later proved to be inaccurate.

Her mistake may have saved the Ripper from arrest three months later. A prostitute named Jean Jordan was killed near some allotments in Manchester on 1 October, 1977. When the body was found nine days later – with twenty-four stab wounds

– the police discovered a new £5 note in her handbag. Since it had been issued on the other side of the Pennines, in Yorkshire, it was obviously a vital clue. The police checked with the banks, and located twenty-three firms in the Leeds area who had paid their workers with £5 notes in the same sequence. Among the workers who were interviewed was a thirty-one-year-old lorry driver named Peter Sutcliffe, who worked at T and W. H. Clark (Holdings) Ltd, and lived in a small detached house at 6 Garden Lane in Bradford. But Sutcliffe had dark curly hair and a beard, and his wife Sonia was able to provide him with an alibi. The police apologized and left, and the Yorkshire Ripper was able to go on murdering for three more years.

As the murders continued – four in 1977, three in 1978, three in 1979 – the police launched the largest operation that had ever been mounted in the north of England, and thousands of people were interviewed. Police received three letters signed "Jack the Ripper", threatening more murders, and a cassette on which a man with a "Geordie" accent taunted George Oldfield, the officer in charge of the case; these later proved to be false leads. The cassette caused the police to direct enormous efforts to the Wearside area, and increased the murderer's sense of invulnerability.

The final murder took place more than a year later. Twenty-year-old Jacqueline Hill, a Leeds University student, had attended a meeting of voluntary probation officers on 17 November 1980, and caught a bus back to her lodgings soon after 9 p.m. An hour later, her handbag was found near some waste ground by an Iraqi student, and he called the police. It was a windy and rainy night and they found nothing. Jacqueline Hill's body was found the next morning on the waste ground. She had been battered unconscious with a hammer, then undressed and stabbed repeatedly. One wound was in the eye – Sutcliffe later said she seemed to be looking at him reproachfully, so he drove the blade into her eye.

This was the Ripper's last attack. On 2 January, 1981 a black prostitute named Olive Reivers had just finished with a client in the centre of Sheffield when a Rover car drove up, and a bearded man asked her how much she charged; she said it would be £10 for sex in the car, and climbed in the front. He seemed tense and asked if she would object if he talked for a while about his family problems. When he asked her to get in

In June 1983, a serial killer named Gerald Gallego was sentenced to death in California for ten murders. Gallego, with the help of his common-law wife Charlene Williams, daughter of a wealthy Sacramento businessman, had committed the murders because he had an obsessional desire to find "the perfect sex slave". (He had been practising incest with his daughter since she was eight.) Charlene, a spoilt only child, had already been married twice when, at the age of twenty-one, she met the ex-convict Gallego, whose father had been executed in 1954 for three murders. Fascinated by his macho brutality, she finally agreed to help him in his search for the "perfect sex slave". In 1978; she approached two teenage girls in a supermarket and asked them if they would like to smoke some pot. When they got back to the van, Gallego was waiting for them with a gun. He raped them both on a mattress in the back before killing them with bullets in the head. Two years - and six murders - later, they kidnapped a young couple who were leaving a dance in Sacramento. The man was 'executed" and the woman raped and subsequently shot. A friend of the kidnapped couple had seen their abduction and taken the license number of the car. The Gallegos fled, but were captured a few weeks later. In exchange for testifying against her "husband", Charlene was allowed to plead guilty to a lesser charge, and received a sixteen-year jail sentence. Gallego was sentenced to die by lethal injection.

Gallego had told a social worker in prison: "My only interest is in killing God" It echoes a comment made by Ian Brady to Chief Superintendent Topping. Although Brady declared that it was nonsense to believe in God, he admitted that after murdering John Kilbride, he had shaken his fist and the sky and shouted: "Take that, you bastard". Nothing could more clearly demonstrate the "magical thinking" of the serial killer.

the back of the car, she said she would prefer to have sex in the front; this may have saved her life – Sutcliffe had stunned at least one of his victims as she climbed into the back of the car. He moved on top of her, but was unable to maintain an erection. He moved off her again, and at this point, a police car pulled up in front. Sutcliffe hastily told the woman to say she was his girlfriend. The police asked his name, and he told them it was Peter Williams. Sergeant Robert Ring and PC Robert Hydes were on patrol duty, and they were carrying out a standard check. Ring noted the number-plate then went off to check it with the computer; while he radioed, he told PC Hydes to get into the back of the Rover. Sutcliffe asked if he could get out to urinate and Hydes gave permission: Sutcliffe stood by an oil storage tank a few feet away, then got back into the car. Meanwhile, the sergeant had discovered that the number-plates did not belong to the Rover, and told Sutcliffe he would have to return to the police station. In the station, Sutcliffe again asked to go to the lavatory and was given permission. It was when the police made him empty his pockets and found a length of clothes-line that they began to suspect that they might have trapped Britain's most wanted man.

To begin with, Sutcliffe lied fluently about why he was carrying the rope and why he was in the car with a prostitute. It was the following day that Sergeant Ring learned about Sutcliffe's brief absence from the car to relieve himself, and went to look near the oil storage tank. In the leaves, he found a ball-headed hammer and a knife. Then he recalled Sutcliffe's trip to the lavatory at the police station. In the cistern he found a second knife. When Sutcliffe was told that he was in serious trouble, he suddenly admitted that he was the Ripper, and confessed to eleven murders. (It seems odd that he got the number wrong – he was later charged with thirteen – but it is possible that he genuinely lost count. He was originally suspected of fourteen murders, but the police later decided that the killing of another prostitute, Jean Harrison – whose body was found in Preston, Lancashire – was not one of the series. She had been raped and the semen was not of Sutcliffe's blood group.)

A card written by Sutcliffe and displayed in his lorry read: "In this truck is a man whose latent genius, if unleashed, would rock the nation, whose dynamic energy would overpower those around him. Better let him sleep?"

The story that began to emerge was of a lonely and shy individual, brooding and introverted, who was morbidly fascinated by prostitutes and red-light areas. He was born on 2 June 1946, the eldest of five children and his mother's favourite. His school career was undistinguished and he left at fifteen. He drifted aimlessly from job to job, including one as a grave-digger in the Bingley cemetery, from which he was dismissed for bad timekeeping. (His later attempt at a defence of insanity rested on a claim that a voice had spoken to him from a cross in the cemetery telling him he had a God-given mission to kill prostitutes.)

In 1967, when he was twenty-one, he met a sixteen-year-old Czech girl, Sonia Szurma, in a pub, and they began going out together. It would be another seven years before they married. The relationship seems to have been stormy; at one point, she was going out with an ice-cream salesman, and Sutcliffe picked up a prostitute "to get even". He was unable to have intercourse, and the woman went off with a £10 note and failed to return with his £5 change. When he saw her in a pub two weeks later and asked for the money, she jeered at him and left him with a sense of helpless fury and humiliation. This, he claimed, was the source of his hatred of prostitutes. In 1969 he made his first attack on a prostitute, hitting her on the head with a sock full of gravel. In October of that year, he was caught carrying a hammer and charged with being equipped for theft; he was fined £25. In 1971 he went for a drive with a friend, Trevor Birdsall, and left the car in the red-light area of Bradford. When he returned ten minutes later he said, "Drive off quickly," and admitted that he had hit a woman with a brick in a sock. Sutcliffe was again driving with Birdsall in 1975 on the evening that Olive Smelt was struck down with a hammer.

In 1972 Sonia Szurma went to London for a teacher's training course and had a nervous breakdown; she was diagnosed as schizophrenic. Two years later, she and Sutcliffe married, but the marriage was punctuated by violent rows – Sutcliffe said he became embarrassed in case the neighbours heard the shouts, implying that it was she who was shouting rather than he. He also told the prostitute Olive Reivers that he had been arguing with his wife "about not being able to go with her", which Olive Reivers took to mean that they were having sexual problems. Certainly, this combination of two introverted people can hardly have improved Sutcliffe's mental condition.

Sutcliffe's first murder – of Wilma McCann – took place in the year after he married Sonia. He admitted: "I developed and played up a hatred for prostitutes . . ." Unlike the Düsseldorf sadist of the 1920s, Peter Kürten, Sutcliffe never admitted to having orgasms as he stabbed his victims; but anyone acquainted with the psychology of sexual criminals would take it for granted that this occurred, and that in most of the cases where the victim was not stabbed, or was left alive, he achieved orgasm at an earlier stage than usual. The parallels are remarkable. Kürten, like Sutcliffe, used a variety of weapons, including a hammer. On one occasion when a corpse remained undiscovered, Kürten also returned to inflict fresh indignities on it. Sutcliffe had returned to the body of Jean Jordan and attempted to cut off the head with a hacksaw.

It was when he pulled up Wilma McCann's clothes and stabbed her in the breast and abdomen that Sutcliffe realized that he had discovered a new sexual thrill. With the second victim, Emily Jackson, he pulled off her bra and briefs, then stabbed her repeatedly – he was, in effect, committing rape with a knife, Sutcliffe was caught in the basic trap of the sex criminal: the realization that he had found a way of inducing a far, more powerful sexual satisfaction than he was able to obtain in normal intercourse, and that he was pushing himself into the position of a social outcast. He admitted sobbing in his car after one of the murders, and being upset to discover that Jayne MacDonald had not been a prostitute (and later, that her father had died of a broken heart). But the compulsion to kill was becoming a fever, so that he no longer cared that the later victims were not prostitutes. He said, probably with sincerity, "The devil drove me."

Sutcliffe's trial began on 5 May 1981. He had pleaded not guilty to murder on grounds of diminished responsibility, and told the story of his "mission" from God. But a warder had overheard him tell his wife that if he could convince the jury that he was mad, he would only spend ten years in a "loony bin". The Attorney-General, Sir Michael Havers, also pointed out that Sutcliffe had at first behaved perfectly normally, laughing at the idea that he might be mentally abnormal, and had introduced the talk of "voices" fairly late in his admissions to the police.

On 22 May Sutcliffe was found guilty of murder, and jailed for life, with a recommendation that he should serve at least thirty years.

# Dennis Nilsen

On the evening of 8 February 1983, a drains maintenance engineer named Michael Cattran was asked to call at 23 Cranley Gardens, in Muswell Hill, north London, to find out why tenants had been unable to flush their toilets since the previous Saturday. Although Muswell Hill is known as a highly respectable area of London – it was once too expensive for anyone but the upper middle classes – No. 23 proved to be a rather shabby house, divided into flats. A tenant showed Cattran the manhole cover that led to the drainage system. When he removed it, he staggered back and came close to vomiting; the smell was unmistakably decaying flesh. And when he had climbed down the rungs into the cistern, Cattran discovered what was blocking the drain: masses of rotting meat, much of it white, like chicken flesh. Convinced this was human flesh, Cattran rang his supervisor, who decided to come and inspect it in the morning. When they arrived the following day, the drain had been cleared. And a female tenant told them she had heard footsteps going up and down the stairs for much of the night. The footsteps seemed to go up to the top flat, which was rented by a thirty-seven-year-old civil servant named Dennis Nilsen.

Closer search revealed that the drain was still not quite clear; there was a piece of flesh, six inches square, and some bones that resembled fingers. Detective Chief Inspector Peter Jay, of Hornsey CID, was waiting in the hallway of the house that evening when Dennis Nilsen walked in from his day at the office – a Jobcentre in Kentish Town. He told Nilsen he wanted to talk to him about the drains. Nilsen invited the policeman into his flat, and Jay's face wrinkled as he smelt the odour of decaying flesh. He told Nilsen that they had found human remains in the drain, and asked what had happened to the rest of the body.

"It's in there, in two plastic bags," said Nilsen, pointing to a wardrobe.

In the police car, the Chief Inspector asked Nilsen whether the remains came from one body or two. Calmly, without emotion, Nilsen said: "There have been fifteen or sixteen altogether."

At the police station, Nilsen – a tall man with metal rimmed glasses – seemed eager to talk. (In fact, he proved to be something of a compulsive talker, and his talk overflowed into a series of school exercise books in which he later wrote his story for the use of Brian Masters, a young writer who contacted him in prison.) He told police that he had murdered three men in the Cranley Gardens house – into which he moved in the autumn of 1981 – and twelve or thirteen at his previous address, 195 Melrose Avenue, Cricklewood.

The plastic bags from the Muswell Hill flat contained two severed heads, and a skull from which the flesh had been stripped – forensic examinaation revealed that it had been boiled. The bathroom contained the whole lower half of a torso, from the waist down, intact. The rest was in bags in the wardrobe and in the tea chest. At Melrose Avenue, thirteen days and nights of digging revealed many human bones, as well as a cheque book and pieces of clothing.

The self-confessed mass murderer – he seemed to take a certain pride in being "Britain's biggest mass murderer" – was a Scot, born at Fraserburgh on 23 November 1945. His mother, born Betty Whyte, married a Norwegian soldier named Olav Nilsen in 1942. It was not a happy marriage; Olav was seldom at home, and was drunk a great deal; they were divorced seven years after their marriage. In 1954, Mrs Nilsen married again and became Betty Scott. Dennis grew up in the house of his grandmother and grandfather, and was immensely attached to his grandfather, Andrew Whyte, who became a father substitute. When Nilsen was seven, his grandfather died and his mother took Dennis in to see the corpse. This seems to have been a traumatic experience; in his prison notes he declares "My troubles started there." The death of his grandfather was such a blow that it caused his own emotional death, according to Nilsen. Not long after this, someone killed the two pigeons he kept in an air raid shelter, another severe shock. His mother's remarriage when he was nine had the effect of making him even more of a loner.

In 1961, Nilsen enlisted in the army, and became a cook. It was during this period tht he began to get drunk regularly, although he remained a loner, avoiding close relationships. In 1972 he changed the life of a soldier for that of a London policeman, but disliked the relative lack of freedom – compared to the army – and resigned after only eleven months. He became a security guard for a brief period, then a job-interviewer for the Manpower Services Commission.

In November 1975, Nilsen began to share a north London flat – in Melrose Avenue – with a young man named David Gallichan, ten years his junior. Gallachan was later to insist that there was no homosexual relationship, and this is believable. Many heterosexual young men would later accept Nilsen's offer of a bed for the night, and he would make no advances, or accept a simple "No" without resentment. But in May 1977, Gallichan decided he could bear London no longer, and accepted a job in the country. Nilsen was furious; he felt rejected and deserted. The break-up of the relationship with Gallichan – whom he had always dominated – seems to have triggered the homicidal violence that would claim fifteen lives.

The killings began more than a year later, in December 1978. Around Christmas, Nilsen picked up a young Irish labourer in the Cricklewood Arms, and they went back to his flat to continue drinking. Nilsen wanted him to stay over the New Year but the Irishman had other plans. In a note he later wrote for his biographer Brian Masters, Nilsen gives as his motive for this first killing that he was lonely and wanted to spare himself the pain of separation. In another confession he also implies that he has no memory of the actual killing. Nilsen strangled the unnamed Irishman in his sleep with a tie. Then he undressed the body and carefully washed it, a ritual he observed in all his killings. After that he placed the body under the floorboards where – as incredible as it seems – he kept it until the following August. He eventually burned it on a bonfire at the bottom of the garden, burning some rubber at the same time to cover the smell.

In November 1979, Nilsen attempted to strangle a young Chinaman who had accepted his offer to return to the flat; the Chinaman escaped and reported the attack to the police. But the police believed Nilsen's explanation that the Chinaman was trying to "rip him off" and decided not to pursue the matter.

The next murder victim was a twenty-three-year-old Canadian

called Kenneth James Ockendon, who had completed a tech- **451** nical training course and was taking a holiday before starting his career. He had been staying with an uncle and aunt in Carshalton after touring the Lake District. He was not a homosexual, and it was pure bad luck that he got into conversation with Nilsen in the Princess Louise in High Holborn around 3 December 1979. They went back to Nilsen's flat, ate ham, eggs and chips, and bought £20 worth of alcohol. Ockendon watched television, then listened to rock music on Nilsen's hi-fi system. Then he sat listening to music wearing earphones, watching television at the same time. This may have been what cost him his life; Nilsen liked to talk, and probably felt "rejected". "I thought bloody good guest this . . ." And sometime after midnight, while Ockendon was still wearing the headphones, he strangled him with a flex. Ockendon was so drunk that he put up no struggle. And Nilsen was also so drunk that after the murder, he sat down, put on the headphones, and went on playing music for hours. When he tried to put the body under the floorboards the next day, rigor mortis had set in and it was impossible. He had to wait until the rigor had passed. Later, he dissected the body. Ockendon had large quantities of Canadian money in his moneybelt, but Nilsen tore this up. The rigorous Scottish upbringing would not have allowed him to steal.

Nilsen's accounts of the murders are repetitive, and make them sound mechanical and almost identical. The third victim in May 1980, was a sixteen-year-old butcher named Martyn Duffey, who was also strangled and placed under the floorboards. Number four was a twenty-six year old Scot named Billy Sutherland – again strangled in his sleep with a tie and placed under the floorboards. Number five was an unnamed Mexican or Philipino, killed a few months later. Number six was an Irish building worker. Number seven was an undernourished down-and-out picked up in a doorway. (He was burned on the bonfire all in one piece.) The next five victims, all unnamed, were killed equally casually between late 1980 and late 1981. Nilsen later insisted that all the murders had been without sexual motivation – a plea that led Brian Masters to entitle his book on the case *Killing for Company*. There are moments in Nilsen's confessions when it sounds as if, like so many serial killers, he felt as if he was being taken over by a Mr Hyde personality or possessed by some demonic force.

In October 1981, Nilsen moved into an upstairs flat in Cranley Gardens, Muswell Hill. On 25 November, he took a homosexual student named Paul Nobbs back with him, and they got drunk. The next day, Nobbs went into University College Hospital for a check-up, and was told that bruises on his throat indicated that someone had tried to strangle him. Nilsen apparently changed his mind at the last moment.

The next victim, John Howlett, was less lucky. He woke up as Nilsen tried to strangle him and fought back hard; Nilsen had to bang his head against the headrest of the bed to subdue him. When he realized Howlett was still breathing, Nilsen drowned him in the bath. He hacked up the body in the bath, then boiled chunks in a large pot to make them easier to dispose of. (He also left parts of the body out in plastic bags for the dustbin men to take away.)

In May 1982, another intended victim escaped – a drag-artiste called Carl Stottor. After trying to strangle him, Nilsen placed him in a bath of water, but changed his mind and allowed him to live. When he left the flat, Stottor even agreed to meet Nilsen again – but decided not to keep the appointment. He decided not to go to the police.

The last two victims were both unnamed, one a drunk and one a drug-addict. In both cases, Nilsen claims to be unable to remember the actual killing. Both were dissected, boiled and flushed down the toilet. It was after this second murder – the fifteenth in all – that the tenants complained about blocked drains, and Nilsen was arrested.

The trial began on 24 October 1983, in the same court where Peter Sutcliffe had been tried two years earlier. Nilsen was charged with six murders and two attempted murders, although he had confessed to fifteen murders and seven attempted murders. He gave the impression that he was enjoying his moment of glory. The defence pleaded diminished responsibility, and argued that the charge should be reduced to manslaughter. The jury declined to accept this, and on 4 November 1983, Nilsen was found guilty by a vote of 10 to 2, and sentenced to life imprisonment.

# • chapter six •

# AMERICA'S SERIAL EPIDEMIC

*During the 1970s, it became increasingly clear that America's law enforcement agencies were facing a new problem: the killer who murdered repeatedly and compulsively – not just half a dozen times, like Jack the Ripper, or even a dozen, like the Boston Strangler, but twenty, thirty, forty, even a hundred times. In Houston, Texas, a homosexual with a taste for boys, Dean Corll, murdered about thirty teenagers – the precise number has never been established – and buried most of the bodies in a hired boatshed; Corll was shot to death by his lover and accomplice, Wayne Henley, in August 1973. In 1979, Chicago builder John Gacy lured thirty-three boys to his home and buried most of the bodies in a crawl space under his house. In 1983, a drifter named Henry Lee Lucas experienced some kind of religious conversion, and confessed to three hundred and sixty murders, mostly of women, killed and raped as he wandered around the country with his homosexual companion Ottis Toole. In 1986, in Ecuador, another drifter named Pedro Lopez confessed to killing and raping three hundred and sixty young girls. Lopez has so far claimed the highest number of victims – Lucas is believed to have exaggerated, although his victims undoubtedly run to more than a hundred.*

# Ted Bundy

During the Seventies, the killer who was most responsible for making Americans aware of this new type of criminal was a personable young law student named Theodore Robert Bundy.

On 31 January 1974, a student at the University of Washington, in Seattle, Lynda Ann Healy, vanished from her room; the bedsheets were bloodstained, suggesting that she had been struck violently on the head. During the following March, April, and May, three more girl students vanished; in June, two more. In July, two girls vanished on the same day. It happened at a popular picnic spot, Lake Sammanish; a number of people saw a good-looking young man, with his arm in a sling, accost a girl named Janice Ott and ask her to help him lift a boat onto the roof of his car; she walked away with him and did not return. Later, a girl named Denise Naslund was accosted by the same young man; she also vanished. He had been heard to introduce himself as "Ted".

In October 1974 the killings shifted to Salt Lake City; three girls disappeared in one month. In November, the police had their first break in the case: a girl named Carol DaRonch was accosted in a shopping centre by a young man who identified himself as a detective, and told her that there had been an attempt to break into her car; she agreed to accompany him to headquarters to view a suspect. In the car he snapped a handcuff on her wrist and pointed a gun at her head; she fought and screamed, and managed to jump from the car. That evening, a girl student vanished on her way to meet her brother. A handcuff key was found near the place from which she had been taken.

Meanwhile, the Seattle police had fixed on a young man named Ted Bundy as a main suspect. For the past six years, he had been involved in a close relationship with a divorcee named Meg Anders, but she had called off the marriage when she realized he was a habitual thief. After the Lake Sammanish disappearances, she had seen a photofit drawing of the wanted "Ted" in the *Seattle Times* and thought it looked like Bundy; moreover, "Ted" drove a Volkswagen like Bundy's. She had seen crutches and plaster of Paris in Bundy's room, and the coincidence seemed too great; with immense misgivings, she telephoned the police. They told her that they had already checked on Bundy; but at the suggestion of the Seattle police, Carol DaRonch was shown Bundy's photograph. She tentatively identified it as resembling the man who had tried to abduct her, but was obviously far from sure. (Bundy had been wearing a beard at the time.)

In January, March, April, July, and August 1975, more girls vanished in Colorado. (Their bodies – or skeletons – were found later in remote spots.) On 16 August 1975, Bundy was arrested for the first time. As a police car was driving along a dark street in Salt Lake City, a parked Volkswagen launched into motion; the policeman followed, and it accelerated. He caught up with the car at a service station, and found in the car a pantyhose mask, a crow-bar, an icepick and various other tools; there was also a pair of handcuffs.

Bundy, twenty-nine years old, seemed an unlikely burglar. He was a graduate of the University of Washington, and was in Utah to study law; he had worked as a political campaigner, and for the Crime Commission in Seattle. In his room there was nothing suspicious – except maps and brochures of Colorado, from which five girls had vanished that year. But strands of hair were found in the car, and they proved to be identical with those of Melissa Smith, daughter of the Midvale police chief, who had vanished in the previous October. Carol DaRonch had meanwhile identified Bundy in a police line-up as the fake policeman, and bloodspots on her clothes – where she had scratched her assailant – were of Bundy's group. Credit card receipts showed that Bundy had been close to various places from which girls had vanished in Colorado.

In theory, this should have been the end of the case – and if it had been, it would have been regarded as a typical triumph of scientific detection, beginning with the photofit drawing and concluding with the hair and blood evidence. The evidence was, admittedly, circumstantial, but taken all together, it formed a powerful case. The central objection to it became apparent as soon as Bundy walked into court. He looked so obviously decent and clean-cut that most people felt there must be some mistake. He was polite, well-spoken, articulate, charming, the kind of man who could have found himself a girlfriend for each night of the week. Why *should* such a man be a sex killer? In spite of which, the impression he made was of brilliance and plausibility rather than innocence. For example, he insisted that he had driven away from the police car because he was smoking marijuana, and that he had thrown the joint out of the window.

The case seemed to be balanced on a knife-edge – until the judge pronounced a sentence of guilty of kidnapping. Bundy sobbed and pleaded not to be sent to prison; but the judge sentenced him to a period between one and fifteen years.

The Colorado authorities now charged him with the murder of a girl called Caryn Campbell, who had been abducted from a ski resort where Bundy had been seen by a witness. After a morning courtroom session in Aspen, Bundy succeeded in wandering into the library during the lunch recess, and jumping out of the window. He was recaptured eight days later, tired and hungry, and driving a stolen car.

Legal arguments dragged on for another six months – what evidence was admissible and what was not. And on 30 December 1977, Bundy escaped again, using a hacksaw blade to cut through an imperfectly welded steel plate above the light fixture in his cell. He made his way to Chicago, then south to Florida; there, near the Florida State University in Tallahassee, he took a room. A few days later, a man broke into a nearby sorority house and attacked four girls with a club, knocking them unconscious; one was strangled with her pantyhose and raped; another died on her way to hospital. One of the strangled girl's nipples had been almost bitten off, and she had a bite mark on her left buttock. An hour and a half later, a student woke up in another sorority house when she heard bangs next door, and a girl whimpering. She dialled the number of the room, and as the telephone rang, someone could be heard running out. Cheryl Thomas was found lying in bed, her skull fractured but still alive.

Three weeks later, on 6 February 1978, Bundy – who was calling himself Chris Hagen – stole a white Dodge van and left Tallahassee; he stayed in the Holiday Inn, using a stolen credit card. The following day a twelve-year-old girl named Kimberly Leach walked out of her classroom in Lake City, Florida, and vanished. Bundy returned to Tallahassee to take a girl out for an expensive meal – paid for with a stolen credit card – then absconded via the fire escape, owing large arrears of rent. At 4 a.m. on 15 February, a police patrolman noticed an orange Volkswagen driving suspiciously slowly, and radioed for a check on its number; it proved to be stolen from Tallahassee. After a struggle and a chase, during which he tried to kill the policeman, Bundy was captured yet again. When the police learned his real name, and that he had just left a town in which five girls had been attacked, they suddenly understood the importance of their capture. Bundy seemed glad to be in custody, and began to unburden himself. He explained that "his problem" had begun when he had seen a girl on a bicycle in Seattle, and "had to have her". He had followed her, but she escaped. "Sometimes", he admitted, "I feel like a vampire."

On 7 April, a party of searchers along the Suwanee river found the body of Kimberly Leach in an abandoned hut; she had been strangled and sexually violated. Three weeks later, surrounded by hefty guards, Bundy allowed impressions of his teeth to be taken, for comparison with the marks on the buttocks of the dead student, Lisa Levy.

Bundy's lawyers persuaded him to enter into "plea bargaining": in exchange for a guarantee of life imprisonment – rather than a death sentence – he would confess to the murders of Lisa Levy, Margaret Bowman, and Kimberly Leach. But Bundy changed his mind at the last moment and decided to sack his lawyers.

Bundy's trial began on 25 June 1979, and the evidence against him was damning; a witness who had seen him leaving the sorority house after the attacks; a pantyhose mask found in the room of Cheryl Thomas, which resembled the one found in Bundy's car; but above all, the fact that Bundy's teeth matched the marks on Lisa Levy's buttocks. The highly compromising taped interview with the Pensacola police was judged inadmissible in court because his lawyer had not been present. Bundy again dismissed his defence and took it over himself; the general impression was that he was trying to be too clever. The jury took only six hours to find him guilty on all counts. Judge Ed Cowart pronounced sentence of death by electrocution, but evidently felt some sympathy for the good-looking young defendant. "It's a tragedy for this court to see such a total waste of humanity. You're a bright young man. You'd have made a good lawyer . . . But you went the wrong way, partner. Take care of yourself . . ."

Bundy was taken to Raiford prison, Florida, where he was

placed on Death Row. On 2 July 1986, when he was due to die a few hours before Gerald Stano, both were granted a stay of execution.

The Bundy case illustrates the immense problems faced by investigators of serial murders. When Meg Anders – Bundy's mistress – telephoned the police after the double murder near Lake Sammanish, Bundy's name had already been suggested by three people. But he was only one of 3,500 suspects. Later Bundy was added to the list of one hundred "best suspects" which investigators constructed on grounds of age, occupation, and past record. Two hundred thousand items were fed into computers, including the names of 41,000 Volkswagen owners, 5,000 men with a record of mental illness, every student who had taken classes with the dead girls, and all transfers from other colleges they had attended. All this was programmed into thirty-seven categories, each using a different criterion to isolate the suspect. Asked to name anyone who came up on any three of these programs, the computer produced 16,000 names. When the number was raised to four, it was reduced to 600. Only when it was raised to twenty-five was it reduced to ten suspects, with Bundy seventh on the list. The police were still investigating number six when Bundy was detained in Salt Lake City with burgling tools in his car. Only after that did Bundy become suspect number one. And by that time, he had already committed a minimum of seventeen murders. (There seems to be some doubt about the total, estimates varying between twenty and forty; Bundy himself told the Pensacola investigators that it ran into double figures.) Detective Robert Keppel, who worked on the case, is certain that Bundy would have been revealed as suspect number one even if he had not been arrested. But in 1982, Keppel and his team were presented with another mass killer in the Seattle area, the so-called Green River Killer, whose victims were mostly prostitutes picked up on the "strip" in Seattle. Seven years later, in 1989, he has killed at least forty-nine women, and the computer has still failed to identify an obvious suspect number one.

The Bundy case is doubly baffling because he seems to contradict the basic assertions of every major criminologist from Lombroso to Yochelson. Bundy is not an obvious born criminal, with degenerate physical characteristics; there is (as far as is known) no history of insanity in his family; he was

not a social derelict or a failure. In her book *The Stranger Beside*
*Me*, his friend Ann Rule describes him as "a man of unusual
accomplishment". How could the most subtle "psychological
profiling" target such a man as a serial killer?

The answer to the riddle emerged fairly late in the day, four
years after Bundy had been sentenced to death. Before his
conviction, Bundy had indicated his willingness to co-operate on
a book about himself, and two journalists, Stephen G. Michaud
and Hugh Aynesworth, went to interview him in prison. They
discovered that Bundy had no wish to discuss guilt, except to
deny it, and he actively discouraged them from investigating
the case against him. He wanted them to produce a gossipy
book focusing squarely on himself, like best-selling biographies
of celebrities such as Frank Sinatra. Michaud and Aynesworth
would have been happy to write a book demonstrating his innocence, but as they looked into the case, they found it impossible
to accept this; instead, they concluded that he had killed at least
twenty-one girls. When they began to probe, Bundy revealed
the characteristics that Yochelson and Samenow had found
to be so typical of criminals: hedging, lying, pleas of faulty
memory, and self-justification: "Intellectually, Ted seemed pro-
foundly dissociative, a compartmentalizer, and thus a superb
rationalizer." Emotionally, he struck them as a severe case of
arrested development: "he might as well have been a twelve year
old, and a precocious and bratty one at that. So extreme was his
childishness that his pleas of innocence were of a character very
similar to that of the little boy who'll deny wrongdoing in the
face of overwhelming evidence to the contrary." So Michaud had
the ingenious idea of suggesting that Bundy should "speculate
on the nature of a person capable of doing what Ted had been
accused (and convicted) of doing". Bundy embraced this idea
with enthusiasm, and talked for hours into a tape recorder. Soon
Michaud became aware that there were, in effect, two "Teds"
– the analytical human being, and an entity inside him that
Michaud came to call the "hunchback". (We have encountered
this "other person" – Mr Hyde – syndrome in many killers,
including Peter Sutcliffe.)

After generalizing for some time about violence in modern
society, the disintegration of the home, and so on, Bundy got
down to specifics, and began to discuss his own development.

He had been an illegitimate child, born to a respectable young girl in Philadelphia. She moved to Seattle to escape the stigma, and married a cook in the Veterans' Hospital. Ted was an oversensitive and self-conscious child who had all the usual day-dreams of fame and wealth. And at an early stage he became a thief and something of a habitual liar – as many imaginative children do. But he seems to have been deeply upset by the discovery of his illegitimacy.

Bundy was not, in fact, a brilliant student. Although he struck his fellow students as witty and cultivated, his grades were usually Bs. In his late teens he became heavily infatuated with a fellow student, Stephanie Brooks, who was beautiful, sophisticated, and came of a wealthy family. Oddly enough, she responded and they became "engaged". To impress her he went to Stanford University to study Chinese; but he felt lonely away from home and his grades were poor. "I found myself thinking about standards of success that I just didn't seem to be living up to." Stephanie wearied of his immaturity, and threw him over – the severest blow so far. He became intensely moody. "Dogged by feelings of wothlessness and failure", he took a job as a busboy in a hotel dining-room. And at this point, he began the drift that eventually turned him into a serial killer. He became friendly with a drug addict. One night, they entered a cliffside house that had been partly destroyed by a landslide, and stole whatever they could find. "It was really thrilling." He began shoplifting and stealing "for thrills", once walking openly into someone's greenhouse, taking an eight-foot tree in a pot, and putting it in his car with the top sticking out of the sunroof.

He also became a full-time volunteer worker for Art Fletcher, the black Republican candidate for Lieutenant-Governor. He enjoyed the sense of being a "somebody" and mixing with interesting people. But Fletcher lost, and Bundy became a salesman in a department store. He met Meg Anders in a college beer joint, and they became lovers – she had a gentle, easy-going nature, which brought out Bundy's protective side. But she was shocked by his kleptomania.

In fact, the criminal side – the "hunchback" – was now developing fast. He acquired a taste for violent pornography – easy to buy openly in American shops. Once, walking round the university district, he saw a girl undressing in a lighted room. This was the turning point in his life. He began to devote hours to walking around, hoping to see more girls undressing.

He was back at university, studying psychology, but his night prowling prevented him from making full use of his undoubted intellectual capacities. He obtained his degree in due course – this may tell us more about American university standards than about Bundy's abilities – and tried to find a law school that would take him. He failed all the aptitude tests and was repeatedly turned down. A year later, he was finally accepted – he worked for the Crime Commission for a month, as an assistant, and for the Office of Justice Planning. His self-confidence increased by leaps and bounds. When he flew to San Francisco to see Stephanie Brooks, the girl who had jilted him, she was deeply impressed, and willing to renew their affair. He was still having an affair with Meg Anders, and entered on this new career as a Don Juan with his usual enthusiasm. He and Stephanie spent Christmas together and became "engaged". Then he dumped her as she had dumped him.

By this time, he had committed his first murder. For years, he had been a pornography addict and a peeping tom. ("He approached it almost like a project, throwing himself into it, literally, for years.") Then the "hunchback" had started to demand "more active kinds of gratification". He tried disabling women's cars, but the girls always had help on hand. He felt the need to indulge in this kind of behaviour after drinking had reduced his inhibitions. One evening, he stalked a girl from a bar, found a piece of heavy wood, and managed to get ahead of her and lie in wait. Before she reached the place where he was hiding, she stopped at her front door and went in. But the experience was like "making a hole in a dam". A few evenings later, as a woman was fumbling for her keys at her front door, he struck her on the head with a piece of wood. She collapsed, screaming, and he ran away. He was filled with remorse, and swore he would never do such a thing again. But six months later, he followed a woman home and peeped in as she undressed. He began to do this again and again. One day, when he knew the door was unlocked, he sneaked in, entered her bedroom, and jumped on her. She screamed and he ran away. Once again, there was a period of self-disgust and revulsion.

This was in the autumn of 1973. On 4 January 1974, he found a door that admitted him to the basement room of eighteen-year-old Sharon Clarke. Now, for the first time, he employed the technique he later used repeatedly, attacking her with a crow-bar until she was unconscious. Then he thrust a speculum, or vaginal probe, inside her, causing internal injuries. But he left her alive.

On the morning of 1 February 1974, he found an unlocked front door in a students' rooming-house and went in. He entered a bedroom at random; twenty-one-year-old Lynda Healy was asleep in bed. He battered her unconscious, then carried the body out to his car. He drove to Taylor Mountain, twenty miles east of Seattle, made her remove her pyjamas, and raped her. When Bundy was later "speculating" about this crime for Stephen Michaud's benefit, the interviewer asked: "Was there any conversation?" Bundy replied: "There'd be some. Since this girl in front of him represented not a person, but again the image of something desirable, the last thing we would expect him to want to do would be to personalize this person."

So Lynda Healy was bludgeoned to death; Bundy always insisted that he took no pleasure in violence, but that his chief desire was "possession" of another person.

Now the "hunchback" was in full control, and there were five more victims over the next five months. Three of the girls were taken to the same spot on Taylor Mountain and there raped and murdered – Bundy acknowledged that his sexual gratification would sometimes take hours. The four bodies were found together in the following year. On the day he abducted the two girls from Lake Sammanish, Bundy "speculated" that he had taken the first, Janice Ott, to a nearby house and raped her, then returned to abduct the second girl, Denise Naslund, who was taken back to the same house and raped in view of the other girl; both were then killed, and taken to a remote spot four miles northeast of the park, where the bodies were dumped.

By the time he had reached this point in his "confession", Bundy had no further secrets to reveal; everything was obvious. Rape had become a compulsion that dominated his life. When he moved to Salt Lake City and entered the law school there – he was a failure from the beginning as a law student – he must have known that if he began to rape and kill young girls there, he would be establishing himself as suspect number one. This made no difference; he had to continue. Even the unsuccessful kidnapping of Carol DaRonch, and the knowledge that someone could now identify him, made no difference. He

merely switched his activities to Colorado. Following his arrest,
conviction, and escape, he moved to Florida, and the compulsive attacks continued, although by now he must have known that another series of murders in a town to which he had recently moved must reduce his habitual plea of "coincidence" to an absurdity. It seems obvious that by this time he had lost the power of choice. In his last weeks of freedom, Bundy showed all the signs of weariness and self-disgust that had driven Carl Panzram to contrive his own execution.

Time finally ran out for Bundy on 24 January 1989. Long before this, he had recognized that his fatal mistake was to decline to enter into plea bargaining at his trial; the result was a death sentence instead of life imprisonment. In January 1989, his final appeal was turned down and the date of execution fixed. Bundy then made a last-minute attempt to save his life by offering to bargain murder confessions for a reprieve – against the advice of his attorney James Coleman, who warned him that this attempt to "trade over victims' bodies" would only create hostility that would militate against further stays of execution. In fact, Bundy went on to confess to eight Washington murders, and then to a dozen others. Detective Bob Keppel, who had led the investigation in Seattle, commented: "The game-playing stuff cost him his life." Instead of making a full confession, Bundy doled out information bit by bit. "The whole thing was orchestrated", said Keppel, "We were held hostage for three days." And finally, when it was clear that there was no chance of further delay, Bundy confessed to the Chi Omega Sorority killings, admitting that he had been peeping through the window at girls undressing until he was carried away by desire and entered the building. He also mentioned pornography as being one of the factors that led him to murder. Newspaper columnists showed an inclination to doubt this, but Bundy's earlier confessions to Michaud leave no doubt that he was telling the truth.

At 7 a.m., Bundy was led into the execution chamber at Starke State prison, Florida; behind Plexiglass, an invited audience of forty-eight people sat waiting. As two warders attached his hands to the arms of the electric chair, Bundy recognized his attorney among the crowd; he smiled and nodded. Then straps were placed around his chest and over his mouth; the metal cap with electrodes was fastened onto his head with screws and the face was covered with a black hood. At 7.07 a.m. the executioner threw the switch; Bundy's body went stiff and rose fractionally from the chair. One minute later, as the power was switched off, the body slammed back into the chair. A doctor felt his pulse and pronounced him dead. Outside the prison, a mob carrying "Fry Bundy!" banners cheered as the execution was announced.

# The Hillside Stranglers

Between 18 October 1977 and 17 February 1978, the naked bodies of ten girls were dumped on hillsides in the Los Angeles area; all had been raped, and medical examination of sperm samples indicated that two men were involved. The police kept this information secret, and the press nicknamed the unknown killer the Hillside Strangler.

In January 1979, the bodies of two girl students were found in the back seat of a car in the small town of Bellingham, in Washington state. A security guard named Kenneth Bianchi was known to have offered the girls a "house sitting" job (looking after the house while the tenant was away), and he was arrested. Forensic evidence indicated Bianchi as the killer, and when it was learned that Bianchi had been in Los Angeles during the "strangler" murders, he was also questioned about these crimes, and eventually confessed. For a while, Bianchi succeeded in convincing psychiatrists that he was a "dual personality", a "Dr Jekyll and Mr Hyde", and that his "Hyde" personality had committed the murders in association with his cousin, an older man named Angelo Buono. A police psychiatrist was able to

---

One third of all murderers commit suicide. But this is because most murders are committed within the family, in a state of jealousy or rage, and the killer is overwhelmed with remorse or despair. Unfortunately, few serial killers commit suicide – although it has been argued that the incredible carelessness that often leads to their capture is a kind of psychological suicide.

prove that Bianchi was faking dual personality, and his detailed confessions to the rape-murders – the girls were usually lured or forced to go to Buono's house – finally led to sentences of life imprisonment for both cousins.

# Richard Ramirez

Throughout 1985 handgun sales in Los Angeles soared. Many suburbanites slept with a loaded pistol by their beds. A series of violent attacks upon citizens in their own homes had shattered the comfortably normality of middle class life. Formerly safe neighbourhoods seemed to be the killer's favourite targets. The whole city was terrified.

The attacks were unprecedented in many ways. Neither murder nor robbery seemed to be the obvious motive, although both frequently took place. The killer would break into a house, creep into the main bedroom and shoot the male partner through the head with a .22. He would then rape and beat the wife or girlfriend, suppressing resistance with threats of violence to her or her children. Male children were sometimes sodomized, the rape victims sometimes shot. On occasion he would ransack the house looking for valuables while at other times he would leave empty-handed without searching. During the attacks he would force victims to declare their love for Satan. Survivors described a tall, slim Hispanic male with black, greasy hair and severely decayed teeth. The pattern of crimes seemed to be based less upon a need to murder or rape but a desire to terrify and render helpless. More than most serial killers the motive seemed to be exercising power.

The killer also had unusual methods of victim selection. He seemed to be murdering outside his own racial group, preferring Caucasians and specifically Asians. He also seemed to prefer to break into yellow houses.

In the spring and summer of 1985 there were more than twenty attacks, most of which involved both rape and murder. By the end of March the press had picked up the pattern and splashed stories connecting the series of crimes. After several abortive nicknames, such as "The Walk-In Killer" or "The Valley Invader", the *Herald Examiner* came up with "The Night Stalker", a name sensational enough to stick.

Thus all through the hot summer of 1985 Californians slept with their windows closed. One policeman commented to a reporter: "People are armed and staying up late. Burglars want this guy caught like everyone else. He's making it bad for their business." The police themselves circulated sketches and stopped anyone who looked remotely like The Night Stalker. One innocent man was stopped five times.

Despite these efforts and thorough forensic analysis of crime scenes there was little progress in the search for the killer's identity.

Things were obviously getting difficult for The Night Stalker as well. The next murder that fitted the pattern occurred in San Francisco, showing perhaps that public awareness in Los Angeles had made it too taxing a location. This shift also gave police a chance to search San Francisco hotels for records of a man of The Night Stalker's description. Sure enough, while checking the downmarket Tenderloin district police learned that a thin Hispanic with bad teeth had been staying at a cheap hotel there periodically over the past year. On the last occasion he had checked out the night of the San Francisco attack. The manager commented that his room "smelled like a skunk" each time he vacated it and it took three days for the smell to clear.

Though this evidence merely confirmed the police's earlier description, The Night Stalker's next shift of location was to prove more revealing. A young couple in Mission Viejo were attacked in their home. The Night Stalker shot the man through the head while he slept, then raped his partner on the bed next to the body. He then tied her up while he ransacked the house for money and jewellery. Before leaving he raped her a second time and force her to fellate him with a gun pressed against her head. Unfortunately for the killer, however, his victim caught a glimpse of him escaping in a battered orange Toyota and memorized the license plate. She immediately alerted the police. LAPD files showed that the car had been stolen in Los Angeles' Chinatown district while the owner was eating in a restaurant. An all-points bulletin was put out for the vehicle, and officers were instructed not to try and arrest the driver, merely to observe him. However, the car was not found. In fact,

The Night Stalker had dumped the car soon after the attack, and it was located two days later in a car park in Los Angeles' Rampart district. After plain clothes officers had kept the car under surveillance for twenty-four hours, the police moved in and took the car away for forensic testing. A set of fingerprints was successfully lifted.

Searching police fingerprint files for a match manually can take many days and even then it is possible to miss correlations. However, the Los Angeles police had recently installed a fingerprint database computer system, designed by the FBI, and it was through this that they checked the set of fingerprints from the orange Toyota. The system works by storing information about the relative distance between different features of a print, and comparing them with a digitized image of the suspect's fingerprint. The search provided a positive match and a photograph. The Night Stalker was a petty thief and burglar. His name was Ricardo Leyva Ramirez.

The positive identification was described by the forensic division as "a near miracle". The computer system had only just been installed, this was one of its first trials. Furthermore, the system only contained the fingerprints of criminals born after 1 January, 1960. Richard Ramirez was born in February 1960.

The police circulated the photograph to newspapers, and it was shown on the late evening news. At the time, Ramirez was in Phoenix, buying cocaine with the money he had stolen in Mission Viejo. On the morning that the papers splashed his name and photograph all over their front pages, he was on a bus on the way back to Los Angeles, unaware that he had been identified.

He arrived safely and went into the bus station toilet to finish off the cocaine he had bought. No one seemed to be overly interested in him as he left the station and walked through Los Angeles. Ramirez was a Satanist, and had developed a belief that Satan himself watched over him, preventing his capture.

At 8.15 a.m. Ramirez entered Tito's Liquor Store at 819 Towne Avenue. He selected some Pepsi and a pack of sugared doughnuts; he had a sweet tooth that, coupled with a lack of personal hygiene, had left his mouth with only a few blackened teeth. At the counter other customers looked at him strangely as he produced three dollar bills and awaited his change. Suddenly he noticed the papers' front pages, and his faith in Satan's power must have been shaken. He dodged out of the shop and ran, accompanied by shouts of, "It is him! Call the cops!" He pounded off down the street at a surprising speed for one so ostensibly unhealthy. Within twelve minutes`he had covered two miles. He had headed east. He was in the Hispanic district of Los Angeles.

Ever since the police had confirmed that The Night Stalker was Hispanic there had been a great deal of anger among the Hispanic community of Los Angeles. They felt that racial stereotypes were already against them enough without their being associated with psychopaths. Thus more than most groups, Hispanics wanted The Night Stalker out of action.

Ramirez, by now, was desperate to get a vehicle. He attempted to pull a woman from her car in a supermarket lot until he was chased away by some customers of the barber's shop opposite. He carried on running, though exhausted, into the more residential areas of east Los Angeles. There, he tried to steal a 1966 red mustang having failed to notice that the owner, Faustino Pinon was lying underneath repairing it. As Ramirez attempted to start the car Pinon grabbed him by the collar and tried to pull him from the driver's seat. Ramirez shouted that he had a gun, but Pinon carried on pulling at him even after the car had started, causing it to career into the gatepost. Ramirez slammed it into reverse and accelerated into the side of Pinon's garage, and the vehicle stalled. Pinon succeeded in wrenching Ramirez out of his car, but in the following struggle Ramirez escaped, leaping the fence and running off across the road. There he tried to wrestle Angelina De La Torres from her Ford Granada. "Te voy a matar! (I'm going to kill you!)" screamed Ramirez, "Give me the keys!", but again he was thwarted and he ran away, now pursued by a growing crowd of neighbours. Manuel De La Torres, Angelina's husband succeeded in smashing Ramirez on the head with a gate bar and he fell, but he managed to struggle up and set off running again before he could be restrained. Incredibly, when Ramirez had developed a lead, he stopped, turned around and stuck his tongue out at his pursuers, then sped off once more. His stamina could not hold indefinitely however, and it was De La Torres who again tackled him and held him down. It is possible that Ramirez would have been lynched there and then had not a patrolman called to the scene arrived. Coincidentally the patrolman was the same age as the killer, and he too was called Ramirez. He reached the scene just as The Night Stalker disappeared under the mob. He drove his patrol car to within a few feet of where Ramirez was restrained, got out and prepared to handcuff the captive.

"Save me. Please. Thank God you're here. It's me, I'm the one you want. Save me before they kill me," babbled Ramirez. The patrolman handcuffed him and pushed him into the back of the car. The crowd was becoming restless, and the car was kicked as it pulled away. Sixteen-year-old Felipe Castaneda, part of the mob that captured Ramirez remarked, "He should never, *never* have come to East LA. He might have been a tough guy, but he came to a tough neighbourhood. He was Hispanic. He should have known better."

"The Night Stalker" was in custody, at first in a police holding cell and then in Los Angeles county jail. While in police care he repeatedly admitted to being "The Night Stalker" and begged to be killed.

The case against Ramirez was strong. The murder weapon, a .22 semi-automatic pistol was found in the possession of a woman in Tijuana, who had been given it by a friend of Ramirez. Police also tried to track down some of the jewellery that Ramirez had stolen and fenced, by sending investigators to his birth-place El Paso, a spiralling town on the Texas-Mexico border. Questioning his family and neighbours revealed that Ramirez' early life had been spent in petty theft and smoking a lot of marijuana. He had never joined any of the rival teenage gangs that fight over territory throughout El Paso, preferring drugs and listening to Heavy Metal. It had been common knowledge that Ramirez was a Satanist; a boyhood friend, Tom Ramos said he believed that it was Bible-study classes that had turned the killer that way.

The investigators also found a great deal of jewellery, stashed at the house of Ramirez' sister Rosa Flores. The police were also hoping to find a pair of eyes that Ramirez had gouged from one of his victims that had not been found in any previous searches. Unfortunately they were not recovered.

The evidence against Ramirez now seemed unequivocal. In a controversial move, the Mayor of Los Angeles said that whatever went on in court, he was convinced of Ramirez' guilt. This was later to prove a mainstay in a defence argument that Ramirez could not receive a fair trial in Los Angeles.

The appointed chief prosecutor in the case was deputy District Attorney P. Philip Halpin, who had prosecuted the "Onion Field" cop-killing case twenty years earlier. Halpin hoped to end the trial and have Ramirez in the gas chamber in a relatively short period of time. The prosecutor drew up a set of initial charges and submitted them as quickly as possible. A public defender was appointed to represent Ramirez. However Ramirez' family had engaged an El Paso lawyer, Manuel Barraza, and Ramirez eventually rejected his appointed public defender in favour of the El Paso attorney. Barraza did not even have a license to practise law in California.

Ramirez accepted, then rejected three more lawyers, finally settling upon two defenders, Dan and Arturo Hernandez. The two were not related, although they often worked together. The judge advised Ramirez that his lawyers did not even meet the minimum requirements for trying a death-penalty case in California, but Ramirez insisted, and more than seven weeks after the initial charges were filed, pleas of Not Guilty were entered on all counts.

The Hernandez' and Ramirez seemed to be trying to force Halpin into making a mistake out of sheer frustration, and thus to create a mis-trial. After each hearing the Hernandez' made pleas for, and obtained, more time to prepare their case. Meanwhile one prosecution witness had died of natural causes, and Ramirez' appearance was gradually changing. He had had his hair permed, and his rotten teeth replaced. This naturally introduced more uncertainty into the minds of prosecution witnesses as to Ramirez identity. The racial make-up of the jury was contested by the defence, which caused delays. The defence also argued, with some justification, that Ramirez could not receive a fair trial in Los Angeles, and moved for a change of location. Although the motion was refused it caused yet more delays. It actually took three and a half years for Ramirez' trial to finally get underway.

Halpin's case was, in practical terms, unbeatable. The defence's only real possibility of success was in infinite delay. For the first three weeks of the trial events progressed relatively smoothly. Then Daniel Hernandez announced that the trial would have to be postponed as he was suffering from nervous exhaustion. He had a doctor's report that advised six weeks rest with psychological counselling. It seemed likely that a mis-trial would

be declared. Halpin tried to argue that Arturo Hernandez could **471**
maintain the defence, even though he had failed to turn up at
the hearings and trial for the first seven months. However this
proved unnecessary as the judge made a surprise decision and
denied Daniel Hernandez his time off, arguing that he had failed
to prove a genuine need.

Halpin, by this stage was actually providing the Hernandez'
with all the information that they required to mount an adequate
defence, in order to move things along and prevent mis-trial.
For the same reasons the judge eventually appointed a defence
co-counsel, Ray Clark. Clark immediately put the defence on
a new track: Ramirez was the victim of a mistaken identity.
He even developed an acronym for this defence – SODDI or
Some Other Dude Did It. When the defence case opened Clark
produced testimony from Ramirez' father that he had been in
El Paso at the time of one of the murders of which he was
accused. He also criticized the prosecution for managing to
prove that footprints at one of the crime scenes were made
by a size eleven-and-a-half Avia trainer without ever proving
that Ramirez actually owned such a shoe. When the jury finally
left to deliberate however, it seemed clear that they would find
Ramirez guilty.

Things were not quite that easy however. After thirteen days of
deliberation juror Robert Lee was dismissed for inattention and
replaced by an alternative who had also witnessed the case. Two
days later, juror Phyllis Singletary was murdered in a domestic
dispute. Her live-in lover had beaten her then shot her several
times. She was also replaced.

At last on 20 September, 1989 after twenty-two days of deliberation the jury returned a verdict of guilty on all thirteen counts
of murder, twelve of those in the first degree. The jury also found
Ramirez guilty of thirty other felonies, including burglary, rape,
sodomy and attempted murder. Asked by reporters how he felt
after the verdict, Ramirez replied, "Evil".

There remained only the selection of sentence. At the hearing
Clark argued that Ramirez might actually have been possessed
by the devil, or that alternatively he had been driven to murder
by over-active hormones. He begged the jury to imprison
Ramirez for life rather than put him on death row. If the
jury agreed, Clark pointed out, "he will never see Disneyland
again," surely punishment enough. After five further days

of deliberation, the jury voted for the death penalty. Again, reporters asked Ramirez how he felt about the outcome as he was being taken away, "Big deal. Death always went with the territory. I'll see you in Disneyland."

Any attempt to trace the source of Ramirez' violent behaviour runs up against an insurmountable problem. No external traumas or difficulties seem to have brutalized him. He had a poor upbringing, he was part of a racial minority, but these things alone cannot explain such an incredibly sociopathic personality. Ramirez seems to have created himself. He was an intelligent and deeply religious child and early teenager. Having decided at some stage that counter-culture and drug-taking provided a more appealing lifestyle, he developed pride in his separateness. In the El Paso of his early manhood, people would lock their doors, if they saw him coming down the street. He was known as "Ricky Rabon", Ricky the thief, a nickname he enjoyed as he felt it made him "someone". By the time he moved to Los Angeles, he was injecting cocaine and probably committing burglaries to support himself. He let his teeth rot away, eating only childish sugary foods. He refused to wash. He listened to loud Heavy Metal music.

It has been argued that it was his taste in music that drove him to murder and Satanism, but this would seem to be more part of the mood of censorship sweeping America than a genuine explanation. Anyone who takes the trouble to listen to the music in question, particularly the AC/DC album cited by American newspapers at the time of the murders will find that there is little in it to incite violence.

Ramirez' obvious attempts to repel others in his personal behaviour, and his heavy drug use seem more likely sources of violence than early poverty or music. His assumed "otherness" seems in retrospect sadly underdeveloped, having never progressed beyond a teenager's need to appal staid grown-up society.

This is not to say that Ramirez was unintelligent. His delaying of his trial and his choice of the Hernandez' to continue the delays shows that he had worked out the most effective method of staying alive for the longest period either before, or soon after he was captured. His remarks in court upon being sentenced were not particularly original, yet they are articulate:

"It's nothing you'd understand but I do have something to

say . . . I don't believe in the hypocritical, moralistic dogma
of this so-called civilized society. I need not look beyond this
room to see all the liars, haters, the killers, the crooks, the
paranoid cowards – truly *trematodes* of the Earth, each one
in his own legal profession. You maggots make me sick –
hypocrites one and all . . . I am beyond your experience. I
am beyond good and evil, legions of the night, night breed,
repeat not the errors of the Night Prowler [a name from an
AC/DC song] and show no mercy. I will be avenged. Lucifer
dwells within us all. That's it."

Ramirez remains on death row. It is unlikely that he will be
executed before the year 2000.


# Jeffrey Dahmer

By the beginning of the 1990s, it began to seem that the
American public had become shock-proof where serial killers
were concerned. Killer "duos" like the Hillside Stranglers, or
Lucas and Toole, killed to satisfy their sexual appetites. "Sunset
Slayer" Douglas Clark and his mistress Carol Bundy confessed to
a taste for playing with the severed heads of their female victims.
In 1985, the suicide of a man named Leonard Lake, and the
flight of his companion Charles Ng, led the police to a house in
Calaveras County, California, and to a cache of videos showing
the sexual abuse and torture of female victims – the number
seems to have exceeded thirty. Ex-convict Gerald Gallego and
his mistress Charlene Williams made a habit of abducting and
murdering teenage girls, who were first subjected to an orgy
of rape and lesbian advances, all in the search for the "perfect
sex slave". In Chicago, a group of four young men, led by
twenty-seven-year-old Robin Gecht, abducted at least fifteen
women, and subjected them to an orgy of rape and torture –
which included amputation and ritual eating of the breasts – in
the course of "satanic" ceremonies. There was also evidence to
link the New York Killer "Son of Sam" – David Berkowitz – who
casually shot strangers in cars – with a satanic cult. It was hard
to imagine how human depravity could go any further.

In spite of which, the revelations that burst on to television screens in late July 1991 caused nationwide shock. Just before midnight on 22 July, a young black man came running out of an apartment building in Milwaukee, Wisconsin, with a handcuff dangling from his wrist, and told two police patrolmen that a madman had tried to kill him, and threatened to cut out his heart and eat it. He led the police to the apartment of thirty-one-year-old Jeffrey Dahmer, where they demanded entrance. Dahmer – a white Anglo-Saxon – at first behaved reasonably, claiming to be under stress after losing his job and drinking too much, but when the police asked for the handcuff key, he became hysterical and abusive, and had to be taken into custody. The police soon realized that Dahmer's two-room apartment was a mixture of slaughter house and torture chamber. A freezer proved to contain severed heads, another some severed hands and a male genital organ, while five skulls – some painted grey – were found in various boxes.

Back at the police station, Dahmer confessed to killing seventeen youths, mostly blacks. He also confessed that the plastic bags of human "meat" in the freezer were intended to be eaten, and described how he had fried the biceps of one victim in vegetable oil. The threat to eat the heart of Tracy Edwards – the latest intended victim – had been no idle bluff.

The first problem was to find out the identities of the men to whom these skulls, bones and genitals belonged.

Back at police headquarters, Dahmer was obviously relieved to be co-operating; he seemed glad that his career of murder was over. It had all started, he admitted, when he was only eighteen years old, in 1978. That first victim has been a hitch-hiker. It was almost ten years before he committed his next murder. But recently, the rate of killing had accelerated – as it often does with serial killers – and there had been no less than three murders in the last two weeks. He had attempted to kill Tracy Edwards only three days after his last murder.

Dahmer was also able to help the police towards establishing the identities of the victims – which included twelve blacks, one Laotian, one Hispanic and three whites. Some of their names he remembered; the police had to work out the identities of others from identity cards found in Dahmer's apartment, and from photographs shown to parents of missing youths.

All Dahmer's confessions were sensational; but the story

of one teenage victim was so appalling that it created out-
rage around the world. Fourteen year old Laotian Konerak
Sinthasomphone, had met Dahmer in front of the same shopping mall where the killer was later to pick up Tracy Edwards;
the boy agreed to return to Dahmer's apartment to allow him
to take a couple of photographs.

Unknown to Konerak, Dahmer was the man who had enticed
and sexually assaulted his elder brother three years earlier.
Dahmer had asked the thirteen-year-old boy back to his
apartment in September 1988, and had slipped a powerful
sleeping draught into his drink, then fondled him sexually.
Somehow, the boy succeeded in staggering out into the street
and back home. The police were notified, and Dahmer was
charged with second degree sexual assault and sentenced to a
year in a correction programme, which allowed him to continue
to work in a chocolate factory.

Now the younger brother Konerak found himself in the same
apartment. He was also given drugged coffee, and then, when
he was unconscious, stripped and raped. After that, Dahmer
went out to buy some beer – he had been a heavy drinker since
schooldays. On his way back to the apartment, Dahmer saw,
to his horror, that his naked victim was talking to two black
teenage girls, obviously begging for help. Dahmer hurried up
and tried to grab the boy; the girls clung on to him. One of them
succeeded in ringing the police, and two squad cars arrived
within minutes. Three irritable officers wanted to know what
the trouble was about.

When Dahmer told them that the young man was his lover,
that they lived together in the nearby apartments, and that
they had merely had a quarrel, the policemen were inclined
to believe him – he looked sober and Konerak looked drunk.
They decided to move away from the gathering crowd, and
adjourned to Dahmer's apartment. There Dahmer showed them
polaroid pictures of the boy in his underwear, to convince him
that they were really lovers (the police had no way of knowing
that the photographs had been taken that evening), and told
them that Konerak was nineteen. Meanwhile, Konerak sat on
the settee, dazed but probably relieved that his ordeal was
over. His passivity was his undoing – his failure to deny
what Dahmer was saying convinced the police that Dahmer
must be telling the truth. They believed Dahmer, and went off

leaving Konerak in his apartment. The moment the police had left, Dahmer strangled Konerak, violated the corpse, then took photographs as he dismembered it. After stripping the skull of flesh, he painted it grey – probably to make it look like a plastic replica.

Back at District Three station house, the three policemen made their second mistake of the evening – they joked about the homosexual quarrel they had just broken up. But a tape recorder happened to be switched on, and when Dahmer was arrested two months later, and admitted to killing the Laotian boy, the tape was located and played on radio and television.

The story caused universal uproar. On 26 July, four days after Dahmer's arrest, the three policemen – John Balcerzak, Joseph Gabrish and Richard Portubcan – were suspended from duty with pay. (Later, administrative charges were filed against them, but finally dismissed.) Public anger was now transferred from Jeffrey Dahmer to the police department. Police Chief Philip Arreola found himself assailed on all sides, subjected to harsh criticism from his own force for not supporting his own men (in the following month, the Milwaukee Police Association passed a vote of no-confidence in him), and from Milwaukee's blacks and Asians for racism.

Dahmer's first murder had taken place in 1968, when he was eighteen. According to Dahmer's confession, he had found himself alone in the family house at 4480 West Bath Road; his father had already left, and his mother and younger brother David were away visiting relatives. He had been left with no money, and very little food in the broken refrigerator. That evening, he explained, he decided to go out and look for some company.

It was not hard to find. A nineteen-year-old white youth, who had spent the day at a rock concert, was hitch-hiking home to attend his father's birthday party. When an ancient Oldsmobile driven by someone who looked about his own age pulled up, the boy climbed in. They went back to Dahmer's house and drank some beer, and talked about their lives. Dahmer found he liked his new friend immensely. But when the boy looked at the clock and said he had to go, Dahmer begged him to stay. The boy refused. So Dahmer picked up a dumbbell, struck him on the head, then strangled him. He then dragged the body to the crawl space under the house, and dismembered it with a

carving knife. It sounds an impossible task for an eighteen-year-
old, but Dahmer was not without experience – he had always
had a morbid interest in dismembering animals.

He had wrapped up the body parts in plastic bags. But after a
few days, the smell began to escape. Dahmer's mother was due
back soon, and was sure to notice the stench. He took the plastic
bags out to the wood under cover of darkness and managed to
dig a shallow grave – the soil was rock-hard. But even with the
bags now underground, he still worried – children might notice
the grave. So he dug them up again, stripped the flesh from the
bones, and smashed up the bones with a sledgehammer. He
scattered them around the garden, and the property next door.
When his mother returned a few days later, there was nothing
to reveal that her son was now a killer.

Unfortunately, Dahmer was unable to recall the name of his
victim. The Milwaukee police telephoned the police of Bath
Township and asked them if they had a missing person case
that dated from mid-1978. They had. On 18 June, a youth named
Stephen Mark Hicks had left his home in Coventry Township
to go to a rock concert. Friends had driven him there, and they
agreed to rendezvous with him that evening to take him home.
Hicks failed to turn up at the meeting place, and no trace of him
was ever found.

For nine years after killing Stephen Hicks, Dahmer kept his
homicidal impulses under control. A period of three years in
the army had ended with a discharge for drunkenness. After
a short stay in Florida, he had moved in with his grandmother
Catherine, in West Allis, south of Milwaukee. But he was still
drinking heavily, and was in trouble with the police for causing
a disturbance in a bar. His family was relieved when he at last
found himself a job – in the Ambrosia Chocolate Company in
Milwaukee.

Dahmer soon discovered Milwaukee's gay bars, where he
became known as a monosyllabic loner. But it was soon observed
that he had a more sinister habit. He would sometimes engage a
fellow customer in conversation, and offer him a drink. These
drinking companions often ended up in a drugged coma. Yet
Dahmer's intention was clearly not to commit rape. He seemed
to want to try out his drugs as a kind of experiment, to see
how much he had to administer, and how fast they worked.
But other patrons noticed, and when one of Dahmer's drinking

companions ended up unconscious in hospital, the owner of Club Bath Milwaukee told him that he was barred.

On 8 September, 1986, two twelve-year-old boys reported to the police that Dahmer had exposed himself to them and masturbated. Dahmer alleged that he had merely been urinating. He was sentenced to a year on probation, and told his probation officers, with apparently sincerity: "I'll never do it again." (Judges and probation officers were later to note that Dahmer had a highly convincing manner of donning the sackcloth and ashes.) This period ended on 9 September, 1987.

A year of good behaviour had done nothing to alleviate Dahmer's psychological problems; on the contrary, they had built up resentment and frustration. Six days after his probation ended, the frustration again exploded into murder. On 15 September, Dahmer was drinking at a gay hang-out called Club 219, and met a twenty-four-year-old man called Stephen Tuomi. They decided to go to bed, and adjourned to the Ambassador Hotel, where they took a room that cost $43.88 for the night. Dahmer claims that he cannot recall much of that night, admitting that they drank themselves into a stupor. When Dahmer woke up, he says Tuomi was dead, with blood coming from his mouth, and strangulation marks on his throat.

It was a terrifying situation – alone in a hotel room with a corpse, and the desk clerk likely to investigate whether the room had been vacated at any moment. Dahmer solved it by going out and buying a large suitcase, into which he stuffed the body. Then he got a taxi to take him back to his grandmother's house in West Allis, where he had his own basement flat – the driver helped him to drag the heavy case indoors. There, says Dahmer, he dismembered it, and stuffed the parts into plastic bags which were put out for the garbage collector. He performed his task of disposal so efficiently that the police were unable to find the slightest sign of it, and decided not to charge Dahmer with the murder.

Clearly, this second murder was a watershed in Dahmer's life. The earlier murder of Stephen Hicks might have been put behind him as a youthful aberration, commited in a mood of psychological stress. But the killing of Stephen Tuomi was a deliberate act – whether Dahmer was fully sober or not. Since Tuomi had gone to the room specifically to have sex, there could be no reason whatever to kill him – unless Dahmer's needs involved more than an act of mutual intercourse: that is, unless they actually involved killing and dissecting his sexual partner, as he had killed and dissected animals as a teenager.

As a result of the murder of Stephen Tuomi, Dahmer seems to have acknowledged that murder was, in fact, what he needed to satisfy his deviant sexual impulse. The fifteen murders that followed leave no possible doubt about it.

Precisely four months later, on 16 January, 1988, Dahmer picked up a white young male prostitute named James Doxtator at a bus stop outside Club 219, and asked him if he would like to earn money by posing for a video. They went back to West Allis on the bus, and had sex in the basement. Then Dahmer gave the boy a drink heavily laced with sleeping potion, and, when he was unconscious, strangled him. With his grandmother's garage at his disposal, getting rid of the body was easy. He told the police that he cleaned the flesh from the bones with acid, then smashed the bones with a sledgehammer, and scattered them around like those of his first victim. What he does not seem to have admitted is that the murder and dismemberment of James Doxtator was his primary purpose when he invited the boy back home.

The police interrogator looked up from his notebook to ask if there was anything distinctive about Doxtator by which he might be identified; Dahmer recalled that he had two scars near his nipples that looked like cigarette burns. Doxtator's mother later confirmed that her son had such scars.

Two months elapsed before Dahmer killed again. On 24 March, 1988, in a bar called the Phoenix not far from Club 219, he met a twenty-three-year-old homosexual named Richard Guerrero, who was virtually broke. Attracted by the graceful, slightly built Hispanic youth, Dahmer made the same proposals that he had made to the previous victim and, like the previous victim, Guerrero accompanied him back to his grandmother's house. There they had oral sex, and Guerrero was offered a drugged drink. When he was unconscious, Dahmer strangled him, then dismembered the body in the garage.

Guerrero's frantic family hired a private detective and cir-culated flyers with their son's description. They also hired a psychic. But they were still searching three years later, when Dahmer confessed to the murder.

Dahmer's grandmother was becoming concerned about the

awful smells that came from the garage. Dahmer said it was garbage, but it seemed to persist even when the sacks had been collected. Dahmer's father Lionel came to investigate, and found a black, sticky residue in the garage. Dahmer, confronted with this evidence, said he had been using acid to strip dead animals of their flesh and fur, as he had done in childhood.

In September 1988, Catherine Dahmer finally decided she could no longer put up with the smells and her grandson's drunkenness. On 25 September, Dahmer moved into an apartment at 808 N. 24th Street.

There can be no doubt that Dahmer intended to use his new-found freedom to give full reign to his morbid sexual urges. But an unforeseen hitch occurred. Within twenty four hours, the four-time murderer was in trouble with the police. 26 September, 1988, was the day he met a thirteen-year-old Laotian boy named Sinthasomphone, lured him back to his apartment, and drugged him. But the elder brother of later victim Konerak somehow managed to escape, and Dahmer was charged with sexual assault and enticing a child for immoral purposes. He spent a week in prison, then was released on bail. On 30 January, 1990, he was found guilty; the sentence would be handed out four months later.

But even the possibility of a long prison sentence could not cure Dahmer of his obsessive need to kill and dismember. When he appeared in court to be sentenced on 23 May, 1989, he had already claimed his fifth victim.

Anthony Sears was a good looking twenty-three-year-old who dreamed of becoming a male model; he had a girlfriend and had just been appointed manager of a restaurant. On 25 March, he went drinking in a gay bar called LaCage with a friend called Jeffrey Connor, and Dahmer engaged them in conversation. By the time the bar closed, Sears had agreed to accompany Dahmer back to his grandmother's home. (Dahmer seems to have been worried that the police were watching his own apartment.) Once there, they had sex, then Dahmer offered Sears a drink. The grim routine was repeated almost without variation; strangulation, dismemberment, and disposal of the body parts in the garbage. Dahmer seems to have decided to preserve the skull as a memento; he painted it, and later took it with him when he moved into the Oxford Apartments.

The Assistant DA, Gale Shelton, had recognized instinctively that a man who would drug a teenage boy for sex was highly dangerous, and needed to be kept out of society for a long time. Arguing for a prison sentence of five years, she described Dahmer as evasive, manipulative, uncooperative and unwilling to change. Dahmer's lawyer Gerald Boyle argued that the assault on the Laotian boy was a one-off offense, and would never happen again. Dahmer himself revealed considerable skill as an actor in representing himself as contrite and self-condemned. "I am an alcoholic and a homosexual with sexual problems." He described his appearance in court as a "nightmare come true", declared that he was now a changed man, and ended by begging the judge: "Please don't destroy my life." Judge William Gardner was touched by the appeal. This clean-cut boy obviously needed help, and there was no psychiatric help in prison. So he sentenced Dahmer to five years on probation, and a year in a House of Correction, where he could continue to work at the chocolate factory during the day.

From the Community Correctional Center in Milwaukee, Dahmer addressed a letter to Judge Gardner, stating "I have always believed a man should be willing to assume responsibility for the mistakes he makes in life. The world has enough misery in it without my adding to it. Sir, I assure you that it will never happen again. That is why, Judge Gardner, I am requesting a sentence modification."

Dahmer was released from the Correctional Center two months early – on 2 March, 1990. Eleven days later, he moved into the Oxford Apartments.

Two more victims followed in quick succession. Thirty-three-year-old Eddie Smith, an ex-jailbird, was picked up in the gay Club 219, drugged with one of Dahmer's Mickey Finns, then strangled and dismembered. A few weeks later, on 14 June, twenty-eight-year-old Eddie Smith was killed in the same way and his body disposed of in garbage bags.

So far, Dahmer's murders seem to have been due to a compulsive drive to kill and dismember. Now a new development occurred: psychological sadism. In April 1991, Eddie Smith's sister Carolyn received a telephone call from a soft spoken man who told her that Eddie was dead; when she asked how he knew he replied: "I killed him", and hung up.

Dahmer's career of slaughter almost came to an abrupt end on 8 July, 1990; it was on that day that he made the mistake of varying his method. He approached a fifteen-year-old Hispanic boy outside a gay bar, and offered him $200 to pose for nude photographs. The boy returned to room 213 and removed his clothes. But instead of offering him the usual drugged drink, Dahmer picked up a rubber mallet and hit him on the head. It failed to knock him unconscious, and the boy fought back as Dahmer tried to strangle him. Somehow, the boy succeeded in calming his attacker. And, incredibly, Dahmer allowed him to go, even calling a taxi.

The boy had promised not to notify the police. But when he was taken to hospital for treatment, he broke his promise. For a few moments, Dahmer's future hung in the balance. But when the boy begged them not to allow his foster parents to find out that he was homosexual, the police decided to do nothing about it.

When he saw his probation officer, Donna Chester, the next day, Dahmer looked depressed and unshaven. He said he had money problems and was thinking of suicide. She wanted to know how he could have money problems when he was earning $1,500 a month, and his apartment cost less than $300 a month. He muttered something about hospital bills. And during the whole of the next month, Dahmer continued to complain of depression and stomach pains, and to talk about jumping off a high building. Donna Chester suggested that he ought to find himself another apartment in a less run-down area. She was unaware that Dahmer was an addict who now urgently needed a fix of his favourite drug: murder.

It happened a few weeks later, on 3 September, 1990. In front of a bookstore on Twenty-seventh, Dahmer picked up a young black dancer named Ernest Miller, who was home from Chicago, where he intended to start training at a dance school in the autumn. They had sex in Apartment 213, then Dahmer offered him a drugged drink, and watched him sink into oblivion. Perhaps because he had not killed for three months, Dahmer's craving for violence and its nauseating aftermath was stronger than usual. Instead of strangling his victim, Dahmer cut his throat. He decided that he wanted to keep the skeleton, so after cutting the flesh from the bones, and dissolving most of it in acid, he bleached the skeleton with acid. He also kept the biceps, which he put in the freezer.

Soon after Ernest Miller's disappearance, his grandmother

began receiving telephone calls; the voice at the other end of the line made choking and groaning noises, and sometimes cried: "Help me, help me."

Neighbours were beginning to notice the smell of decaying flesh; some of them knocked on Dahmer's door to ask about it. Dahmer would explain politely that his fridge was broken and that he was waiting to get it fixed.

The last victim of 1990 died almost by accident. Twenty-three-year-old David Thomas had a girlfriend and a three-year-old daughter; nevertheless he accepted Dahmer's offer to return to his apartment in exchange for money. Dahmer gave him a drugged drink, but then decided that Thomas was not his type after all, and that he had no desire for sex. But since Thomas was now drugged, and might be angry when he woke up, he killed him anyway. But he filmed the dismemberment process, and took photographs of his severed head; Thomas's sister later identified him by the photograph.

He had committed nine murders; there were eight still to go.

The first murder of the new year was a nineteen-year-old black homosexual named Curtis Straughter, whose ambition was to become a male model; Dahmer picked him up in freezing, rainy weather on 18 February, 1991. While they were engaging in oral sex in the evil-smelling apartment, Straughter began to flag as the sleeping potion took effect. Dahmer took a leather strap and strangled him, then dismembered the body and recorded the process on camera. Once again, he kept the skull.

On 25 March, there occurred an event that psychiatrists believe may be responsible for the final spate of multiple murder. It was on that day that Dahmer's mother Joyce contacted him for the first time in five years. Joyce Dahmer – now Flint – was working as an AIDS counsellor in Fresco, California, and it may have been her contact with homosexuals that led her to telephone her son. She spoke openly about his homosexuality – for the first time – and told him she loved him. The call was a good idea – or would have been if she had made it a few years earlier. Now it was too late; Dahmer had gone too far in self-damnation.

The murder of nineteen-year-old Errol Lindsey on 7 April has a quality or *déja-vu*. The police report states bleakly that Dahmer met Lindsey on a street corner and offered him money to pose for photographs. Lindsey was drugged and strangled; then Dahmer had oral sex with the body. Errol Lindsey was dismembered, but Dahmer kept his skull.

Thirty-one-year-old Tony Hughes, was a deaf mute who loved to dance. When Dahmer accosted him outside Club 219 on 24 May, he had to make his proposition in writing – $50 for some photographs. Hughes was offered the sleeping potion, then strangled and dismembered. Dahmer had become so casual that he simply left the body lying in the bedroom for a day or so before beginning the dismemberment process – it was, after all, no more dangerous than having an apartment full of skulls and body parts.

With victim number thirteen, Dahmer again varied his method and came close to being caught. This was the fourteen-year-old Laotian boy – already mentioned – Konerak Sinthasomphone. Instead of strangling him after drugging him and committing rape, Dahmer went out to buy a pack of beer. Konerak woke up and almost escaped. But the Milwaukee police returned him, and his skull ended as yet another keepsake.

Sunday 30 June was the day of Chicago's Gay Pride Parade, and Dahmer decided to attend, taking a Greyhound bus for the ninety mile trip. After watching the parade, Dahmer went to the police station to report that a pickpocket had taken his wallet. But he seems to have had enough money left to approach a young black he met at the Greyhound Bus station, another aspiring model named Matt Turner. They travelled back to Milwaukee on the bus, then to Dahmer's apartment by cab. (Dahmer often earned more than $300 a week at the chocolate factory, which explains his frequent extravagance with cabs.) In his later confession, Dahmer said nothing about sex; but he admitted to drugging Turner, strangling him with a strap, then dismembering him and cutting off his head, keeping the skull.

Five days later, Dahmer was back in Chicago, looking for another victim. In a gay club on Wells Street he met twenty-three-year-old Jeremiah Weinberger, and invited him back to Milwaukee. Weinberger consulted a former room mate, Ted Jones, about whether he should accept. "Sure, he looks ok", said Jones. He was later to comment ruefully: "Who knows what a serial killer looks like?"

Dahmer and Weinberger spent Saturday in Room 213 having

sex; Dahmer appeared to like his new acquaintance. But when,
the following day, Weinberger looked at the clock and said it
was time to go, Dahmer offered him a drink. Weinberger's head
joined Matt Turner's in a plastic bag in the freezer.

But Dahmer was nearing the end of his tether, and even drink
could not aesthetize him for long. Neighbours kept complaining
about the smell, and he solved this by buying a fifty-seven gallon
drum of concentrated hydrochloric acid, and disposing of some
of the body parts that were causing the trouble. All this meant
he was frequently late for work, or even absent. On 15 July,
1991, the Ambrosia Chocolate Company finally grew tired of
his erratic behaviour and fired him.

His reaction was typical. The same day he picked up a
twenty-four-year-old black named Oliver Lacy, took him back
to his apartment, and gave him a drugged drink. After strangling
him, he sodomized the body.

But the murder spree was almost over. Four days later, the
head of the final victim joined the others in the freezer. He was
twenty-five-year-old Joseph Bradeholt, an out of work black who
was hoping to move from Minnesota to Milwaukee with his wife
and two children. But he accepted Dahmer's offer of money for
photographs, and willingly joined in oral sex in Room 213. After
that, he was drugged, strangled and dismembered. His body
was placed in the barrel of acid, which was swiftly turning into
a black, sticky mess.

That Dahmer's luck finally ran out may have been due to
the carelessness that leads to the downfall of so many multiple
murderers. The last intended-victim, Tracy Edwards was a
slightly built man, and should have succumbed to the drug
like all the others. For some reason, he failed to do so; it seems
most likely that Dahmer failed to administer a large enough dose.
Equally puzzling is the fact that, having seen that the drug had
failed to work, he allowed Edwards to live, and spent two hours
watching a video with him. Was the homicidal impulse finally
burning itself out? Dahmer knew that if he failed to kill Tracy
Edwards, he would be caught; yet, with a large knife in his
hand, he allowed him to escape from the apartment.

It sounds as if he recognized that the time had come to try
to throw off the burden of guilt and rejoin the human race.

On 27 January, Wisconsin's worst mass murderer came to
trial in Milwaukee before Judge Lawrence Gram, entering a

plea of guilty but insane. On 15 February, the jury rejected Dahmer's plea and found him guilty of the fifteen murders with which he had been charged. (In two cases, the prosecution had decided the evidence was insufficient.) He was sentenced to fifteen terms of life imprisonment (Wisconsin has no death penalty) which means that he can never be released.

# CONCLUSIONS

Perhaps one of the most disturbing things about this survey of serial killers is that the majority of them – from Dumollard and Vacher to the Yorkshire Ripper and Jeffrey Dahmer, were caught by accident. This was the problem that made America's law enforcement agencies aware that a totally new approach was necessary.

Until the early 1980s, cooperation between states had been as loose as between, say, the various police forces in Europe. Clearly, something more like a single force was needed – linked by a single computer. That is why, in November 1982, various crime specialists put forward the idea of a National Centre for the Analysis of Violent Crime (or NCAVC), a proposal that was unanimously adopted seven months later. The result was the formation of the NCAVC at the FBI Academy at Quantico, Virginia.

The Centre was run by agents of the elite Behavioural Science Unit, sometimes known as the Psychological Profiling Unit, because its chief task was to attempt to assess the personalities of unknown killers from the crime itself. For example, in November 1979, when the New York police had appealed to the Quantico unit for help in solving the rape and murder of a schoolteacher named Francine Elveson, the unit had been able to suggest the killer's age, his educational qualifications and his psychological problems; this had led officers working on the case to recognize that the "profile" fitted a suspect named Carmine Calabro, an

The National Center for the Analysis of Violent Crime is in Quantico, Virginia, and includes an underground complex of banks, shops, service station, cleaners, restaurants and cinema. The cinema shows the same programme that was seen by the famous gangster John Dillinger (the Biography was showing *Manhattan Melodrama*, a gangster film with Clark Gable) before he walked out with "the Lady in Red" (Polly Keele) and was shot down by FBI agents.

unemployed actor. Calabro's tooth-prints established his guilt and he was sentenced to life imprisonment.

This was the unit that now became the central coordinator of the new programme, with its vast computer that gathers information on every murder that occurs anywhere in the United States, and looks for similarities that might establish whether the same killer has been responsible for more than one murder. As a result of these new methods, the FBI handbook *Sexual Homicide: Its Patterns and Motives* estimates conservatively that the success rate of the NCAVC has been about seventy-seven per cent.

Cases like the Dahmer murders make it clear that there is still a long way to go. If the disappearance of young blacks in Milwaukee had been recorded on the FBI computer, the presence of a serial killer would have been established long before Dahmer had disposed of seventeen victims. Yet the slowly increasing success rate of the NCAVC suggests that this problem, like the others, is amenable to the scientific approach. In 1986, special agent Roger Depue of the NCAVC expressed the new sense of optimism when he pointed out that the Quantico unit had already contributed significantly to slowing down the spiral of violent crime in America. "We are not only going to fight back – we are going to win."

The hunt for the "Yorkshire Ripper", Peter Sutcliffe, took so long (six years) because of the problem of storing and organizing 22,000 interviews and 150,000 suspects. As soon as murder hunts were computerized (after 1980) the success rate increased dramatically. John Duffy, the "Railway Rapist" and killer of three girls, was caught after he was selected by computer from a list of 4,900 sex offenders.